THE PORTABLE DALÍ

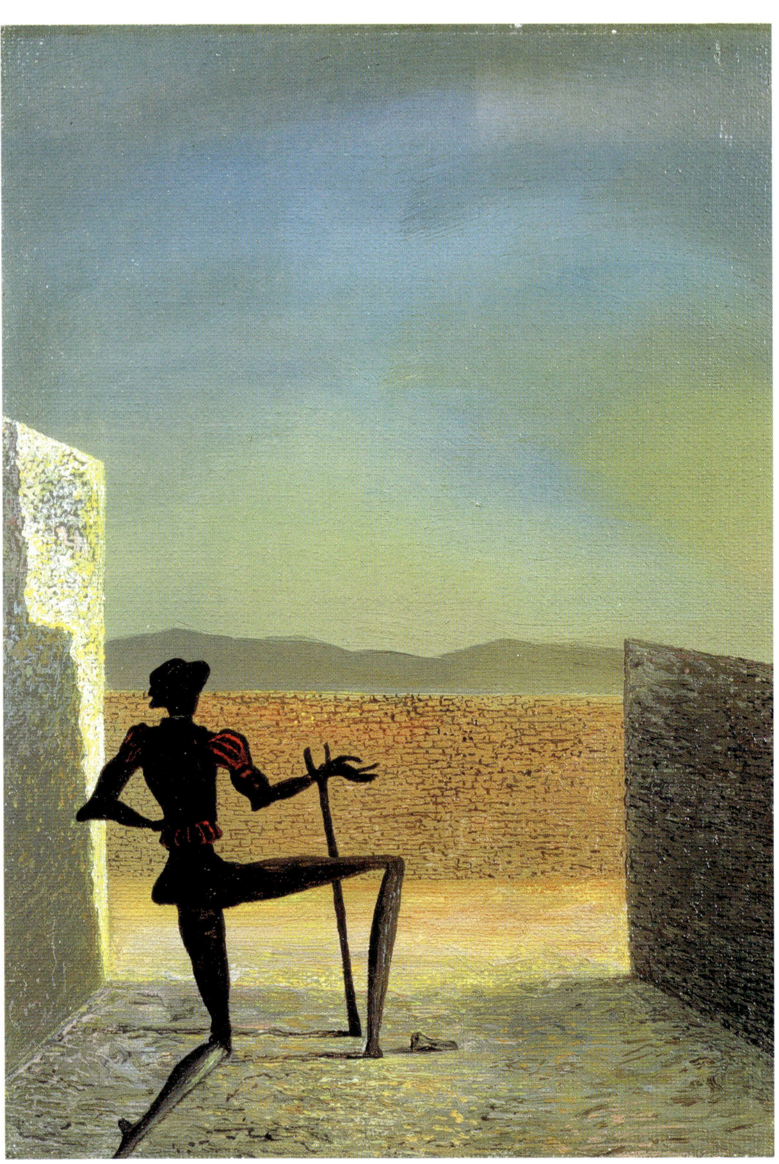

THE PORTABLE
DALÍ

Introduction by *Robert Hughes*

UNIVERSE

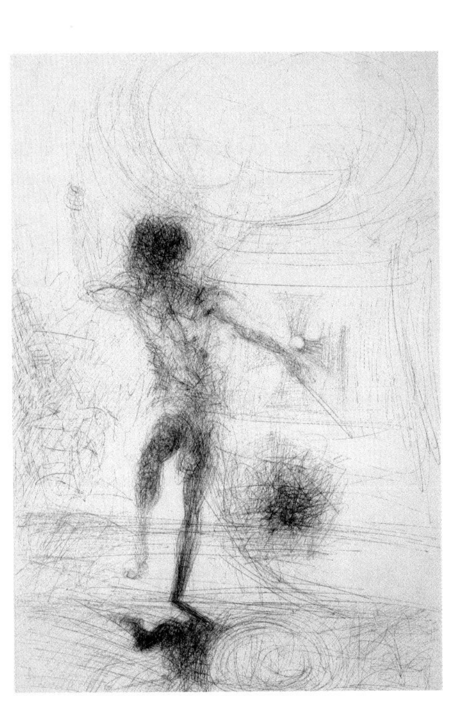

CONTENTS

For almost forty years, Salvador Dalí has been one of the two most famous painters alive. As a bodily trademark, his moustache was the only rival to van Gogh's ear and Picasso's testicles; though unlike them, it was adopted from Velázquez's portrait of Philip IV. Dalí's success, large as it was, coincided with his decline as a serious artist. Painters often imitate themselves, but Dalí did so with unusual zeal, and his celebrity arises from the way in which he fulfilled two ruling clichés about artists. The first was the Painter as Old Master (Raphael, Rubens); the second, the Artist as Freak (Rimbaud, van Gogh). Dalí's public image contrived to give a tacky, vivid caricature of both while fulfilling neither. Here, on one hand, was early Dalí: a manic and unrestrained imagination, immersed in sovereign private fantasy. On the other, the late Dalí convinced an audience that could scarcely tell the difference between a Vermeer and a Velázquez that he was the spiritual heir to both painters. He did both, not so much through art as by the diffusion of small anecdotes and a stoic indifference to the pangs of self-repetition. "The difference between a madman and me," Dalí is often quoted as saying, "is that I am not mad." Indeed, he is not; and in his later years the Catalan promoter, with his moustache-wax, lobster-telephones, and soft watches, managed to annihilate his earlier self—crazy Sal the Andalusian Dog, the insecure and ravenously aggressive young dandy whose tiny, enameled visions helped create one of the extreme moments of modernist disgust and revolt.

Almost all the works of art on which Dalí's fame as a serious artist rests were painted before his thirty-fifth birthday, between 1929 and 1939. Around 1926, he discovered that realism, pressed to an extreme of detail, could subvert one's sense of reality. Instead of presenting a painting as a surface, with all its inherent tensions, Dalí went to the opposite extreme of treating it as a perfectly transparent window, using what he called "all the usual paralyzing tricks of eye-fooling, the most discredited academism" to invoke "sublime hierarchies of thought." The painter Dalí chose as his model was the late nineteenth-century academician Jean-Louis Meissonier, whose detailed canvases stood for everything that was not modern: an accuracy more than photographic, with paint as smooth and licked as bathroom porcelain.

This technique could make any vision, no matter how outrageous and irrational, seem persuasively real. But it needed a system of images, and this Dalí approached through what he called his "paranoiac-critical" method. In essence, it meant looking at one thing and seeing another. This kind of trick double-reading had been used occasionally by artists since the sixteenth century—*capriccio* heads made of vegetables or fish or game, by Arcimboldo and his imitators, had as much of a vogue at the court of Rudolf II of Prague as, after Dalí, they would have among chic interior decorators—but Dalí took it to an extraordinary pitch of ingenuity, linking the most diverse and spatially remote objects into mutually canceling figures-of-sight. Thus in *Metamorphosis of Narcissus*, 1937 (p. 202), the hand sprouting from the ground, holding an enormous egg—from whose cracked shell a narcissus sprouts —can be made to "turn into" the figure of Narcissus in the background, gazing into the pool. These ambiguities usually went on in a dream landscape that Dalí appropriated, with refinements, from de Chirico—the flat, desert-like plane, Lautréamont's operating table, on which strange objects meet, as in the mocking verse in a thirties issue of *Punch*:

> *On the pale yellow sands*
> *There's a pair of clasped hands*
> *And an eyeball entangled in string,*
> *And a plate of raw meat,*
> *And a bicycle seat,*
> *And a Thing that is hardly a Thing.*

Close; but no cigar. The content of vintage Dalí is too weird and obsessive to parody, since parody requires some sense of normality in its subject, and Dalí's work had none. Its intensity placed it beyond satire. That intensity was also bound up with its small scale—the opposite, in this respect, of Abstract Expressionism, whose impact was largely dependent on the engulfing size of the canvas. With Dalí, one is always looking down the wrong end of the telescope at a brilliantly clear, poisoned, and shrunken world, whose deep perspectives and sharp patches of hallucinatory shadow intrigue the eye but do not invite the body; one cannot imagine oneself walking in this landscape, or even touching it, for it is all illusion. His small paintings, like *The Persistence of Memory (Soft Watches)*, 1931 (p.110), preserve their magic because they cannot be verified. One must accept this stretched and satiny beach, these melting watches, and that biomorphic blob (a profile of the artist, in fact, turned nose to the ground).

Dalí had a brilliant sense of provocation, and if his images are to be rightly seen they must be set, in retrospect, into the context of a less sexually frank time. Today, the art world is less easily alarmed by images of sex, blood, excrement, and putrefaction, but fifty years ago it was still quite shockable and had difficulty in digesting a painting like Dalí's *Lugubrious Game*, 1929 (p.89), with its explicit imagery of masturbation—the figure on the plinth, averting its head in shame, with its enormously enlarged right hand—and of coprophilia. The minutely painted smutch of excrement on the shorts of the gibbering man in the foreground even offended Breton, and the Surrealists conducted a serious *enquête* on whether or not turds were an acceptable dream image. Dalí rightly pointed out that a censored dream was no dream at all, but a conscious construction; if his colleagues were interested in the marvelous workings of the unconscious, they must take them warts, dung, and all. Like a gland irritated by constant scratching, Dalí's mind threw off many of these confessional images before the end of the 1930s. As Picasso used his erotic rage as a subject throughout his life, Dalí deployed an imagery of impotence and guilt. He liked anything that was not erect, that spoke of flaccidity—runny Camembert cheese, Gaudi's stonework, melon-like lobes of flesh held up by crutches, soft watches, fried eggs, deliquescent heads. He inherited from Spanish devotional art—not the art of the Prado, rather the gaudy devotional image of the provincial church—an almost paralyzing morbidity about flesh. In Dalí it suffers, scourged by light, and seems ripe as over-hung grouse: there is no such thing as the confident body, but no spiritual transcendence of the flesh either. Hence the peculiarly airless, pessimistic tone of Dalí's work, another characteristic that it, like much Surrealist art, shared with pornography.

—ROBERT HUGHES (1980)

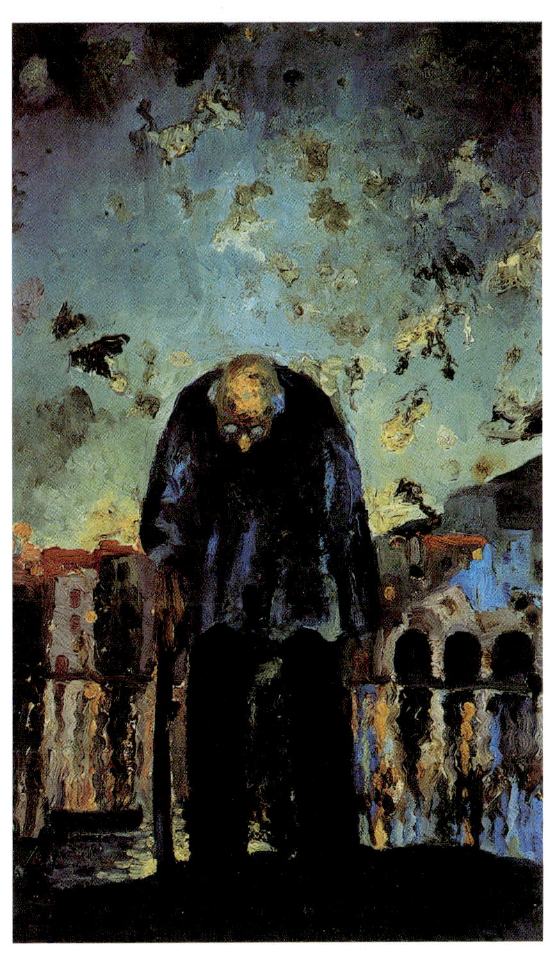

Old Man at Twilight · 1918

Private collection

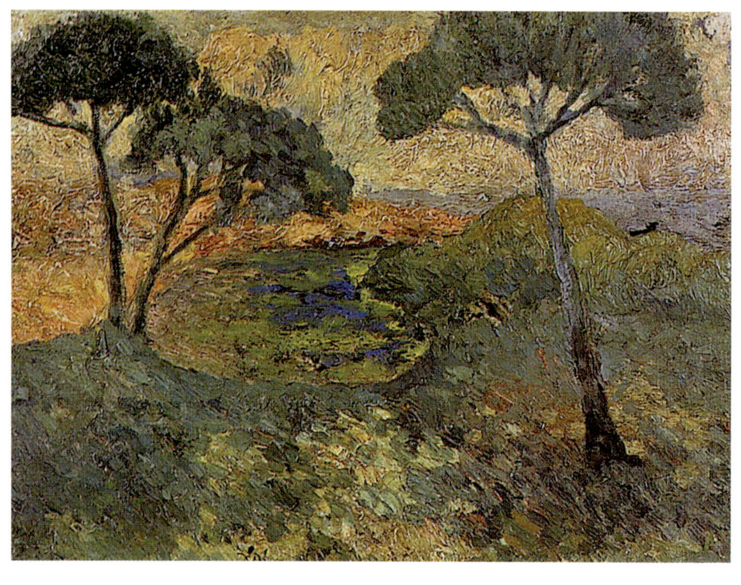

The Three Pines · c. 1919
Private collection

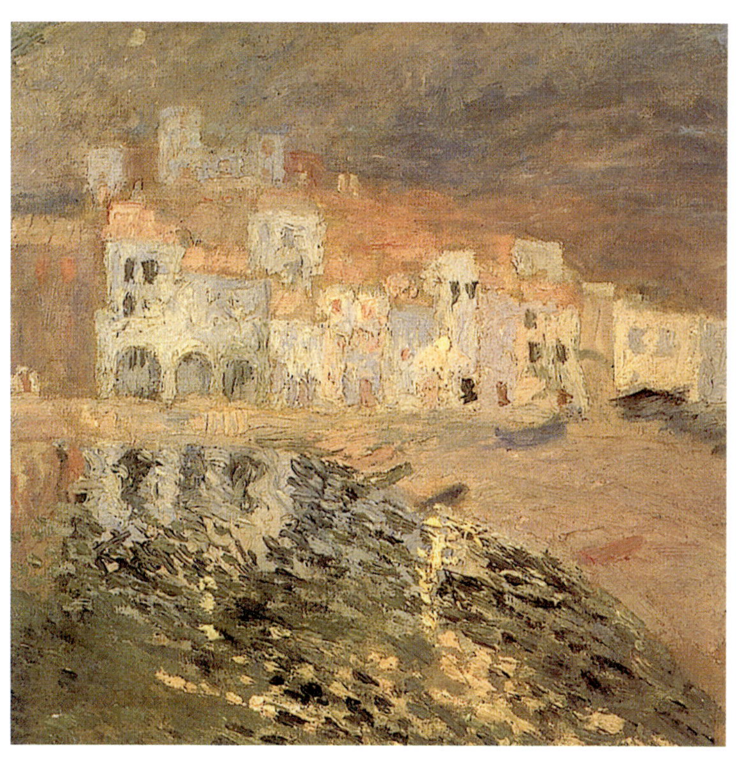

Port Alguer · 1919–20

Fundación Gala-Salvador Dalí, Figueras, gift of Dalí to the Spanish state

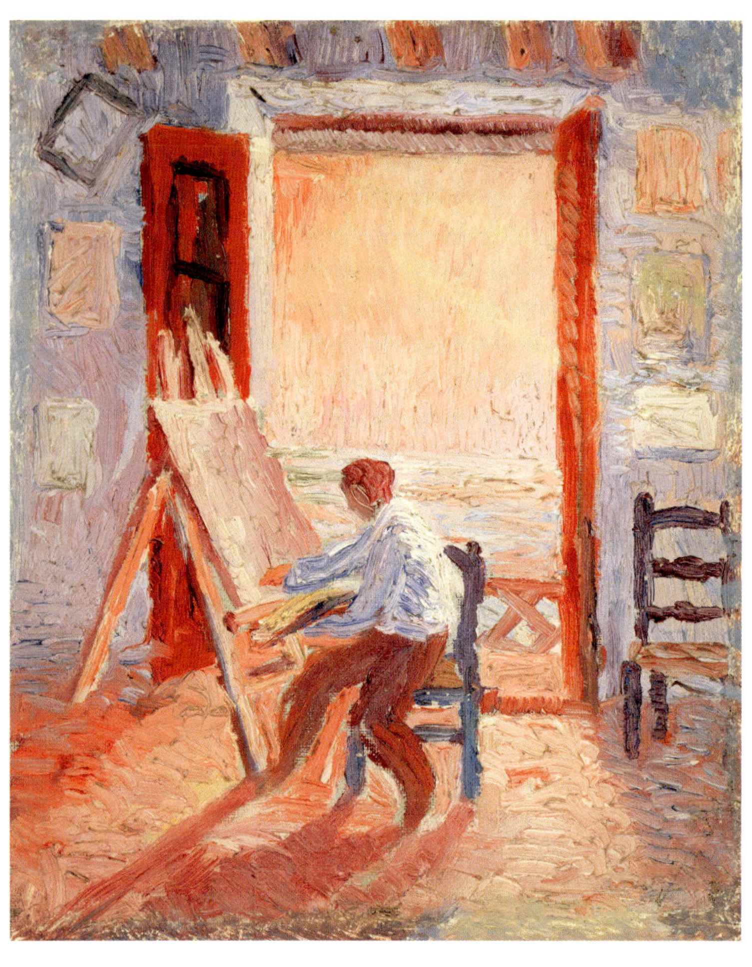

Self-Portrait in the Studio · c. 1919
The Salvador Dalí Museum, St. Petersburg, Florida;
formerly Collection E. and A. Reynolds Morse

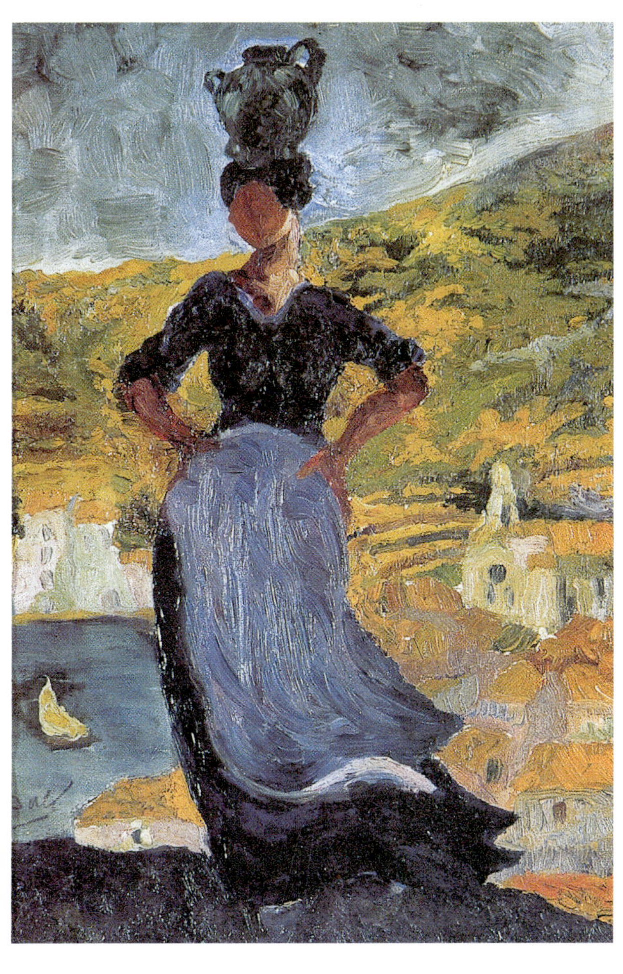

Portrait of Hortensia, Peasant Woman from Cadaqués · 1920
Private collection

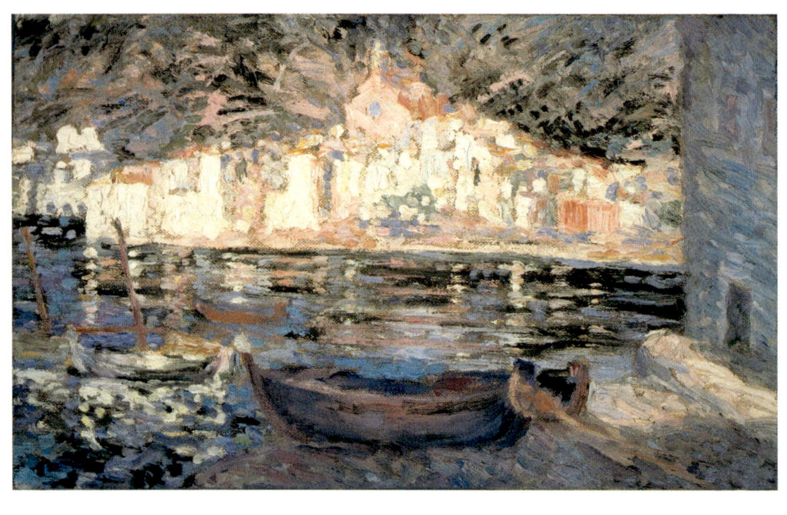

View of Cadaqués from Playa Poal · 1920
The Salvador Dalí Museum, St. Petersburg, Florida;
formerly Collection E. and A. Reynolds Morse

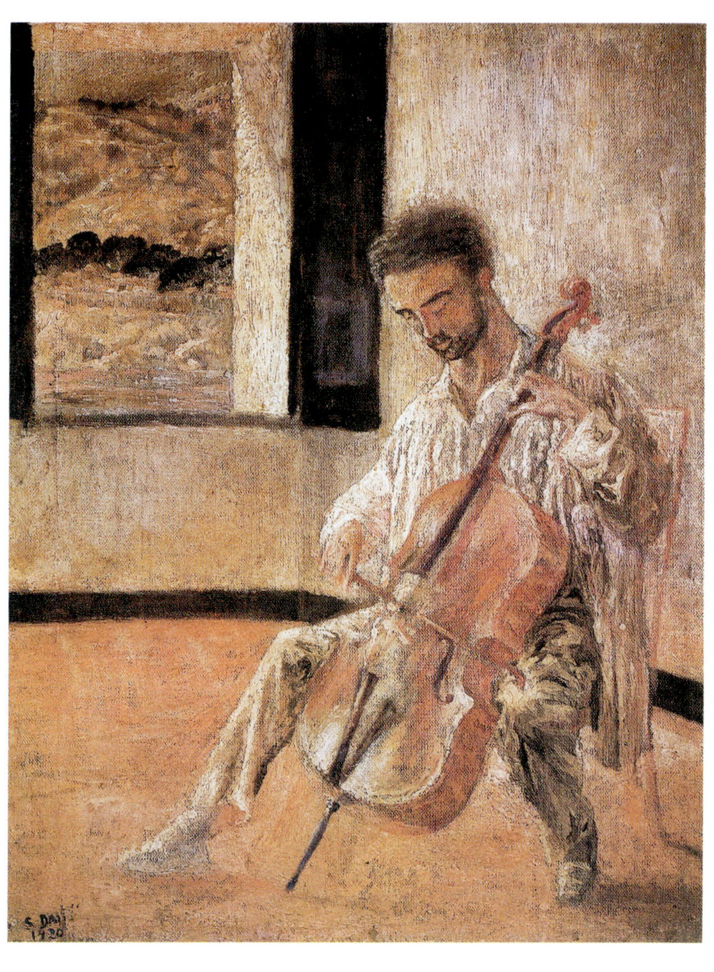

Portrait of the Cellist Ricardo Pichot · 1920
Private collection, Cadaqués

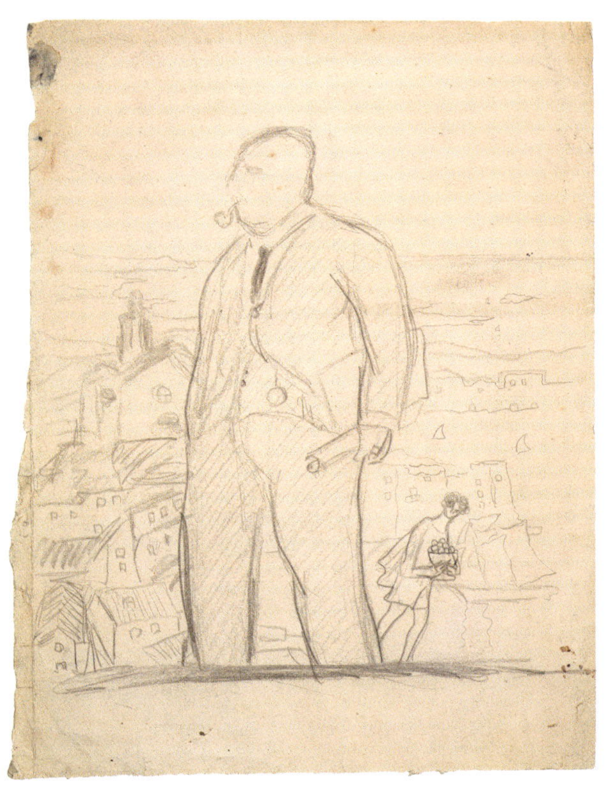

Study for "Portrait of My Father" · 1920
Fundación Gala-Salvador Dalí, Figueras, Dalí Bequest 1989

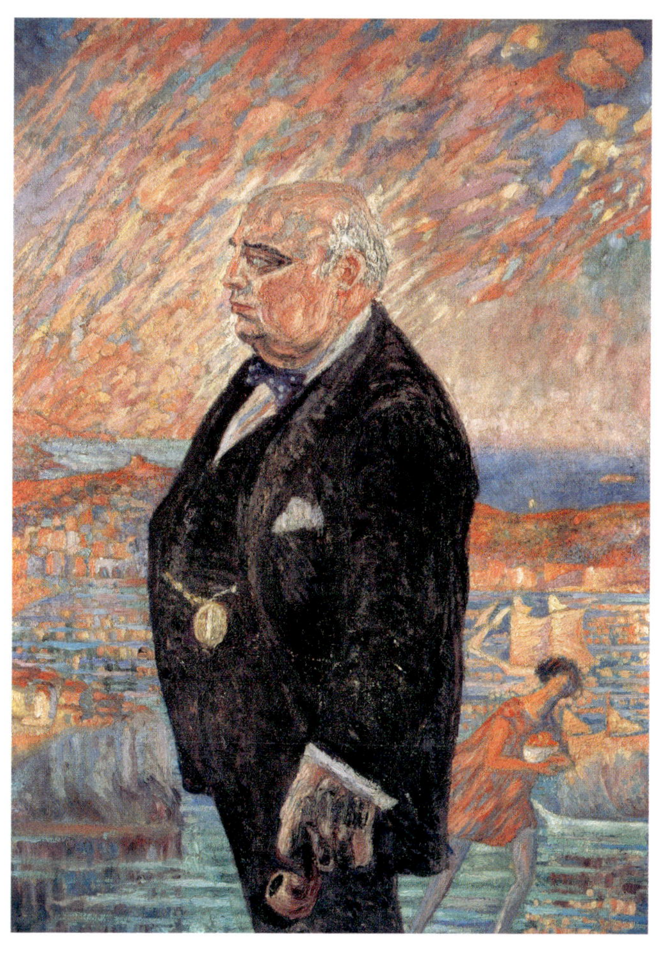

Portrait of My Father · 1920–21
Fundación Gala-Salvador Dalí, Figueras, gift of Dalí to the Spanish state

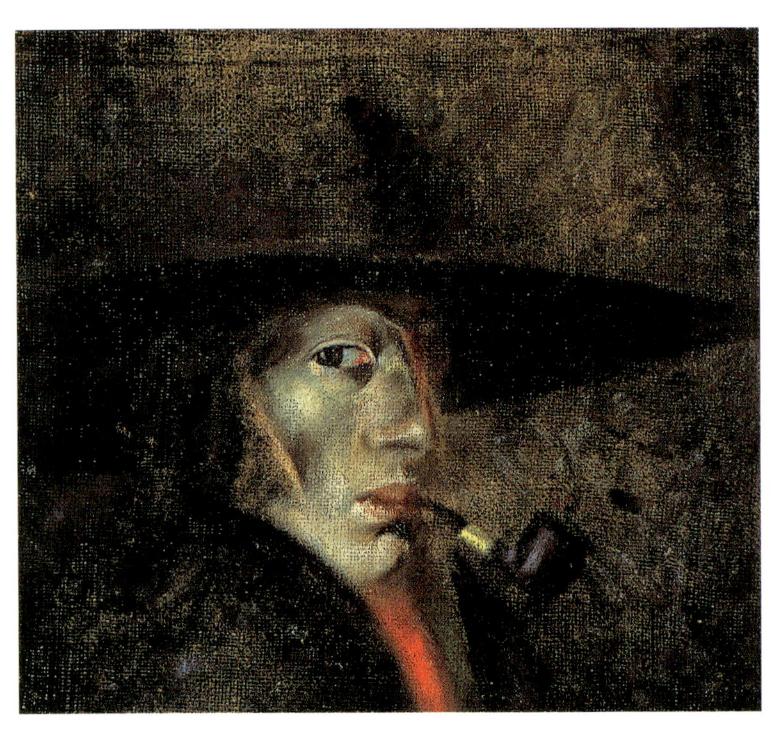

Self-Portrait · C. 1921

The Salvador Dalí Museum, St. Petersburg, Florida

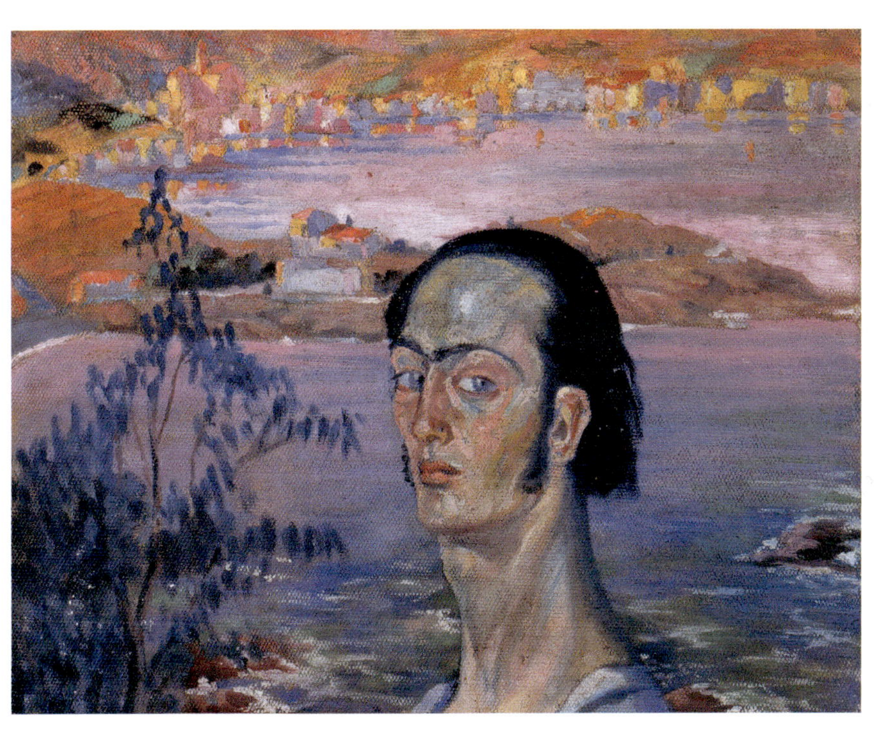

Self-Portrait with the Neck of Raphael · 1920–21
Fundación Gala-Salvador Dalí, Figueras, gift of Dalí to the Spanish state

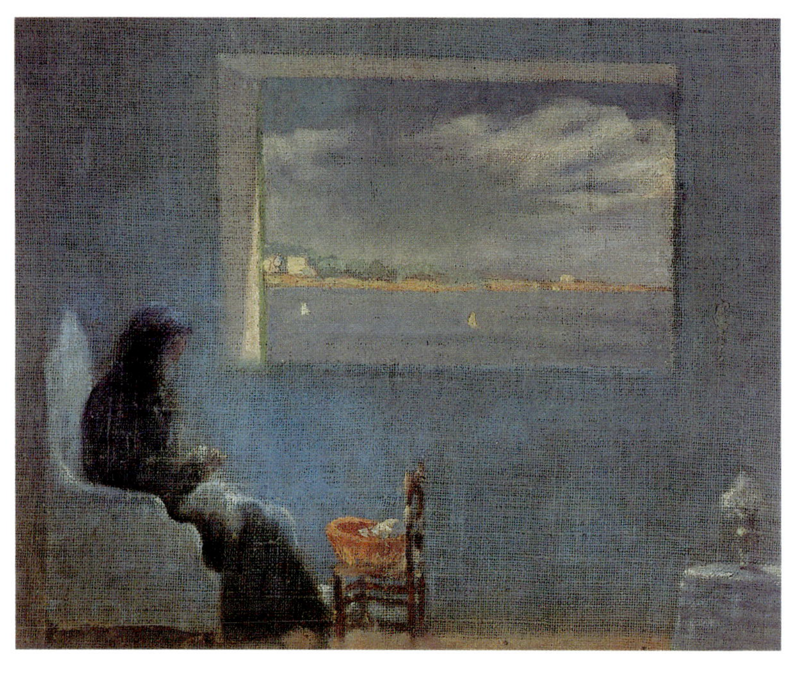

Portrait of Grandmother Ana Sewing · C. 1921
Collection Joaquín Vila Moner, Figueras

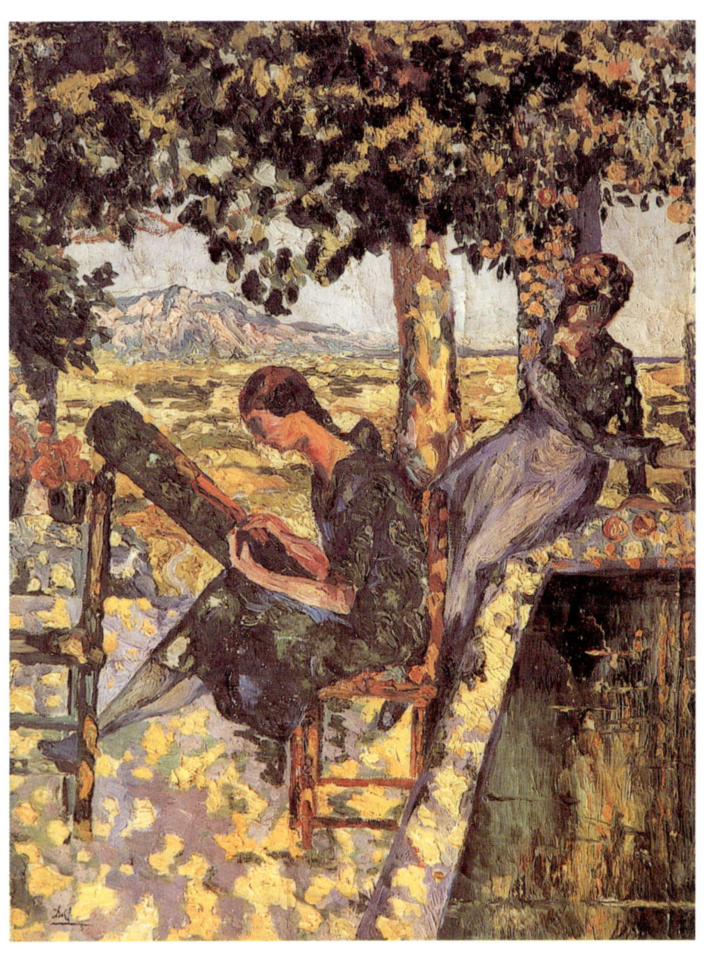

Girls in a Garden (The Cousins) · 1921
André-François Petit, Paris

23

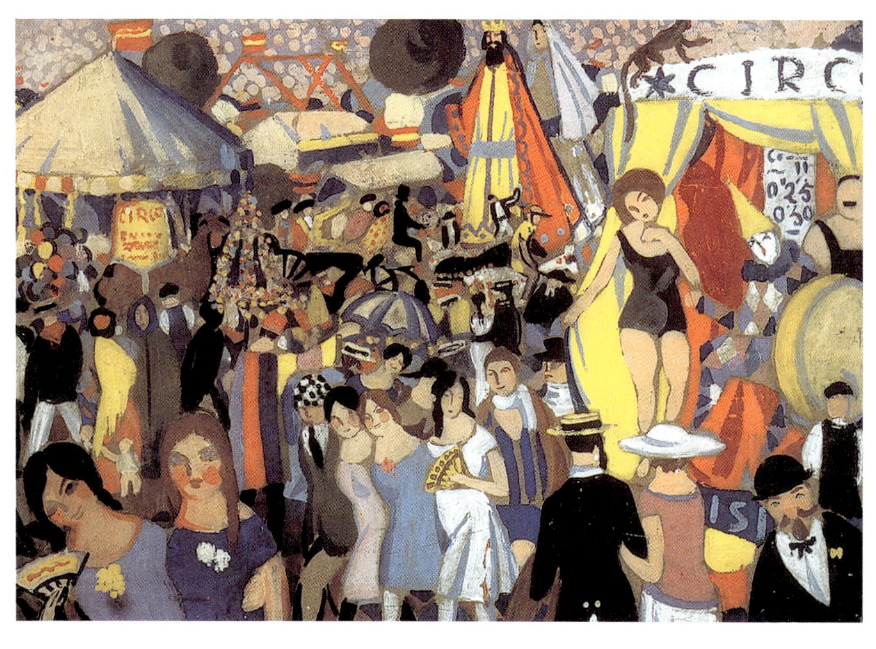

Santa Creus Festival in Figueras—The Circus · 1921

Fundación Gala-Salvador Dalí, Figueras

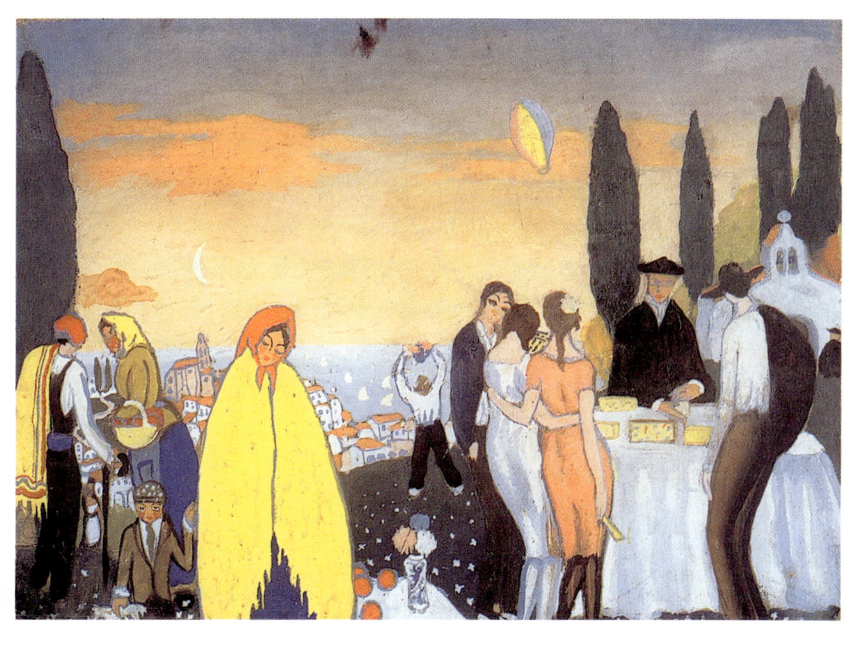

Festival at San Sebastián · 1921
Fundación Gala-Salvador Dalí, Figueras

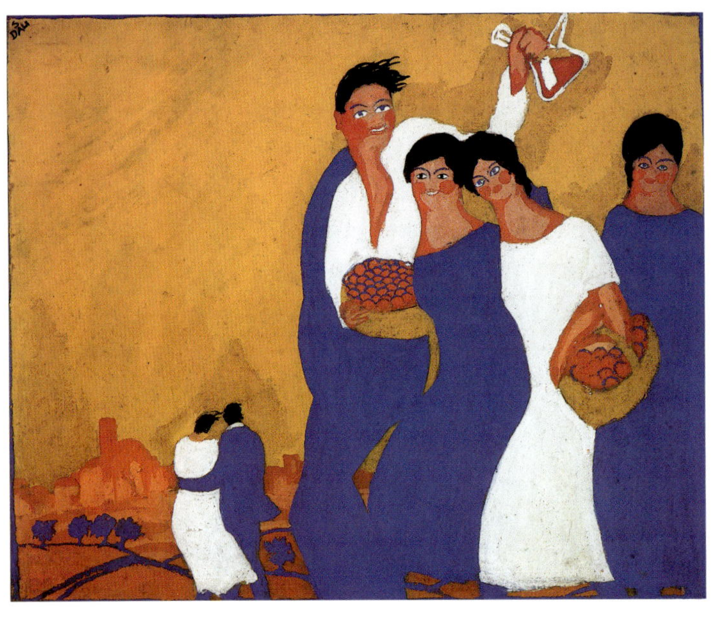

Santa Creus Festival in Figueras · 1920
The Salvador Dalí Museum, St. Petersburg, Florida,
on loan from E. and A. Reynolds Morse

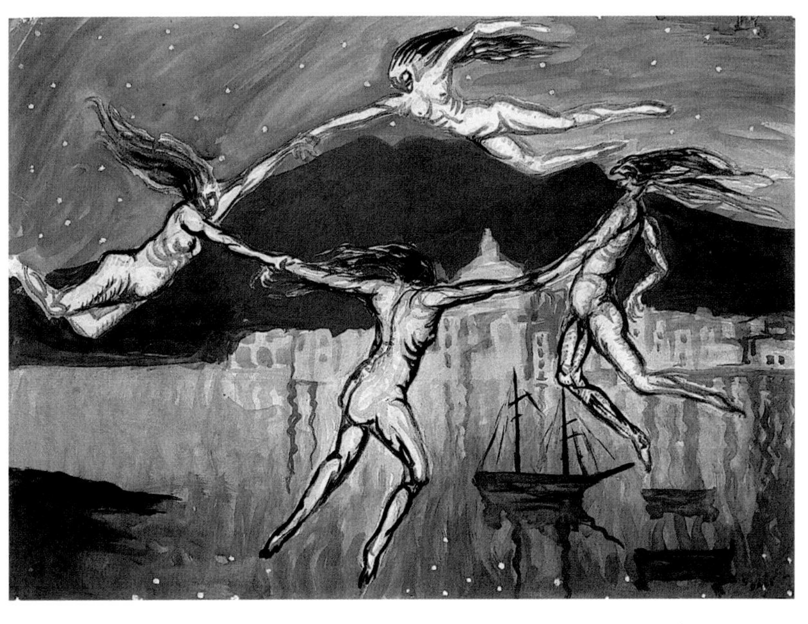

Sardana of the Witches · 1921

The Salvador Dalí Museum, St. Petersburg, Florida

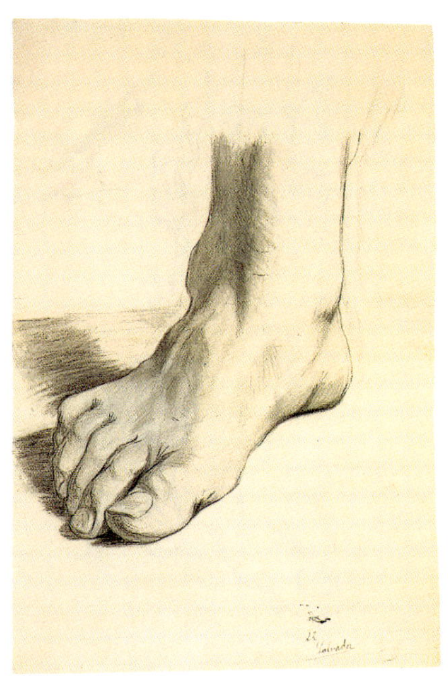

Study of a Foot · 1922

Fundación Gala-Salvador Dalí, Figueras: Dalí Bequest 1989

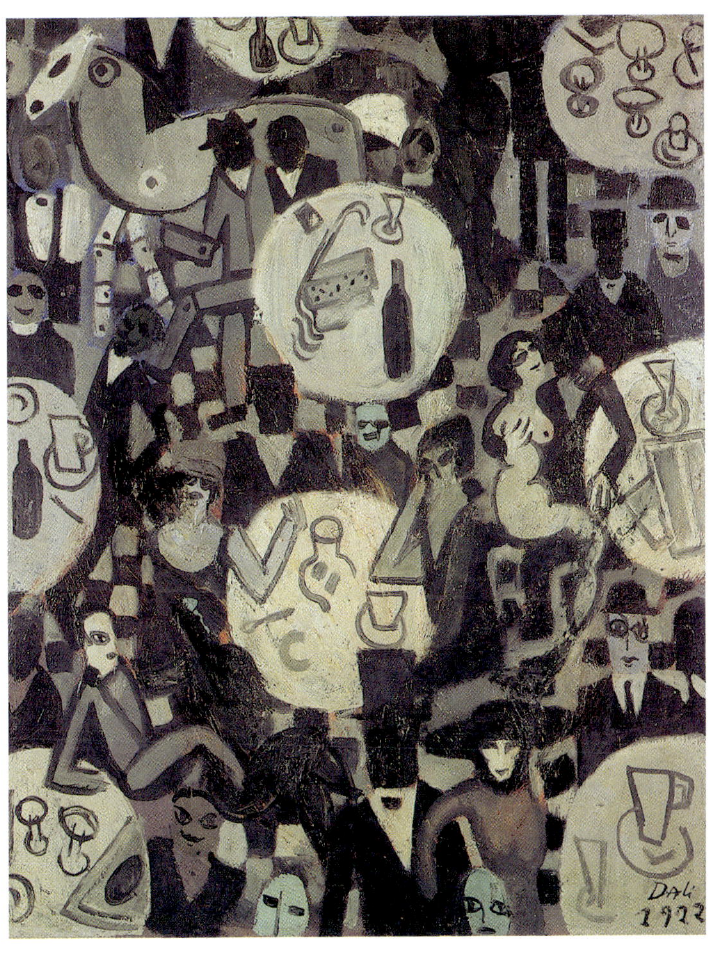

Scene in a Cabaret · 1922

Collection Bénédict Petit, Paris

29

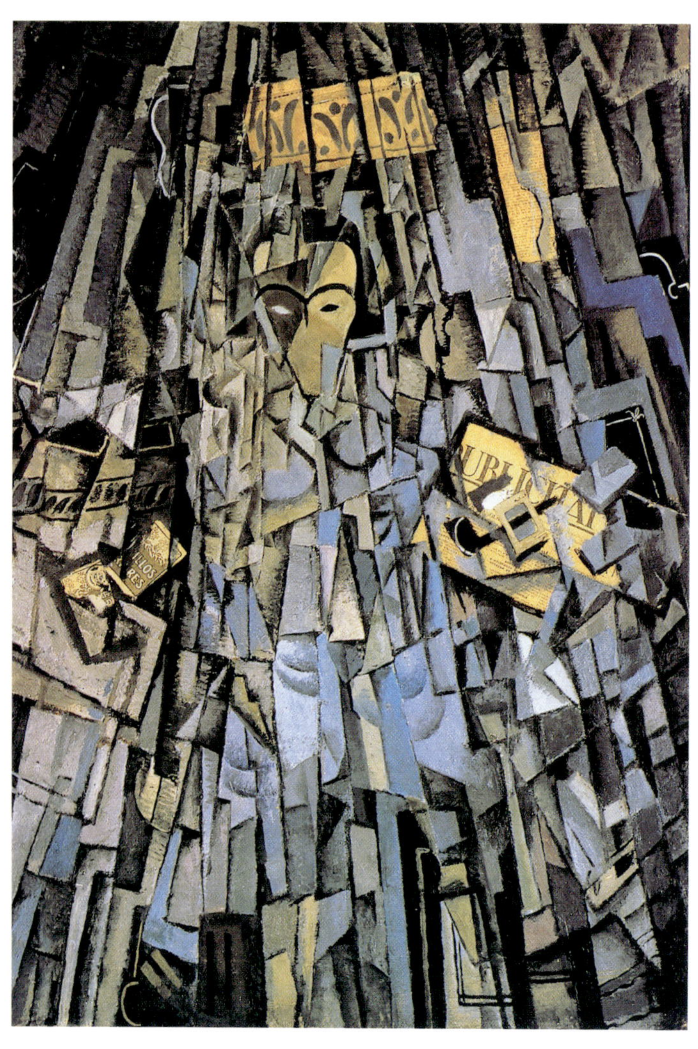

Cubist Self-Portrait · 1923
Museo Nacional Centro de Arte Reina Sofía, Madrid,
gift of Dalí to the Spanish state

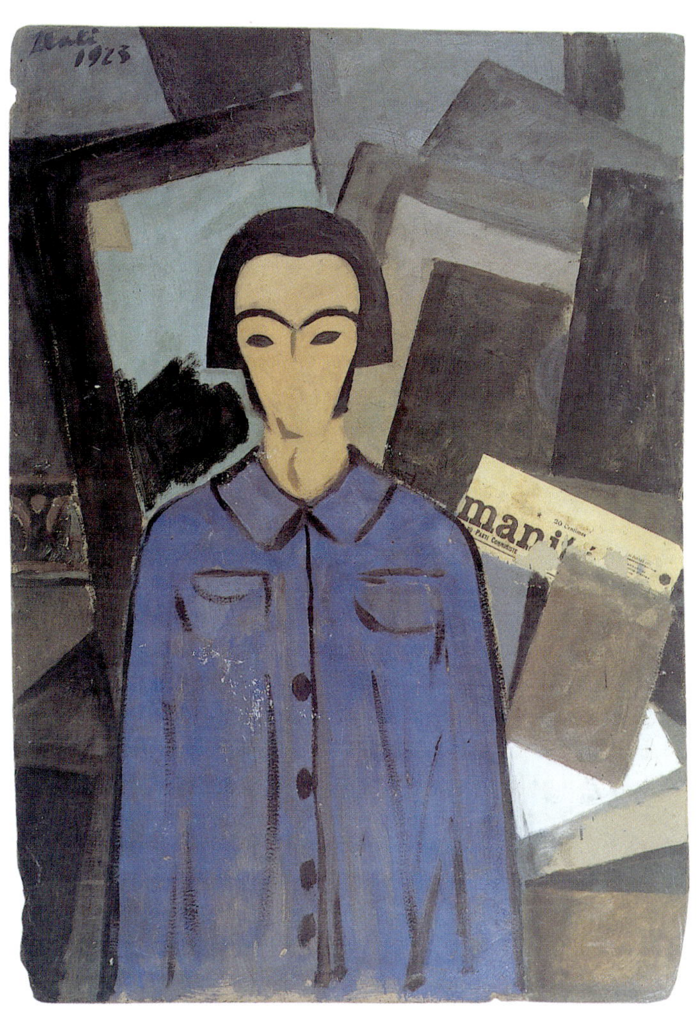

Self-Portrait with "L'Humanité" · 1923
Fundación Gala-Salvador Dalí, Figueras, gift of Dalí to the Spanish state

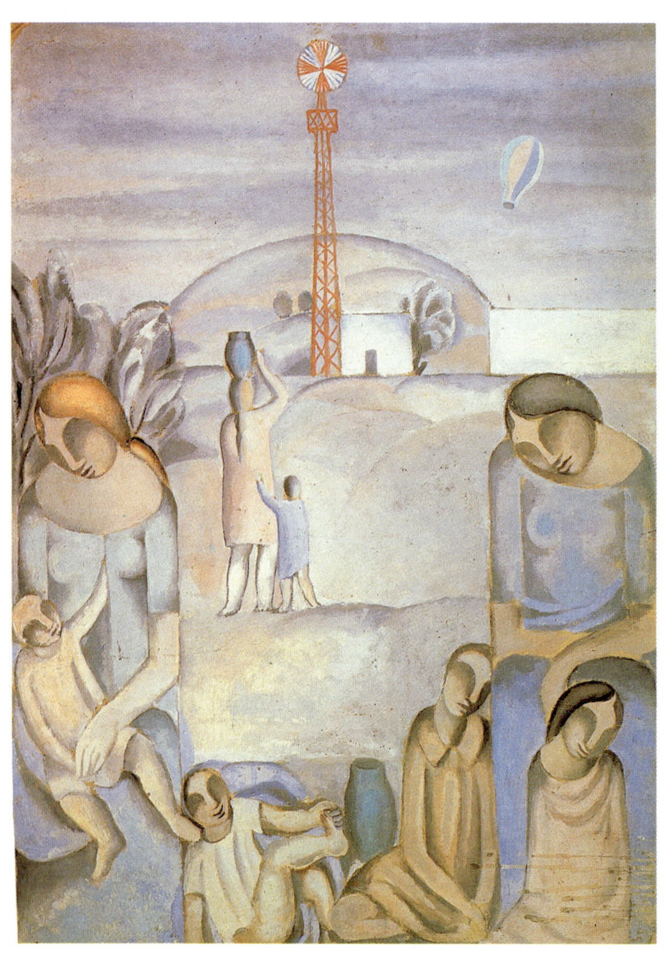

Figures in a Landscape at Ampurdán · 1923
Fundación Gala-Salvador Dalí, Figueras, gift of Dalí to the Spanish state

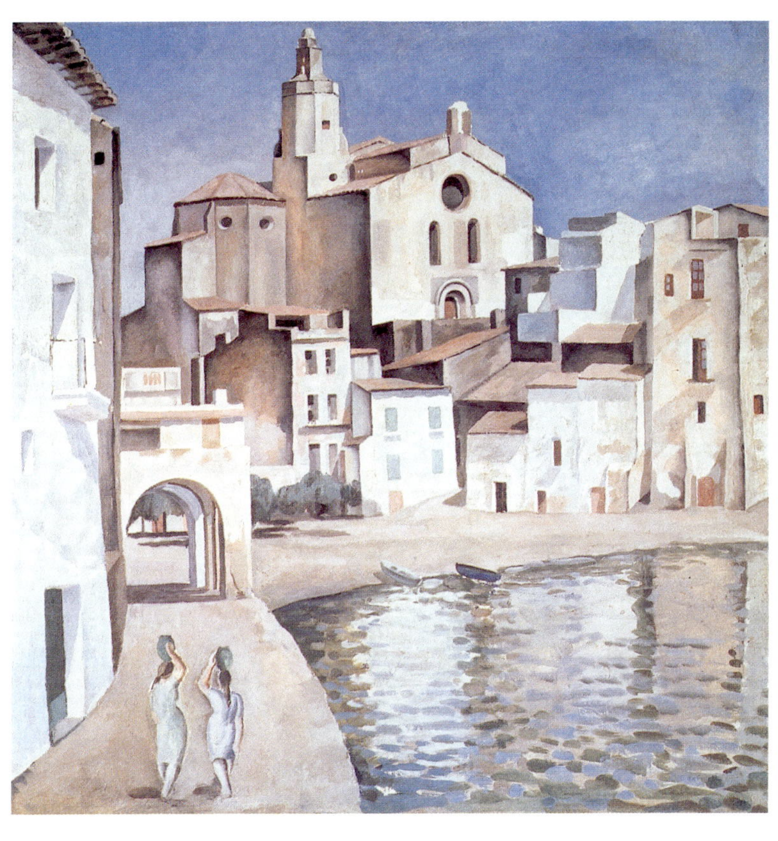

Port Alguer, Cadaqués · 1924
Fundación Gala-Salvador Dalí, Figueras

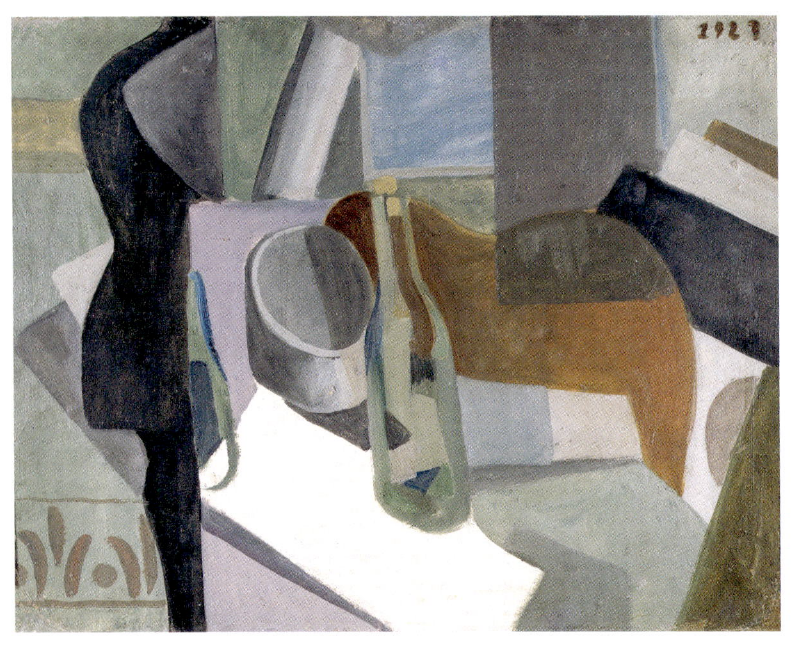

Still Life · 1923
Museo Nacional Centro de Arte Reina Sofía, Madrid, gift of Dalí to the Spanish state

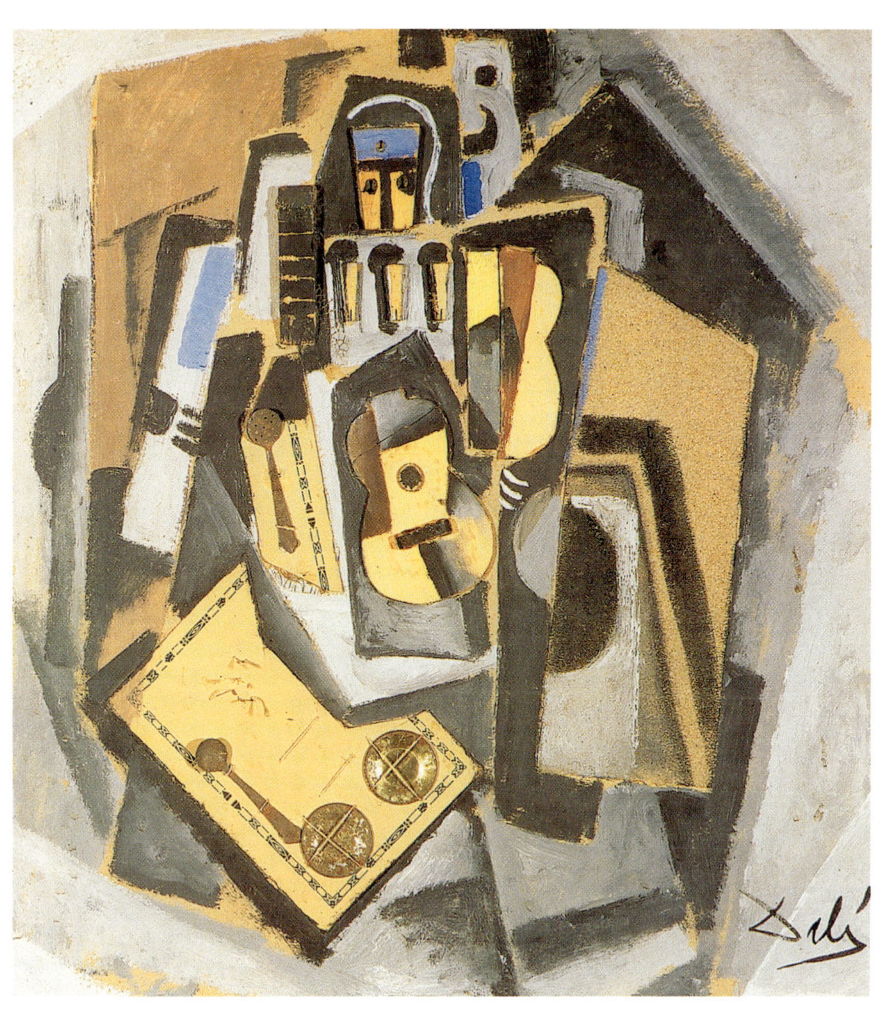

Pierrot and Guitar · 1924
Museo Thyssen-Bornemisza, Madrid;
formerly Collection Montserrat Dalí de Bas

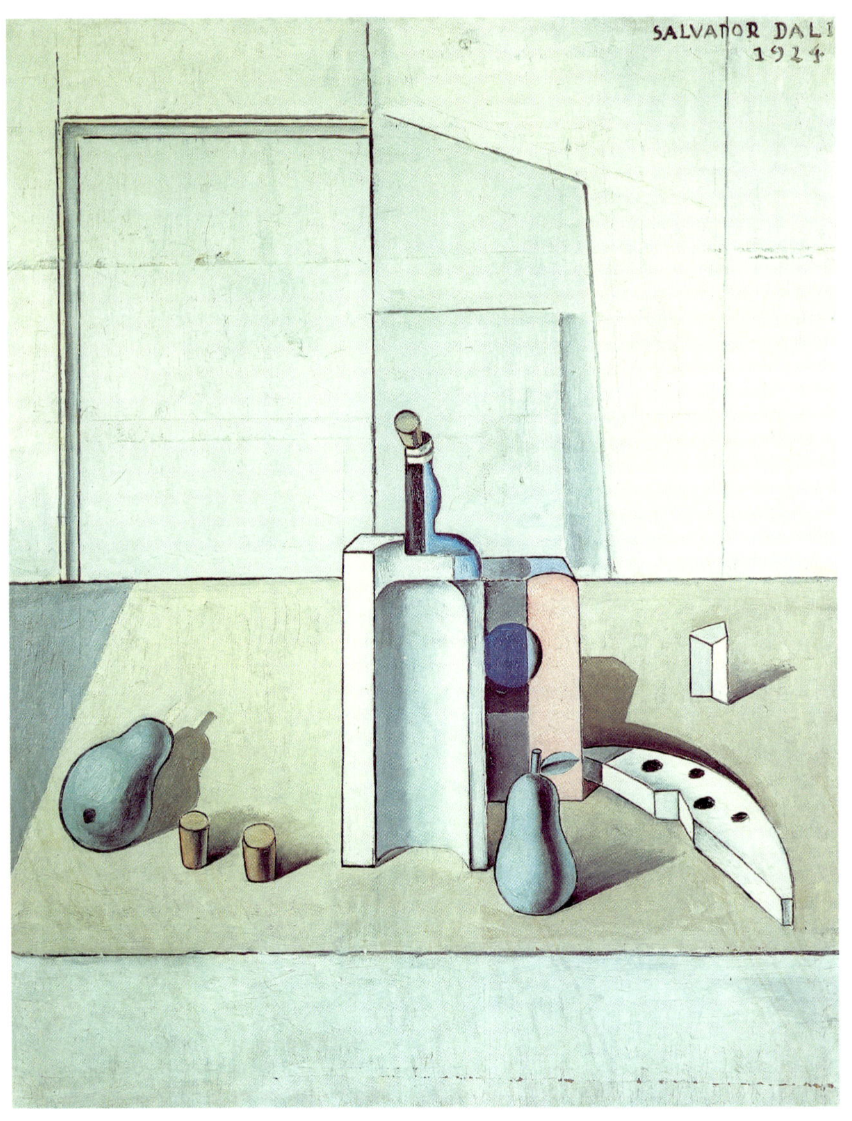

Still Life · 1924
Fundación Federico García Lorca, Madrid

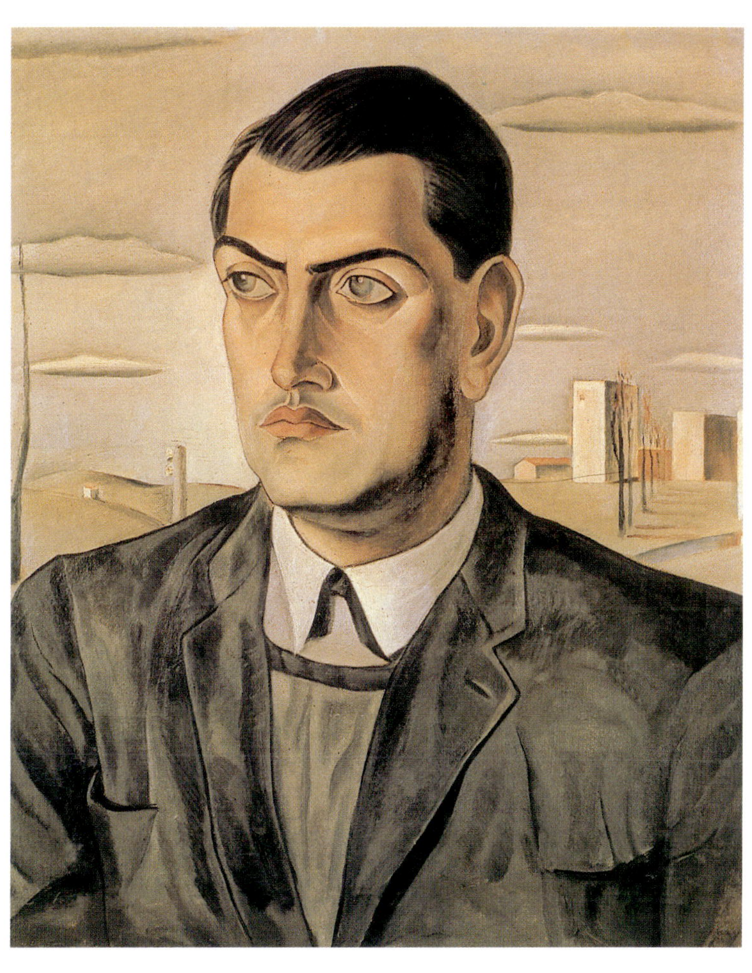

Portrait of Luis Buñuel · 1924

Museo Nacional Centro de Arte Reina Sofía, Madrid; formerly Collection Luis Buñuel

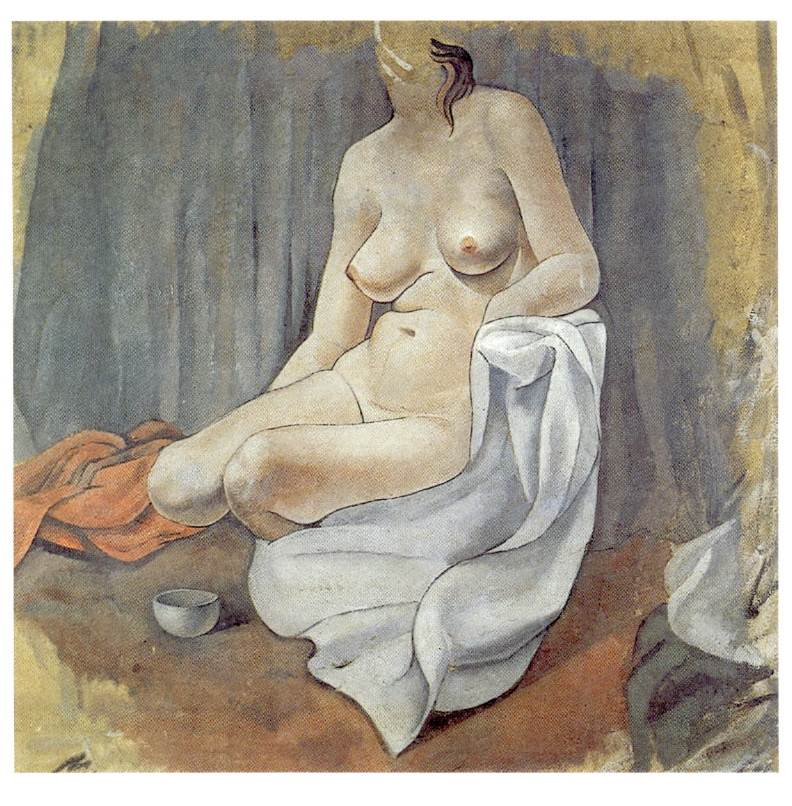

Female Nude · 1925
Private collection

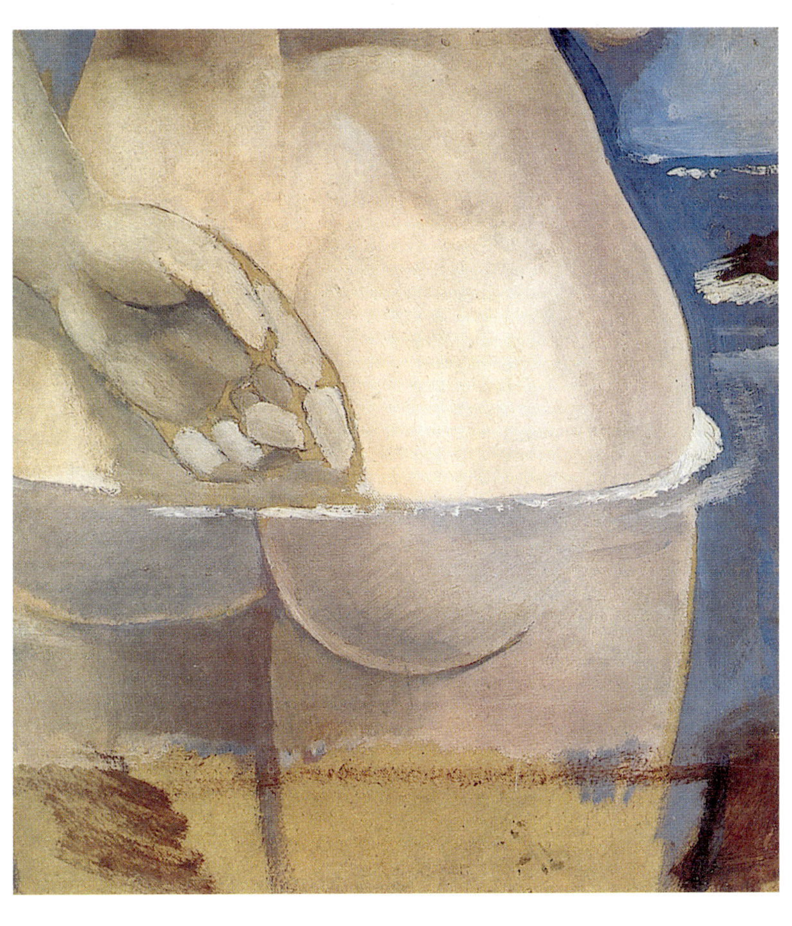

Nude in the Water · 1925
Private collection

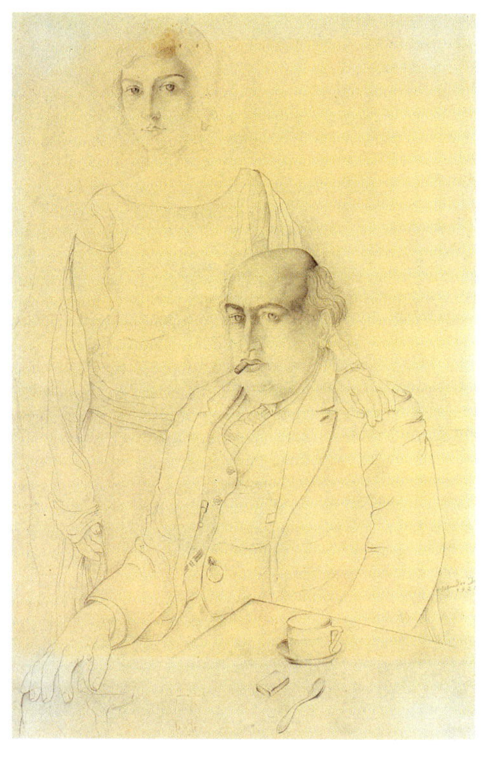

Don Salvador and Ana María Dalí (Portrait of the Artist's Father and Sister) · 1925
Museo de Arte Moderno, Barcelona

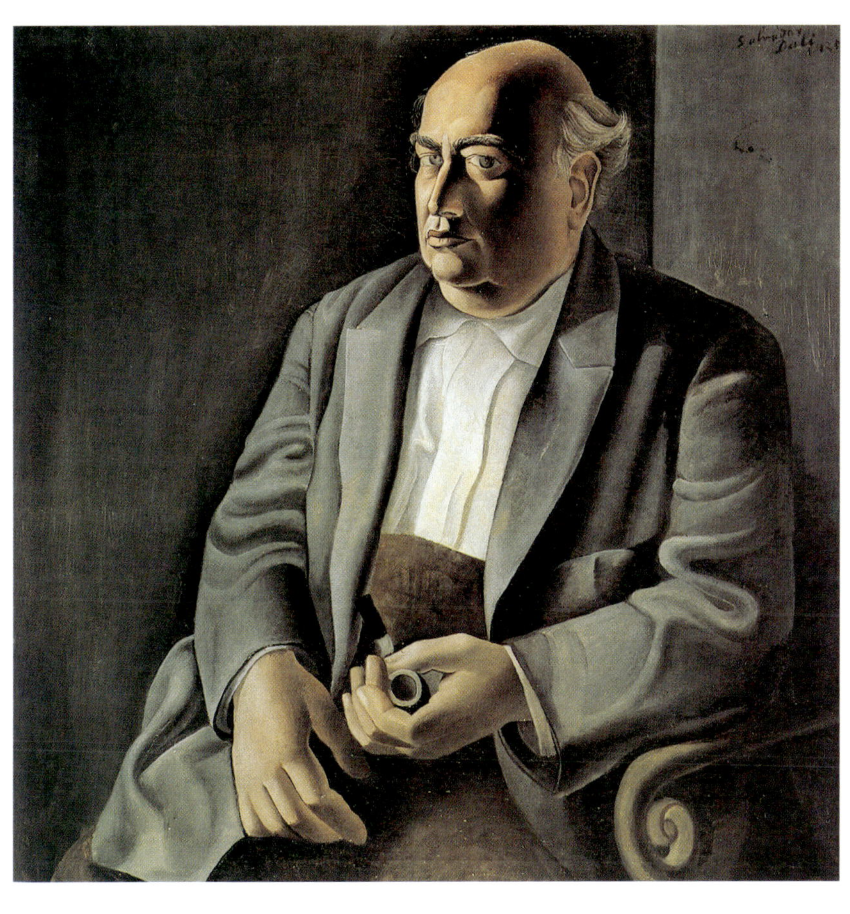

Portrait of My Father · 1925

Museo de Arte Moderno, Barcelona

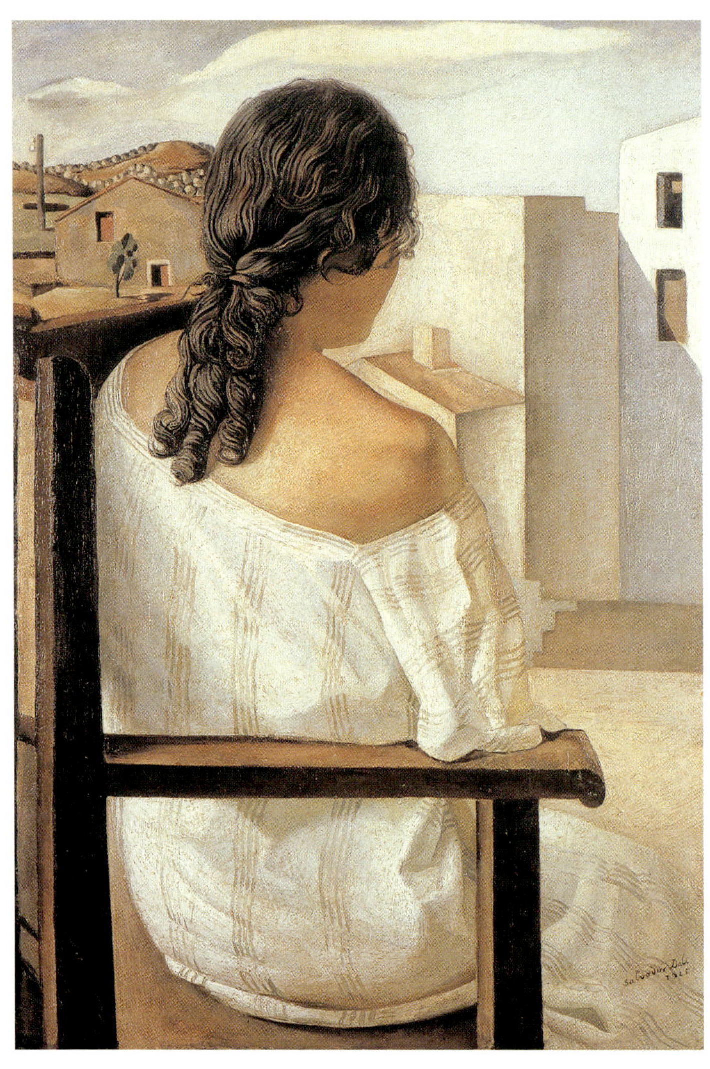

Seated Girl from the Back · 1925
Museo Nacional Centro de Arte Reina Sofía, Madrid

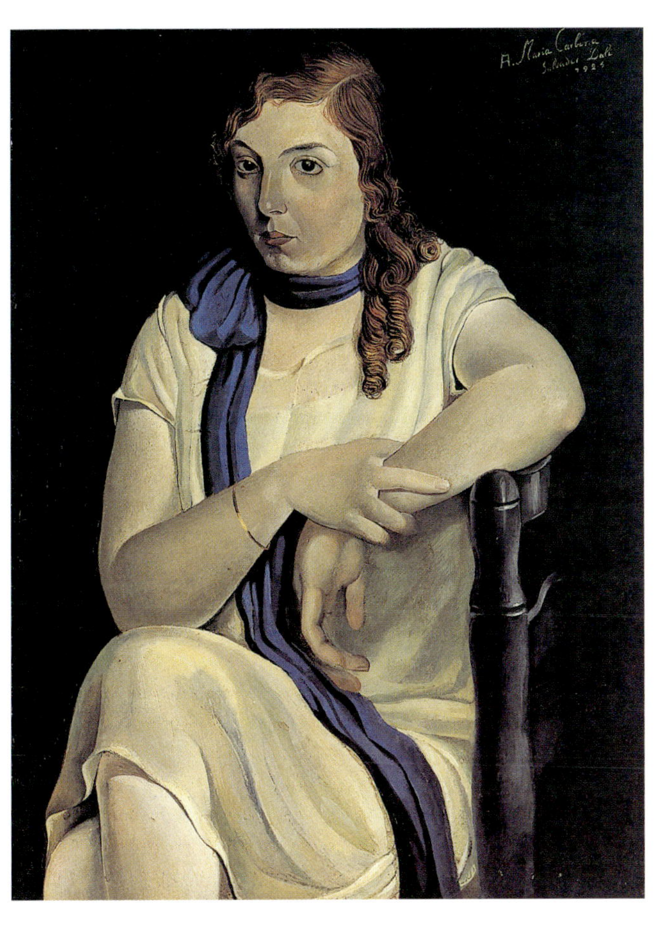

Portrait of María Carbona · 1925
Montreal Museum of Fine Arts

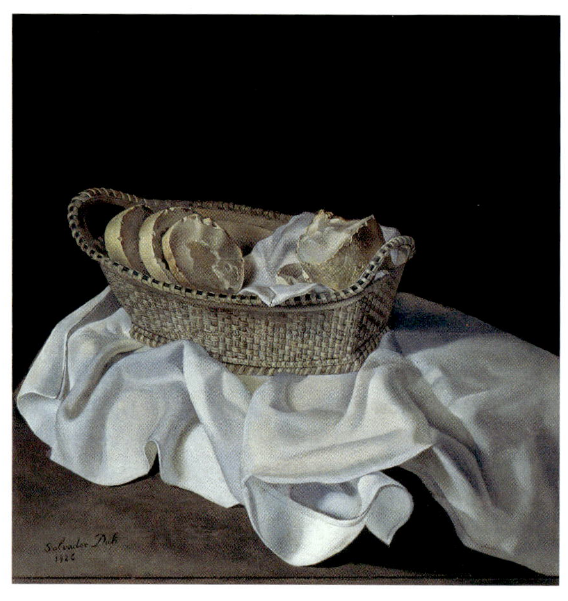

Basket of Bread · 1925

The Salvador Dalí Museum, St. Petersburg, Florida;
formerly Collection E. and A. Reynolds Morse

> **Figure at a Window** · 1925

Museo Nacional Centro de Arte Reina Sofía, Madrid

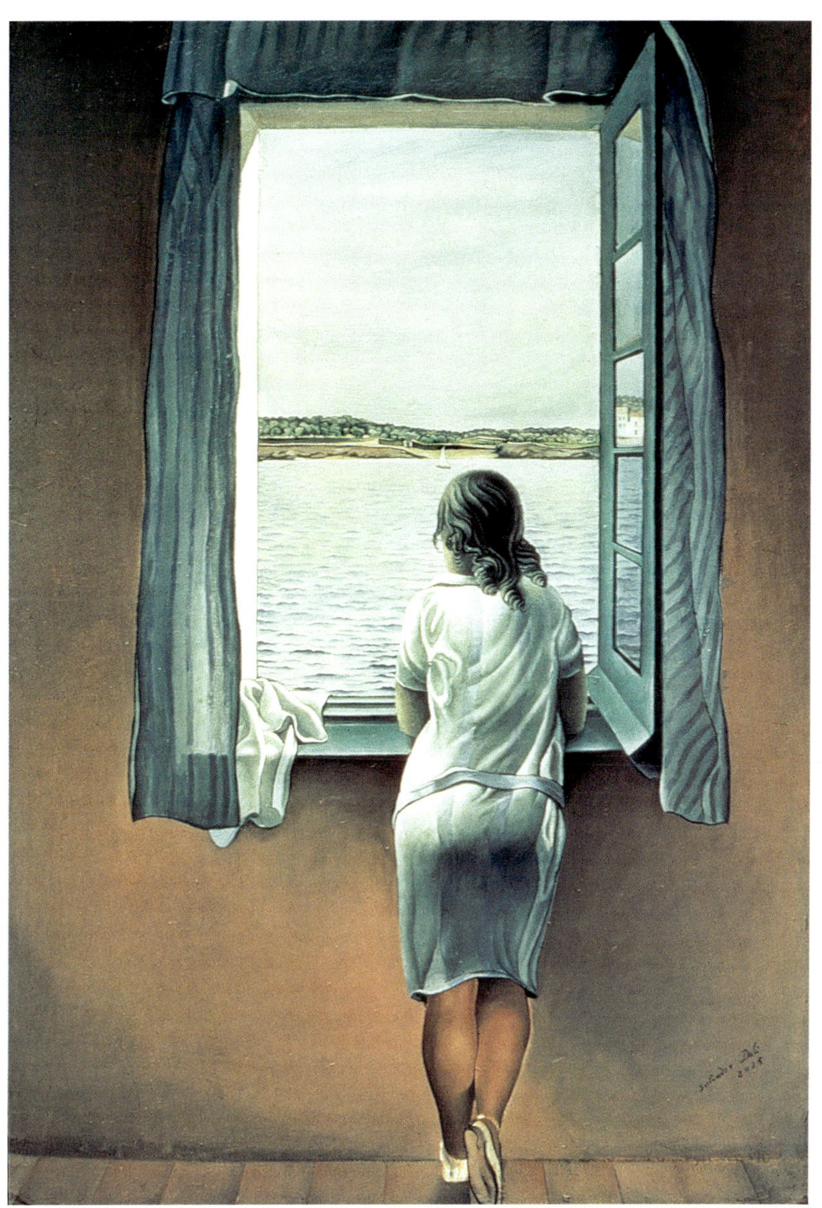

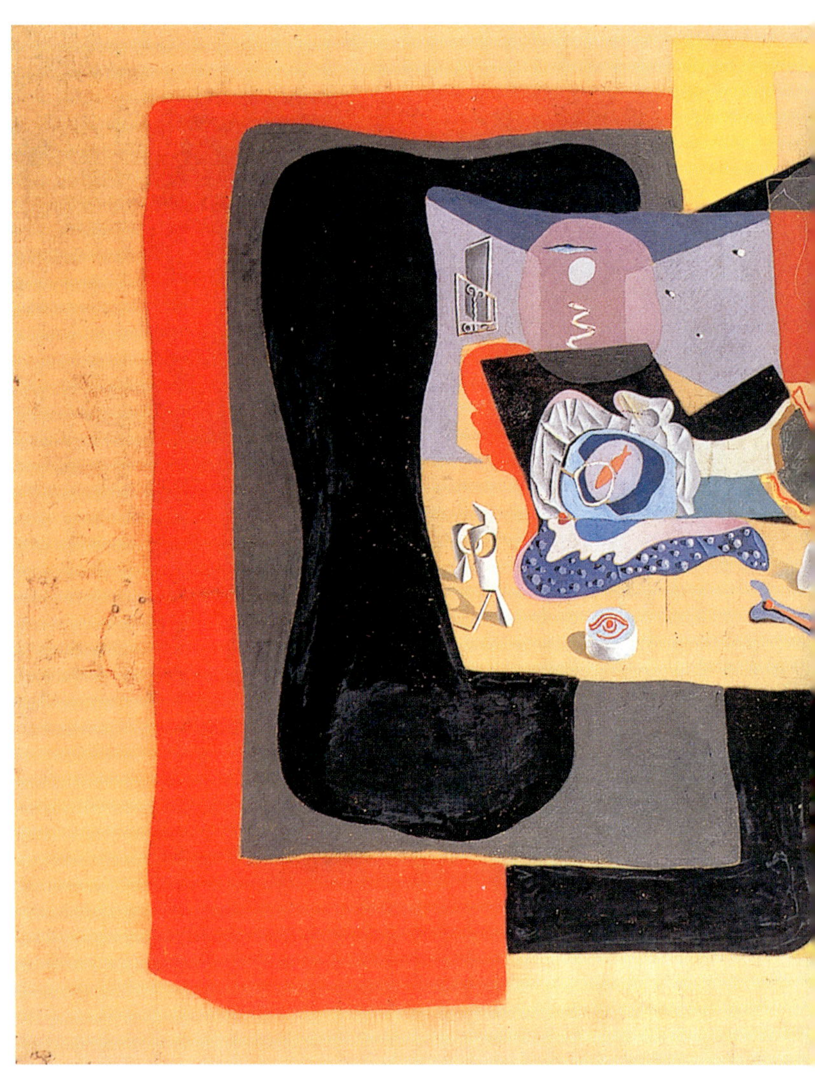

Still Life and Mauve Moonlight · 1926
Fundación Gala-Salvador Dalí, Figueras, gift of Dalí to the Spanish state

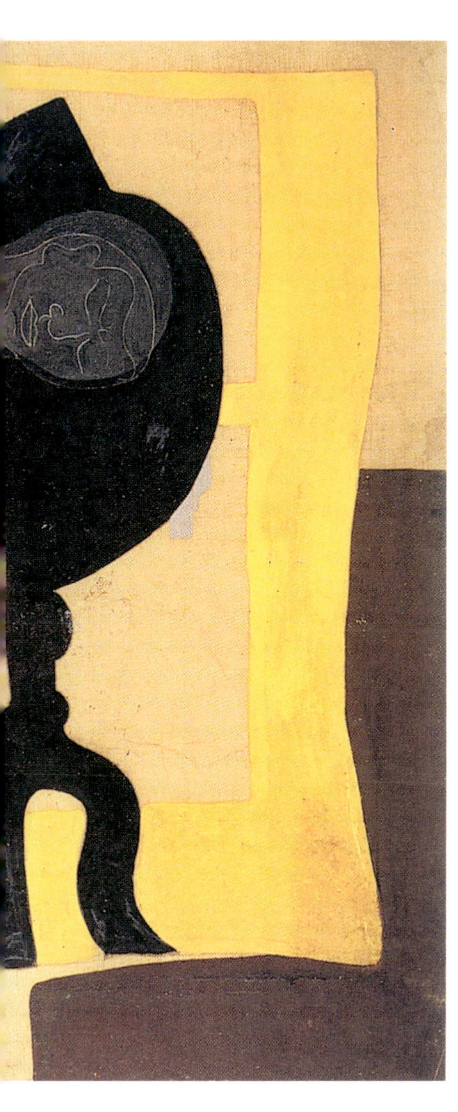

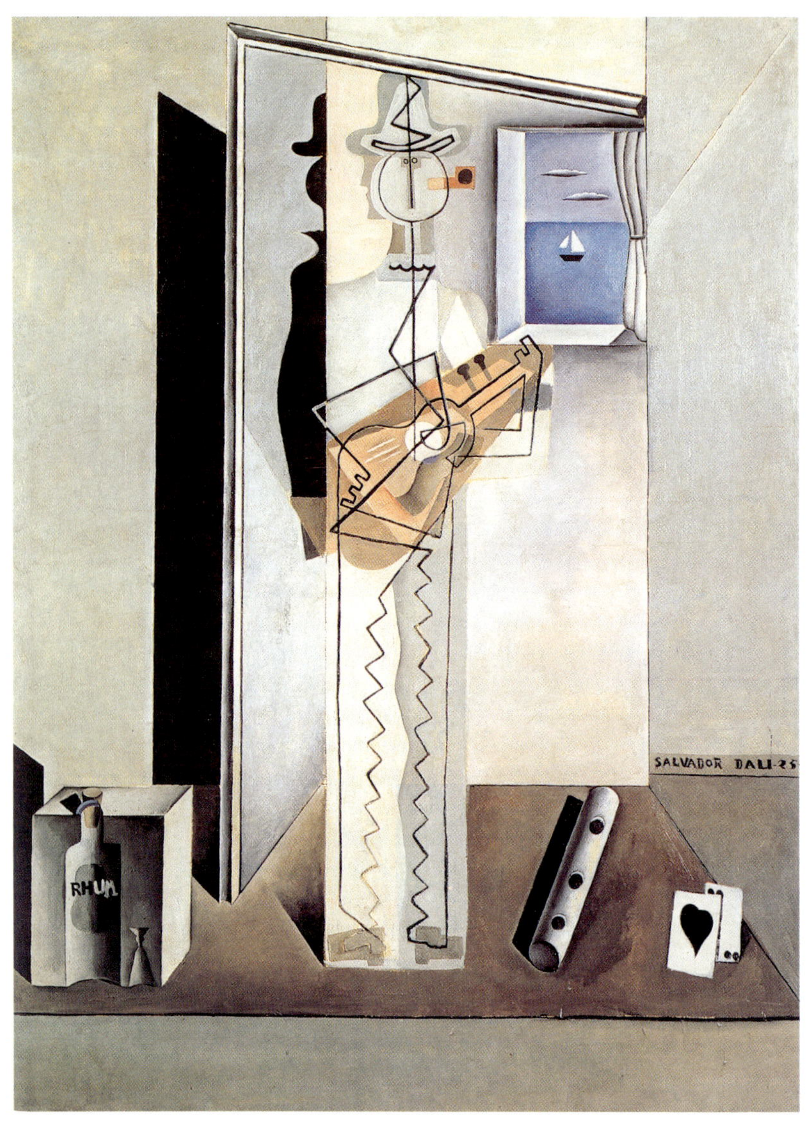

Pierrot Playing the Guitar · 1926
Museo Nacional Centro de Arte Reina Sofía, Madrid, gift of Dalí to the Spanish state

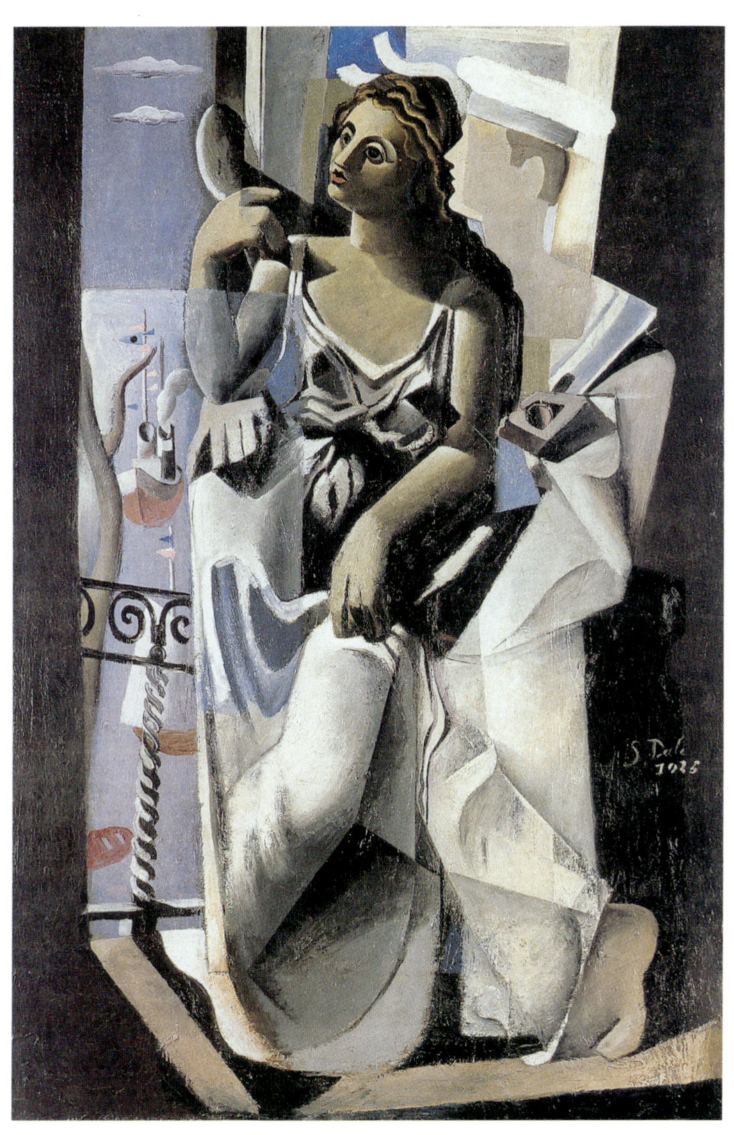

Venus and a Sailor—Homage to Salvat-Papasseit · 1925
Ikeda Museum of 20th Century Art, Shizuoka

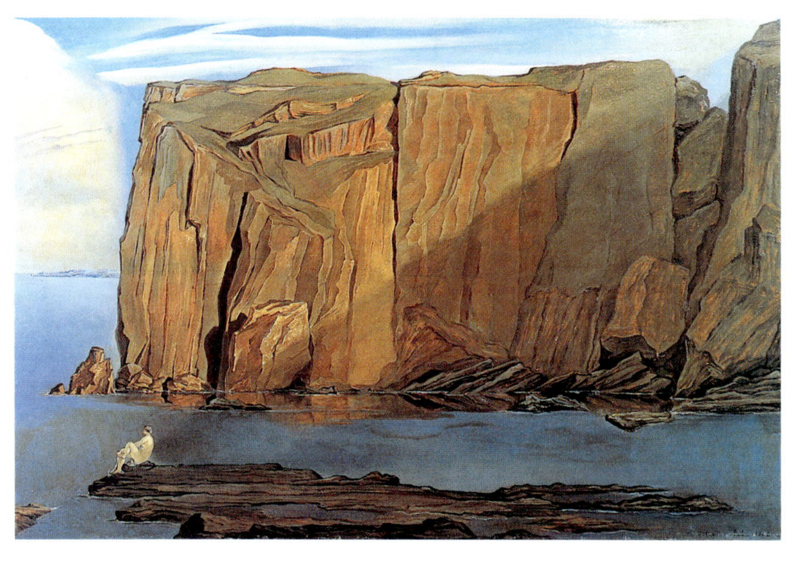

Penya-Segats (Woman on the Rocks) · 1925
Private collection
> **Portrait of Ramoneta Montsalvatge** · 1926
Fundación Gala-Salvador Dalí, Figueras

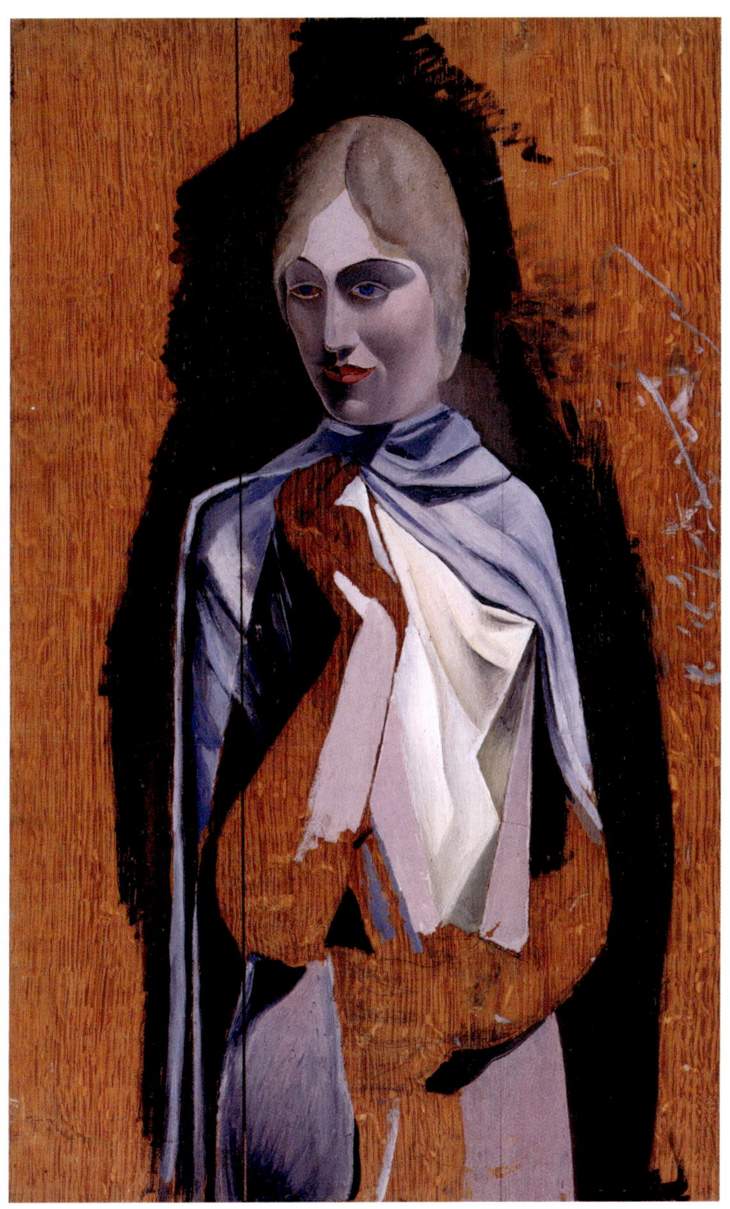

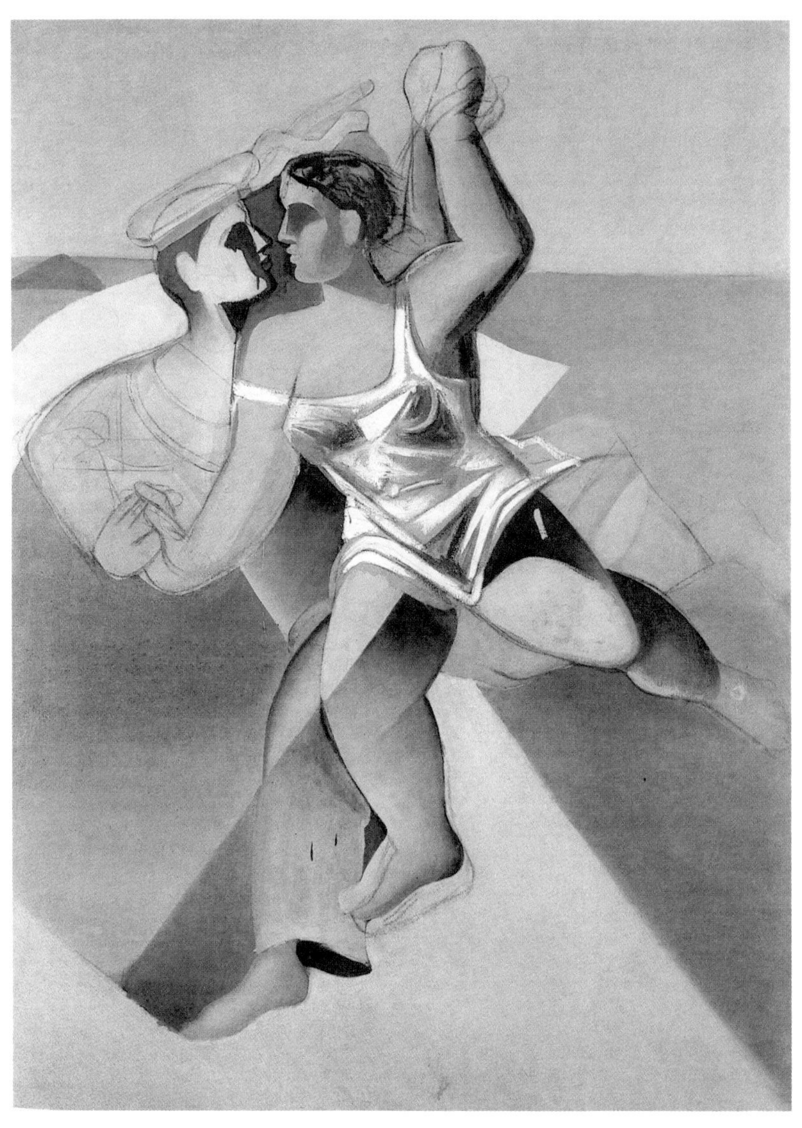

Venus and Sailor · 1924–26
André-François Petit, Paris

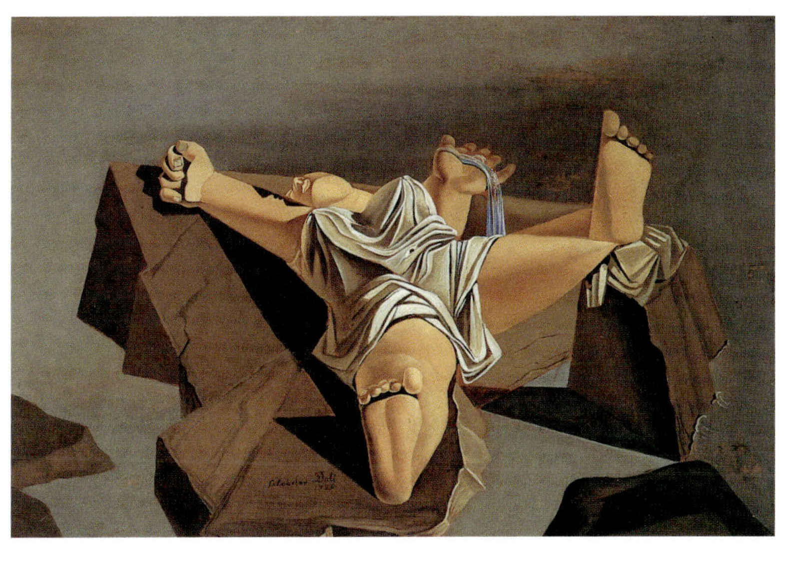

Figure on the Rocks (Sleeping Woman) · 1925

The Salvador Dalí Museum, St. Petersburg, Florida;
formerly Collection E. and A. Reynolds Morse

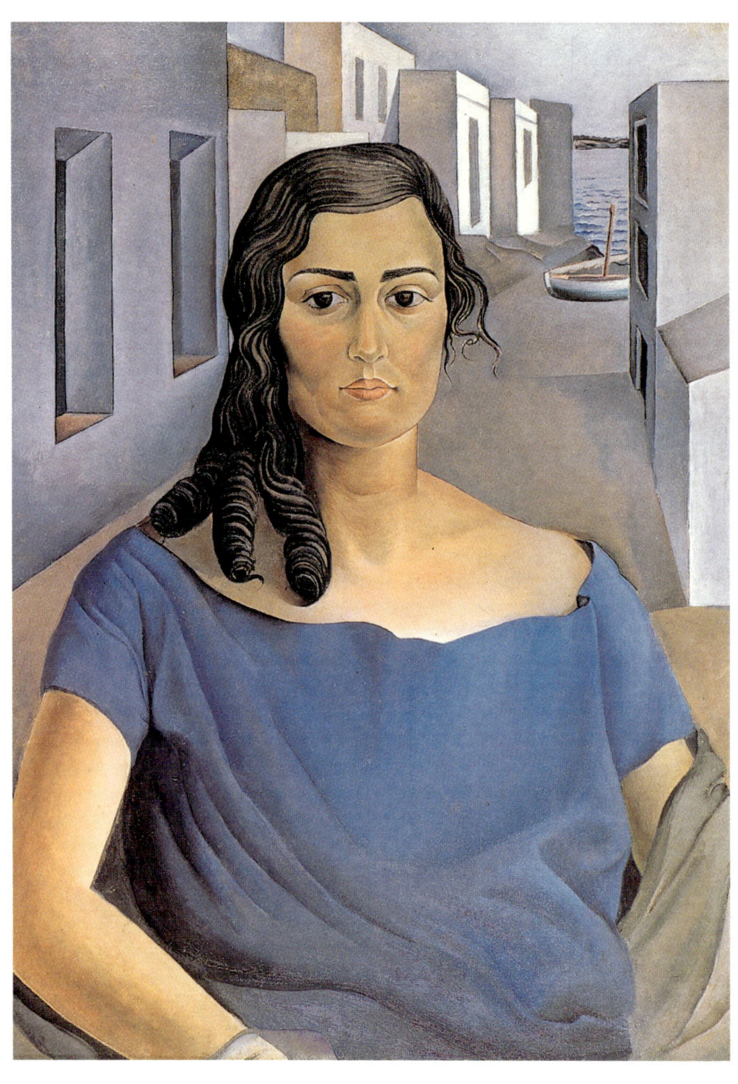

Portrait of a Girl in a Landscape (Cadaqués) · 1926
Fundación Gala-Salvador Dalí, Figueras, gift of Dalí to the Spanish state

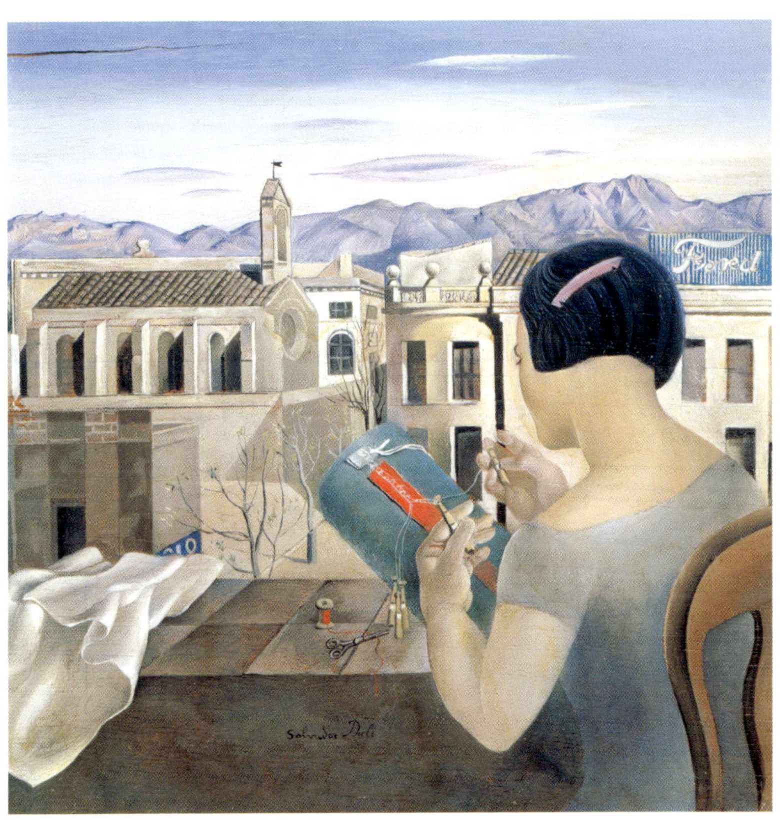

Woman at the Window at Figueras · 1926
Collection Juan Casanelles, Barcelona

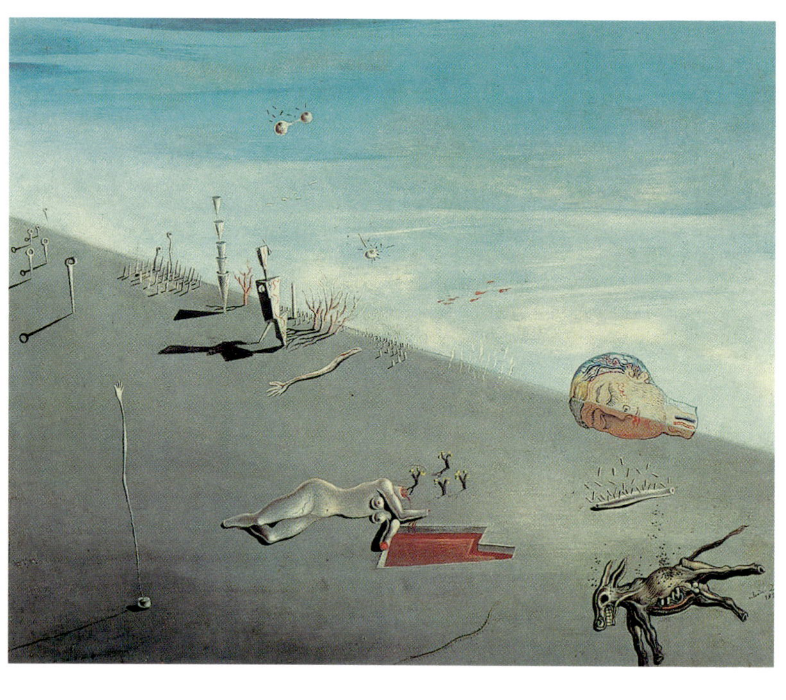

Study for "Honey Is Sweeter than Blood" (Automatic Drawing) · 1926
Private collection

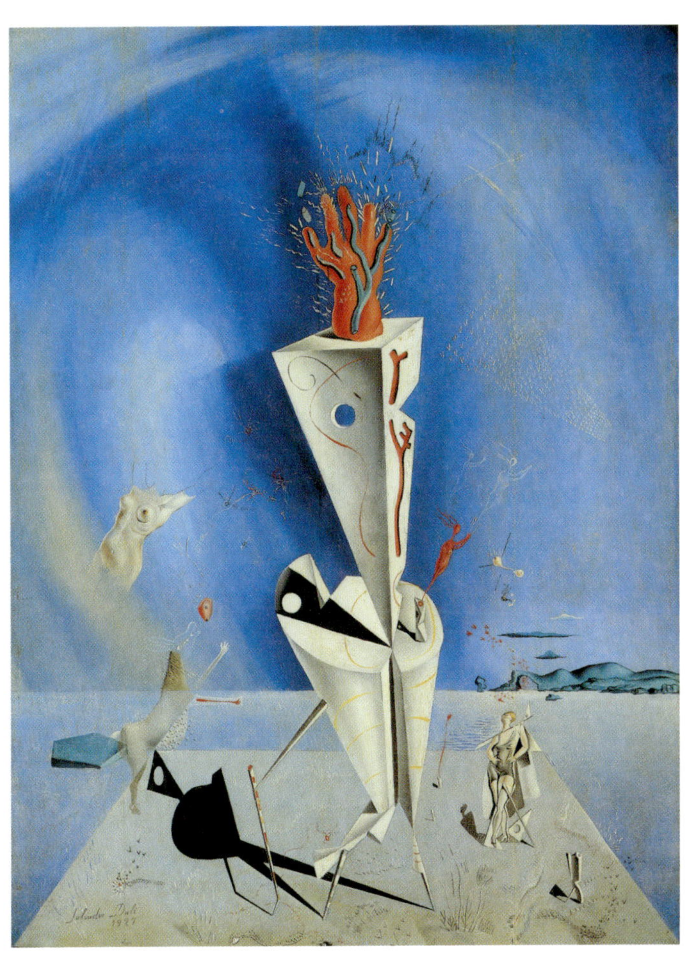

Apparatus and Hand · 1927
The Salvador Dalí Museum, St. Petersburg, Florida;
formerly Collection E. and A. Reynolds Morse

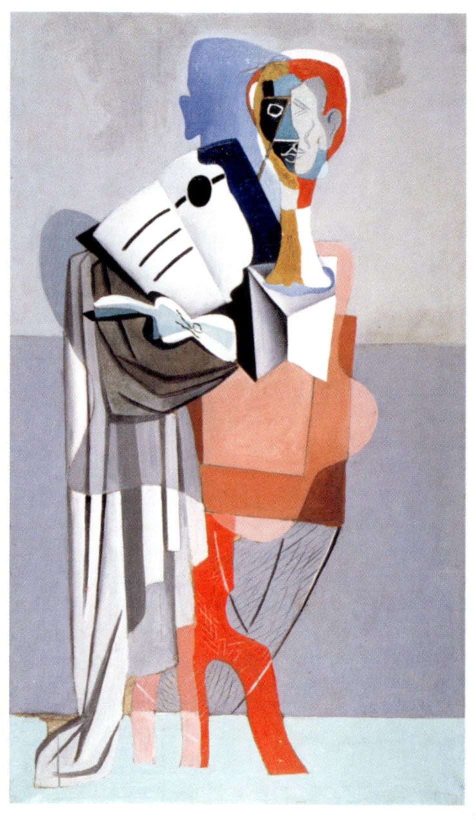

Cubist Figure (Homage to Erik Satie) · 1926
Fundación Gala-Salvador Dalí, Figueras, gift of Dalí to the Spanish state

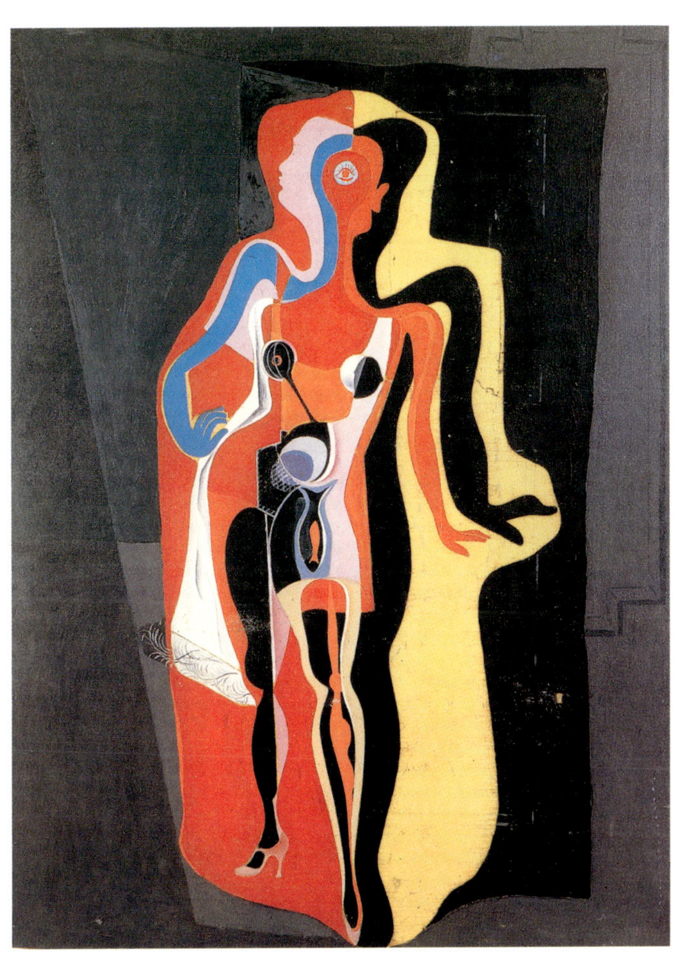

Mannequin · 1926–27
Fundación Gala-Salvador Dalí, Figueras, gift of Dalí to the Spanish state

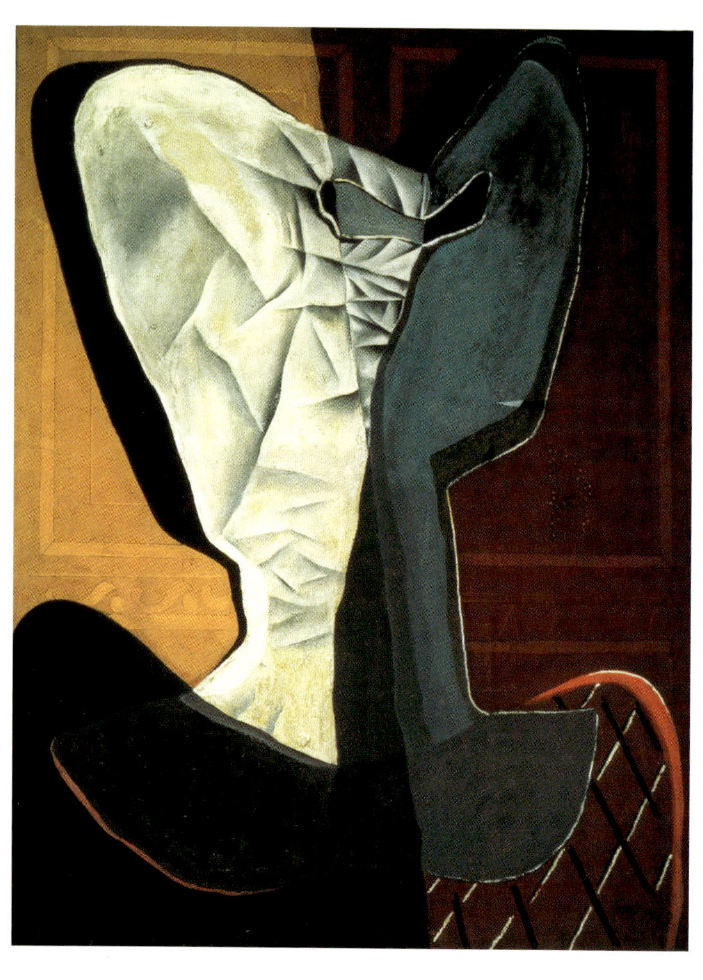

Harlequin · 1927
Museo Nacional Centro de Arte Reina Sofía, Madrid

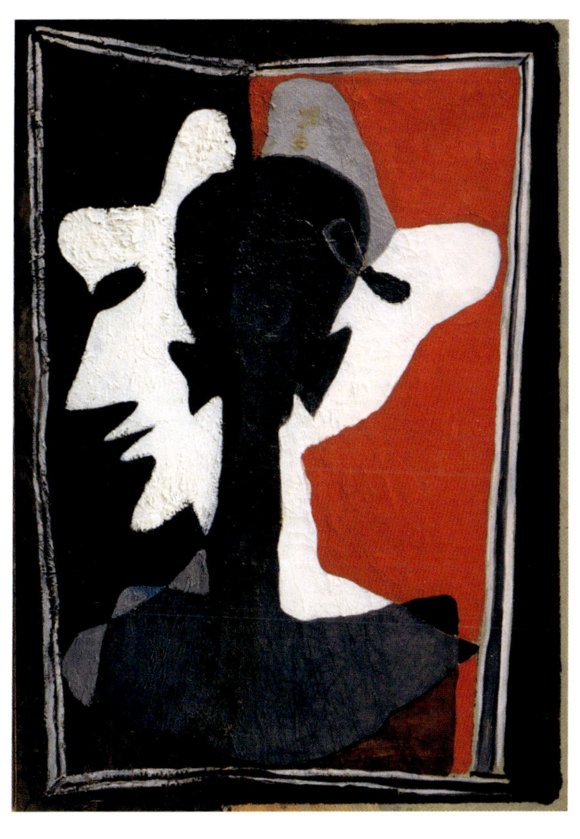

Self-Portrait Splitting into Three · 1927

Fundación Gala-Salvador Dalí, Figueras

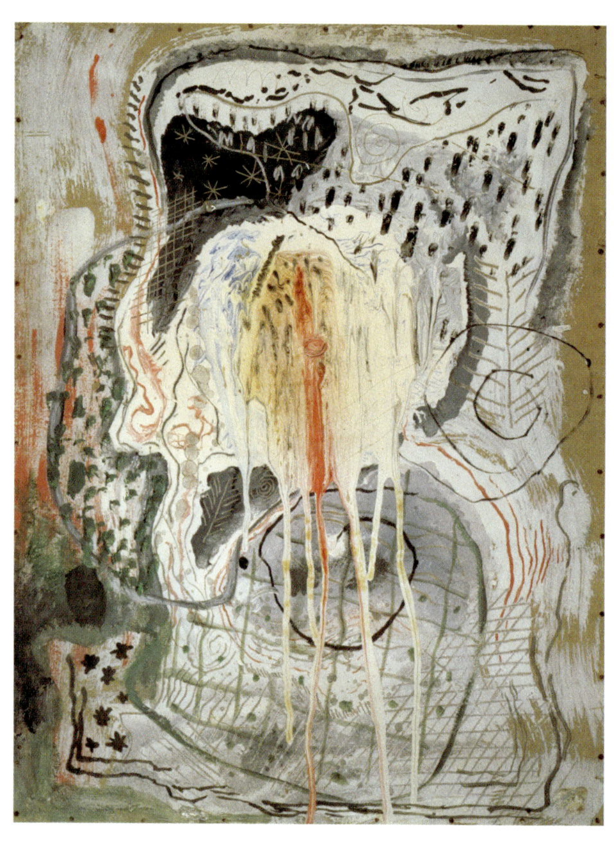

Nude Woman Seated in an Armchair · 1927–28
Fundación Gala-Salvador Dalí, Figueras
> **Still Life by the Light of the Moon** · 1927
Museo Nacional Centro de Arte Reina Sofía, Madrid,
gift of Dalí to the Spanish state

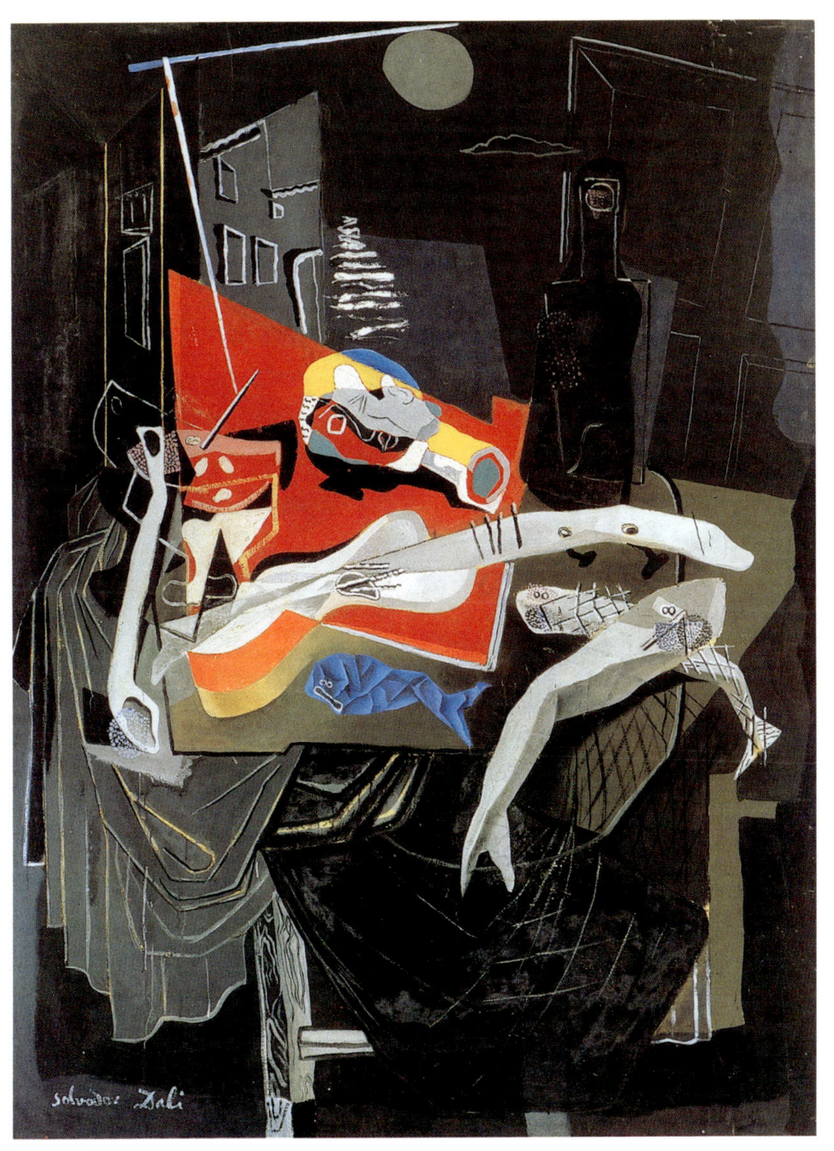

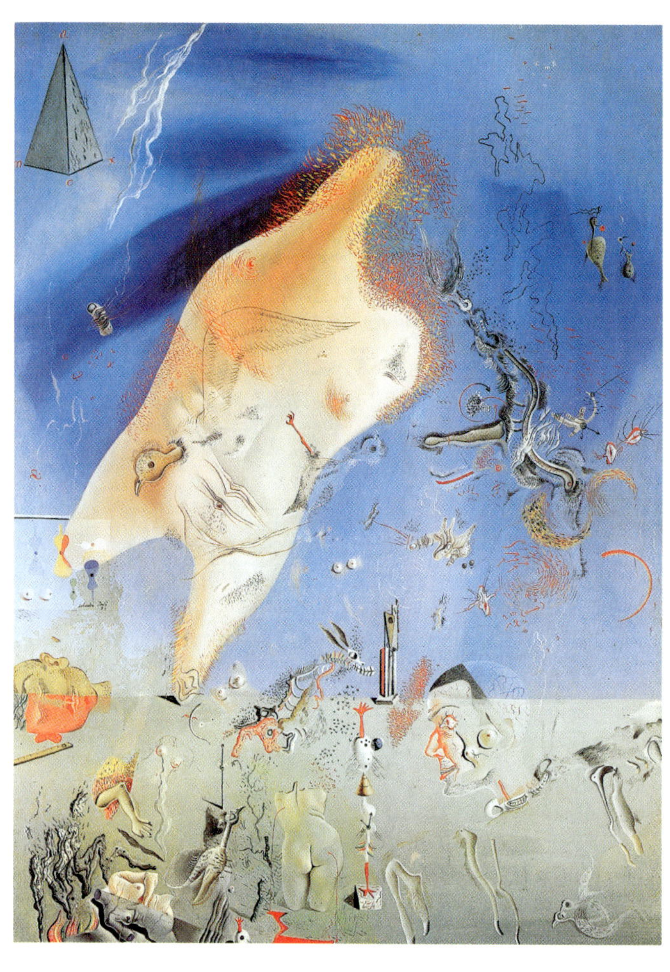

Little Cinders (Cenicitas) · 1927–28

Museo Nacional Centro de Arte Reina Sofía, Madrid

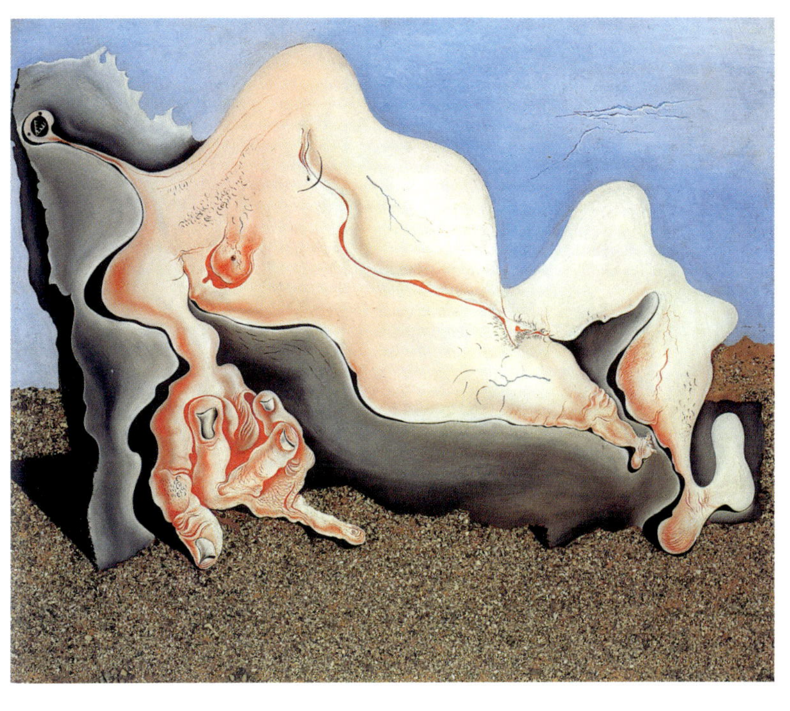

Bather (Female Nude) · 1928
The Salvador Dalí Museum, St. Petersburg, Florida,
on loan from E. and A. Reynolds Morse

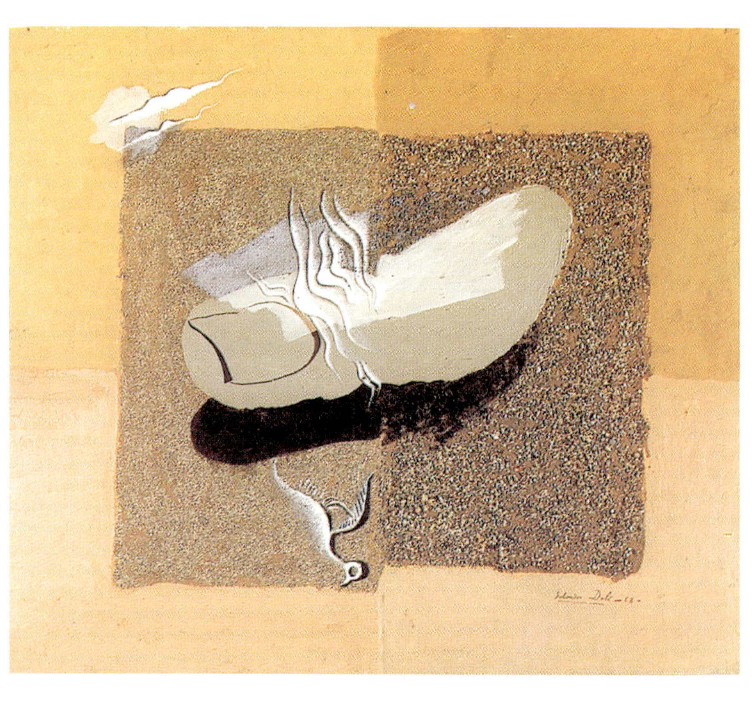

The Wounded Bird · 1928
Collection Mizne-Blumental, Monte Carlo

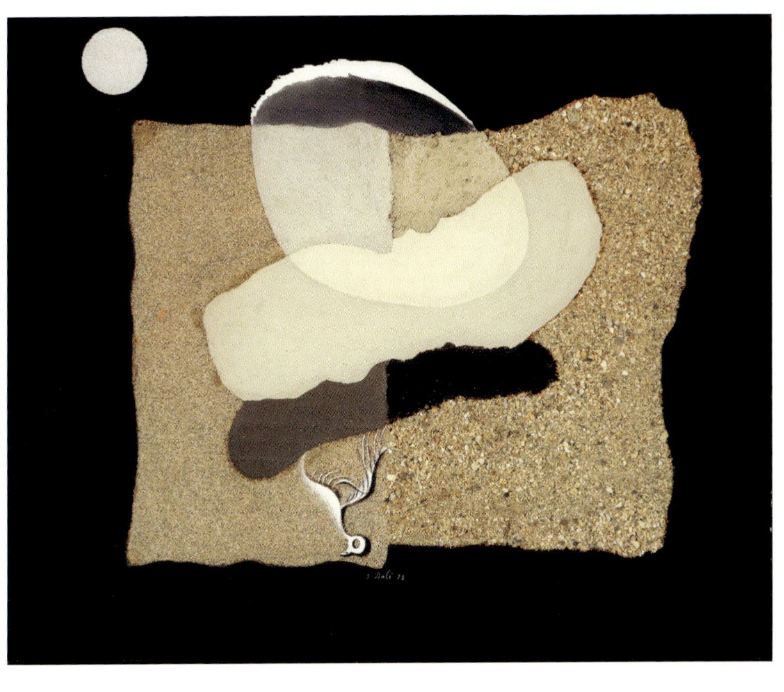

Big Thumb, Beach, Moon, and Decaying Bird · 1928
The Salvador Dalí Museum, St. Petersburg, Florida;
formerly Collection E. and A. Reynolds Morse

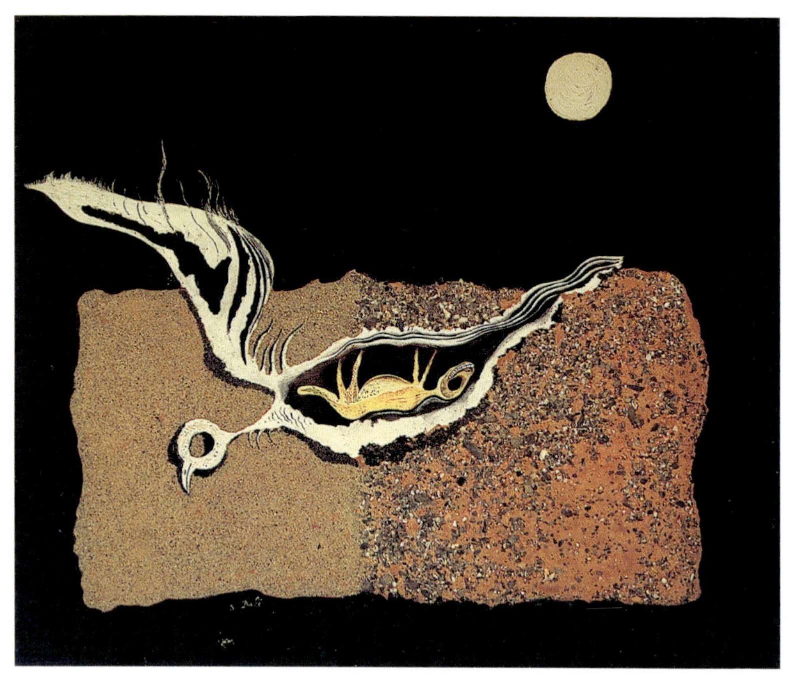

Bird · 1928
Private collection, England; formerly Collection Sir Roland Penrose

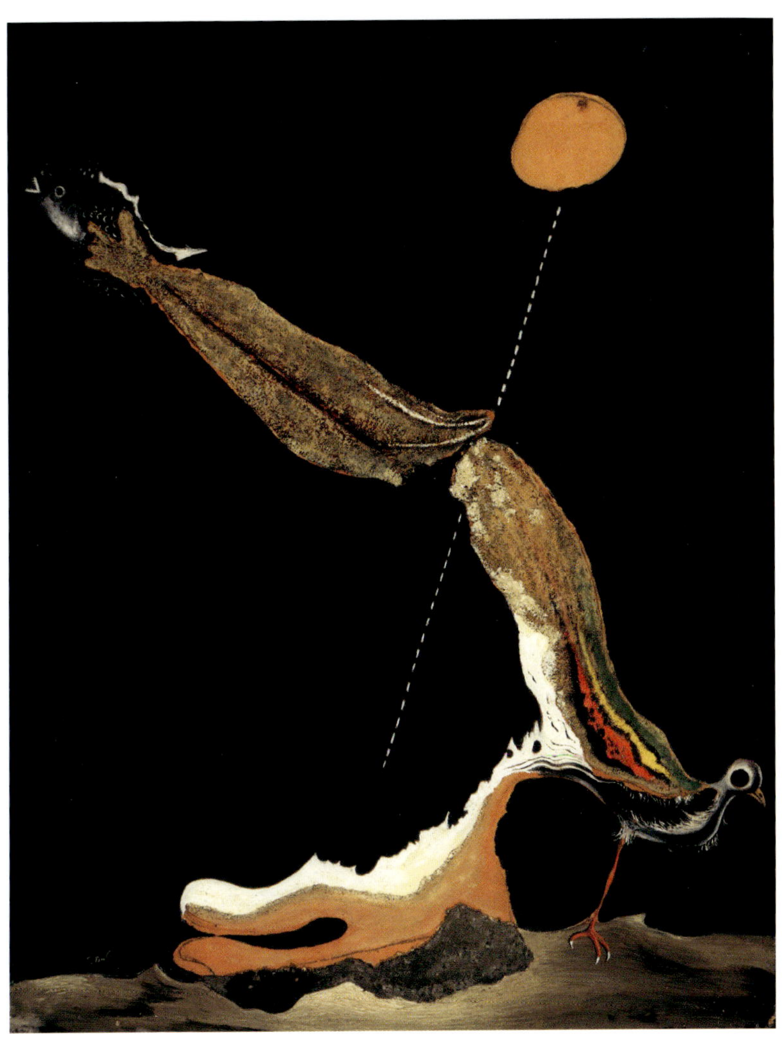

War Fish (Ocell . . . Peix) · 1928
The Salvador Dalí Museum, St. Petersburg, Florida;
formerly Collection E. and A. Reynolds Morse

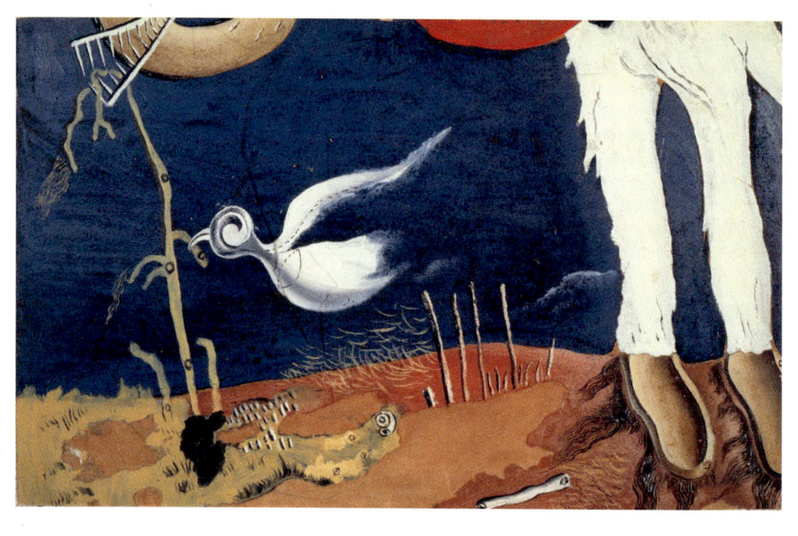

Putrefied Bird · 1928
Fundación Gala-Salvador Dalí, Figueras

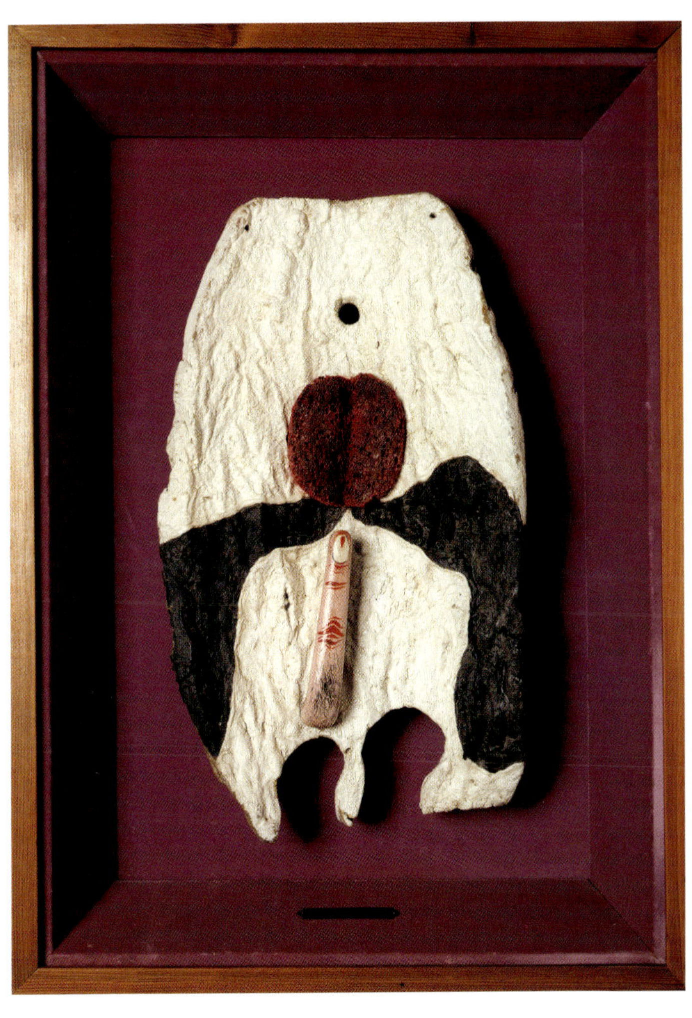

Anthropomorphic Beach · 1928
The Salvador Dalí Museum, St. Petersburg, Florida,
on loan from E. and A. Reynolds Morse

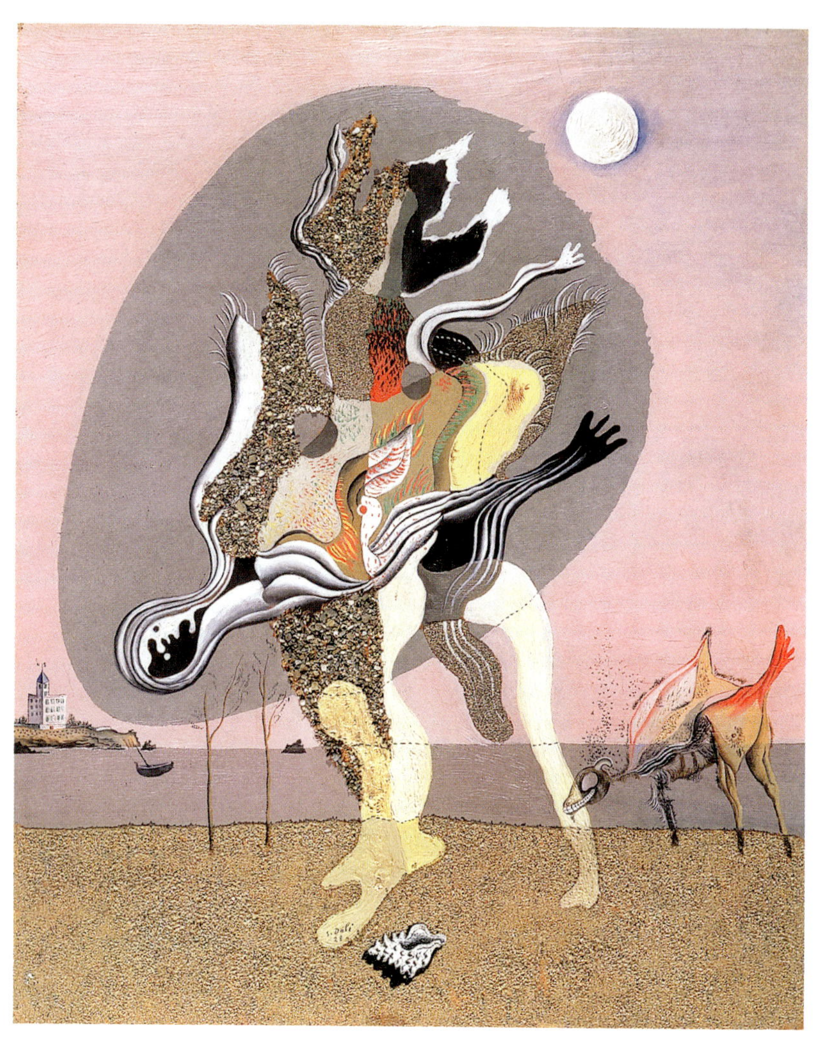

The Putrefied Donkey · 1928
André-François Petit, Paris; formerly Collection Paul Eluard

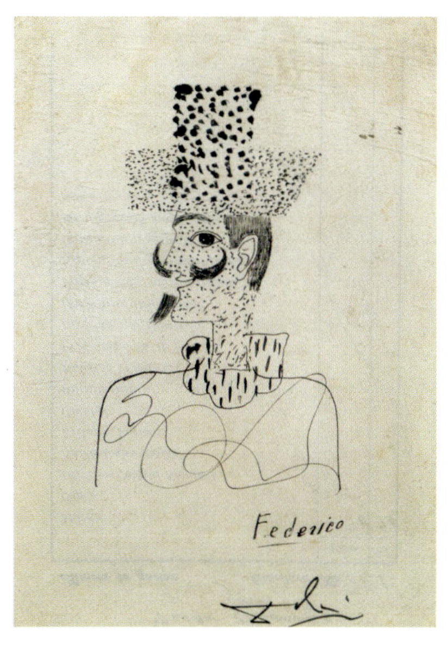

Self-Portrait, Dedicated to Federico García Lorca · 1928
Collection Juan Abello Prat, Mollet

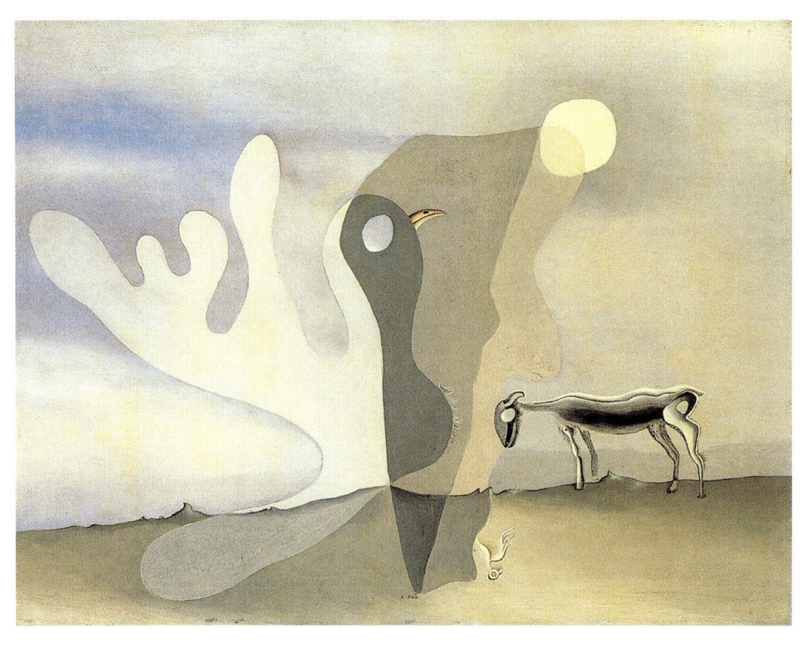

The Ram · 1928
The Salvador Dalí Museum, St. Petersburg, Florida,
on loan from E. and A. Reynolds Morse

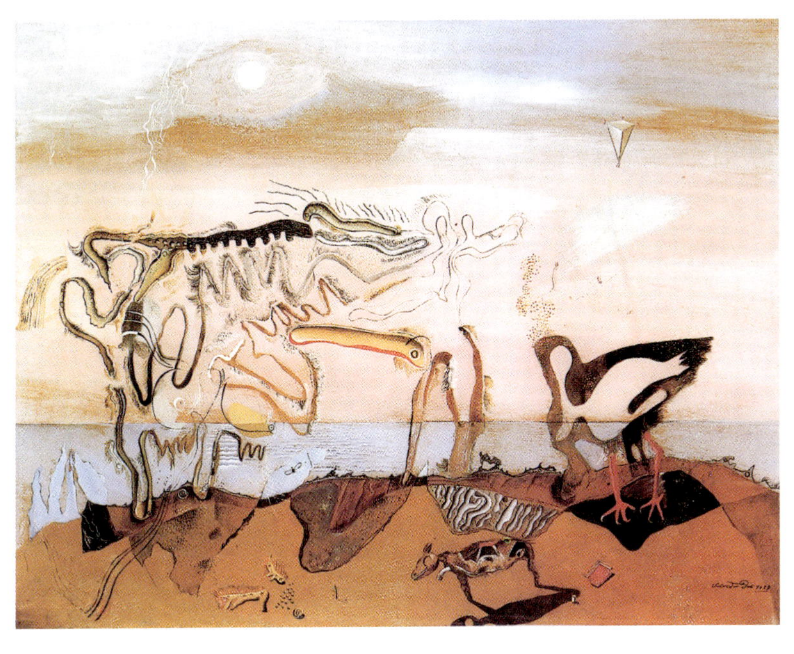

The Spectral Cow · 1928
Musée National d'Art Moderne, Centre Georges Pompidou, Paris

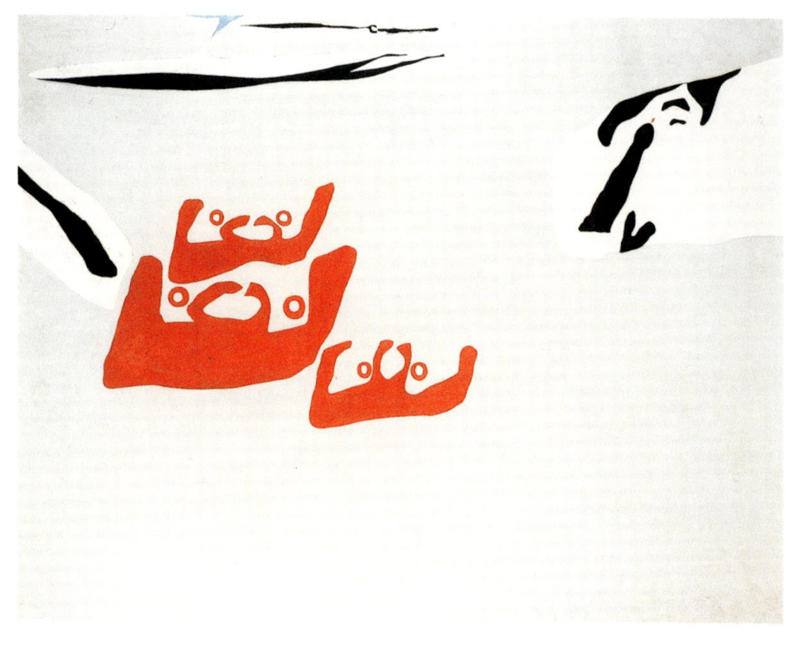

Sun, Four Fisherwomen of Cadaqués · 1928

Museo Nacional Centro de Arte Reina Sofía, Madrid, gift of Dalí to the Spanish state

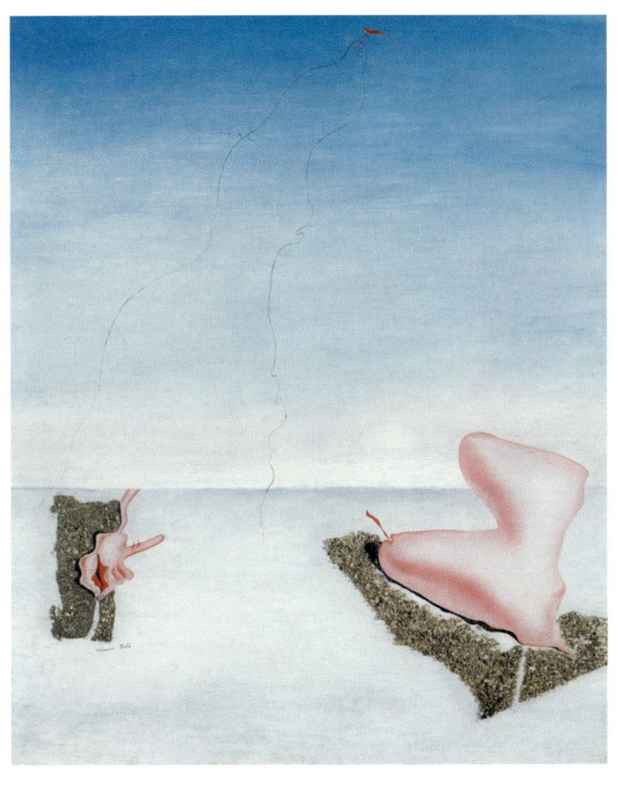

Unsatisfied Desires · 1928
Private collection

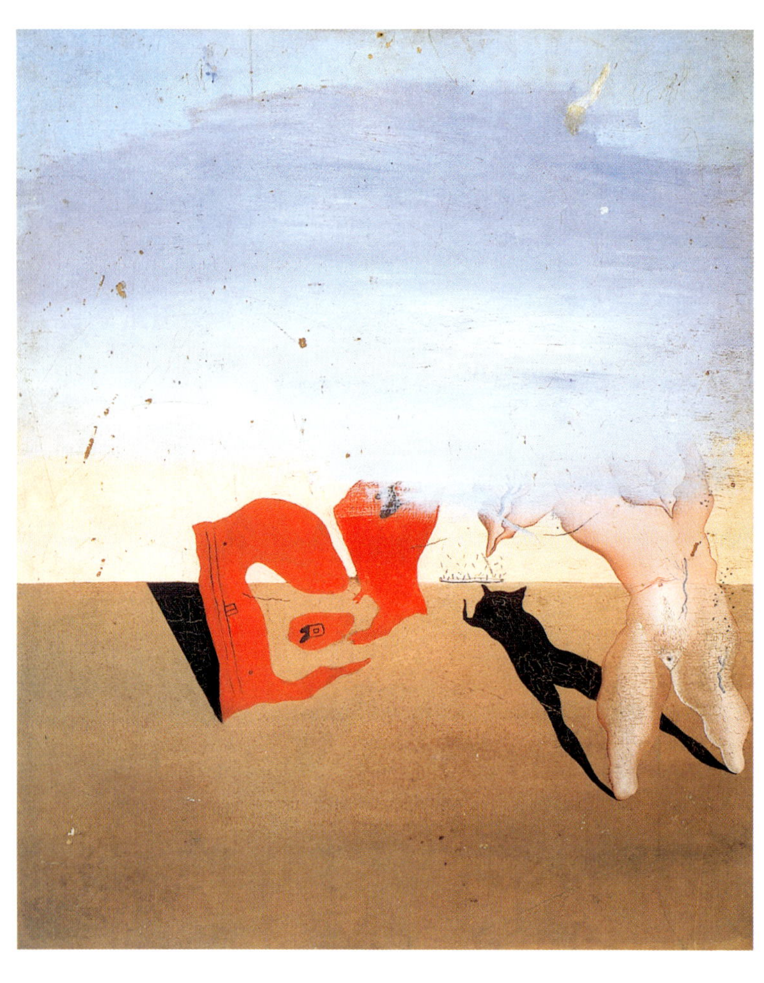

Untitled · 1928

Fundación Gala-Salvador Dalí, Figueras

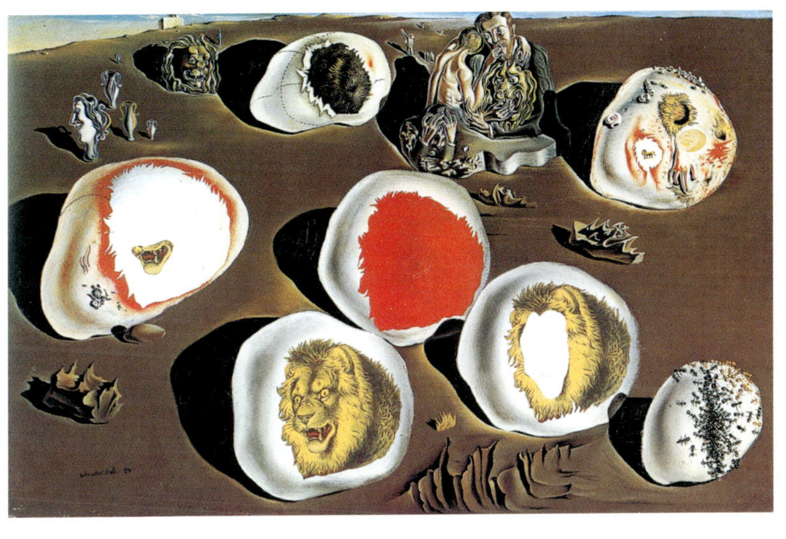

Accommodations of Desire · 1929
Private collection; formerly Julien Levy Collection

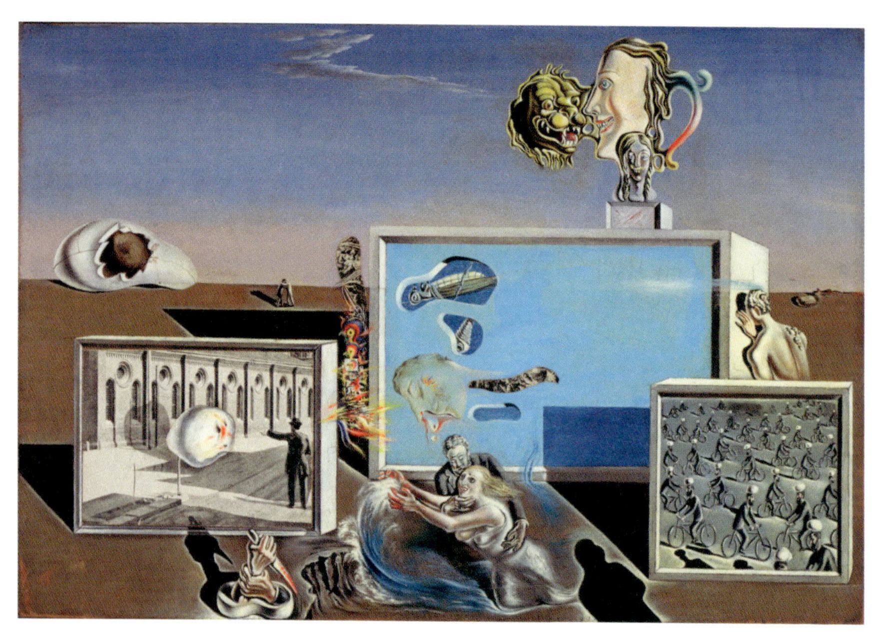

Illuminated Pleasures · 1929
The Museum of Modern Art, New York, Collection Sidney and Harriet Janis, 1957

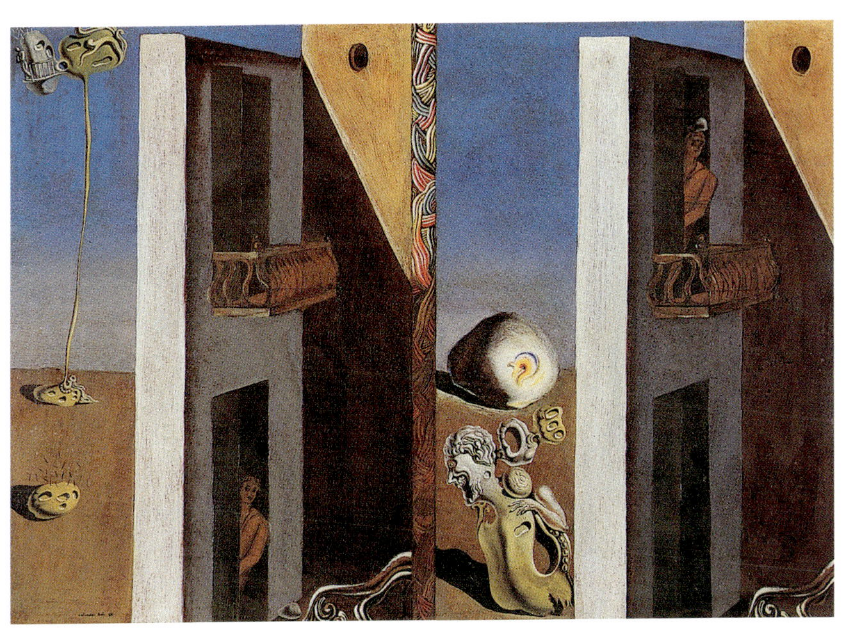

Man of Sickly Complexion Listening to the Sound of the Sea
or **The Two Balconies** · 1929
Museu da Chácara do Céu, Rio de Janeiro, Fundaçao Raymundo Ottoni de Castro Maya

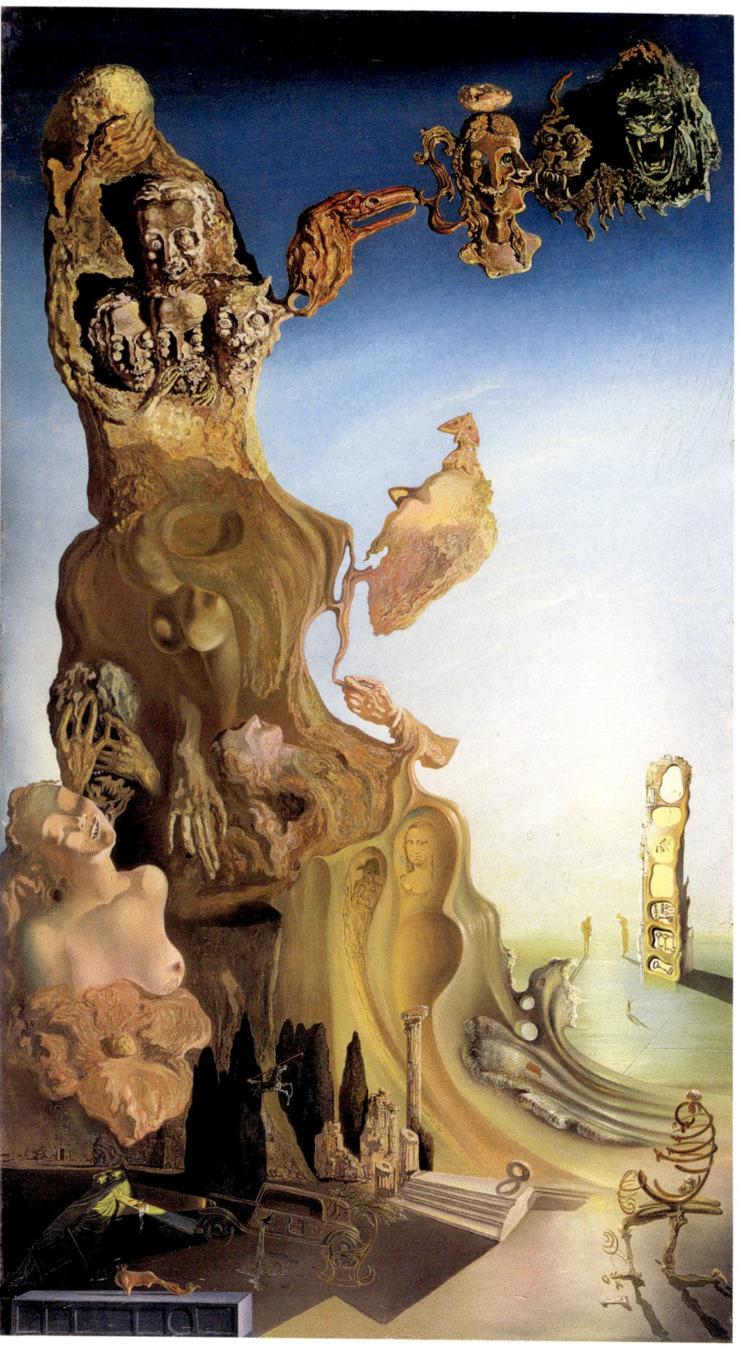

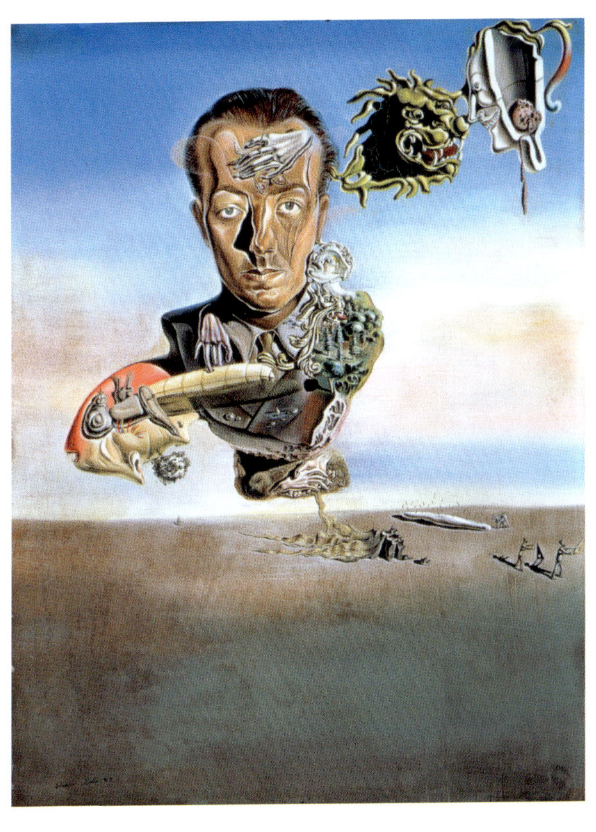

Portrait of Paul Eluard · 1929
Formerly Collection Gala and Salvador Dalí
< **Imperial Monument to the Child-Woman** · 1929
Museo Nacional Centro de Arte Reina Sofía, Madrid,
gift of Dalí to the Spanish state

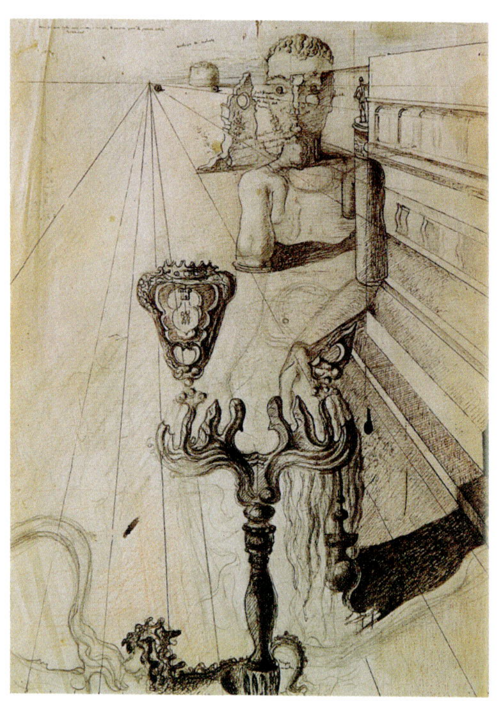

Study for "The Invisible Man" · 1929
Private collection
> **The Invisible Man** · 1929
Museo Nacional Centro de Arte Reina Sofía, Madrid,
gift of Dalí to the Spanish state

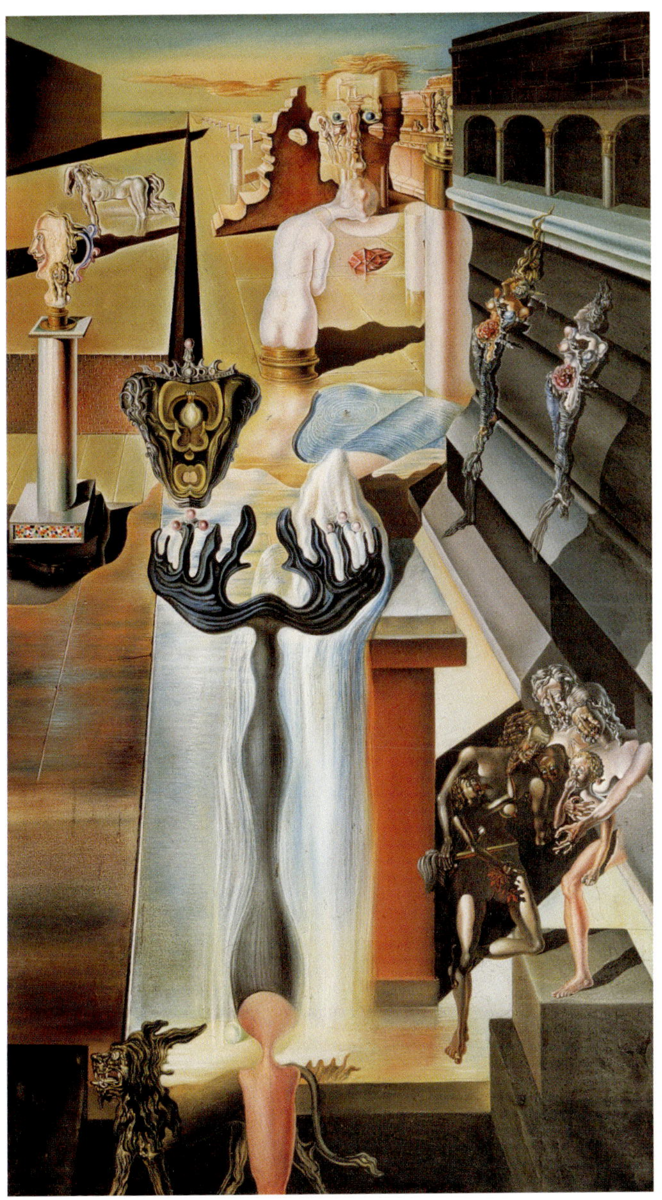

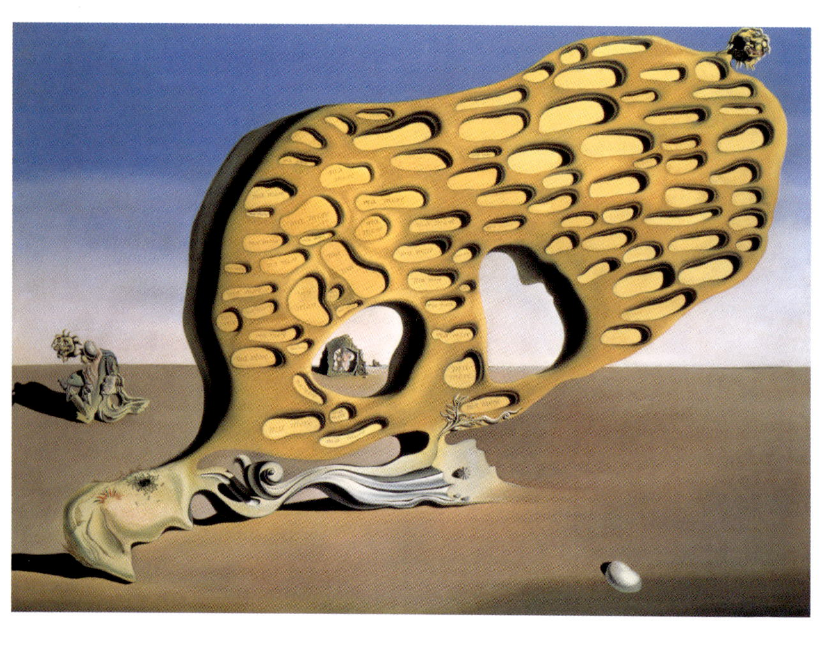

The Enigma of Desire—My Mother, My Mother, My Mother · 1929
Staatsgalerie Moderner Kunst, Munich; formerly Collection Oskar R. Schlag

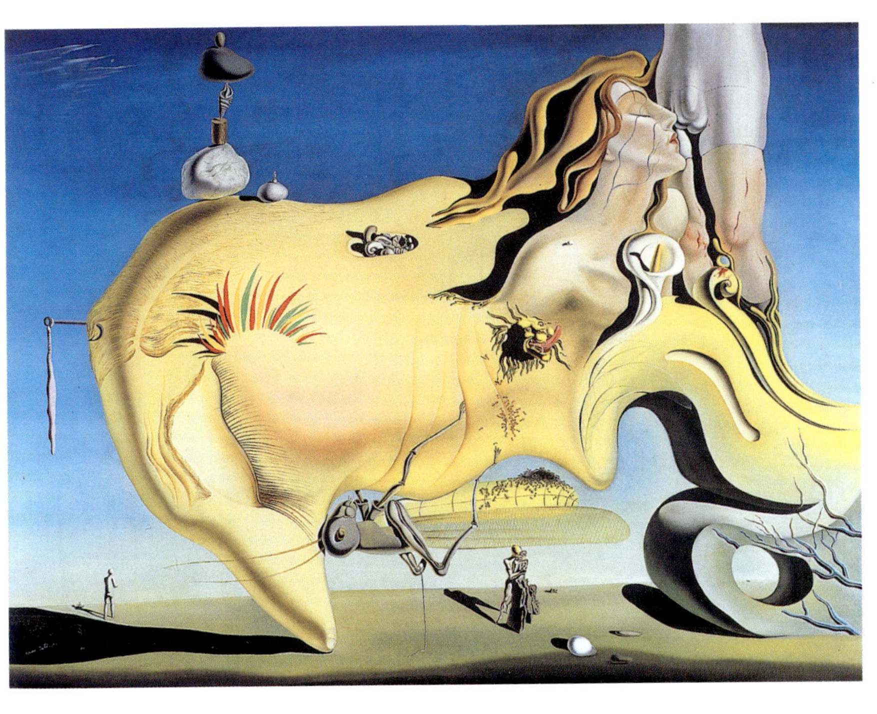

The Great Masturbator · 1929
Museo Nacional Centro de Arte Reina Sofía, Madrid,
gift of Dalí to the Spanish state

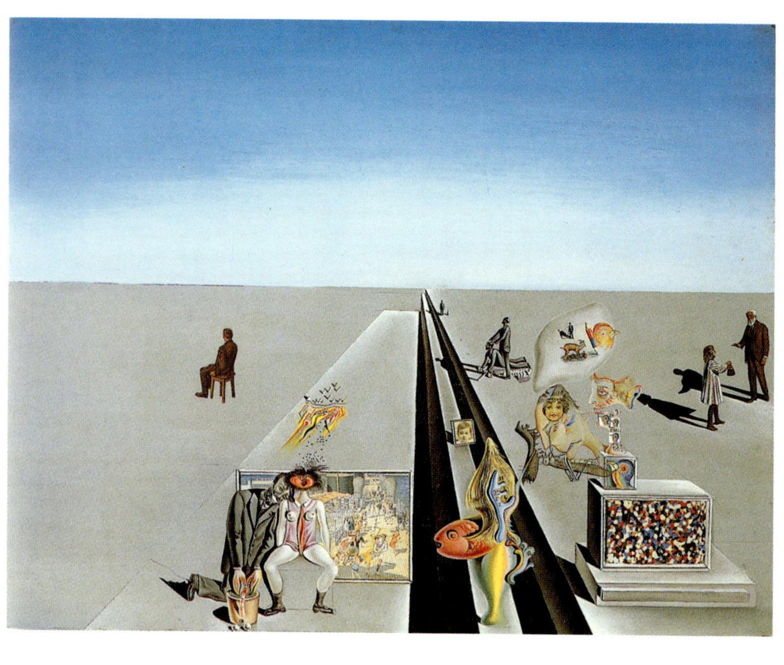

The First Days of Spring · 1929
The Salvador Dalí Museum, St. Petersburg, Florida,
on loan from E. and A. Reynolds Morse

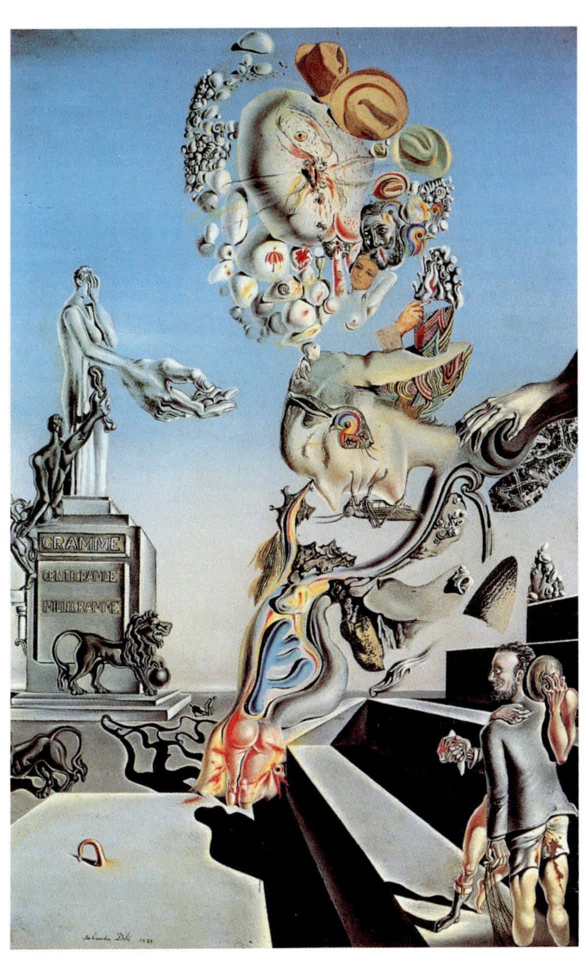

The Lugubrious Game · 1929
Private collection

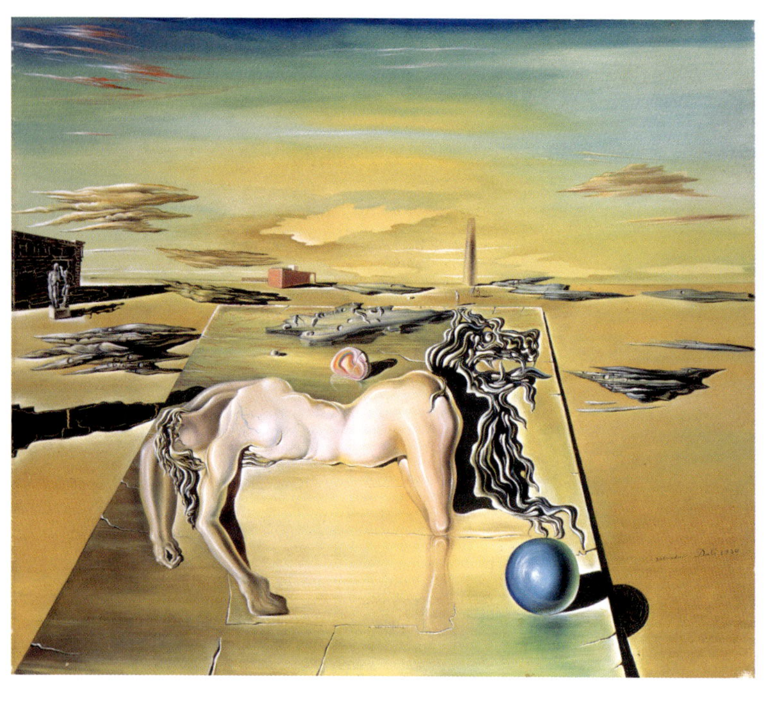

Invisible Sleeping Woman, Horse, Lion · 1930
Private collection, Paris; formerly Collection Vicomte de Noailles

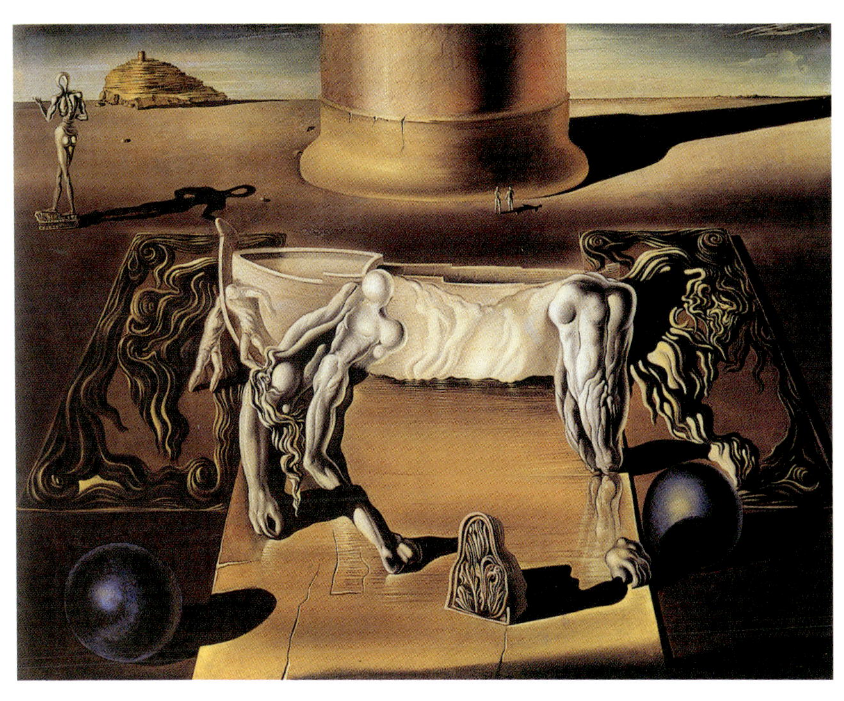

Paranoiac Woman-Horse · 1930

Musée National d'Art Moderne, Centre Georges Pompidou, Paris

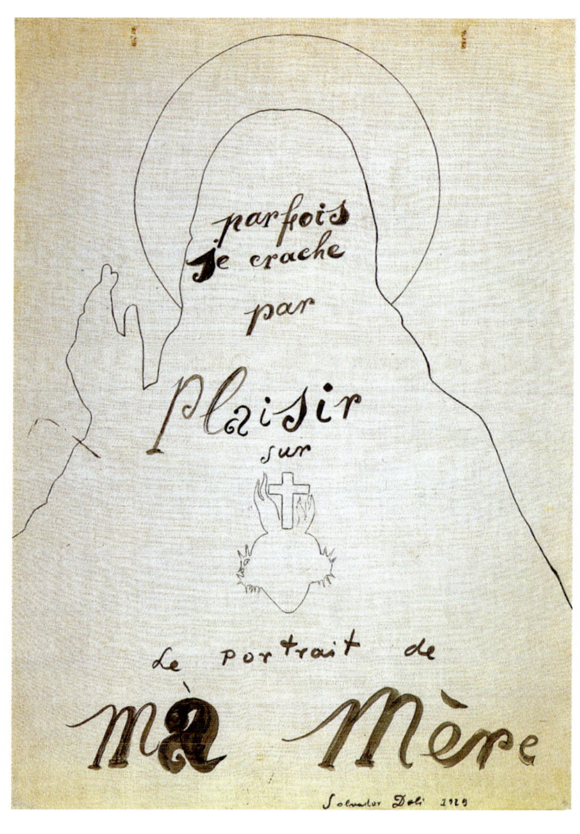

The Sacred Heart · 1929

Musée National d'Art Moderne, Centre Georges Pompidou, Paris

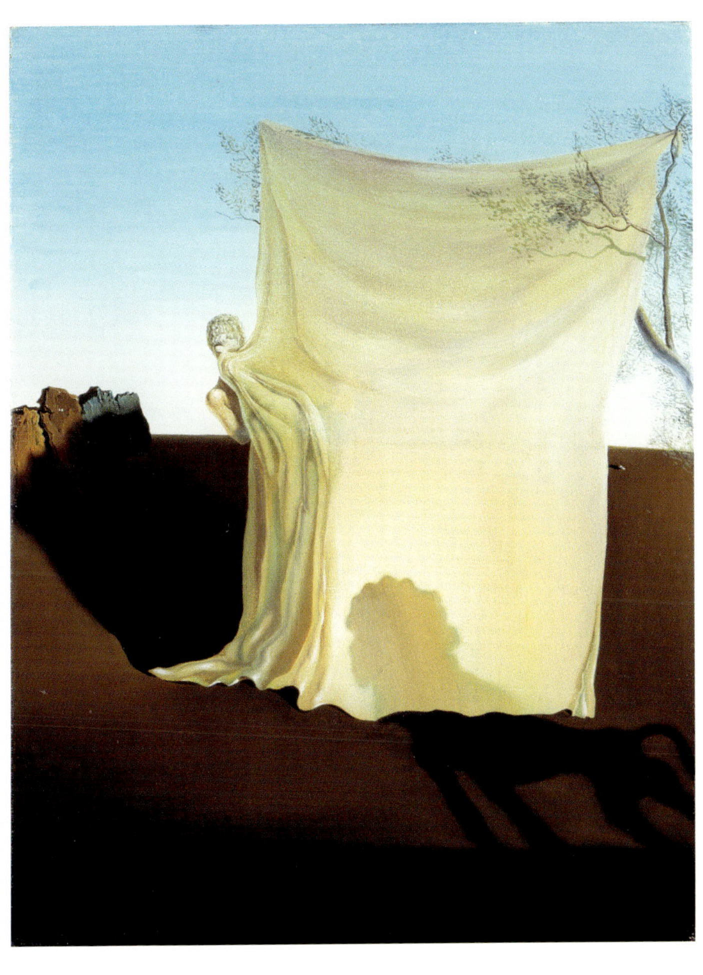

The Feeling of Becoming · 1930

Private collection; formerly Collection Mrs. W. Murray Crane

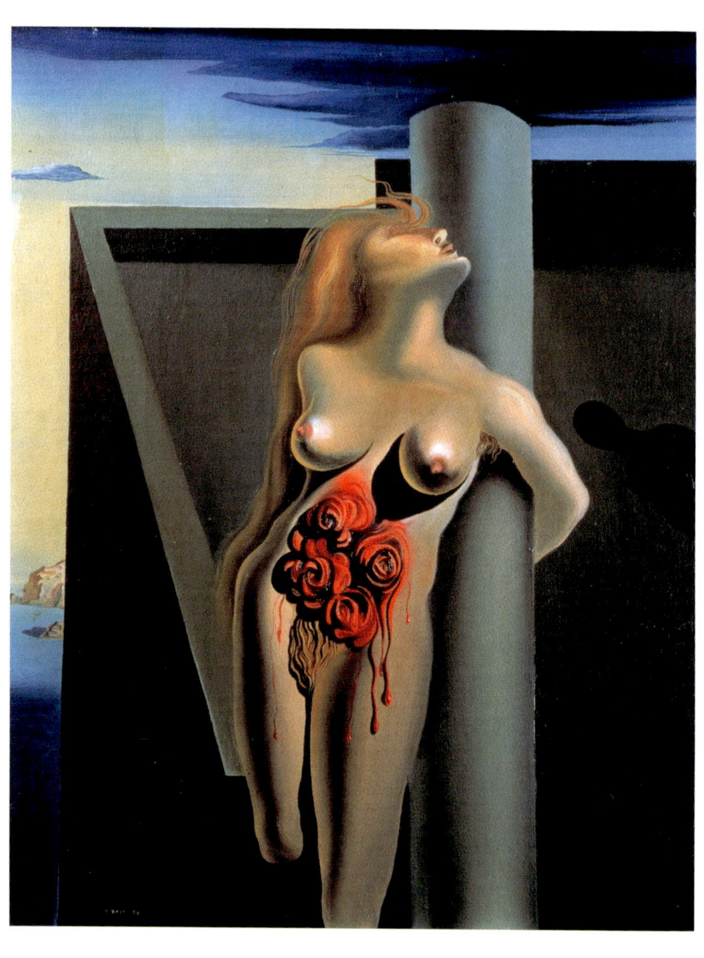

The Bleeding Roses · 1930
Private collection, Geneva

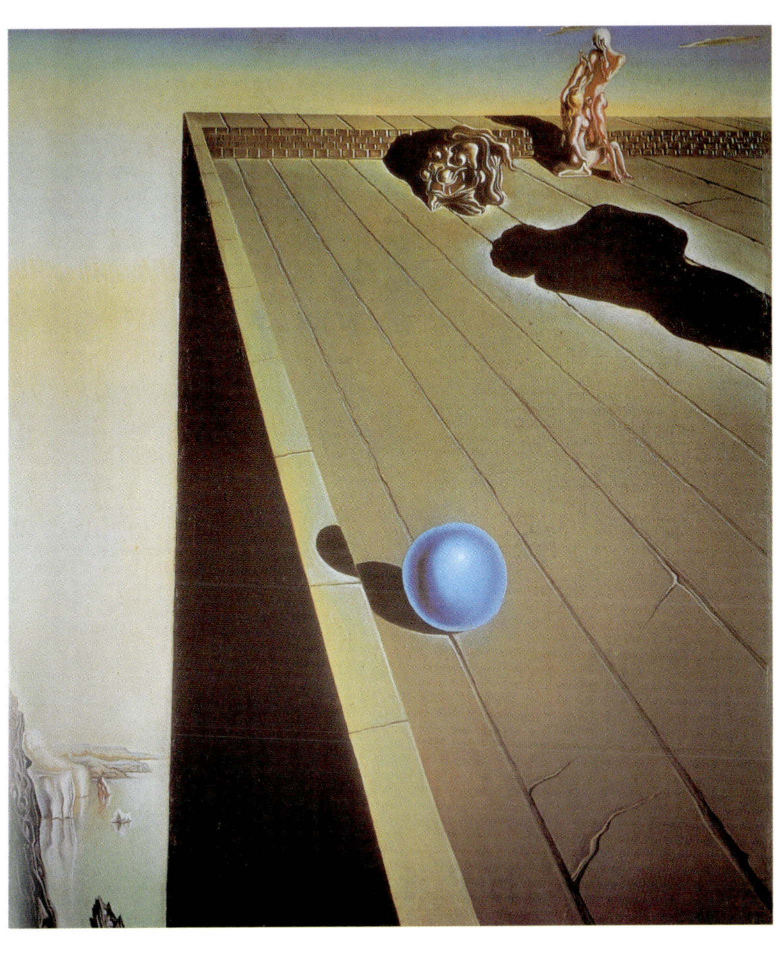

Vertigo—Tower of Pleasure · 1930
Private collection

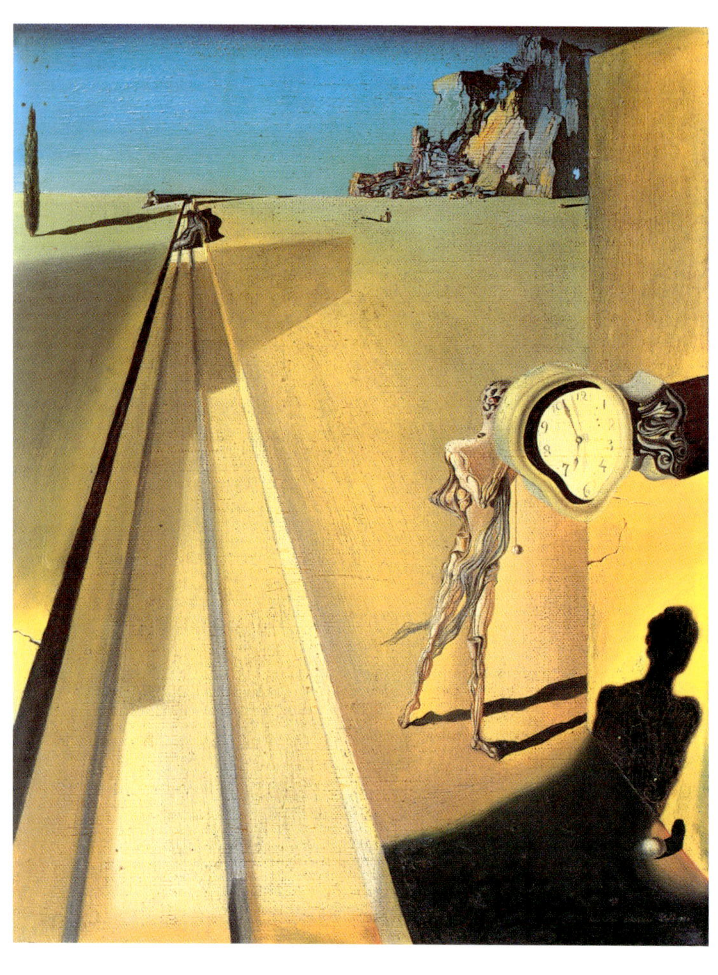

Premature Ossification of a Railway Station · 1930
Private collection; formerly Collection Countess Pecci-Blunt

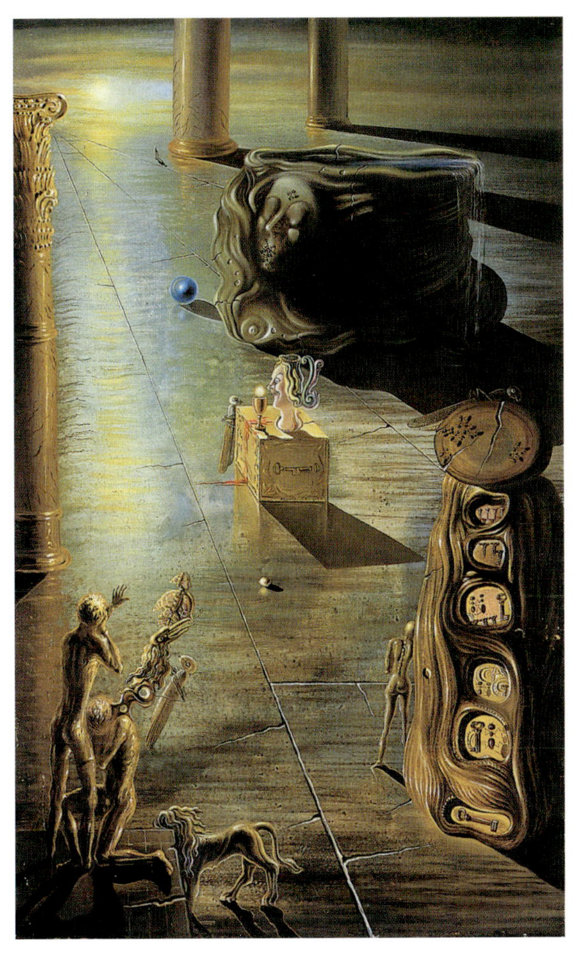

The Font · 1930

The Salvador Dalí Museum, St. Petersburg, Florida;
formerly Collection E. and A. Reynolds Morse

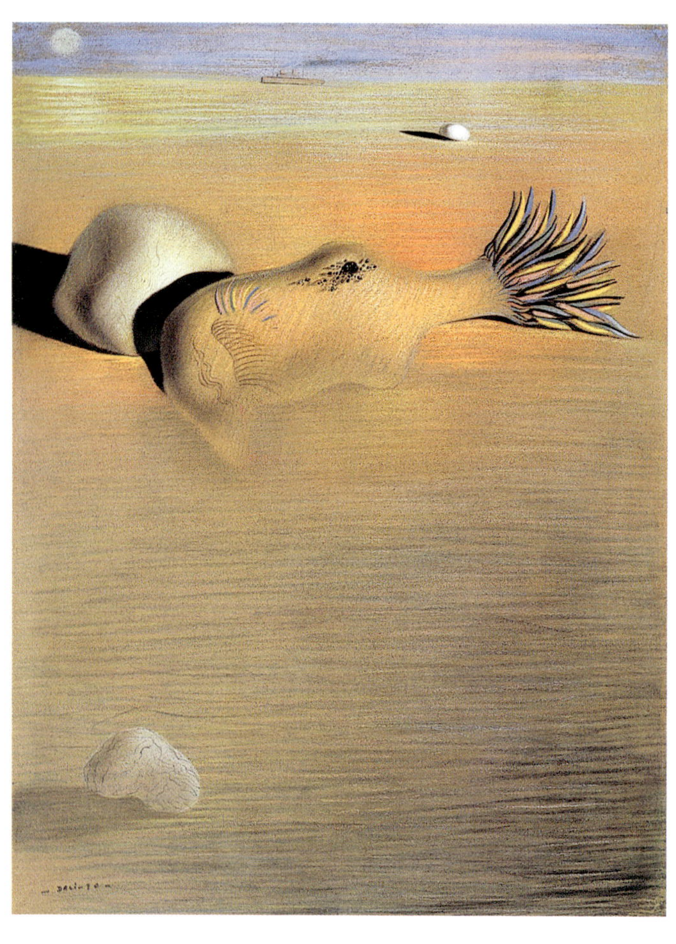

The Lost Face—The Great Masturbator · 1930
The Salvador Dalí Museum, St. Petersburg, Florida
> **William Tell** · 1930
Private collection; formerly Collection André Breton

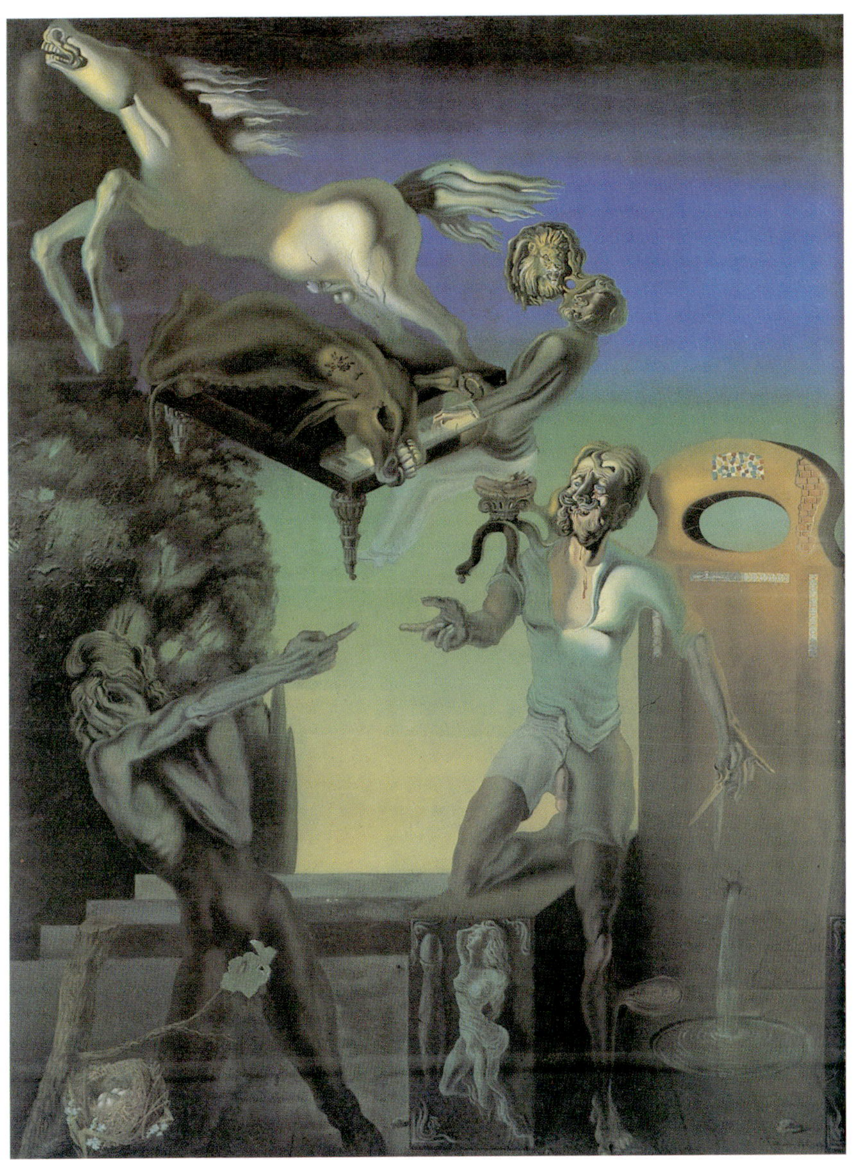

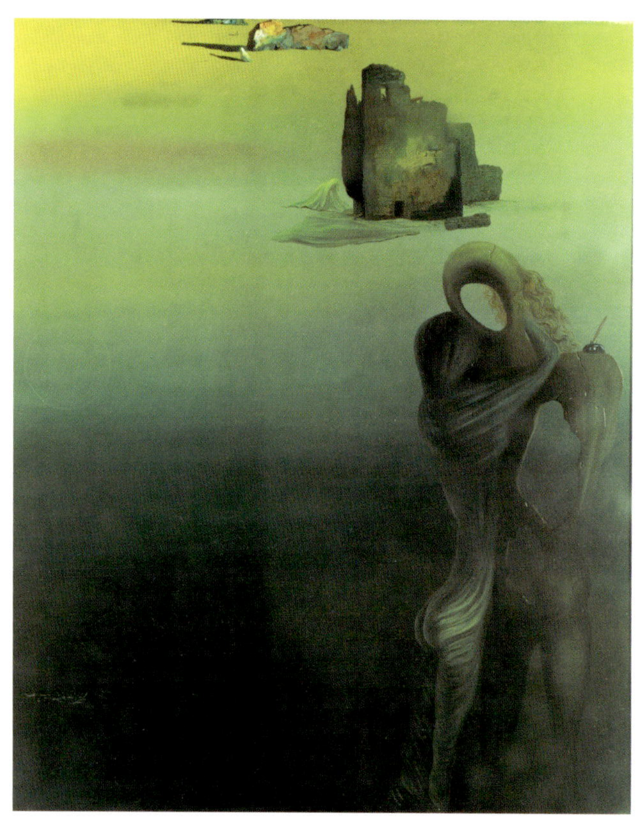

Gradiva Rediscovers the Anthropomorphic Ruins—Retrospective Fantasy · 1931
Museo Thyssen-Bornemisza, Madrid;
formerly Collection Robert de Saint-Jean

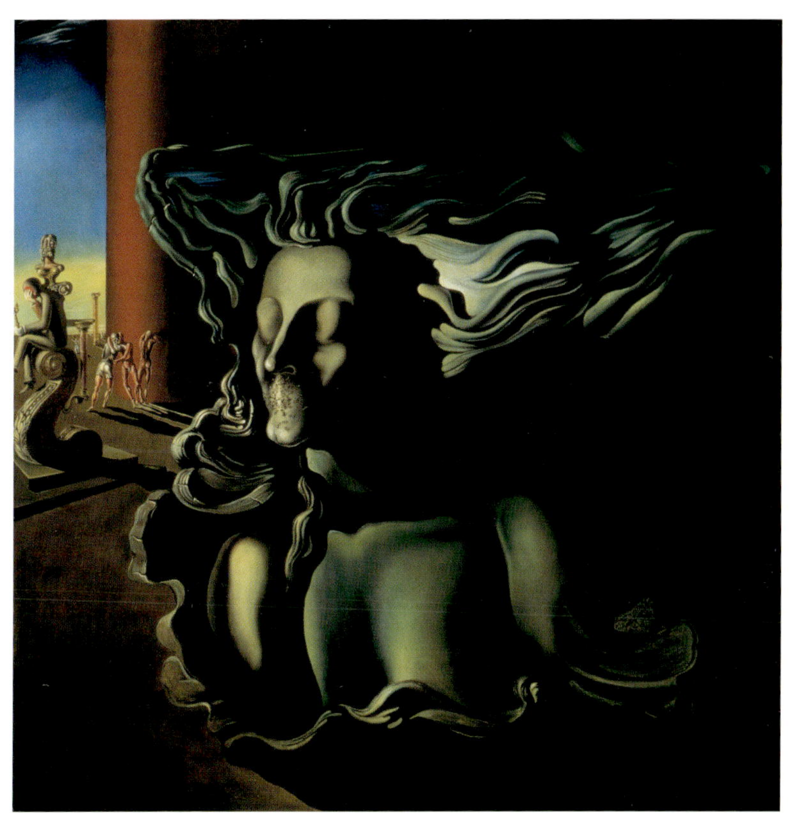

The Dream · 1931

Private collection, New York; formerly Collection Félix Labisse

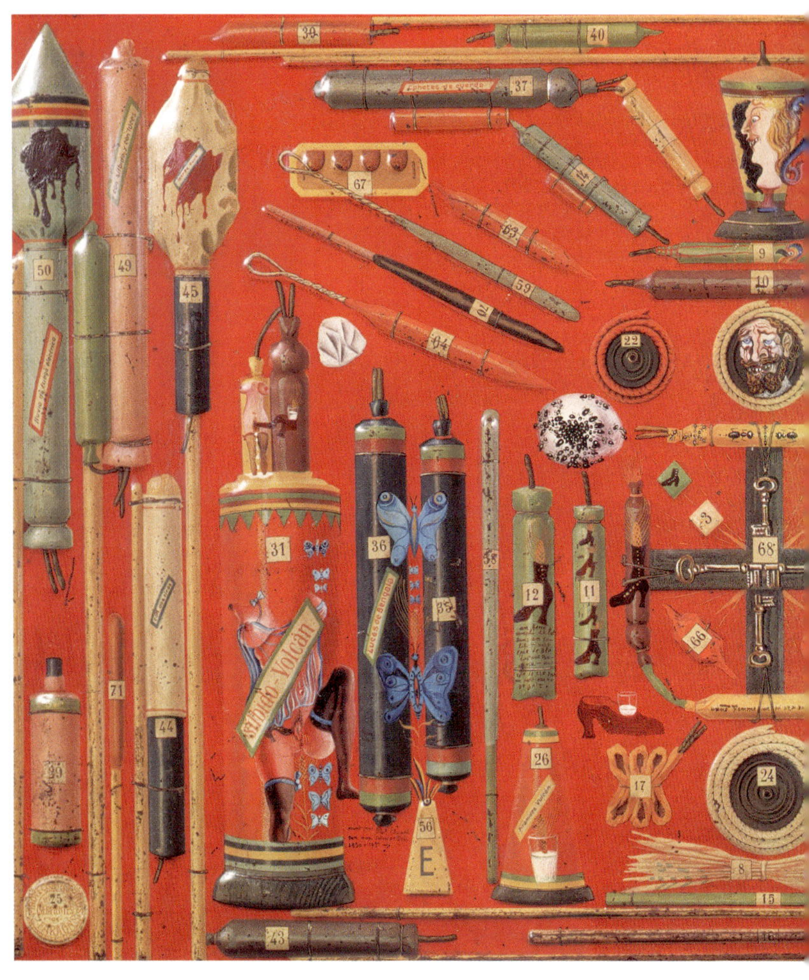

Mad Associations (Board of Fireworks) · 1930–31
Private collection, London

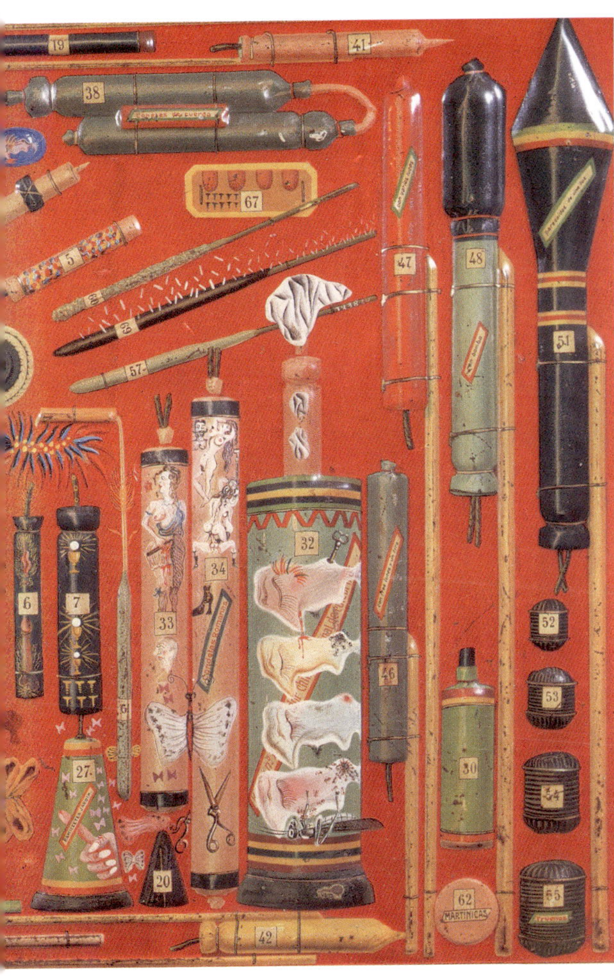

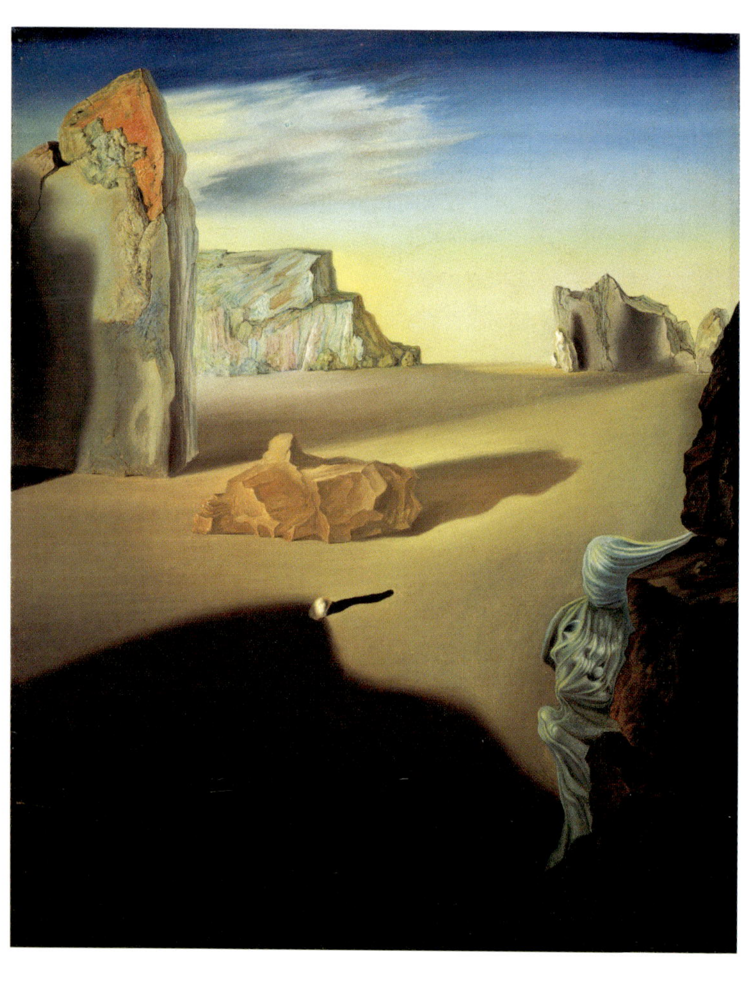

Shades of Night Descending · 1931
The Salvador Dalí Museum, St. Petersburg, Florida,
on loan from E. and A. Reynolds Morse

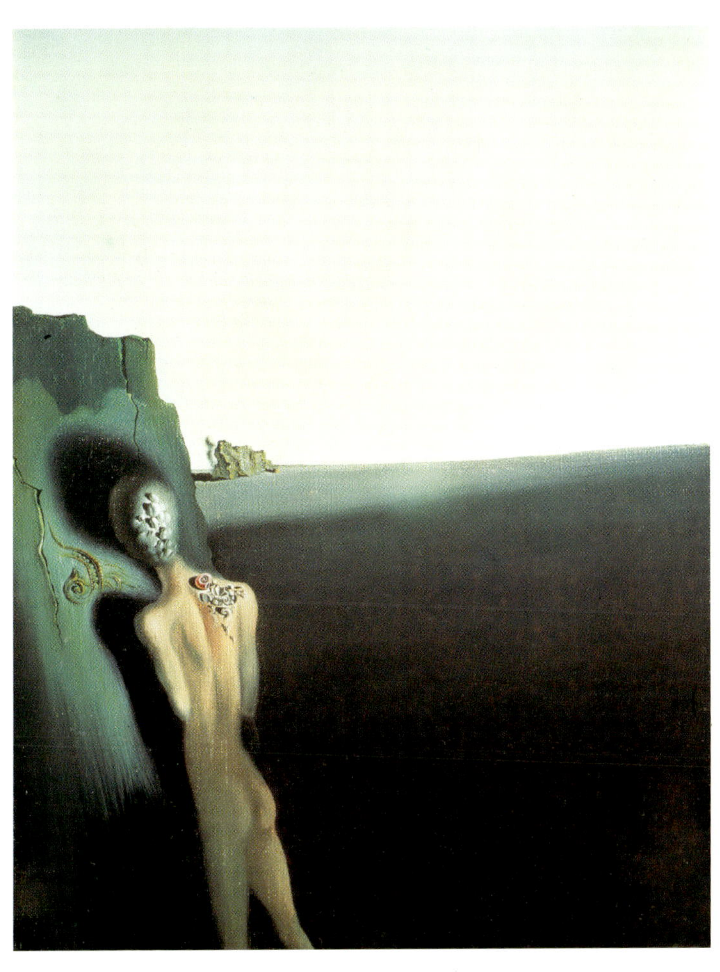

Solitude—Anthropomorphic Echo · 1931
Private collection

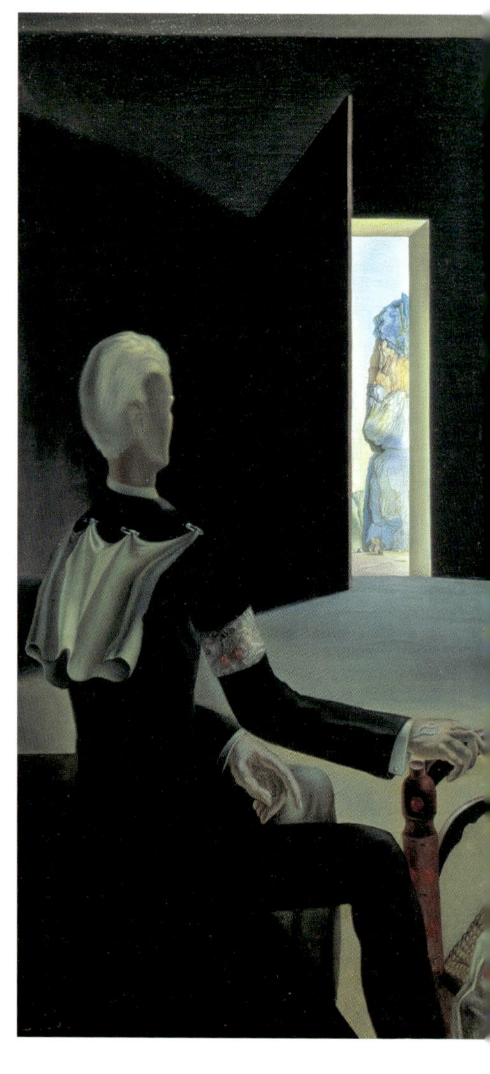

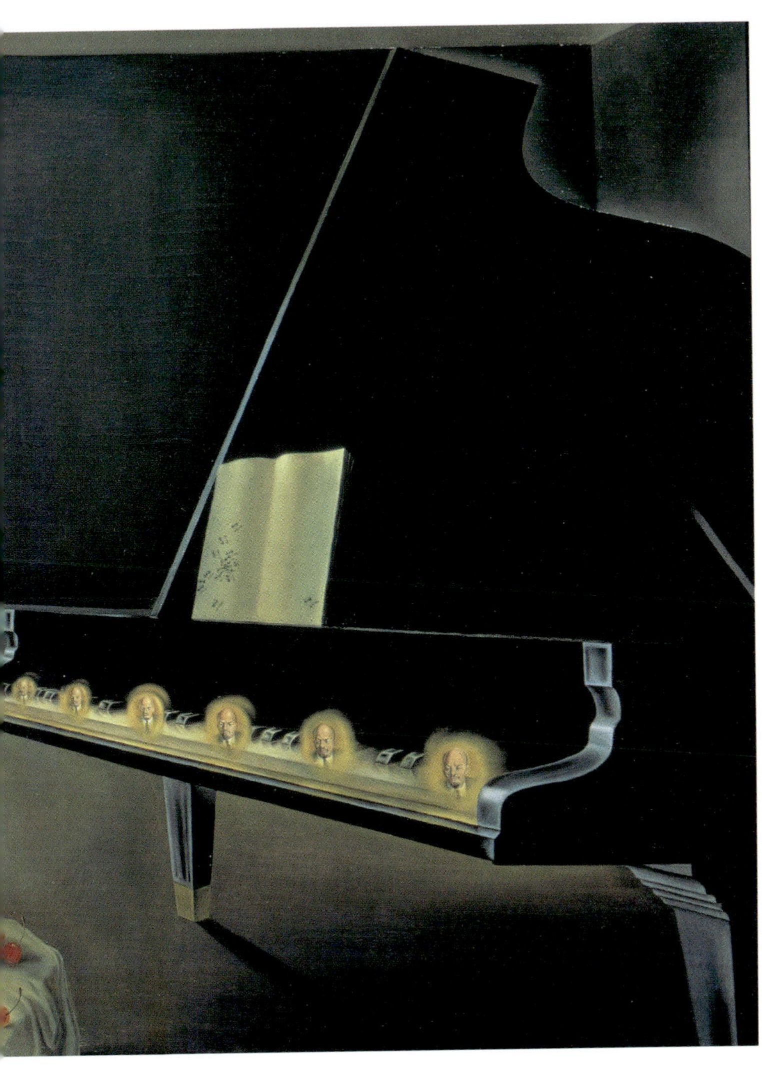

Partial Hallucination. Six Apparitions of Lenin on a Grand Piano · 1931

Musée National d'Art Moderne, Centre Georges Pompidou, Paris

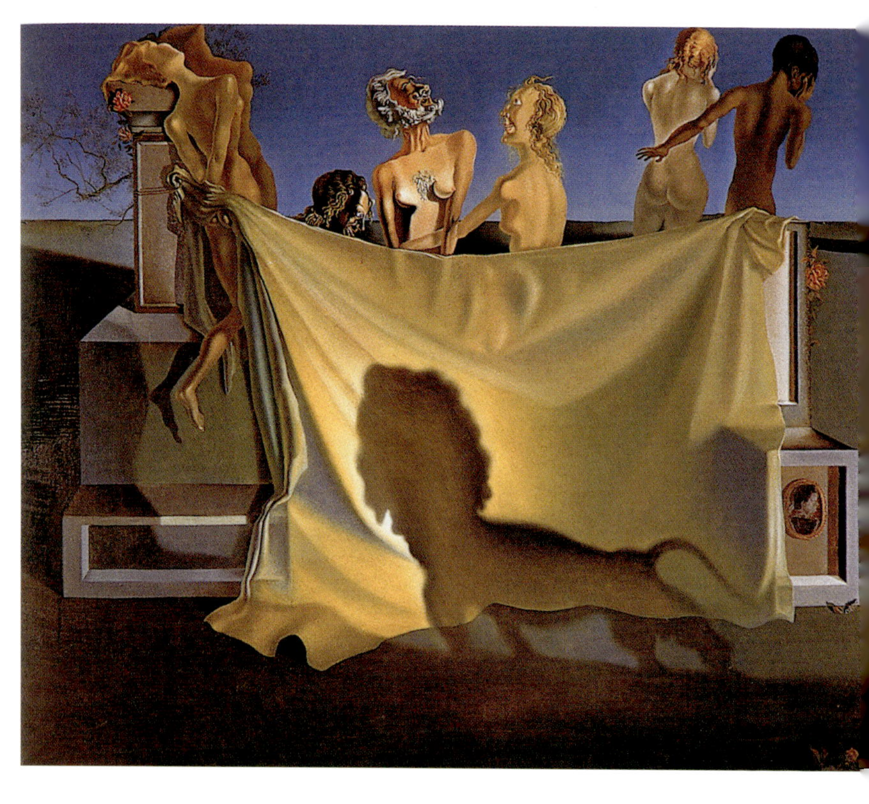

The Old Age of William Tell · 1931
Private collection; formerly Collection Vicomte de Noailles

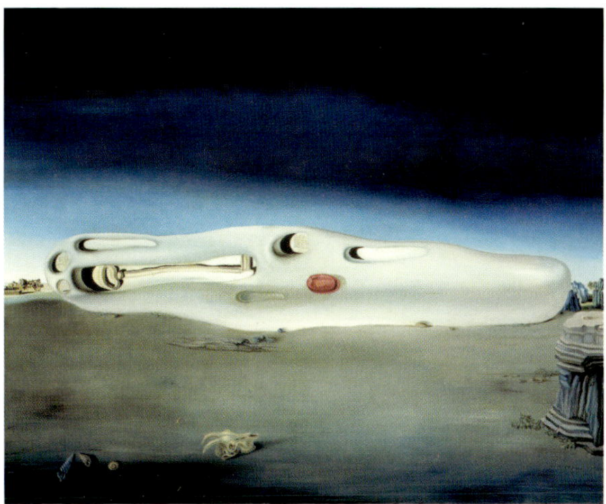

Diurnal Fantasies · 1932
The Salvador Dalí Museum, St. Petersburg, Florida,
on loan from the Morse Charitable Trust

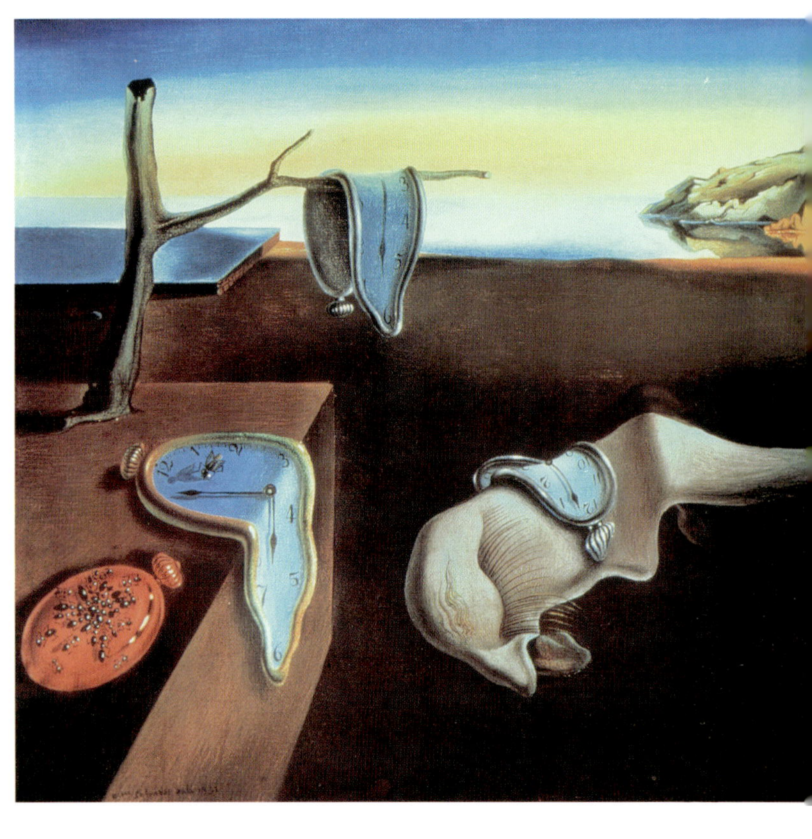

The Persistence of Memory (Soft Watches) · 1931
The Museum of Modern Art, New York (anonymous gift 1934)

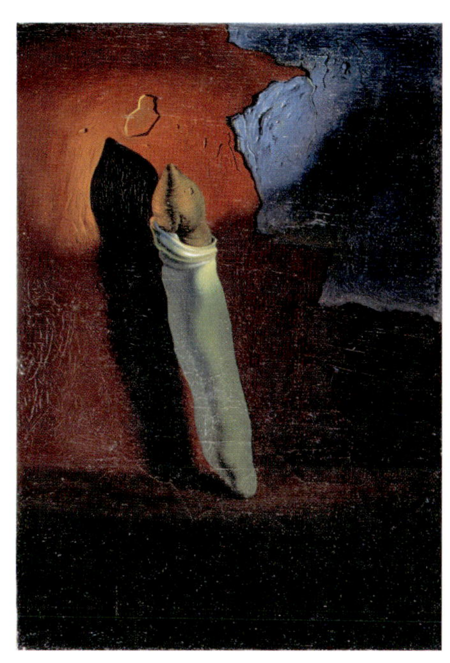

Anthropomorphic Bread · c. 1932
Fundación Gala-Salvador Dalí, Figueras

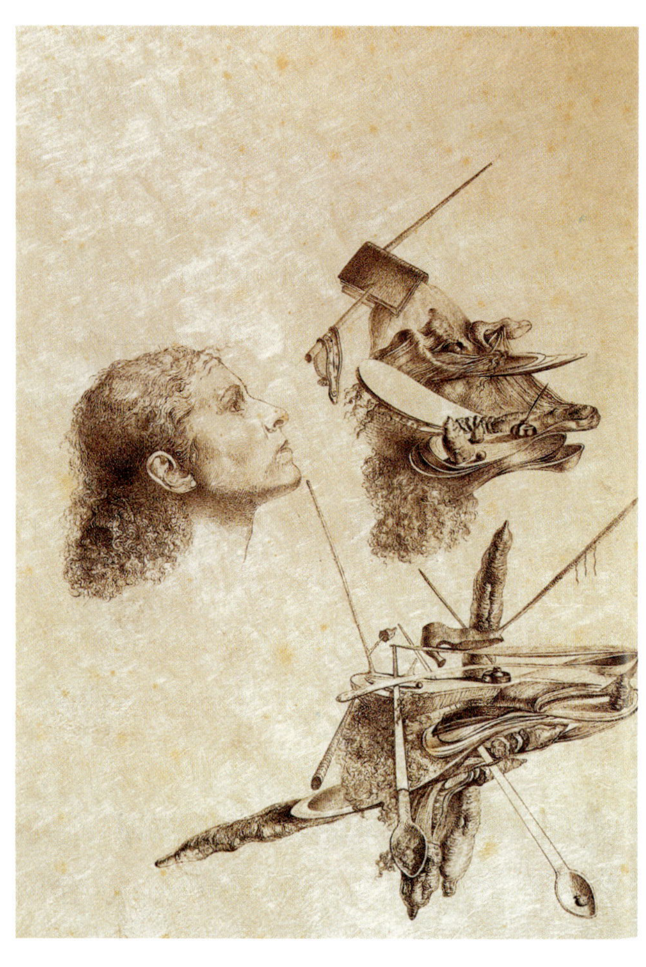

Paranoiac Metamorphosis of Gala's Face · 1932

Fundación Gala-Salvador Dalí, Figueras; formerly Collection Boris Kochno

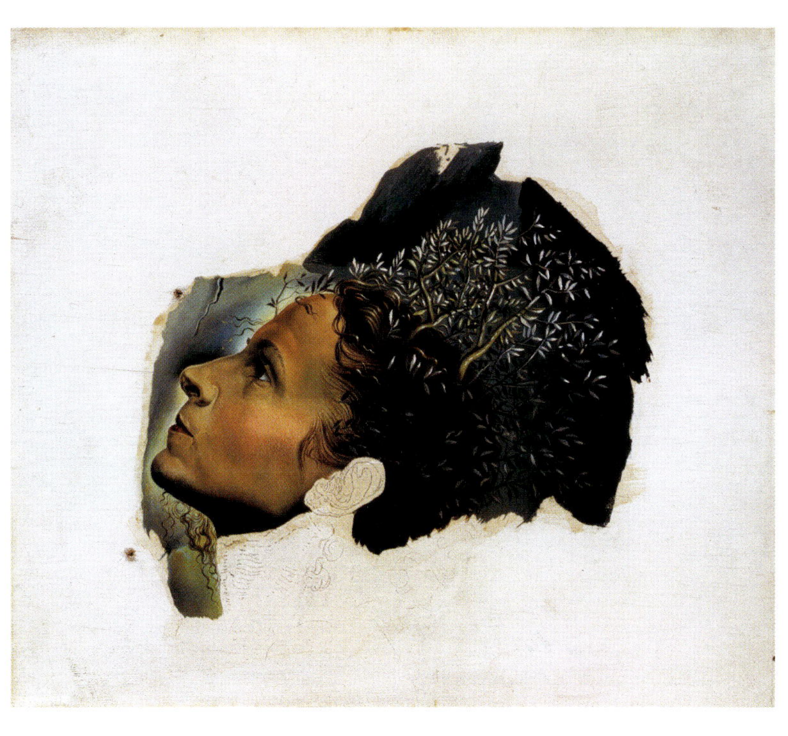

Automatic Beginning of a Portrait of Gala (unfinished) · 1932
Fundación Gala-Salvador Dalí, Figueras

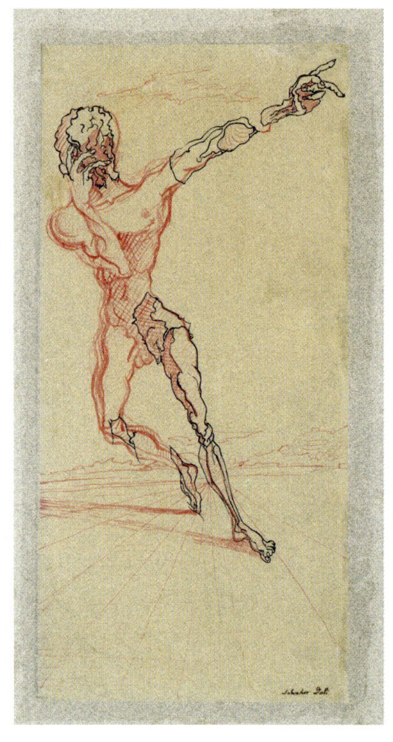

Figure after "William Tell" · 1932
The Salvador Dalí Museum, St. Petersburg, Florida

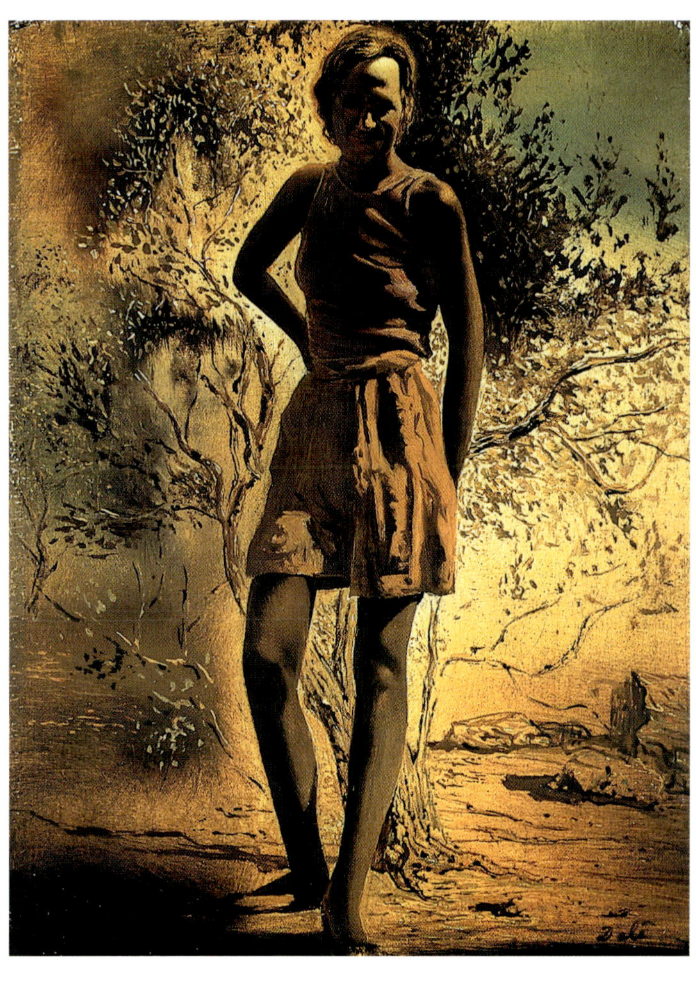

Portrait of Gala · 1932
The Salvador Dalí Museum, St. Petersburg, Florida,
on loan from E. and A. Reynolds Morse

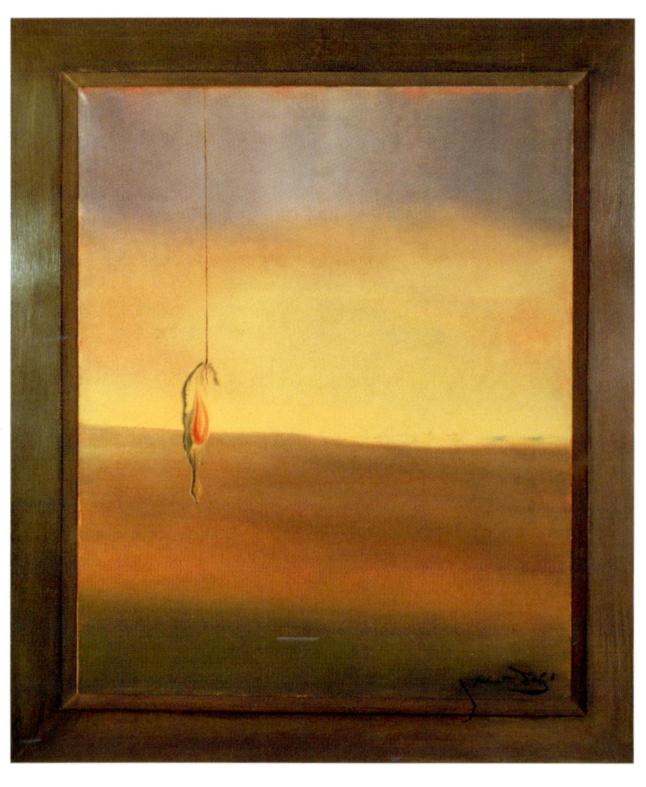

Fried Egg on the Plate without the Plate · 1932
Galería Theo, Madrid

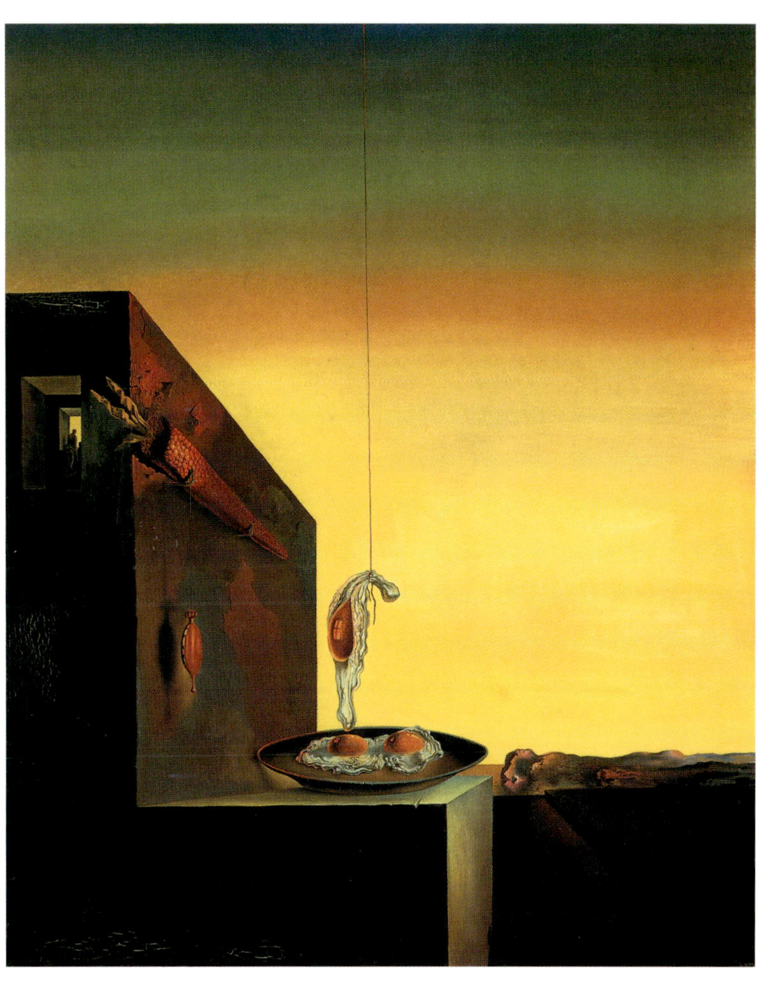

Fried Eggs on the Plate without the Plate · 1932
The Salvador Dalí Museum, St. Petersburg, Florida,
on loan from the Morse Charitable Trust

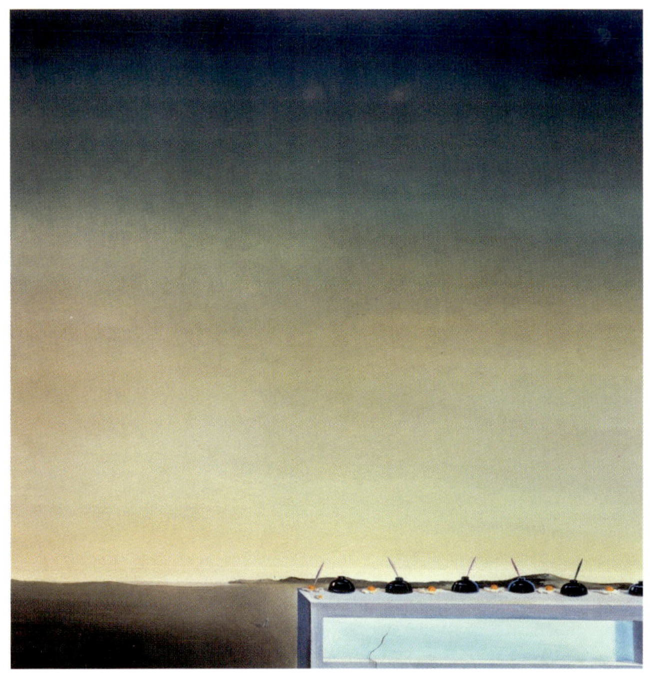

Nostalgia of the Cannibal · 1932
Sprengel Museum, Hanover

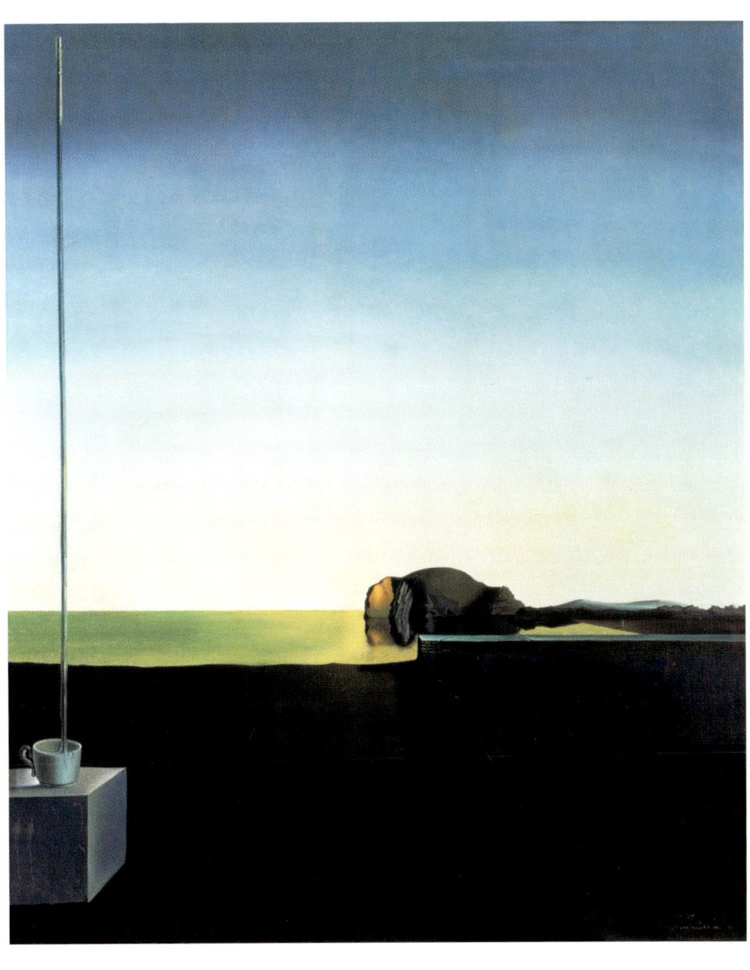

The True Painting of "The Isle of the Dead"
by Arnold Böcklin at the Hour of the Angelus · 1932
Von der Heydt-Museum, Wuppertal

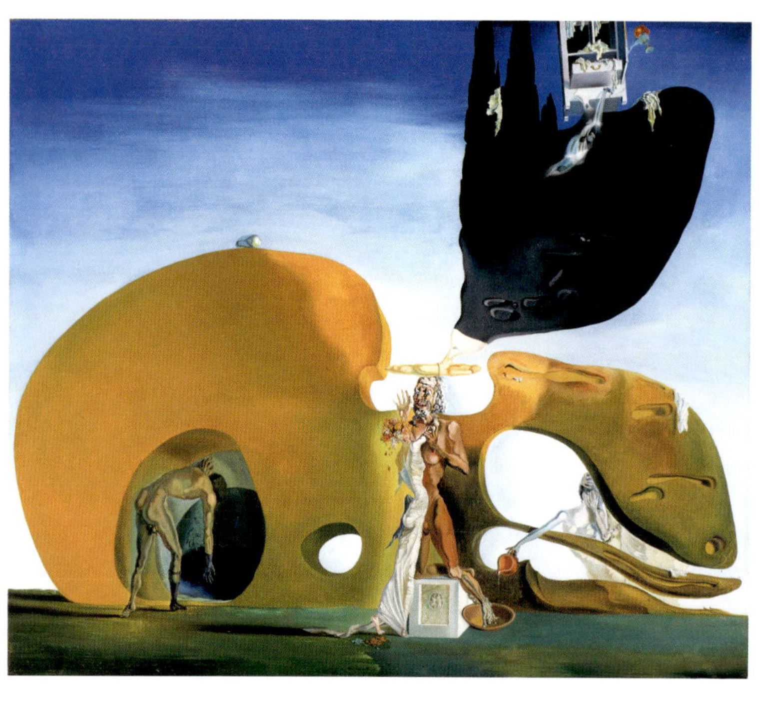

The Birth of Liquid Desires · 1932
Peggy Guggenheim Collection, Venice

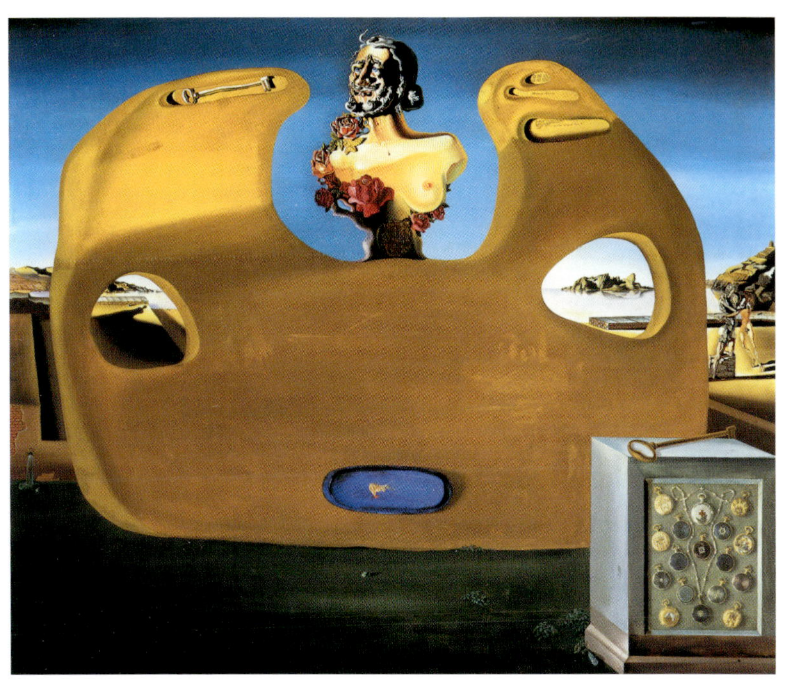

Memory of the Child-Woman · 1932
The Salvador Dalí Museum, St. Petersburg, Florida,
on loan from the Morse Charitable Trust

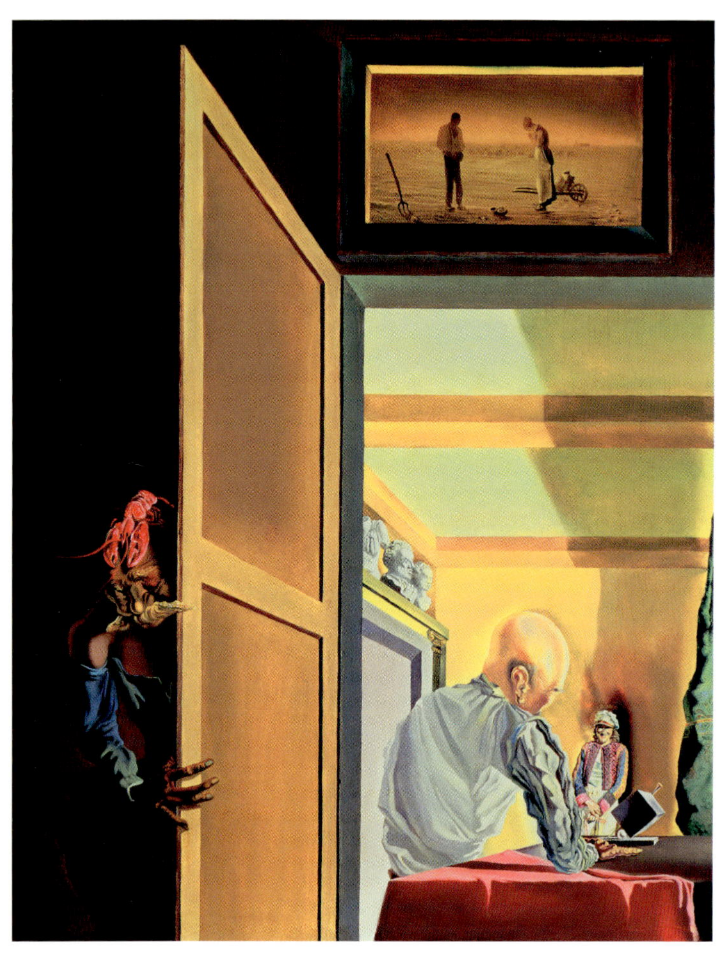

**Gala and the Angelus of Millet Preceding the Imminent Arrival
of the Conical Anamorphoses** · 1933

The National Gallery of Canada, Ottawa; formerly Collection Henry P. McIlhenny

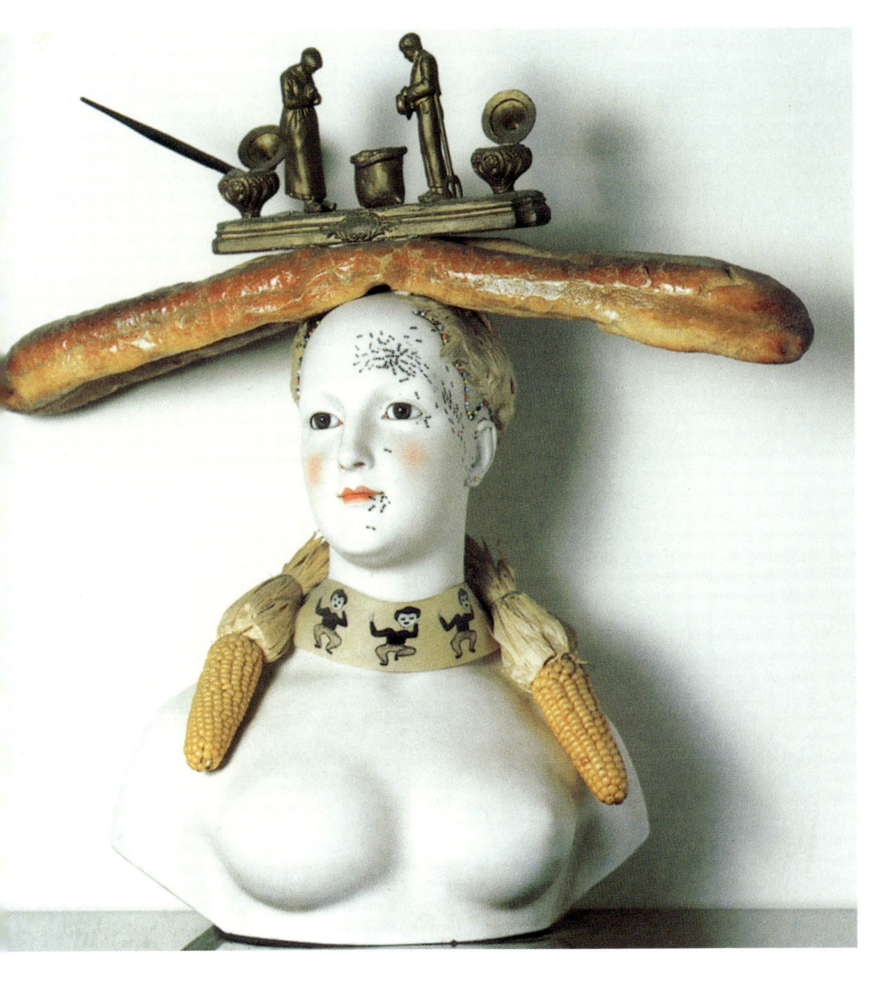

Retrospective Bust of a Woman · 1933
Private collection, Belgium

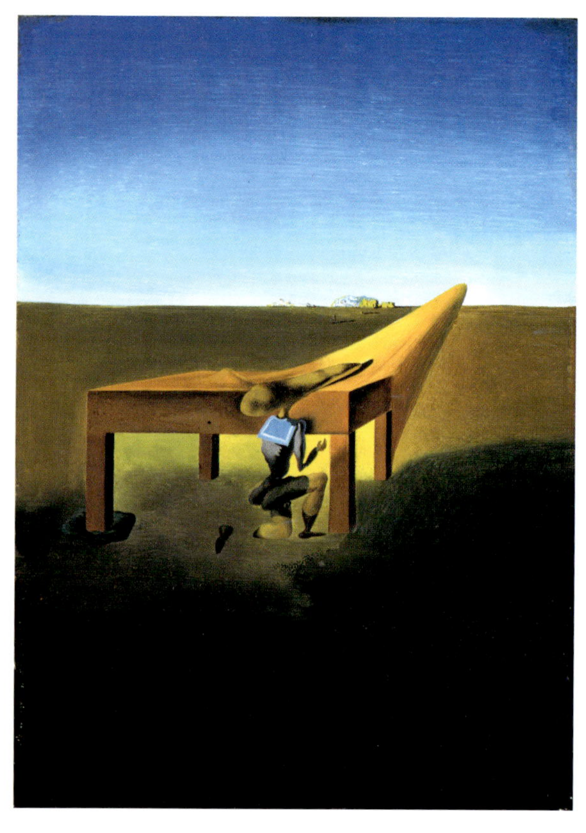

**Myself at the Age of Ten When I Was
the Grasshopper Child—Castration Complex** · 1933
The Salvador Dalí Museum, St. Petersburg, Florida,
on loan from E. and A. Reynolds Morse

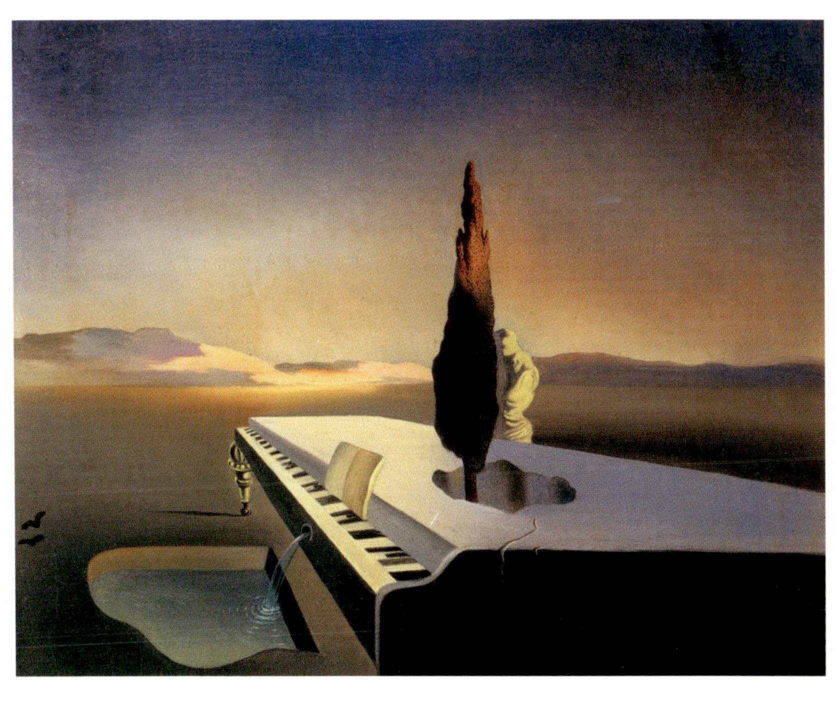

Necrophiliac Fountain Flowing from a Grand Piano · 1933
Private collection

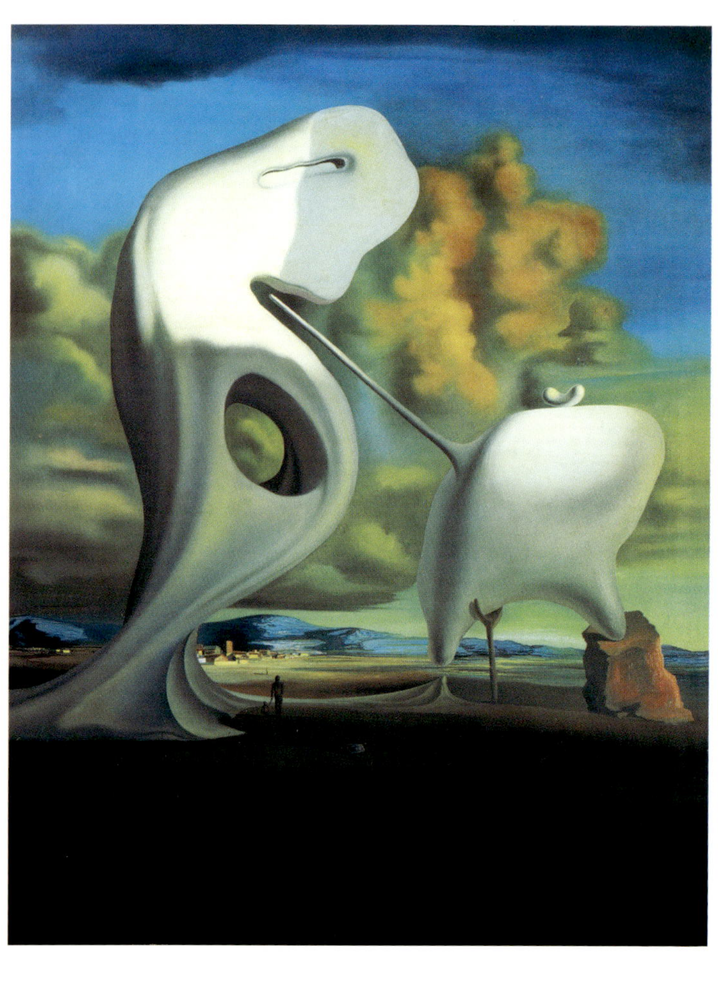

The Architectural Angelus of Millet · 1933

Museo Nacional Centro de Arte Reina Sofía, Madrid

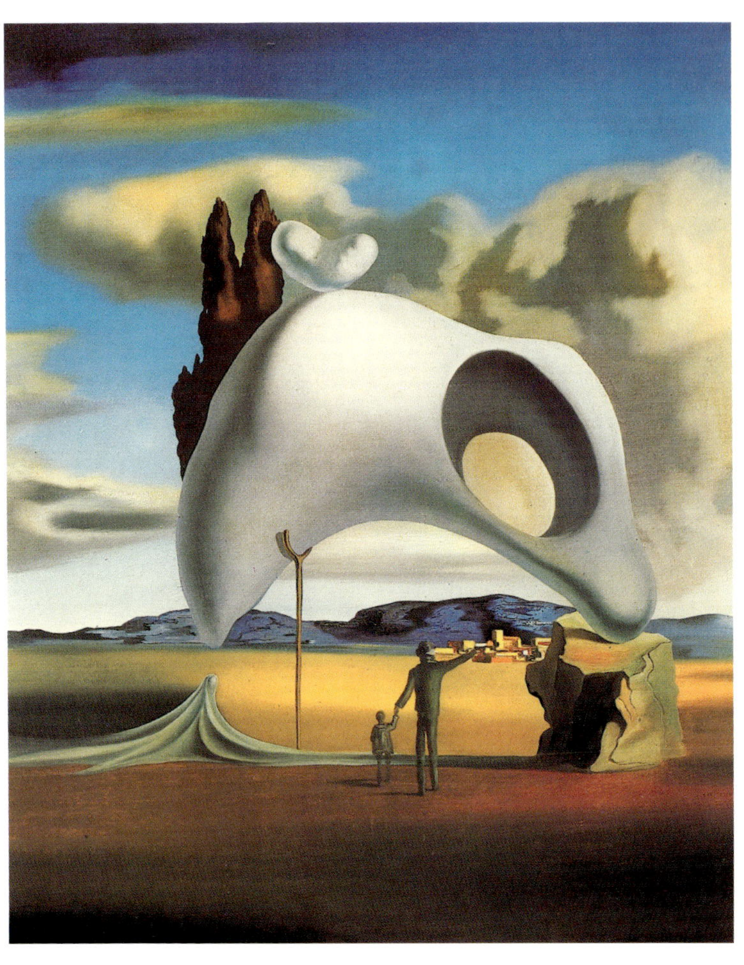

Atavistic Vestiges after the Rain · 1934
Perls Galleries, New York; formerly Collection Carlo Ponti, Rome

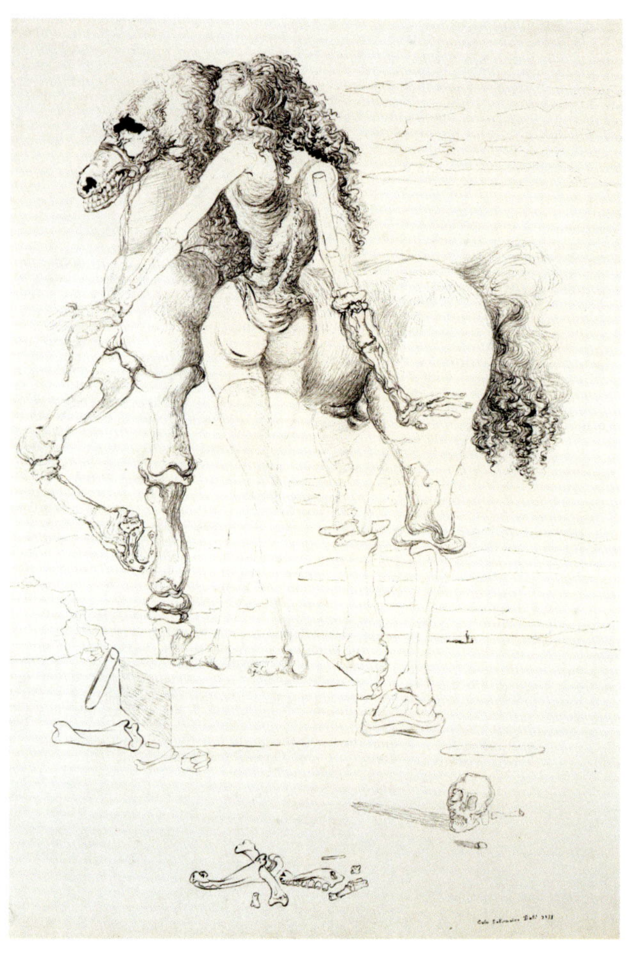

Surrealist Horse—Woman-Horse · 1933
The Salvador Dalí Museum, St. Petersburg, Florida;
formerly Collection E. and A. Reynolds Morse
> **Figure with Drawers. For a four-part screen** · c. 1934
Collection Italcambio

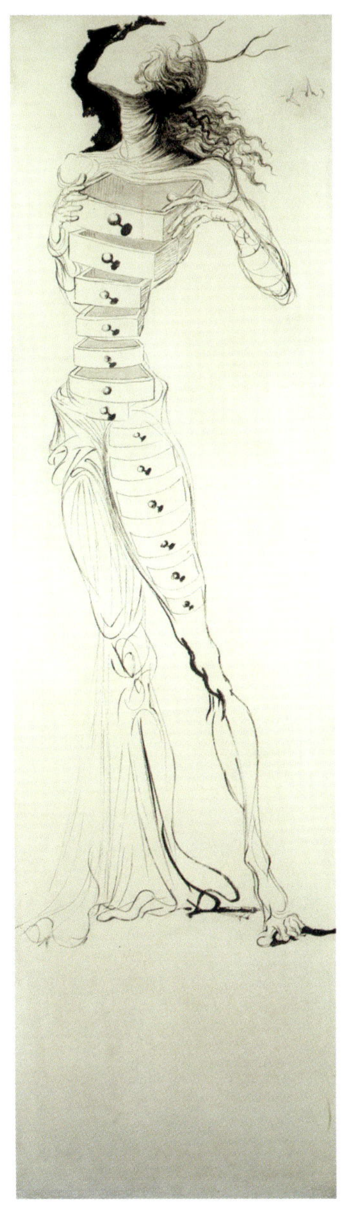

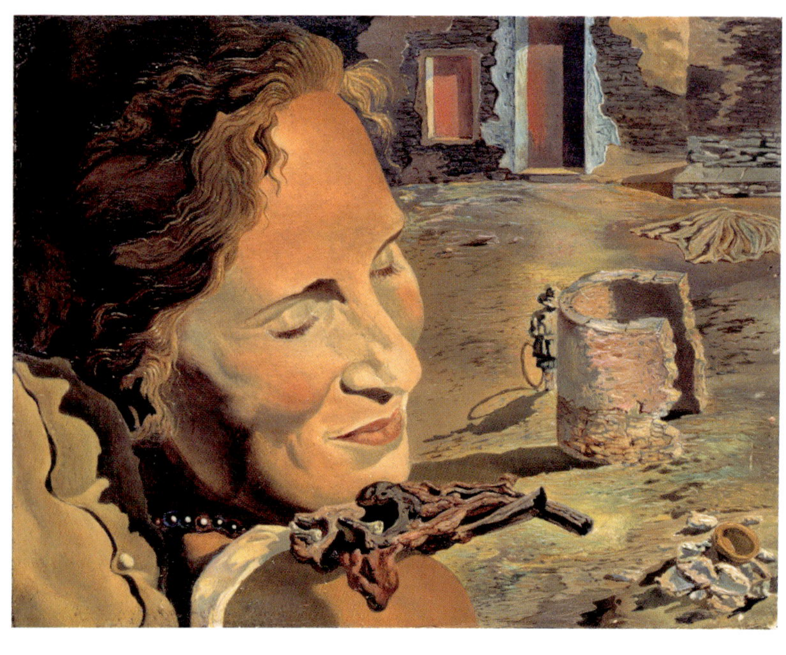

Portrait of Gala with Two Lamb Chops Balanced on Her Shoulder · 1933
Fundación Gala-Salvador Dalí, Figueras

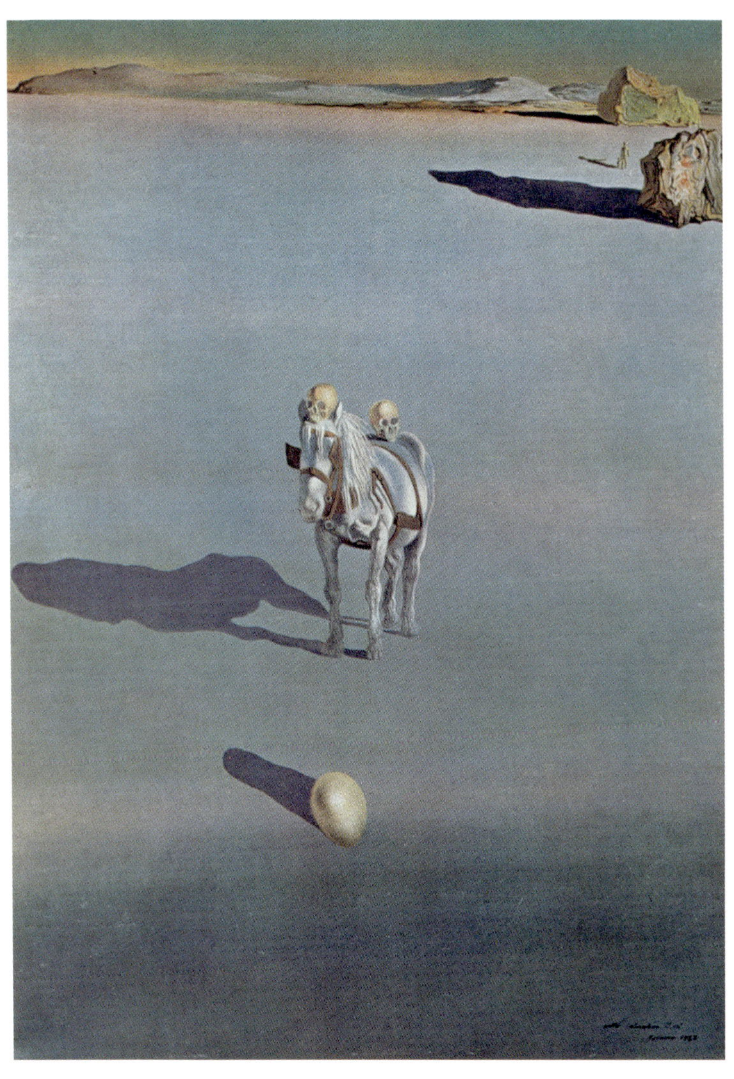

Geological Destiny · 1933
Private collection; formerly Julien Green Collection

131

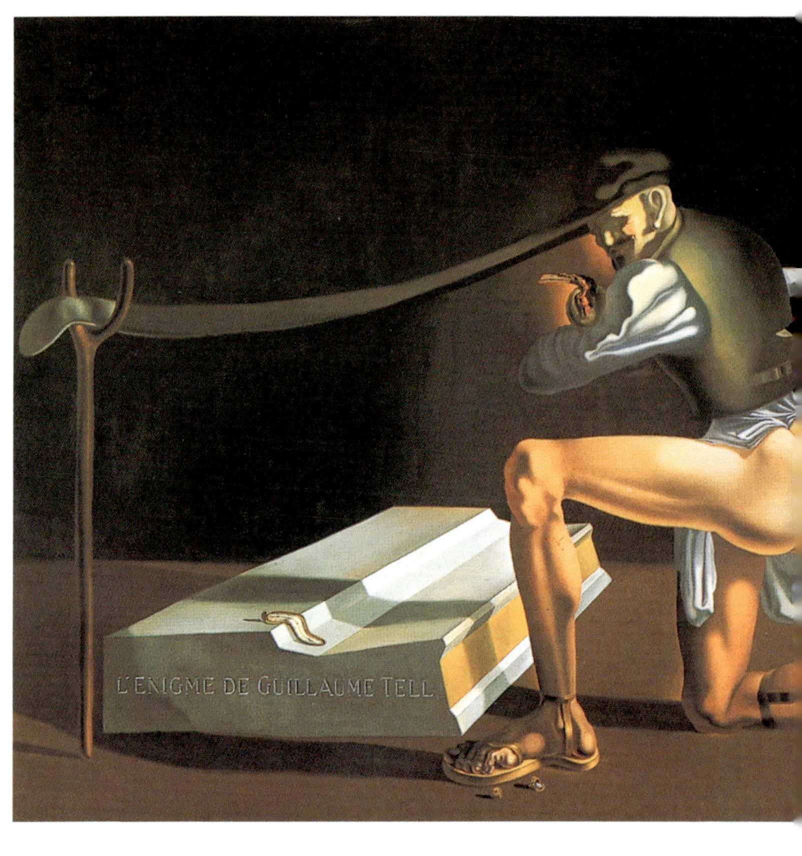

The Enigma of William Tell · 1933

Moderna Museet, Stockholm

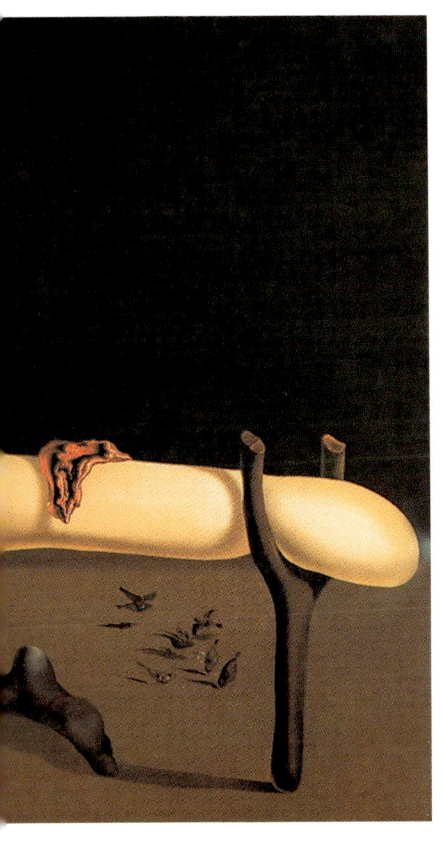

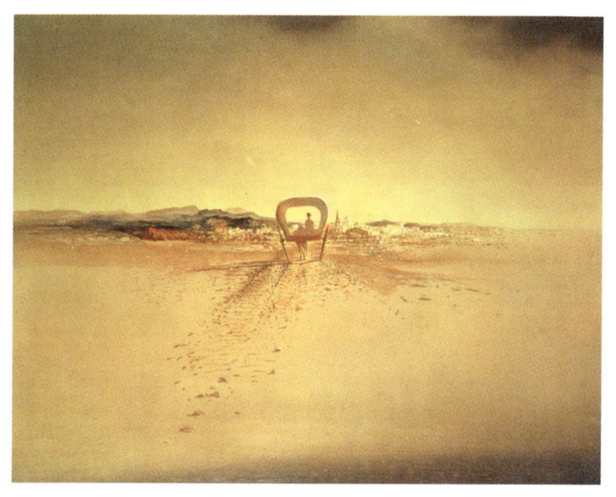

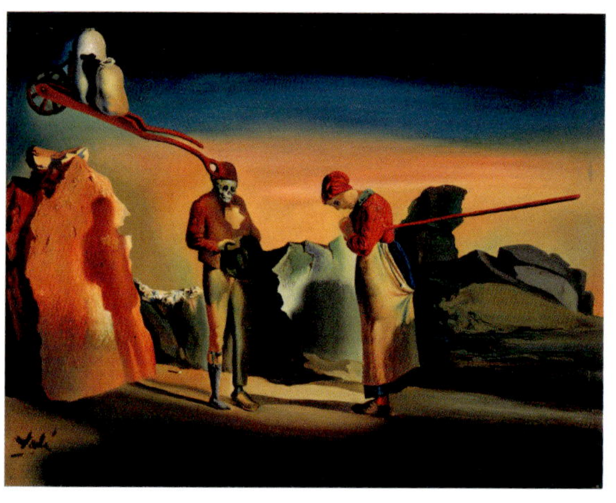

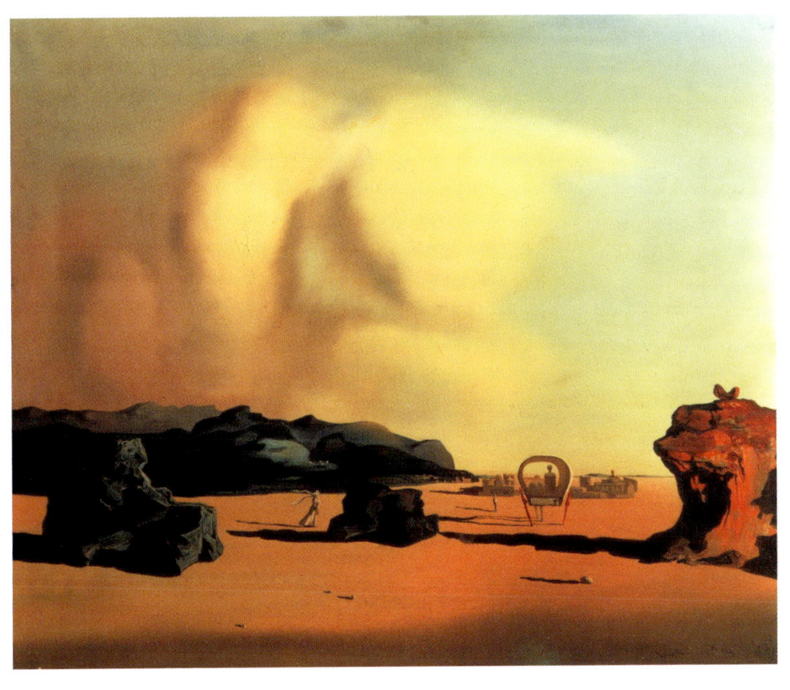

Moment of Transition · 1934
Private collection

< **The Phantom Cart** · 1933
Private collection; formerly Collection Edward James
< **Atavism at Twilight** · 1933–34
Kunstmuseum Bern, Georges F. Keller Bequest 1981

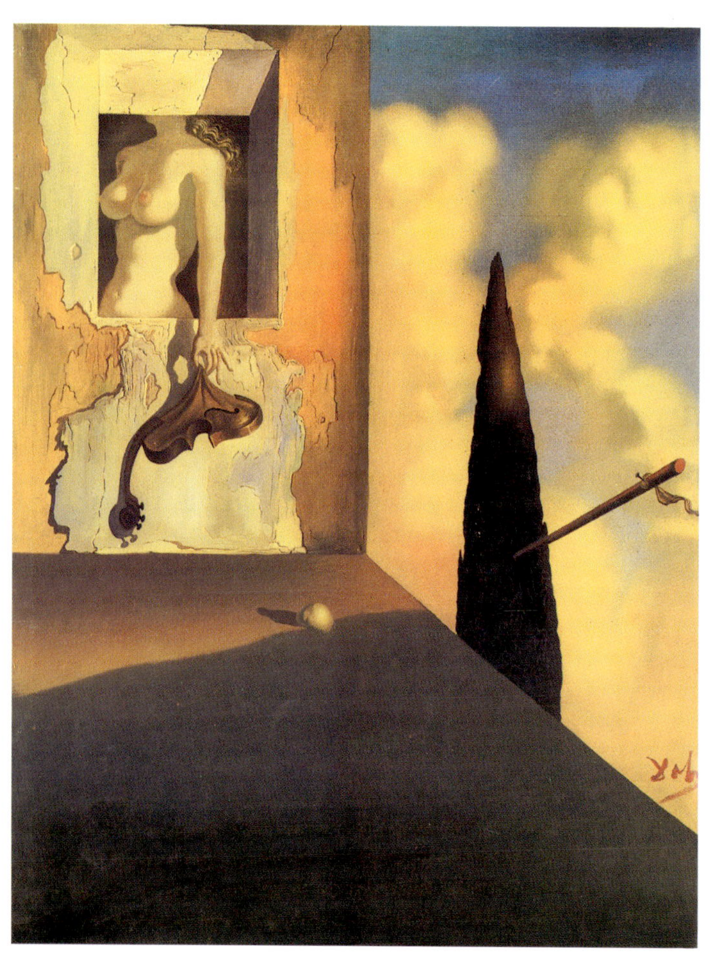

Masochistic Instrument · 1933–34

Private collection; formerly Collection Countess Pecci-Blunt

136

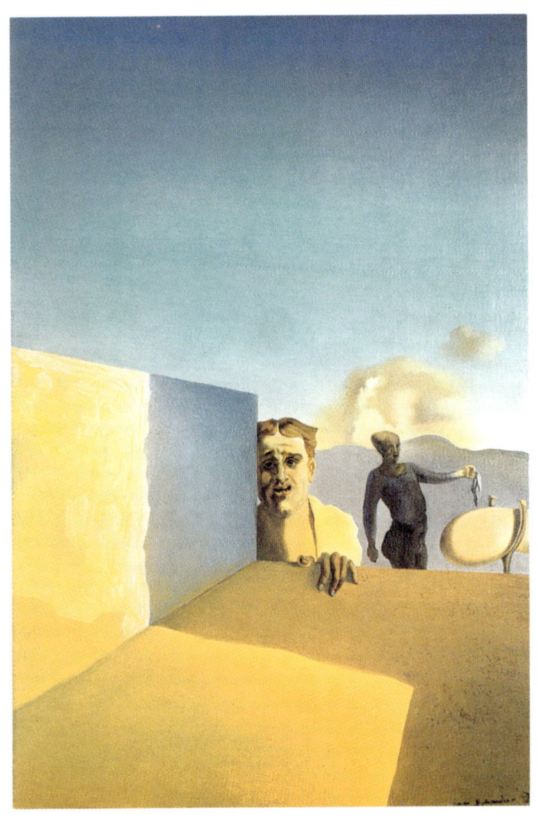

**Barber Saddened by the Persistence of Good Weather
(The Anguished Barber)** · 1934

Collection Klaus G. Perls, New York

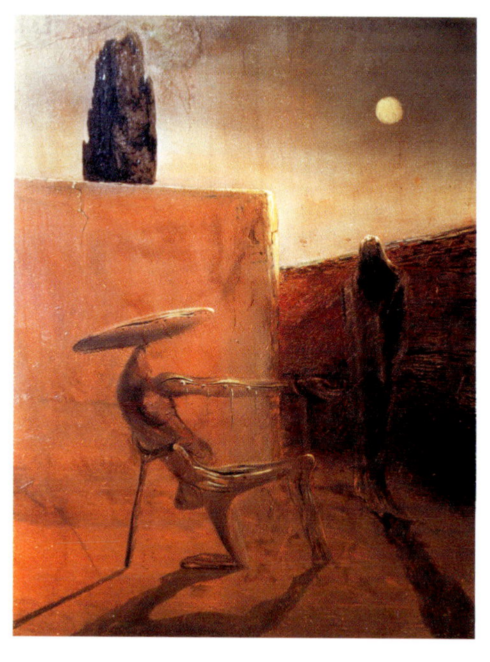

The Ghost of Vermeer van Delft · c. 1934
Private collection, Switzerland

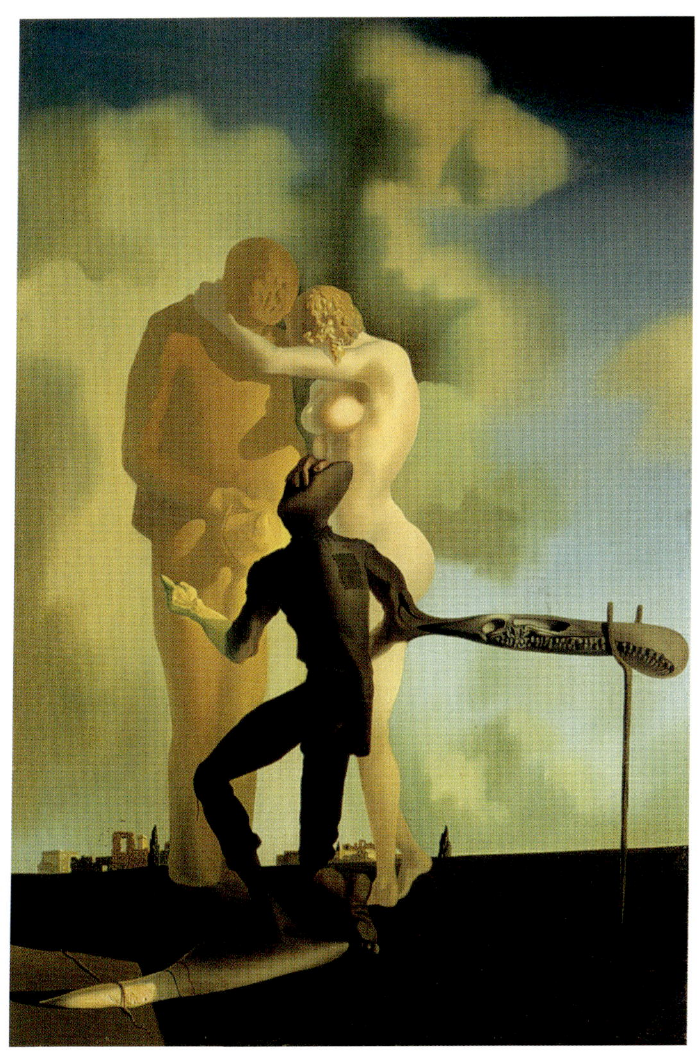

Meditation on the Harp · 1932–34
The Salvador Dalí Museum, St. Petersburg, Florida,
on loan from the Morse Charitable Trust; formerly Collection André Durst

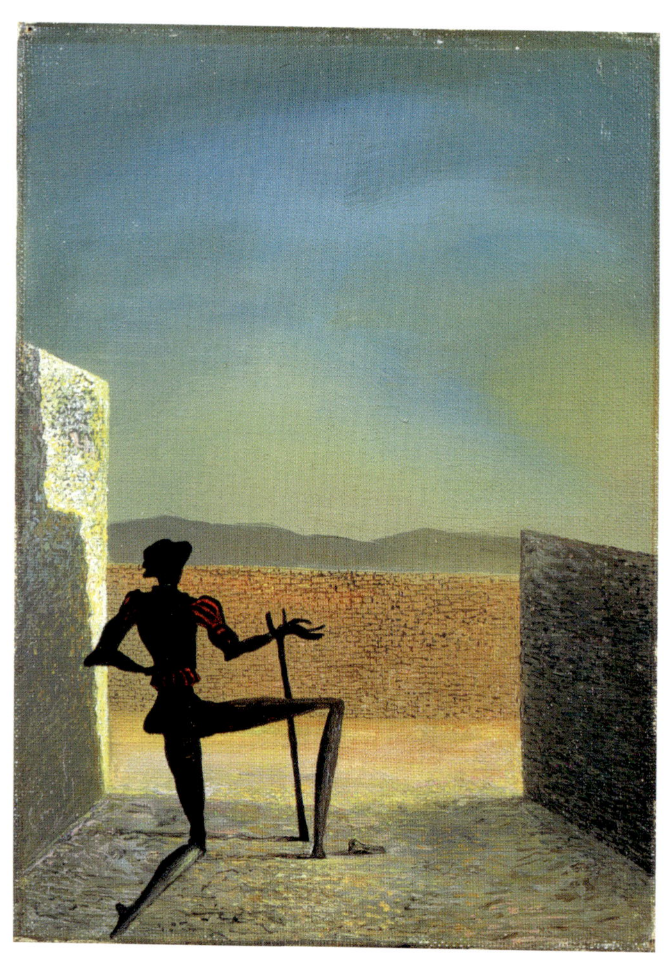

The Ghost of Vermeer van Delft · 1934
Whereabouts unknown

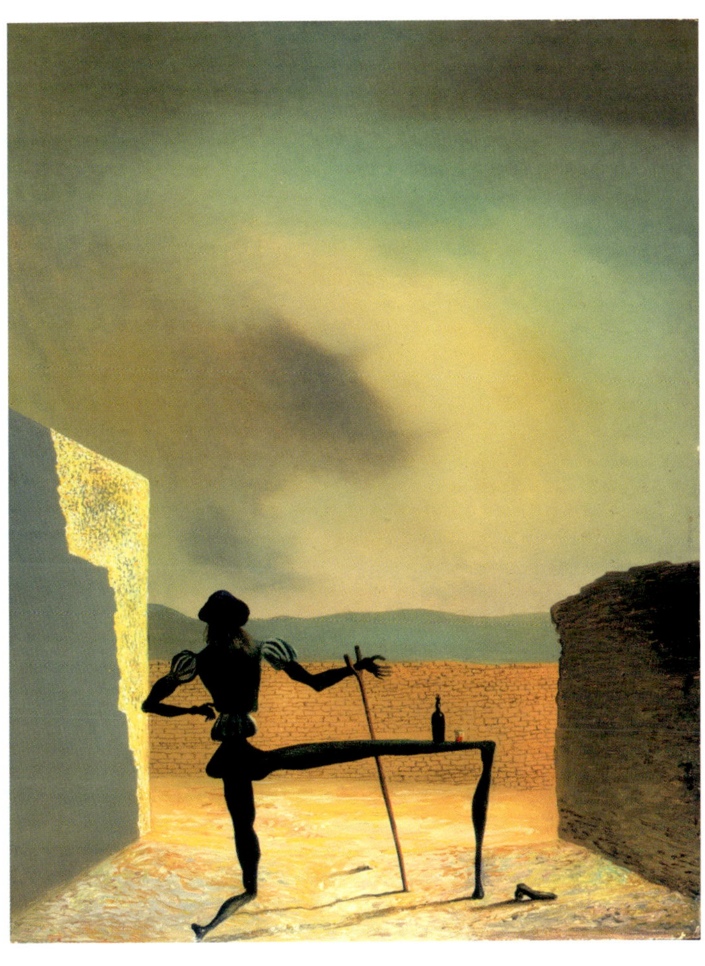

The Ghost of Vermeer van Delft which Can Be Used as a Table · 1934
The Salvador Dalí Museum, St. Petersburg, Florida,
on loan from E. and A. Reynolds Morse

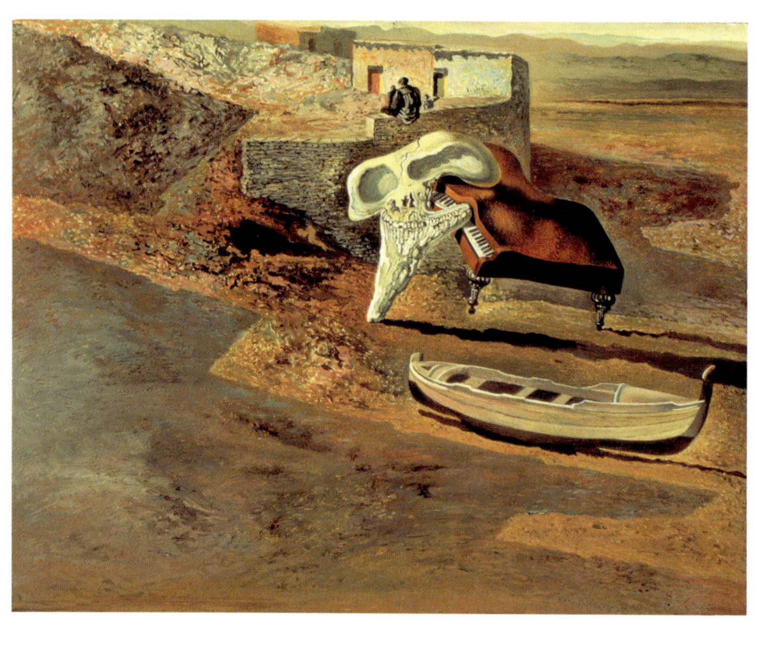

Atmospheric Skull Sodomizing a Grand Piano · 1934
The Salvador Dalí Museum, St. Petersburg, Florida,
on loan from E. and A. Reynolds Morse

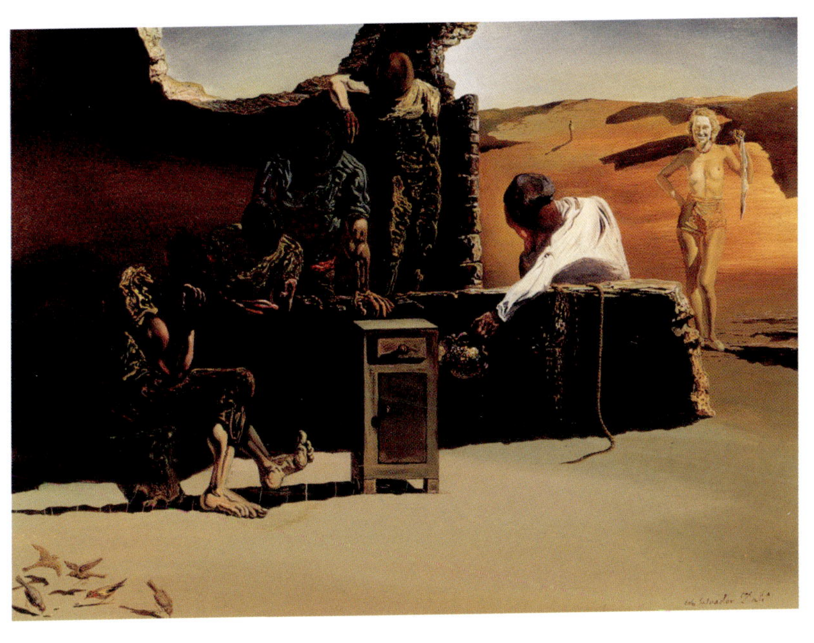

Cardinal, Cardinal! · 1934

Munson-Williams-Proctor Arts Institute, Utica, New York

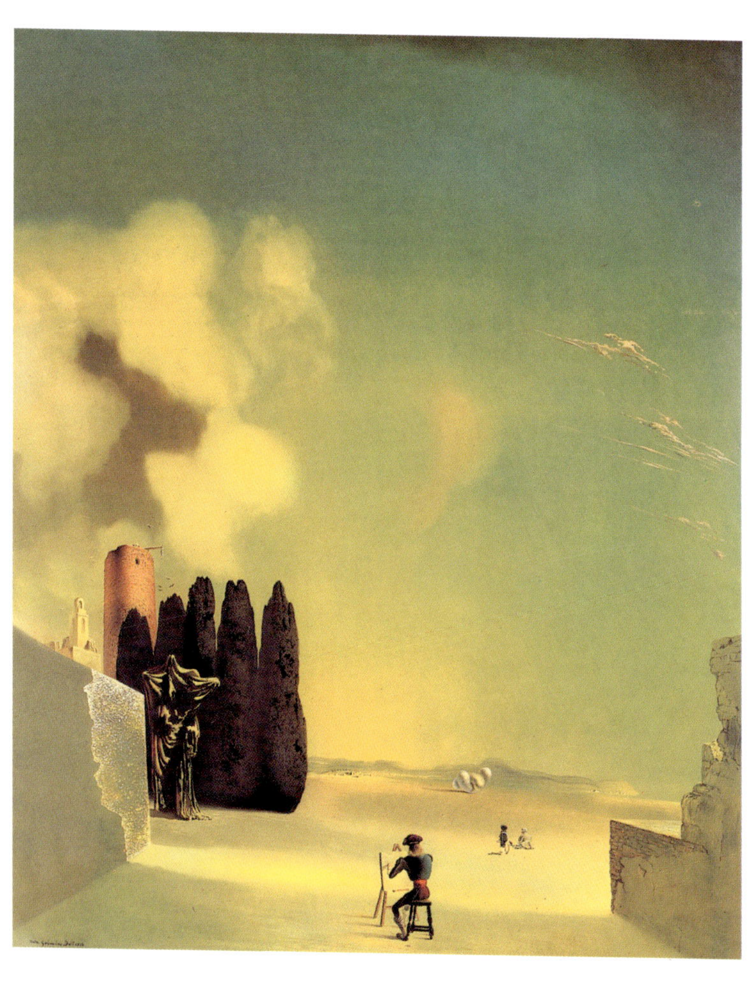

Enigmatic Elements in the Landscape · 1934
Private collection; formerly Collection Cyrus L. Sulzberger, Paris

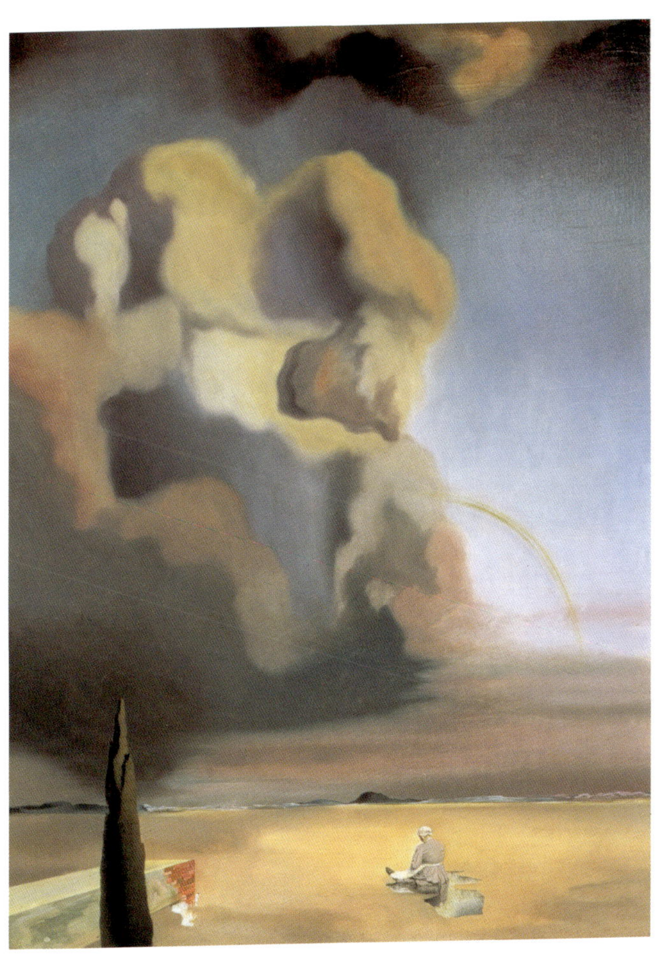

The Spectre and the Phantom · 1934
Five Stars Investment Ltd., New York

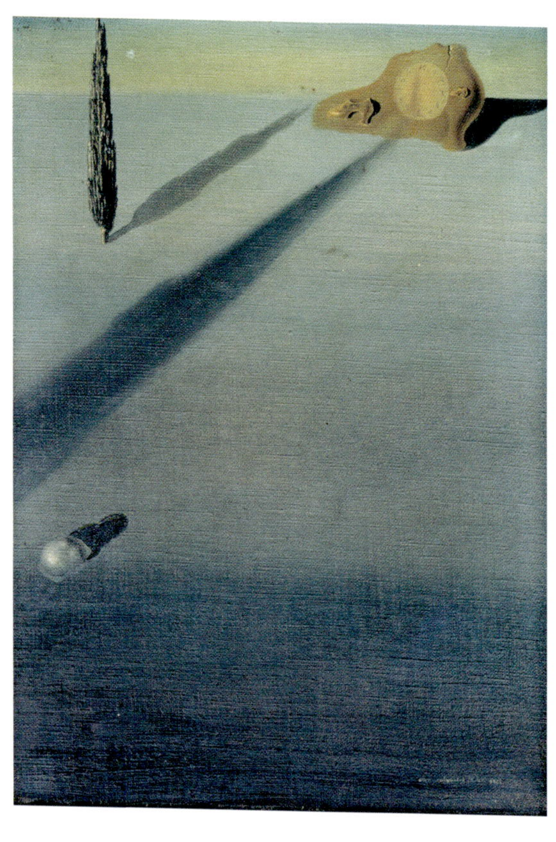

The Sense of Speed · 1934
Private collection; formerly Rothschild Collection

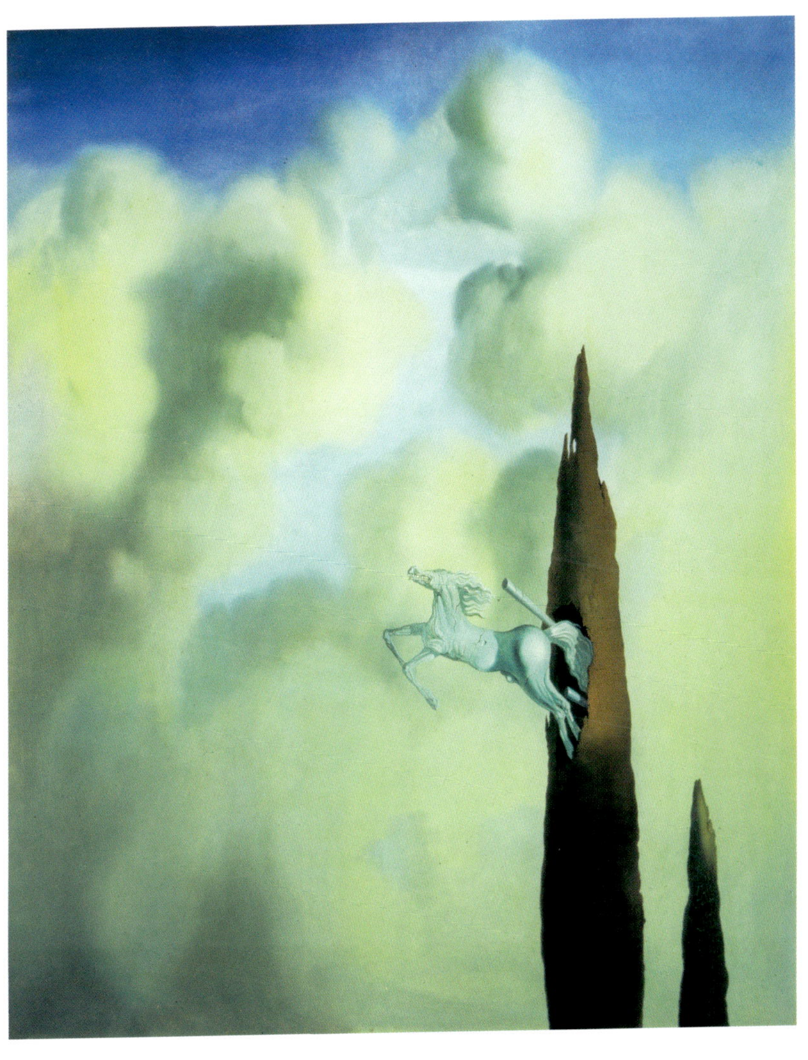

Morning Ossification of the Cypress · 1934
Private collection, Milan; formerly Collection Anne Green

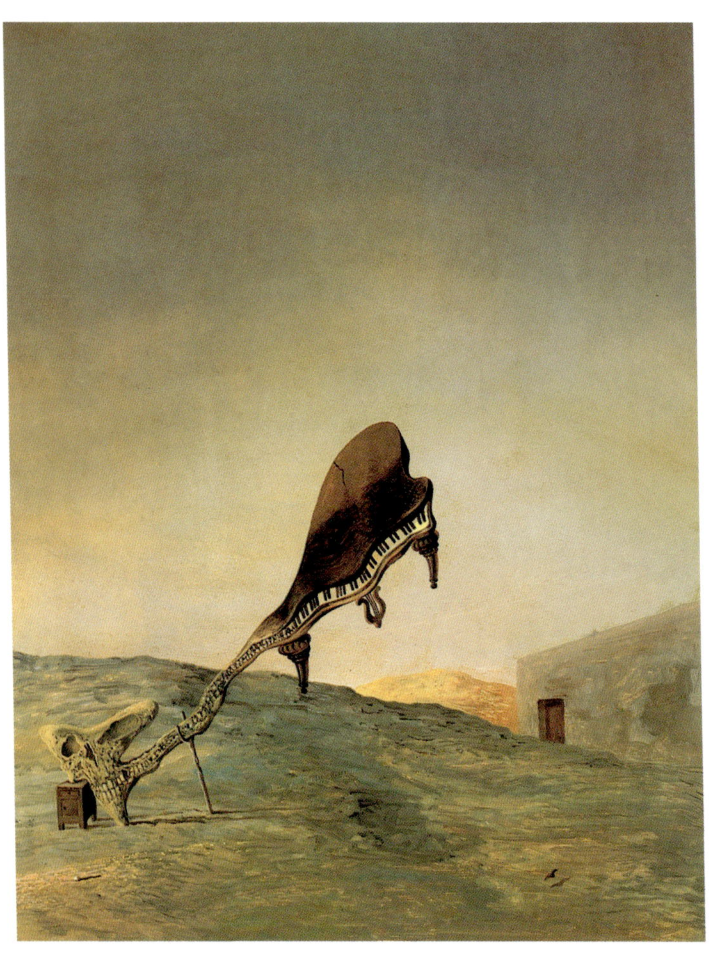

Skull with its Lyric Appendage Leaning on a Bedside Table which Should Have the Exact Temperature of a Cardinal's Nest · 1934
The Salvador Dalí Museum, St. Petersburg, Florida,
on loan from E. and A. Reynolds Morse

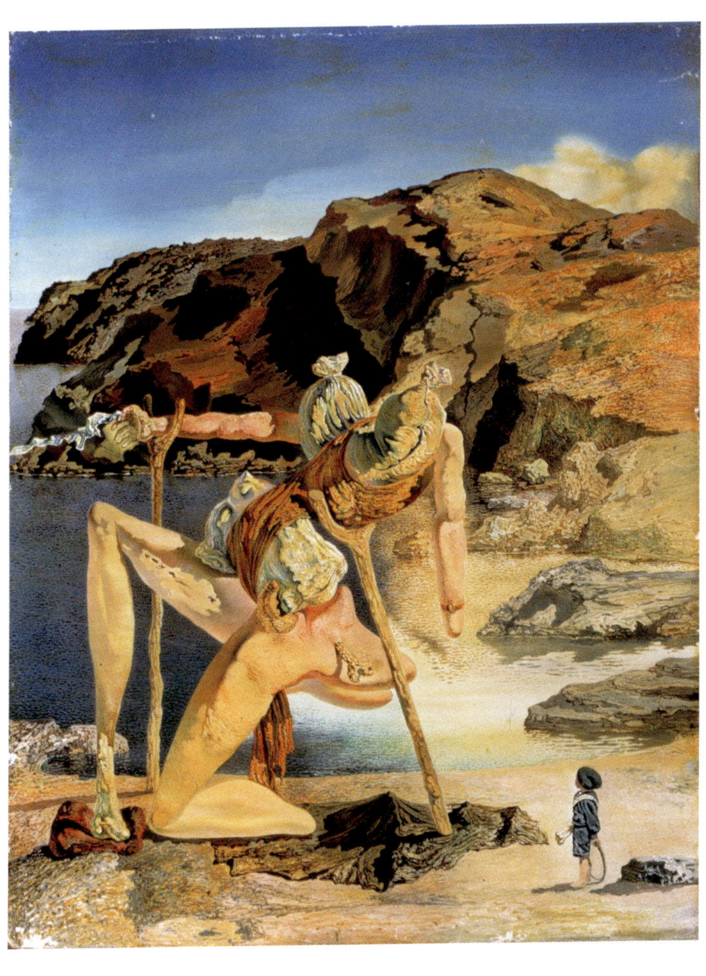

The Spectre of Sex Appeal · 1934
Fundación Gala-Salvador Dalí, Figueras

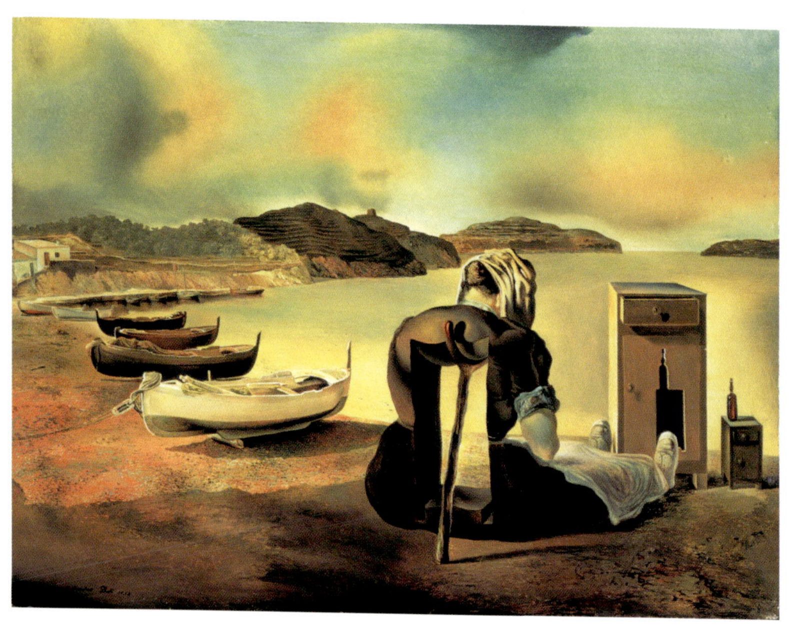

The Weaning of Furniture-Nutrition · 1934
The Salvador Dalí Museum, St. Petersburg, Florida,
on loan from E. and A. Reynolds Morse; formerly Collection Jocelyn Walker

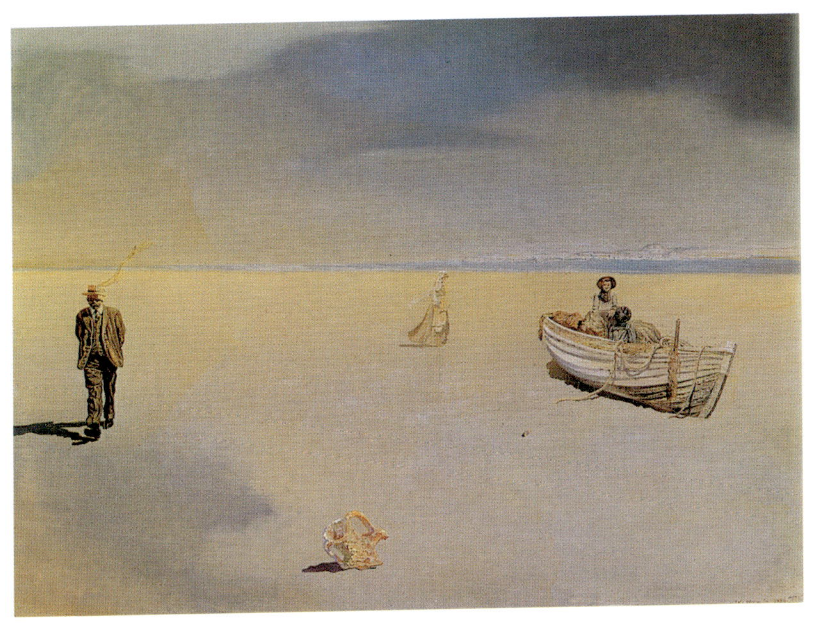

Paranoiac Astral Image · 1934
The Wadsworth Atheneum, Hartford, Connecticut,
Ella Gallup Sumner and Mary Catlin Sumner Collection

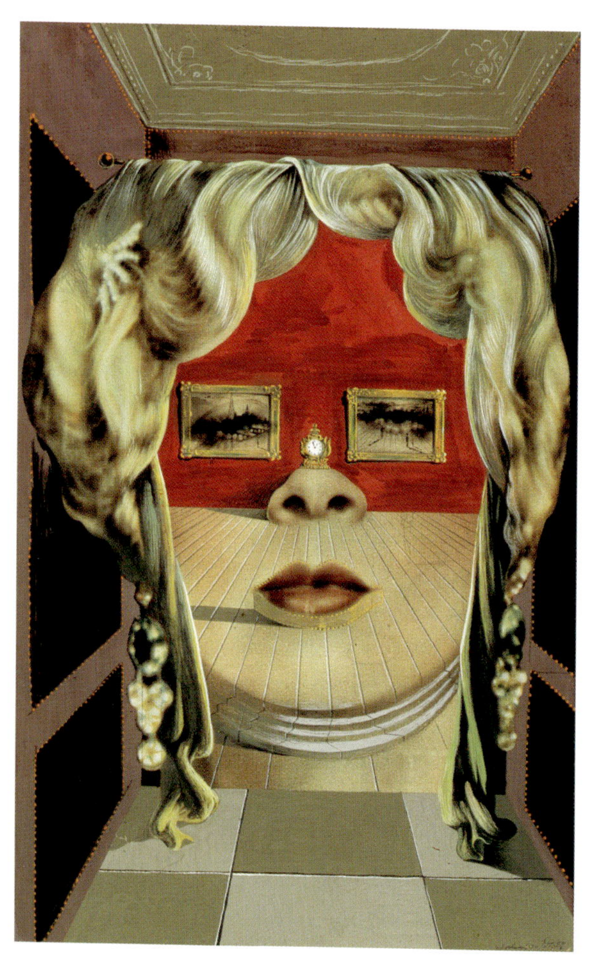

Mae West's Face which May Be Used as a Surrealist Apartment · 1934–35
The Art Institute of Chicago

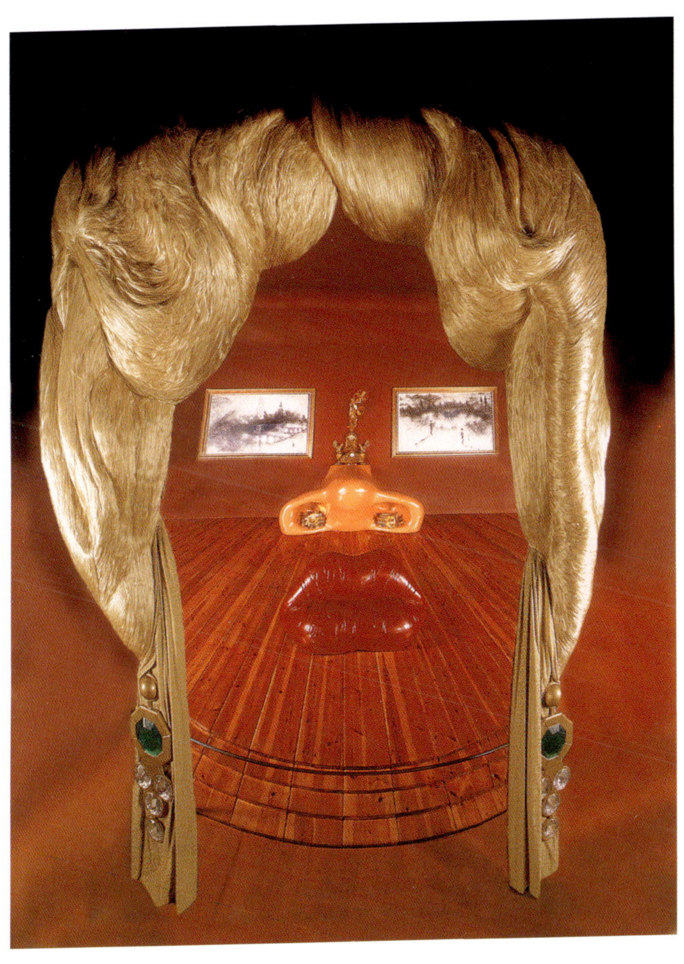

The Face of Mae West

Fundación Gala-Salvador Dalí, Figueras, gift of Dalí to the Spanish state

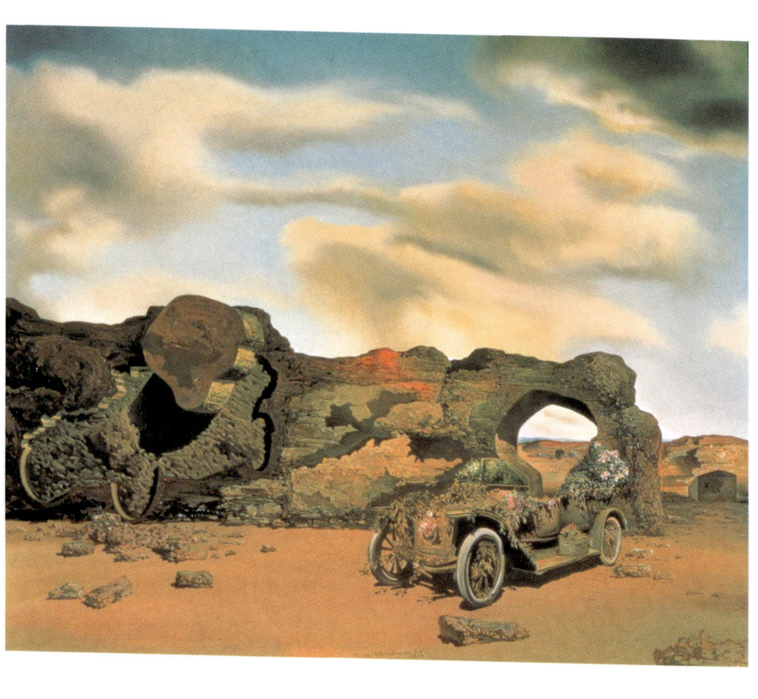

Paranoiac-Critical Solitude · 1935
Private collection; formerly Collection Edward James

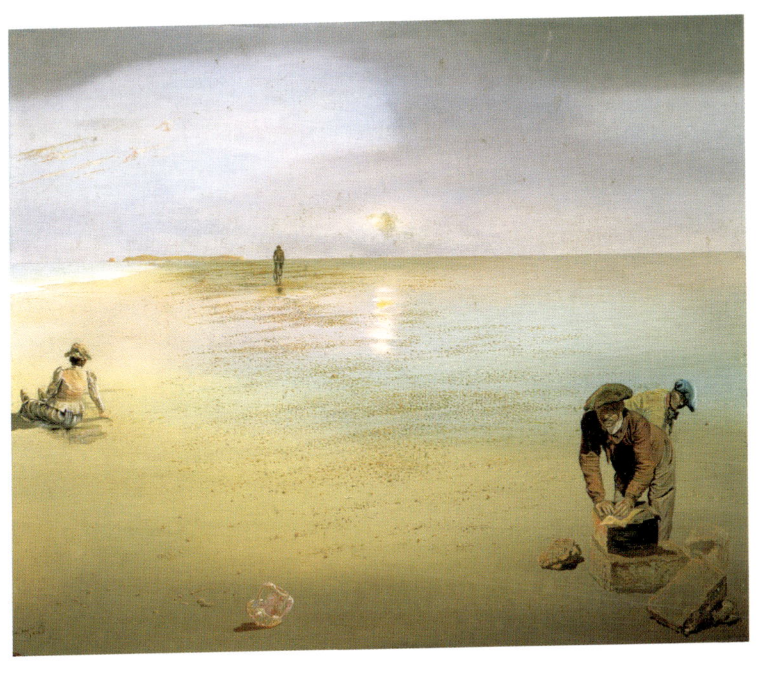

Mediumnistic-Paranoiac Image · 1935
Collection G.E.D. Nahmad, Geneva; formerly Collection Edward James

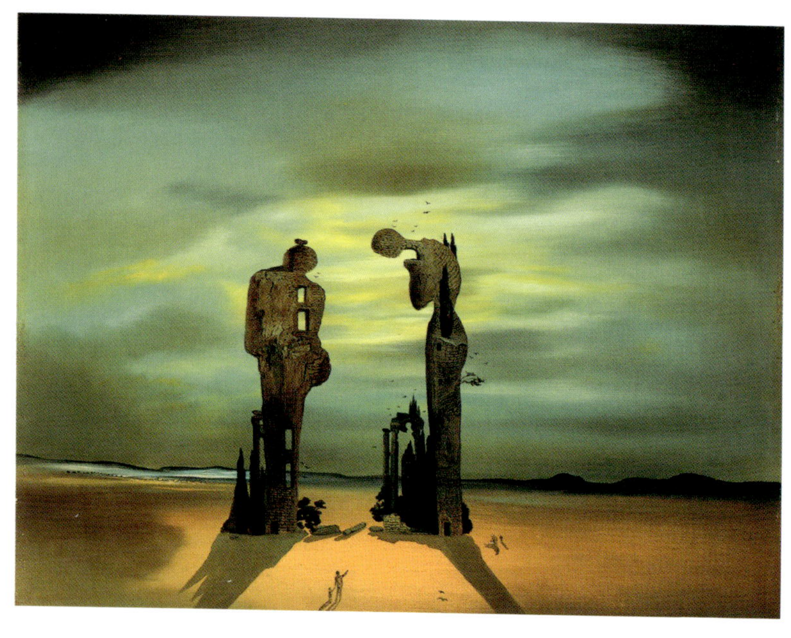

Archaeological Reminiscence of Millet's "Angelus" · 1935
The Salvador Dalí Museum, St. Petersburg, Florida,
on loan from the Morse Charitable Trust; formerly Collection E. Spitzer

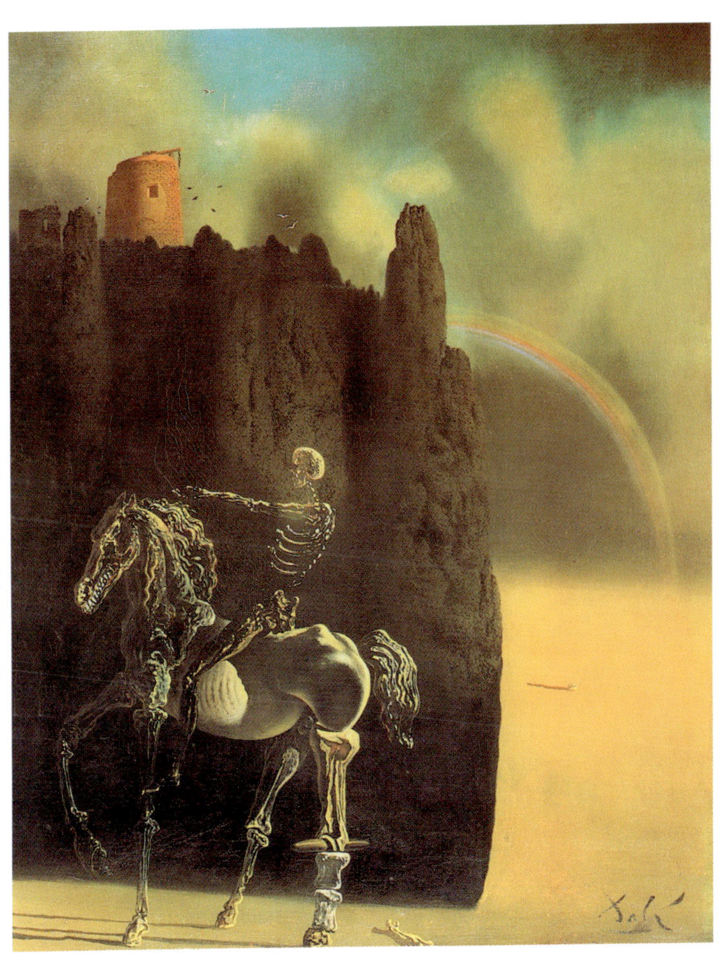

The Horseman of Death · 1935

André-François Petit, Paris

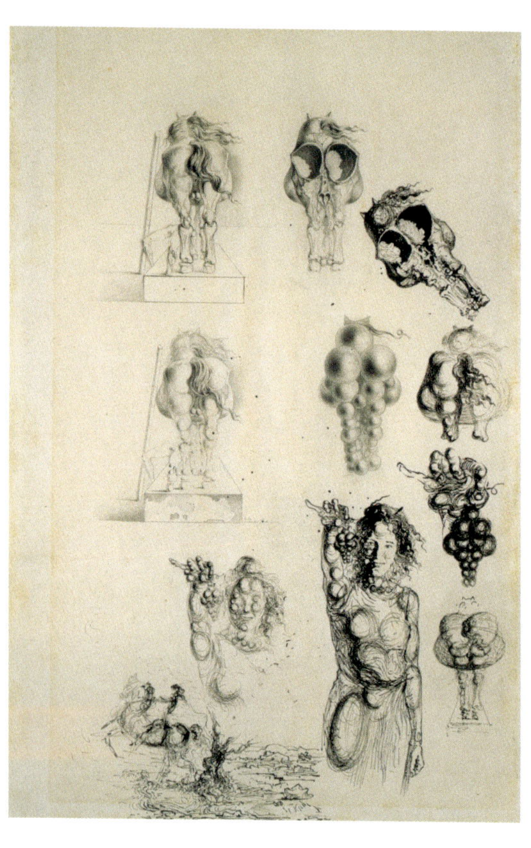

Study for "Suburbs of a Paranoiac-Critical Town" · 1935
Private collection

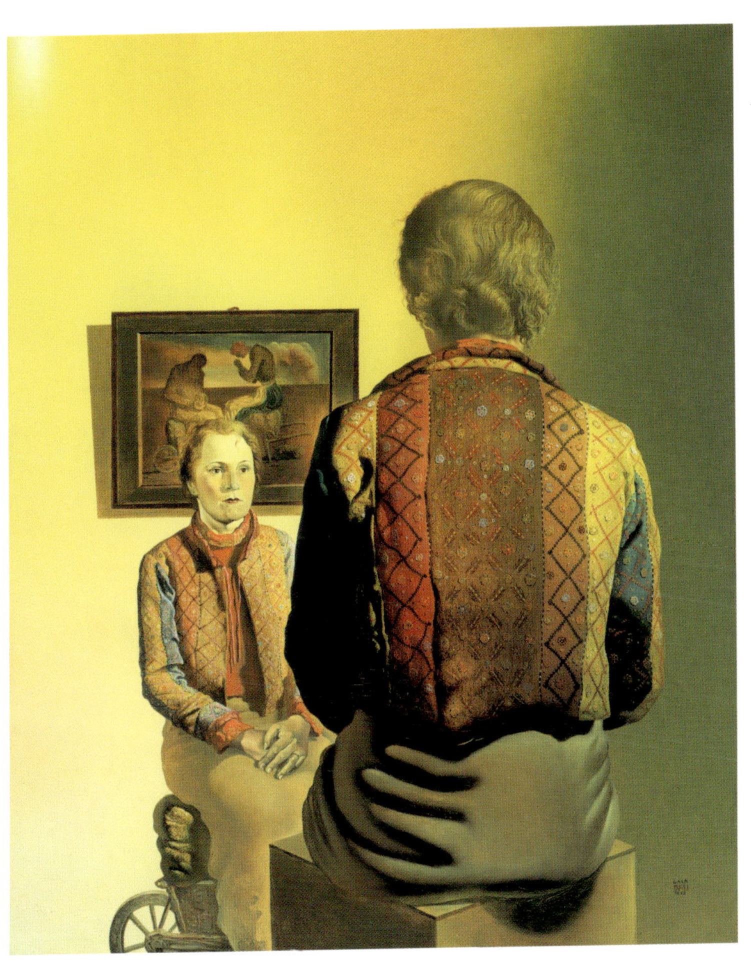

The Angelus of Gala · 1935
The Museum of Modern Art, New York

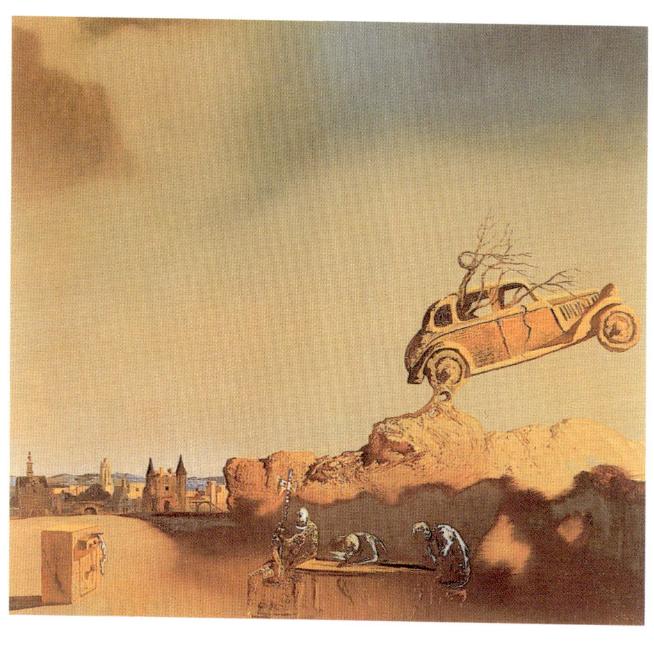

Apparition of the Town of Delft · 1935–36
Private collection

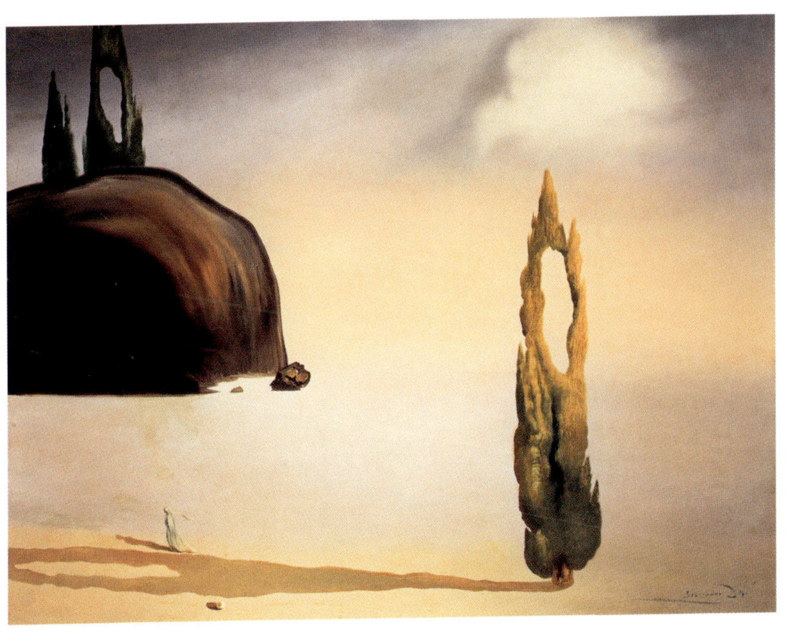

The Echo of the Void · 1935

Private collection

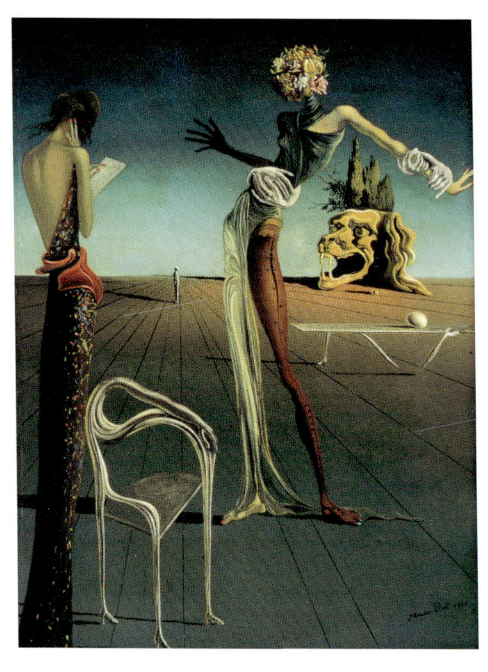

Woman with a Head of Roses · 1935

Kunsthaus Zürich

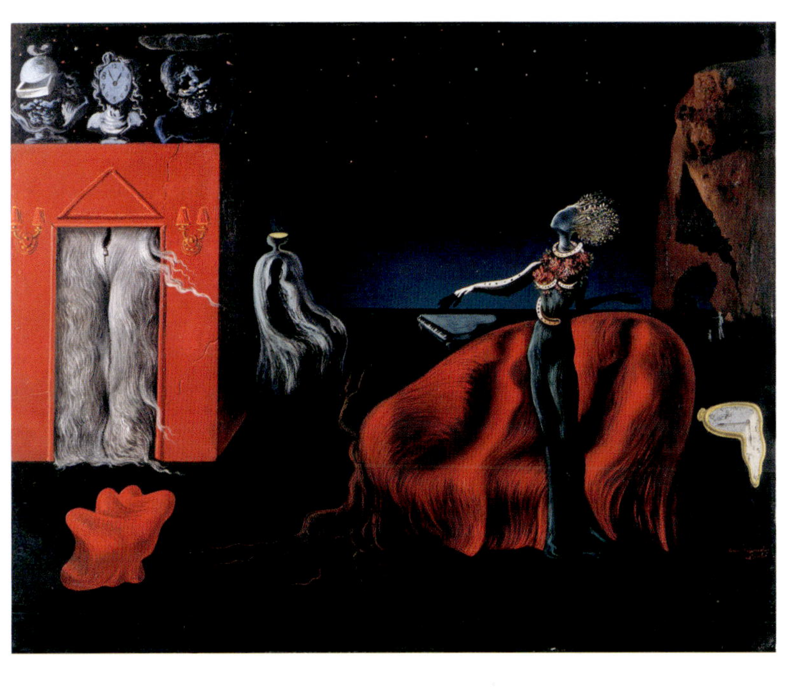

Singularities · 1935–36
Fundación Gala-Salvador Dalí, Figueras

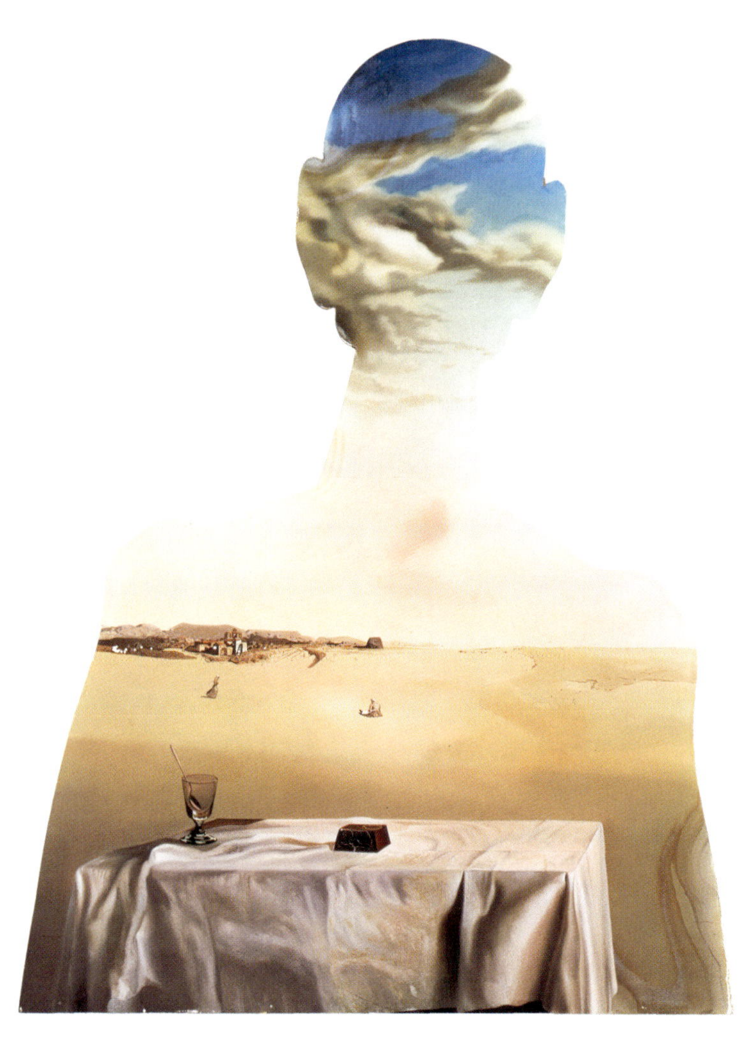

A Couple with Their Heads Full of Clouds · 1936

Museum Boijmans Van Beuningen, Rotterdam; formerly Collection Edward James

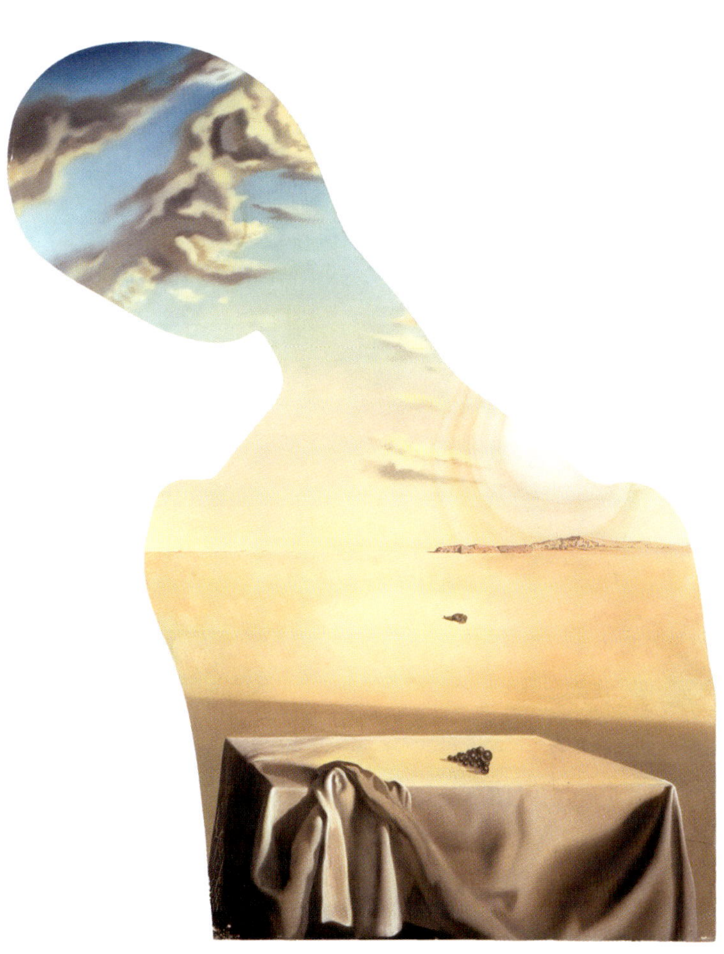

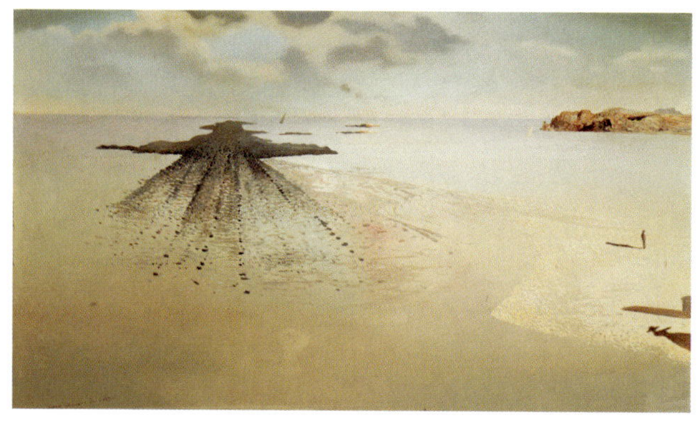

Geological Justice · 1936

Museum Boijmans Van Beuningen, Rotterdam; formerly Collection Edward James

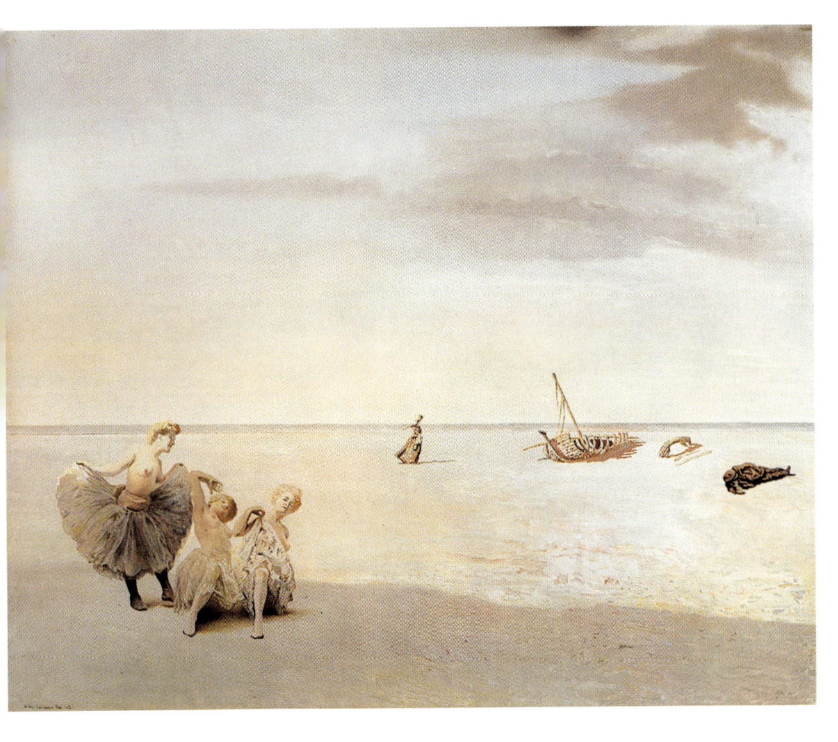

The Forgotten Horizon · 1936
Tate Gallery, London; formerly Collection Edward James

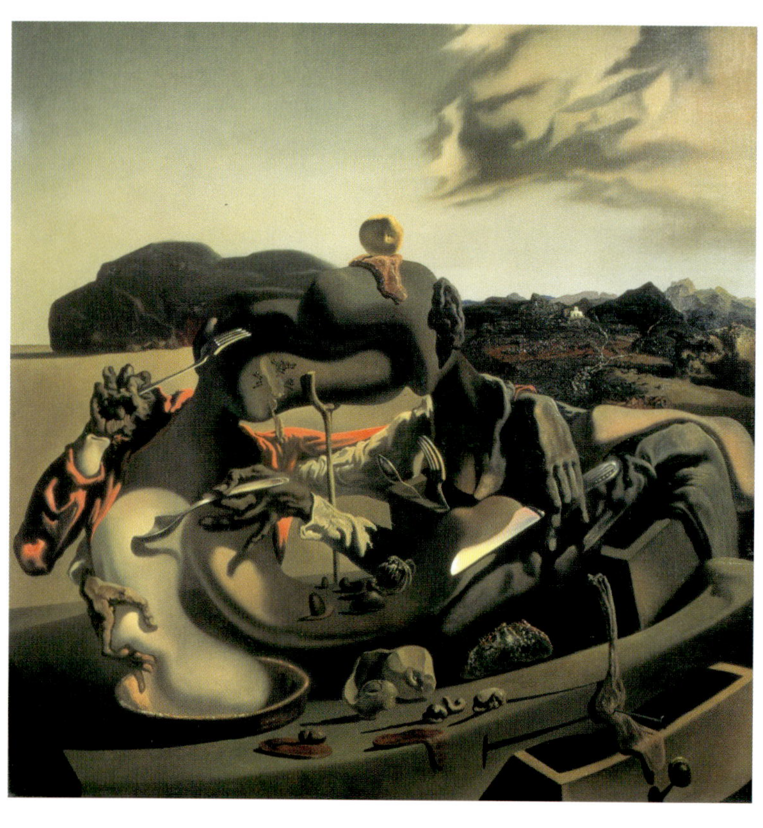

Autumn Cannibalism · 1936
Tate Gallery, London; formerly Collection Edward James

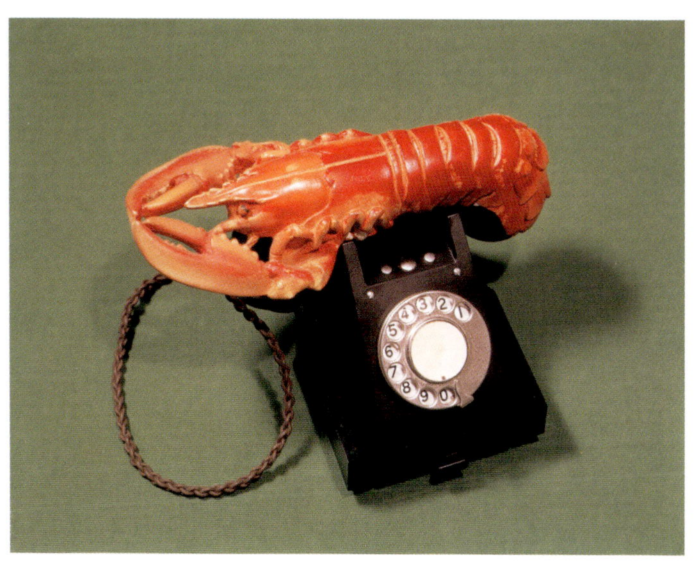

Lobster Telephone · 1936

Museum Boijmans Van Beuningen, Rotterdam; formerly Collection Edward James

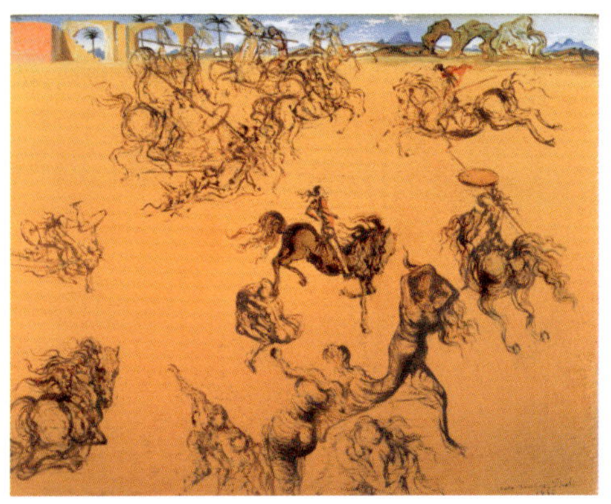 

**Head of a Woman in the Form of a Battle.
Study for "Spain"** · 1936

Private collection; formerly Collection Edward James

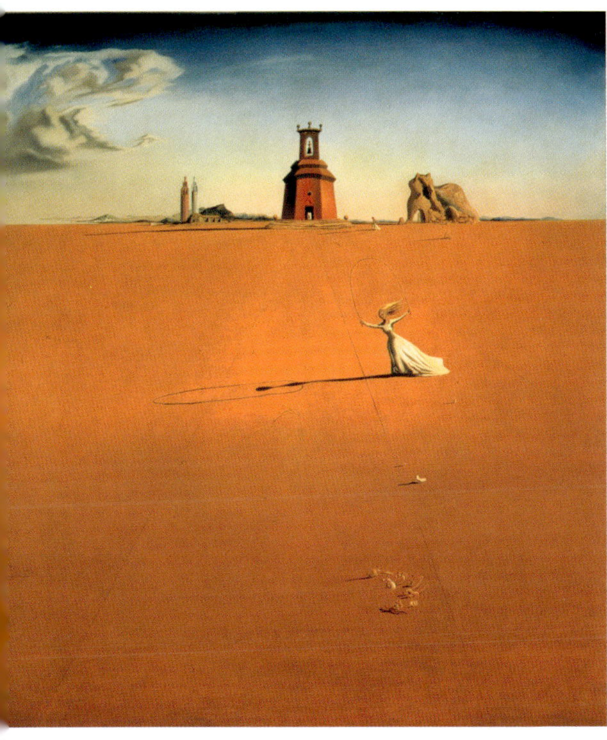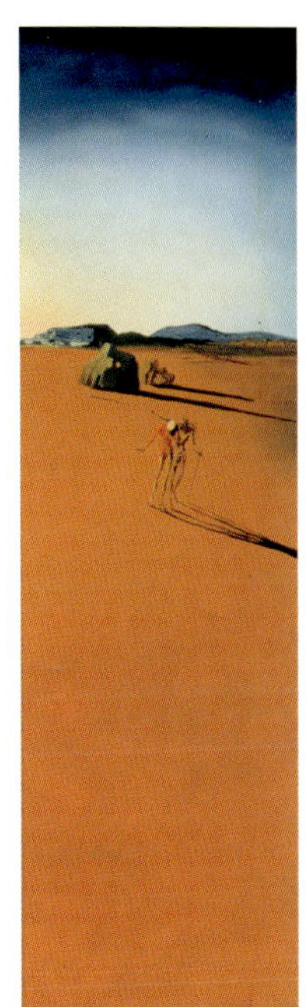

Landscape with a Girl Skipping · 1936

Museum Boijmans Van Beuningen, Rotterdam; formerly Collection Edward James

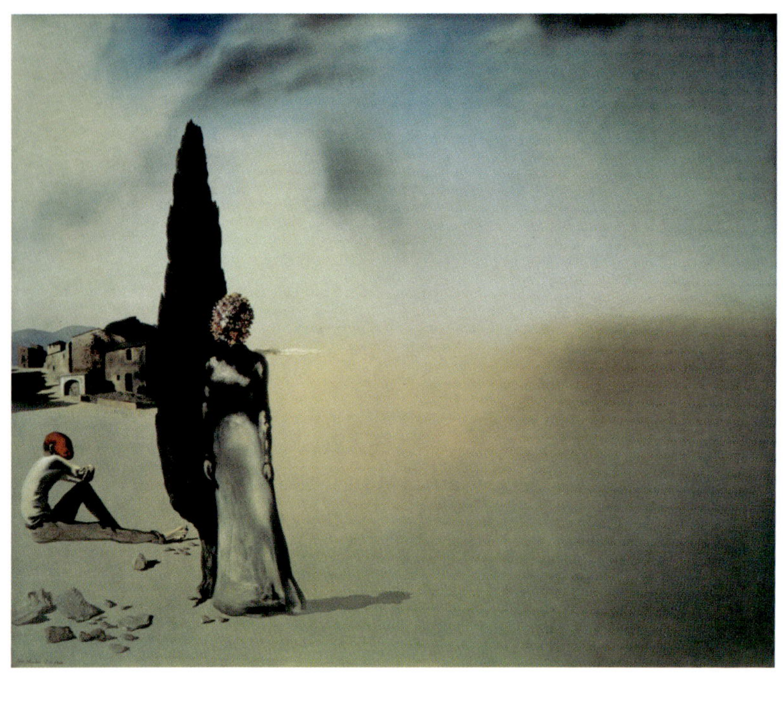

Necrophiliac Springtime · 1936
Private collection; formerly Collection Elsa Schiaparelli

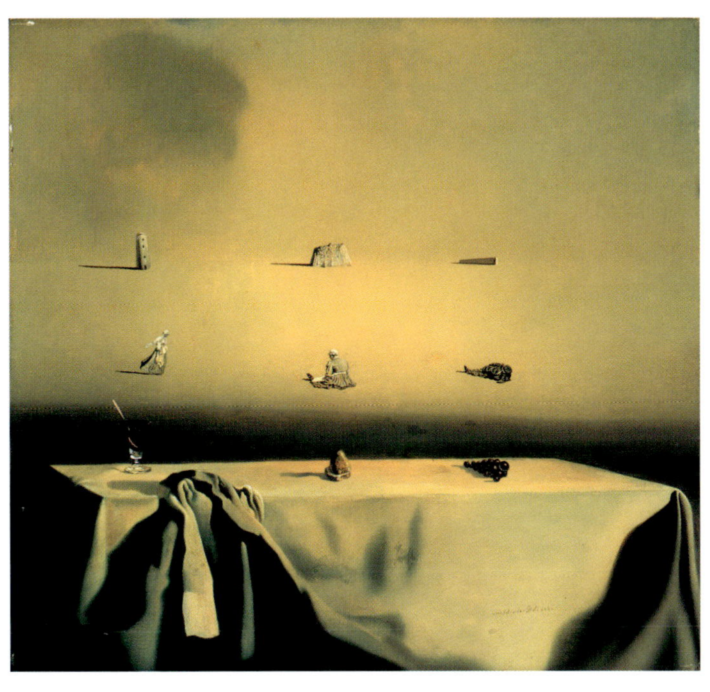

Morphological Echo · 1936
The Salvador Dalí Museum, St. Petersburg, Florida,
on loan from E. and A. Reynolds Morse

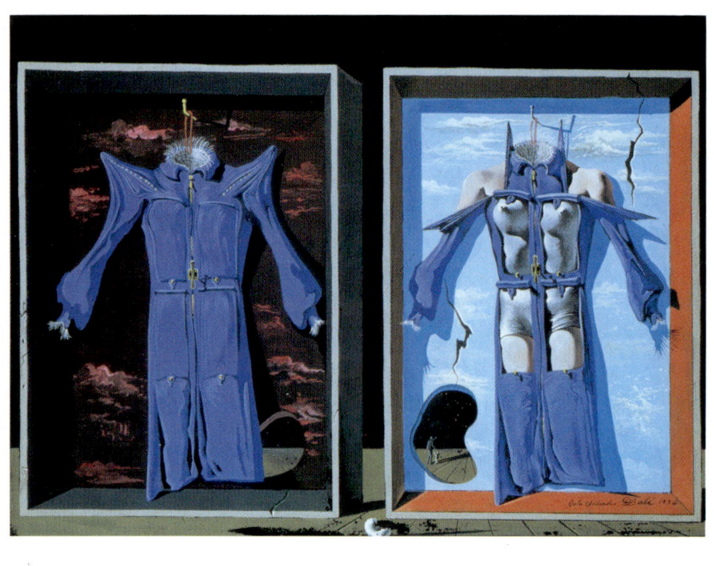

Night and Day Clothes of the Body · 1936
Private collection

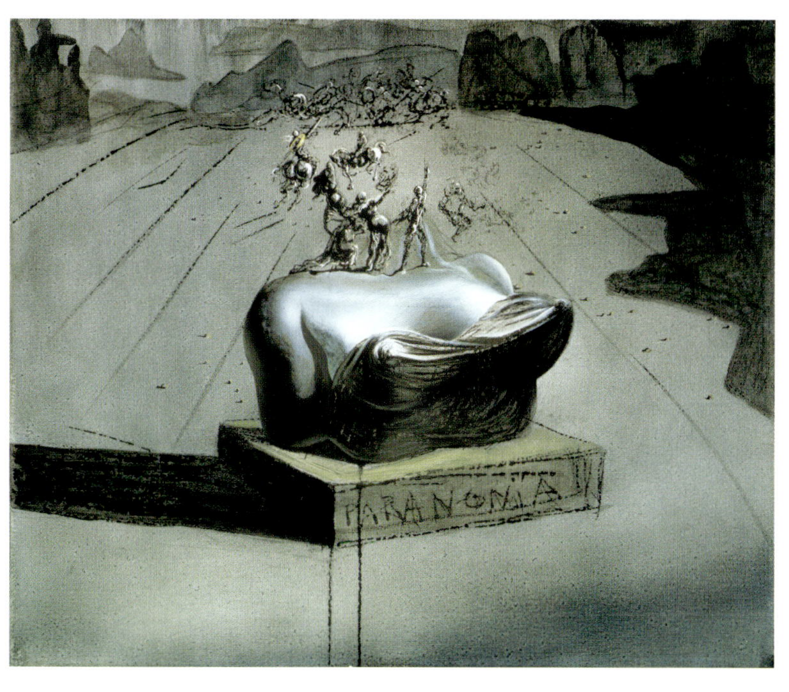

Paranoia · 1936
The Salvador Dalí Museum, St. Petersburg, Florida,
on loan from E. and A. Reynolds Morse

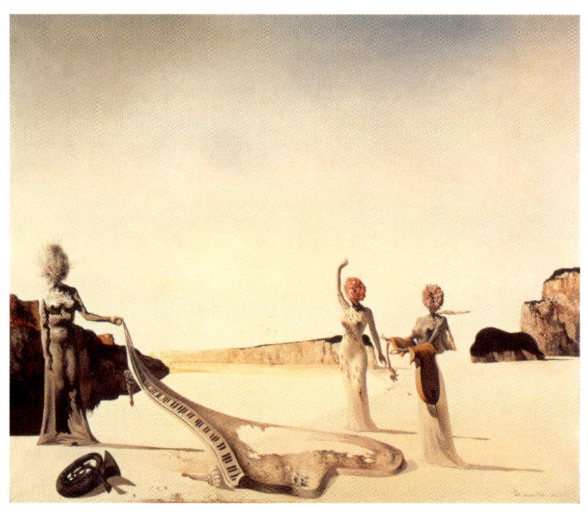

**Three Young Surrealist Women Holding in Their Arms
the Skins of an Orchestra · 1936**
The Salvador Dalí Museum, St. Petersburg, Florida,
on loan from the Morse Charitable Trust

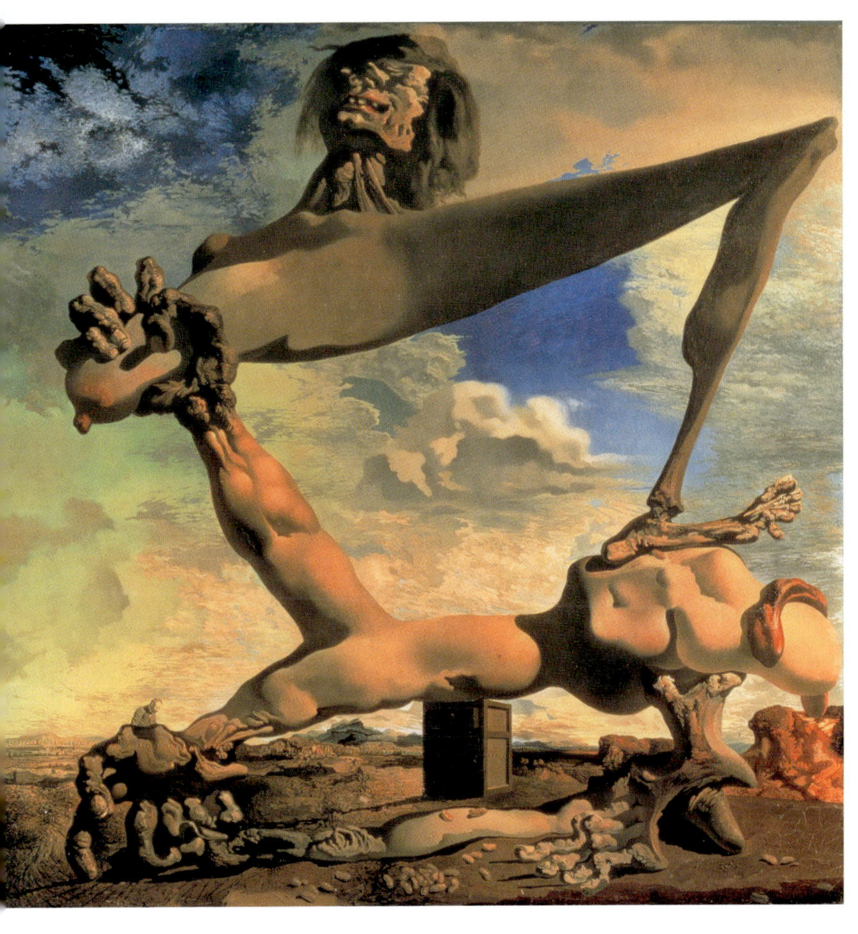

Soft Construction with Boiled Beans—Premonition of Civil War · 1936

The Philadelphia Museum of Art,

The Louise and Walter Arensberg Collection; formerly Collection Peter Watson

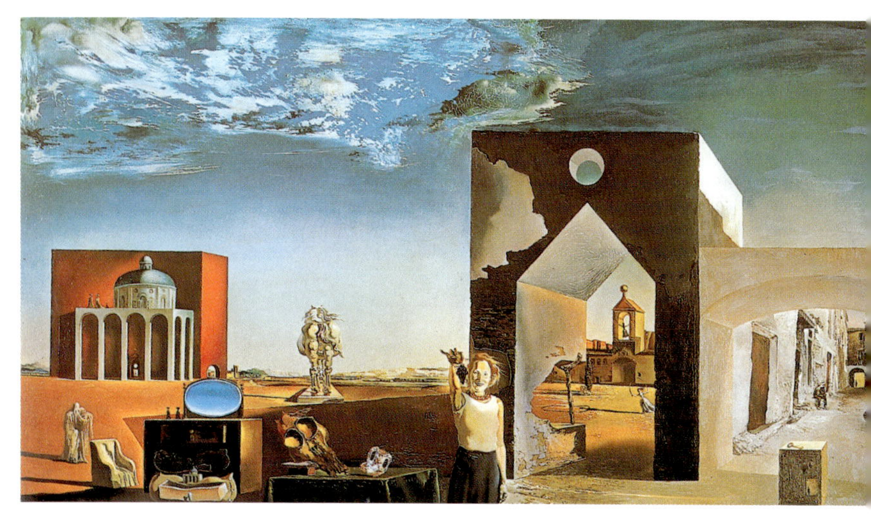

**Suburbs of a Paranoiac-Critical Town: Afternoon on the Outskirts
of European History · 1936**

Museum Boijmans Van Beuningen, Rotterdam; formerly Collection Edward James

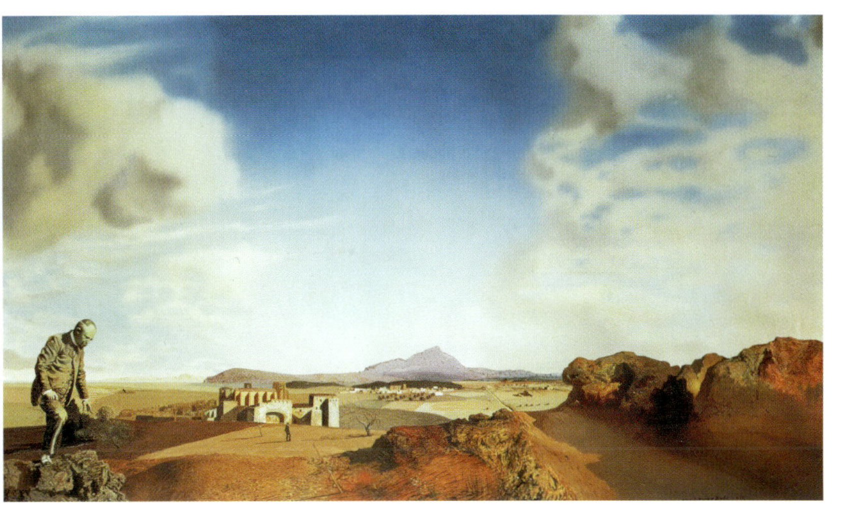

The Chemist of Ampurdán in Search of Absolutely Nothing · 1936

Museum Folkwang, Essen; formerly Collection Edward James

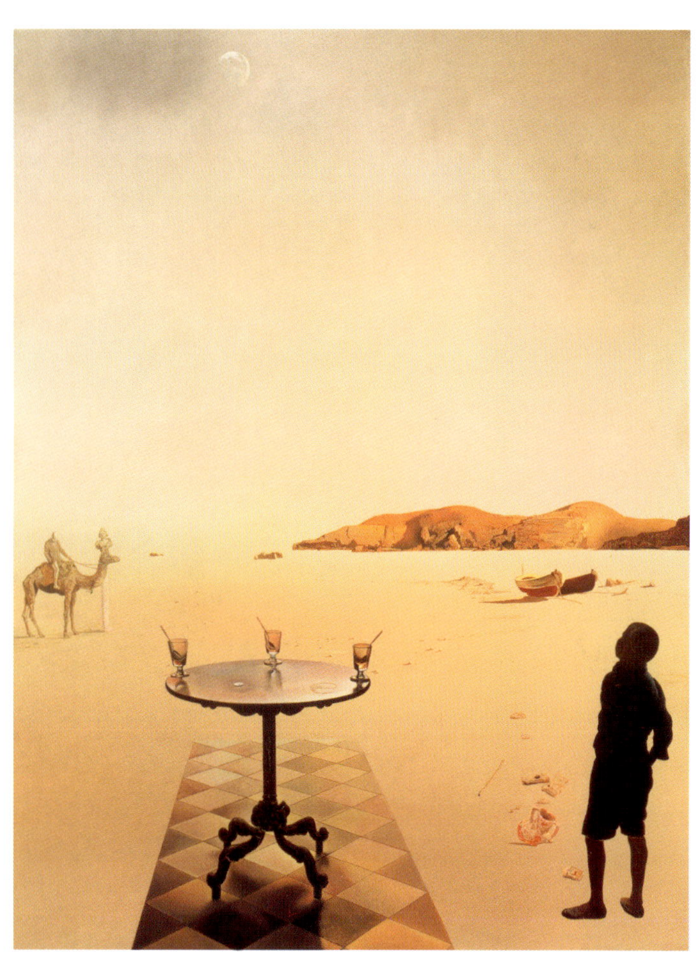

Sun Table · 1936

Museum Boijmans Van Beuningen, Rotterdam; formerly Collection Edward James

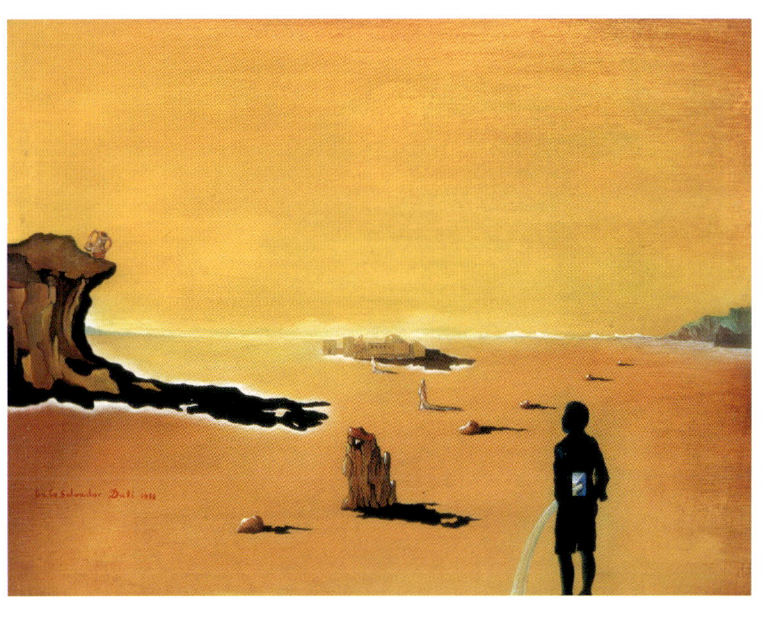

Surrealist Landscape · 1936
Galerie Malingue, Paris

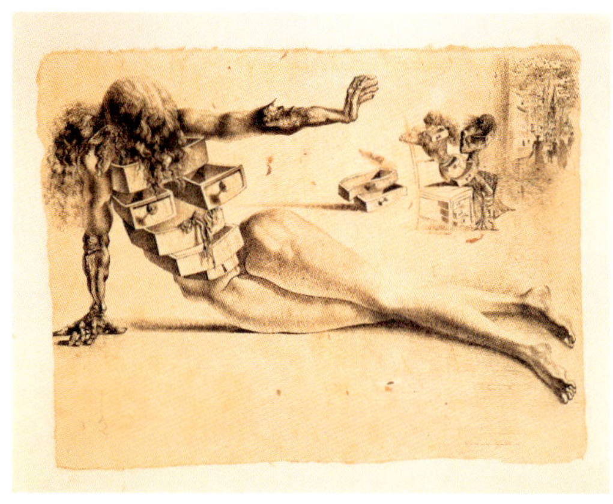

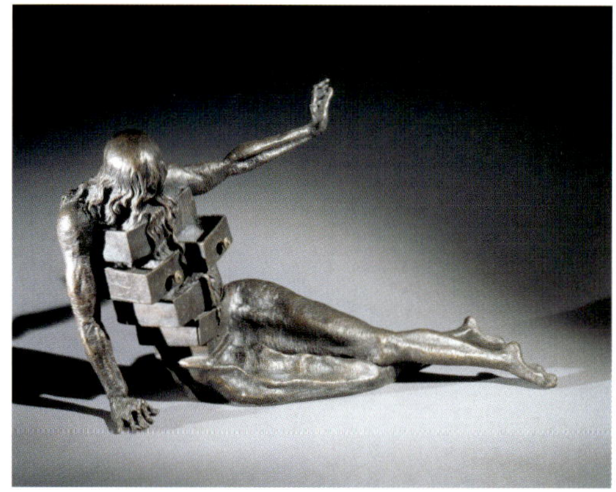

The City of Drawers. Study for the "Anthropomorphic Cabinet" · 1936
Collection Paul L. Herring, New York; formerly Collection Edward James
The Anthropomorphic Cabinet · 1982
Private collection

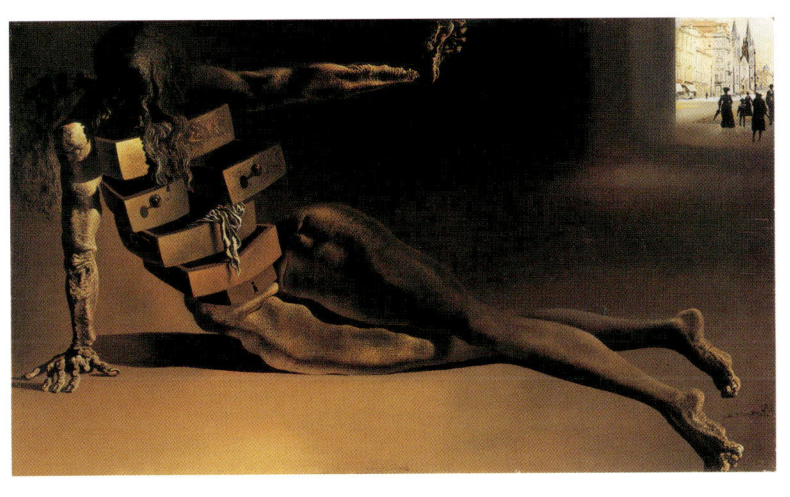

The Anthropomorphic Cabinet · 1936

Kunstsammlung Nordrhein-Westfalen, Düsseldorf;
formerly Collection Edward James

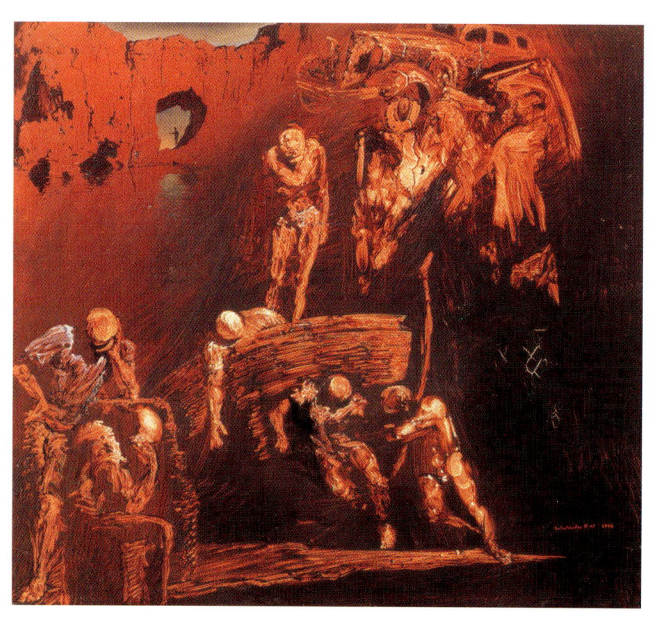

The Fossilized Automobile of Cape Creus · 1936
Collection G.E.D. Nahmad, Geneva; formerly Collection Edward James

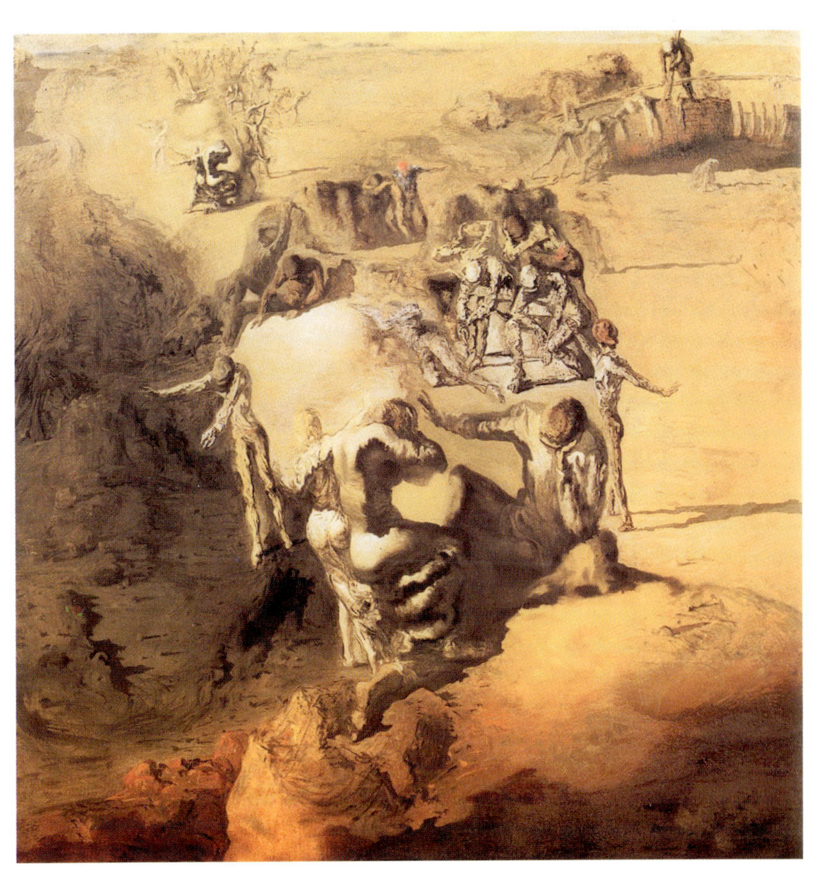

The Great Paranoiac · 1936

Museum Boijmans Van Beuningen, Rotterdam; formerly Collection Edward James

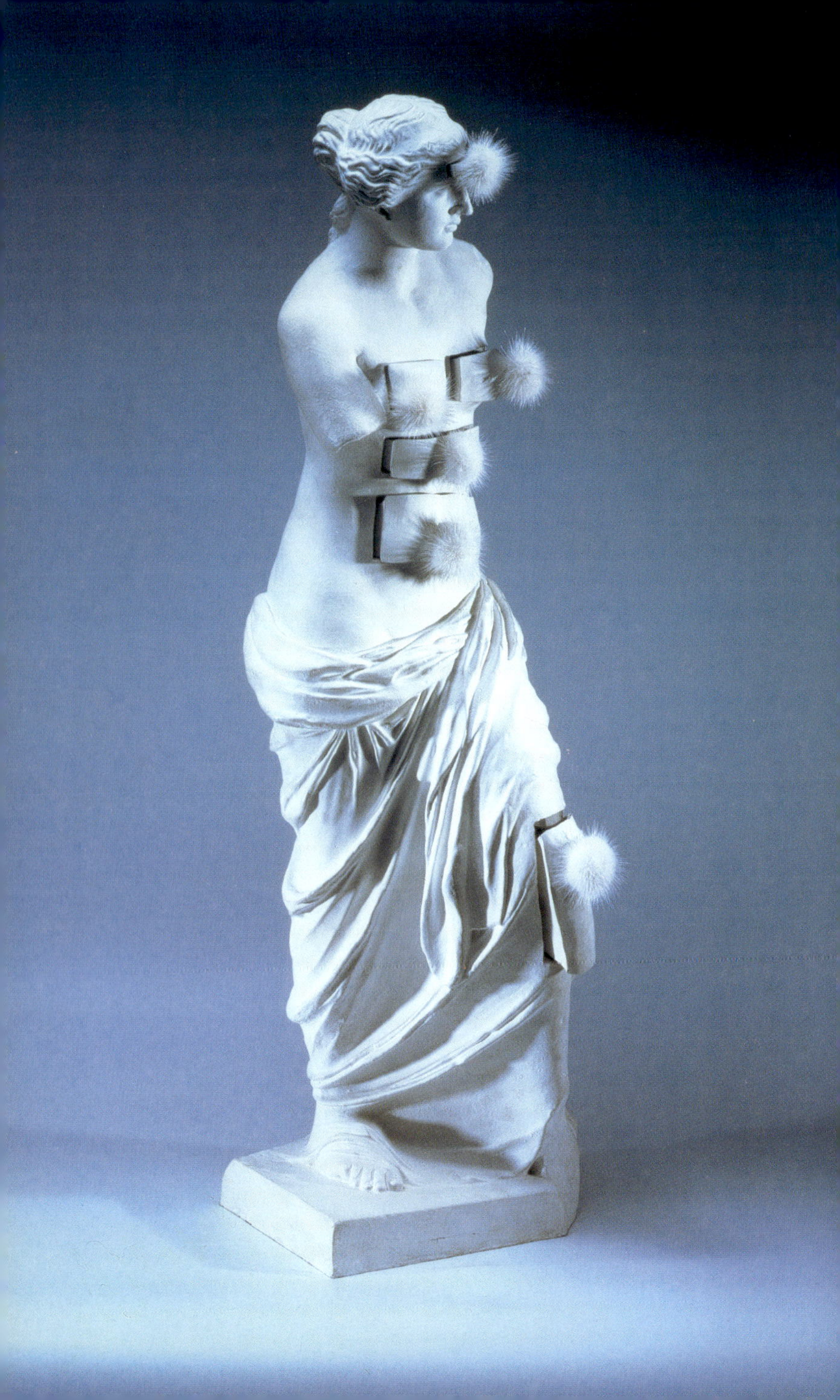

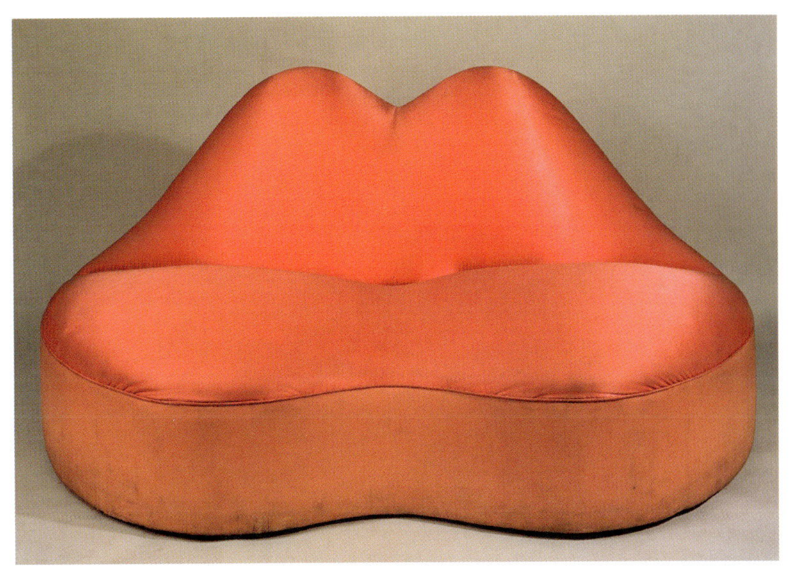

Mae West Lips Sofa · 1936–37
The Royal Pavilion Art Gallery and Museum, Borough of Brighton;
formerly Collection Edward James
‹ **Venus de Milo with Drawers** · 1936
Museum Boijmans Van Beuningen, Rotterdam

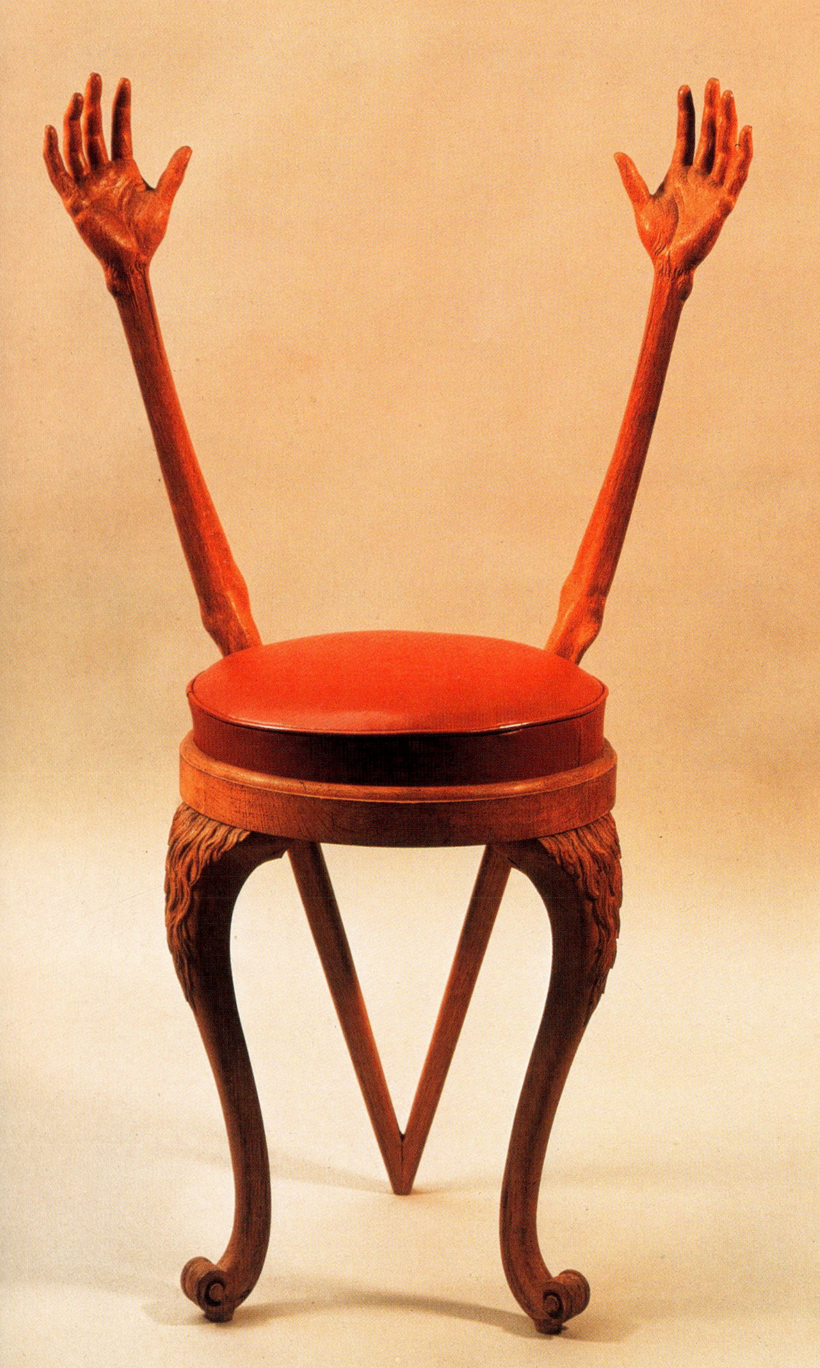

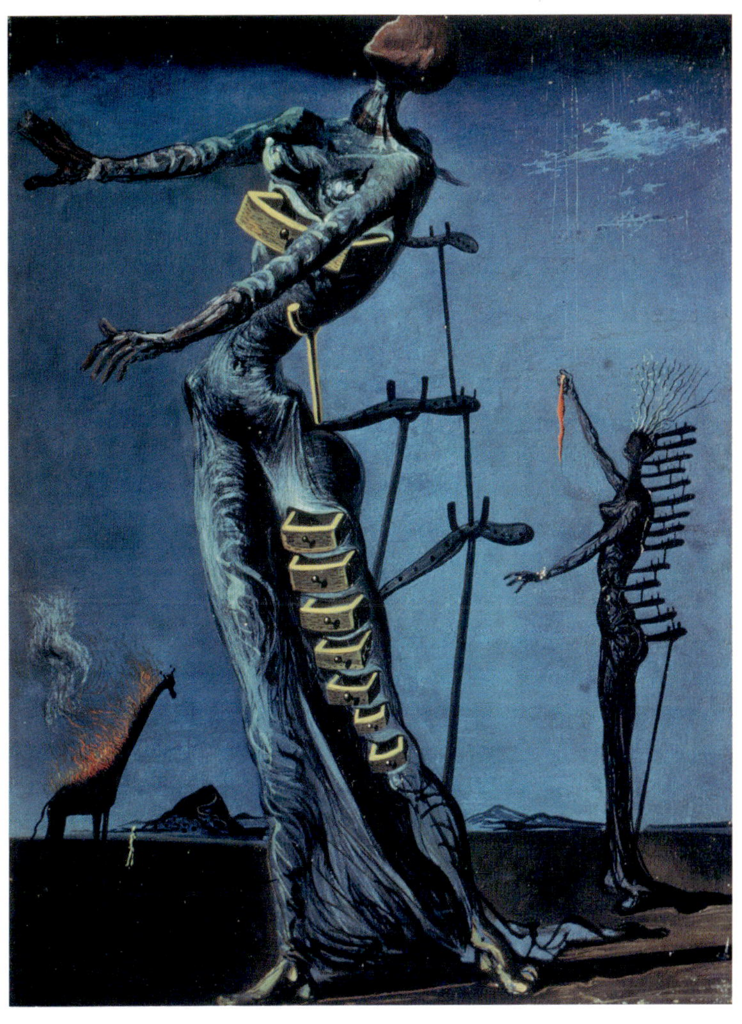

The Burning Giraffe · 1936–37
Kunstmuseum Basel, Öffentliche Kunstsammlung, Basel;
Emanuel Hoffmann Foundation
< **"Hands" Chair** · c. 1936
Formerly Edward James Foundation, Sussex

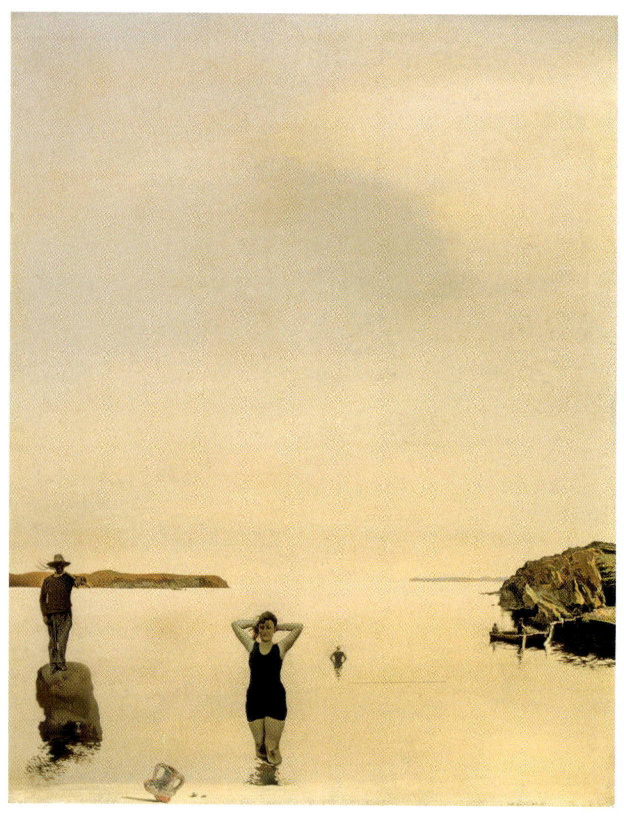

White Calm · 1936
Collection G.E.D. Nahmad, Geneva; formerly Collection Edward James

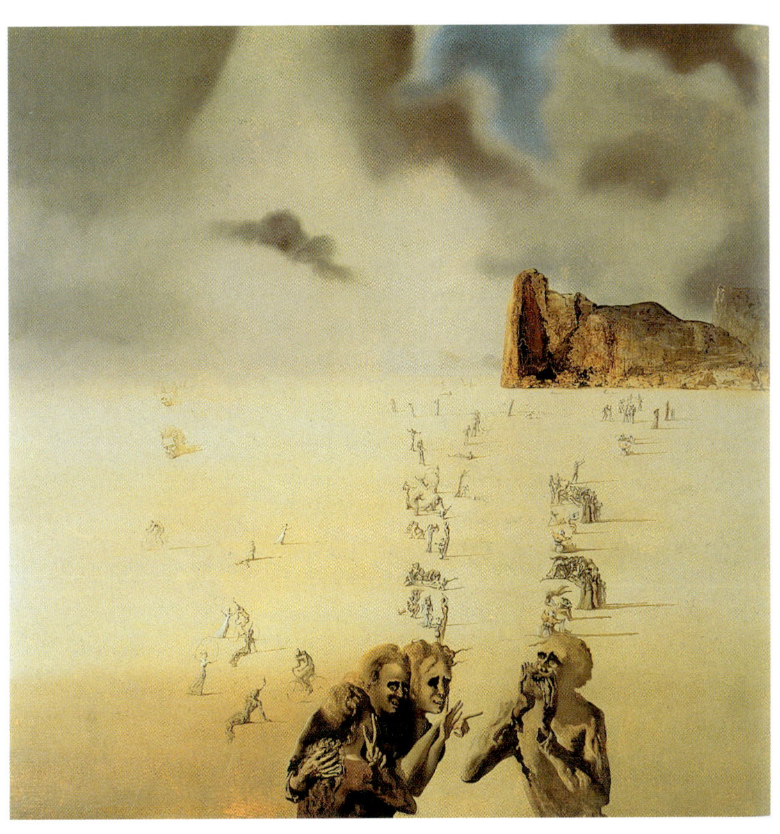

**Perspectives (Premonition of Paranoiac Perspectives
through Soft Structures)** · 1936–37
Kunstmuseum Basel, Öffentliche Kunstsammlung, Basel;
Emanuel Hoffmann Foundation

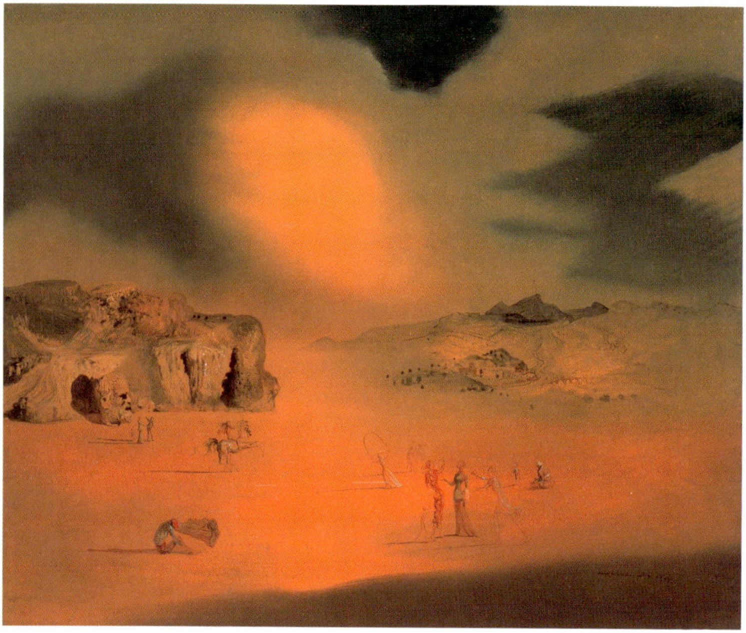

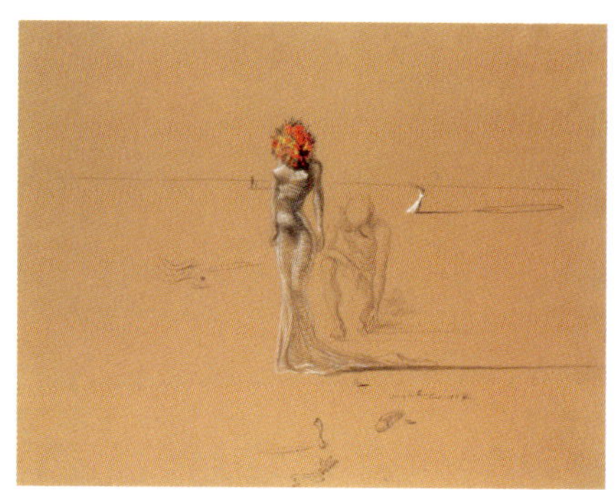

Average Pagan Landscape · 1937
Collection G.E.D. Nahmad, Geneva; formerly Collection Edward James
Untitled (Female Figure with Head of Flowers) · 1937
Private collection

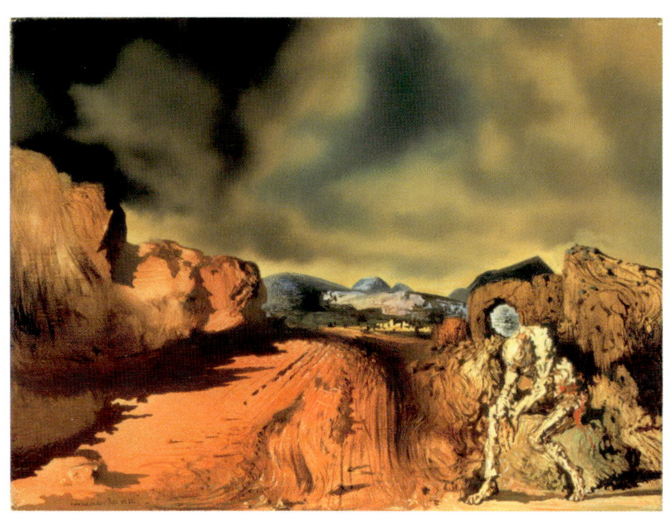

The Man with the Head of Blue Hortensias · 1936
The Salvador Dalí Museum, St. Petersburg, Florida,
on loan from E. and A. Reynolds Morse

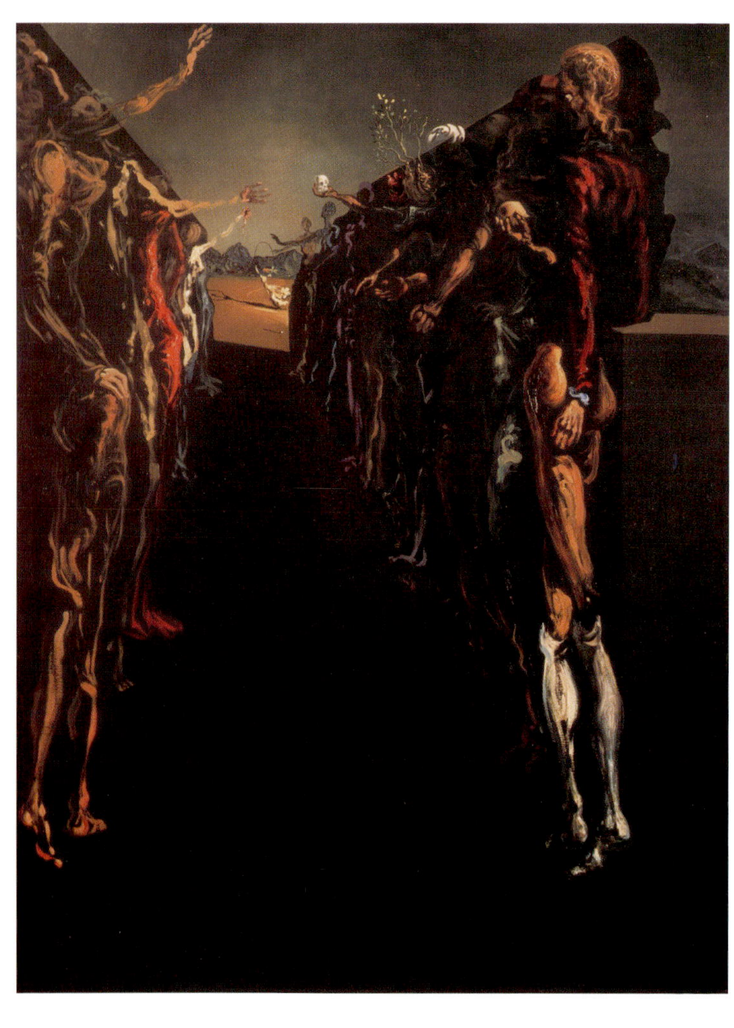

Palladio's Thalia Corridor · 1937

Collection G.E.D. Nahmad, Geneva; formerly Collection Edward James

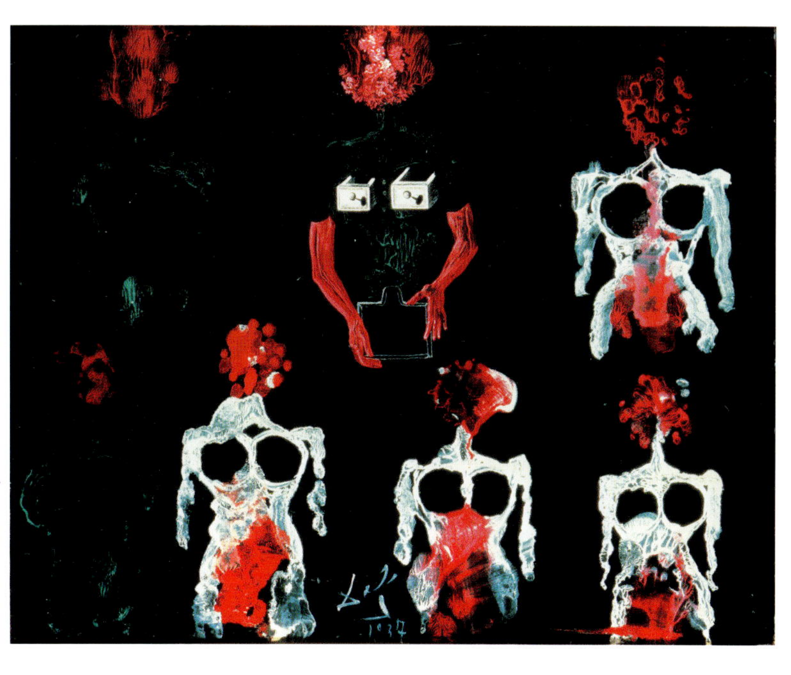

Anatomical Studies—Transfer Series · 1937
Private collection, courtesy Galerie Beyeler, Basel

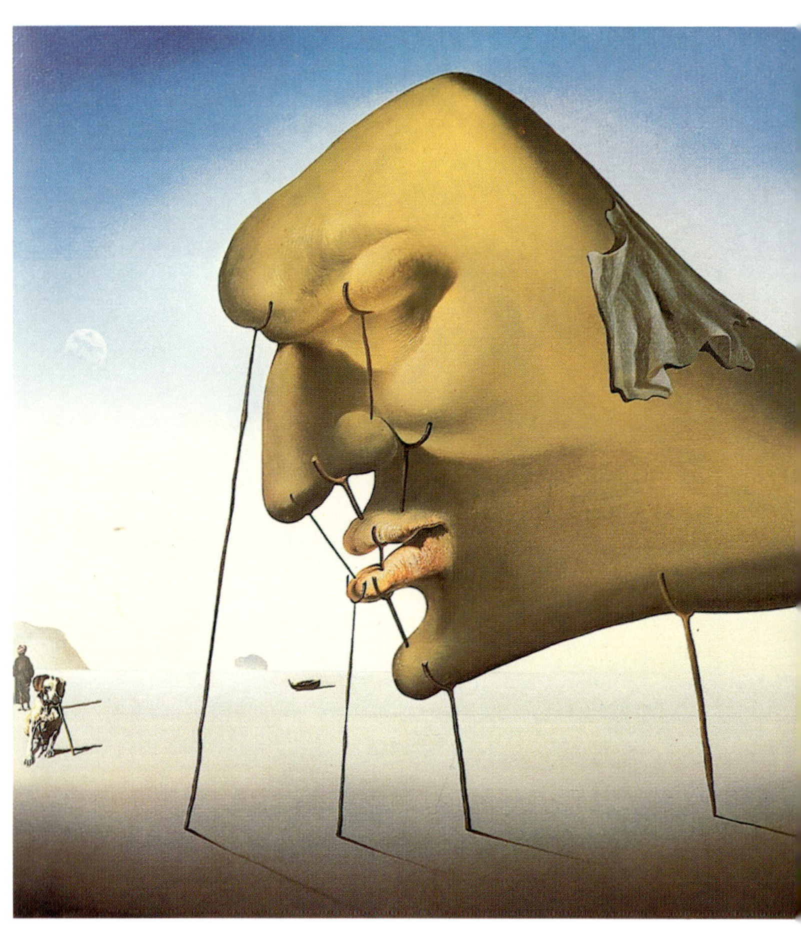

Sleep · 1937
Private collection; formerly Collection Edward James

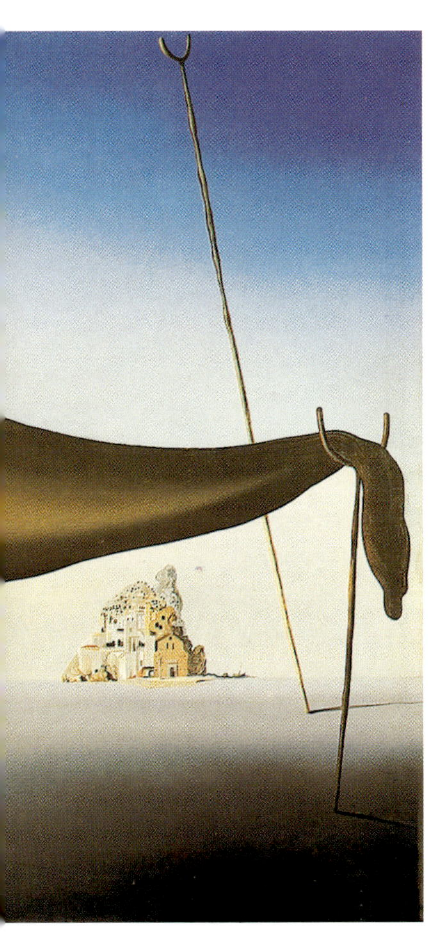

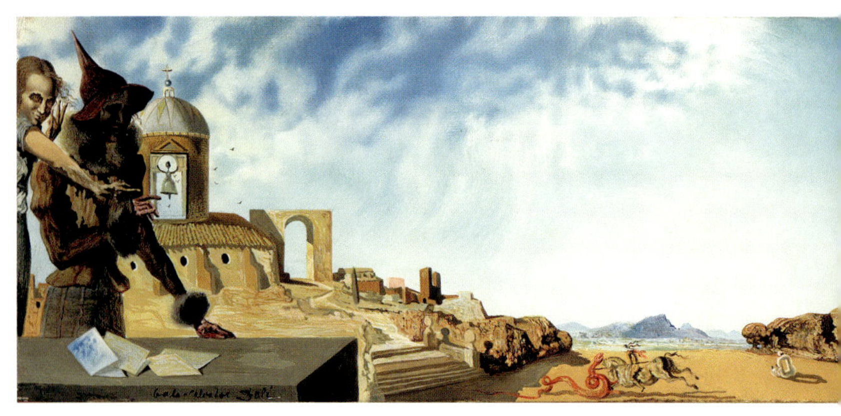

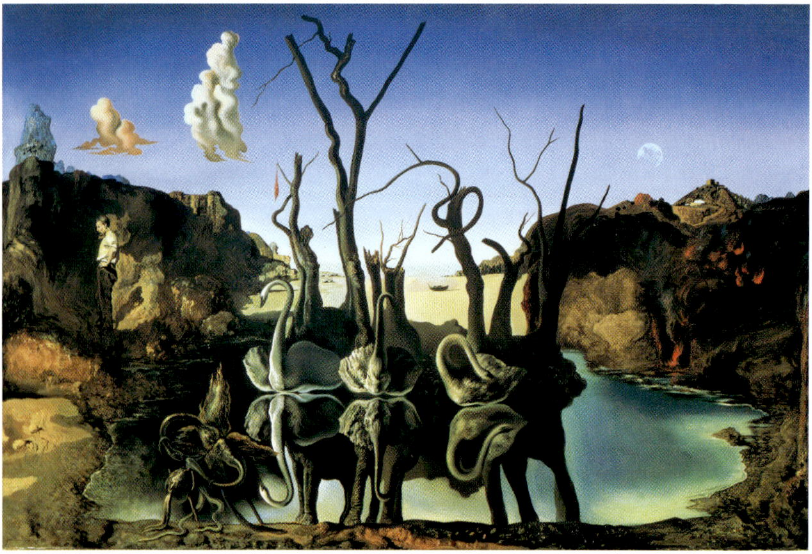

Swans Reflecting Elephants · 1937
Cavalieri Holding Co. Inc., Geneva; formerly Collection Edward James

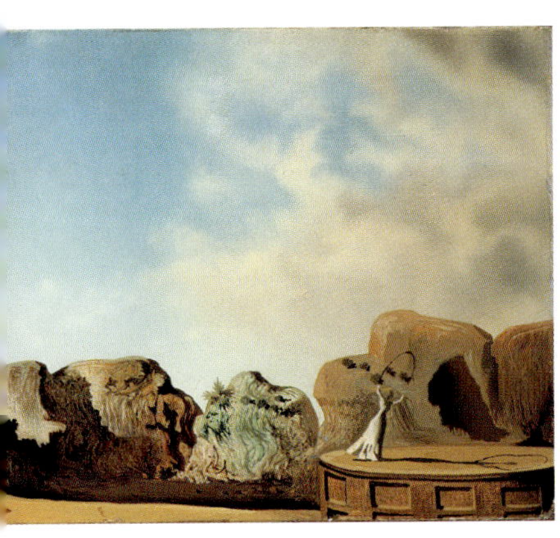

Anthropomorphic Echo · 1937
The Salvador Dalí Museum, St. Petersburg, Florida,
on loan from E. and A. Reynolds Morse

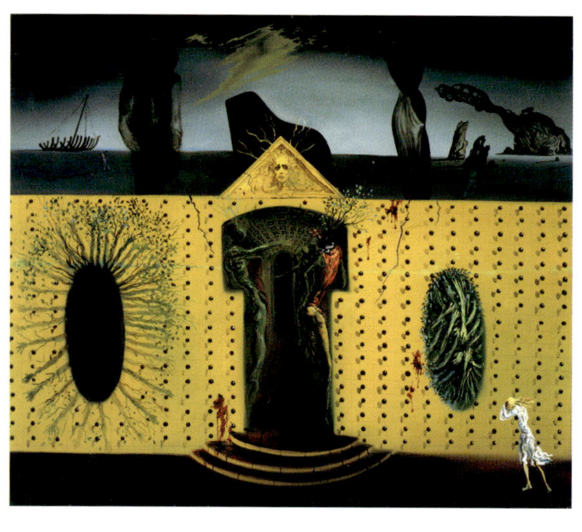

Tristan Insane · c. 1938
The Salvador Dalí Museum, St. Petersburg, Florida,
on loan from E. and A. Reynolds Morse

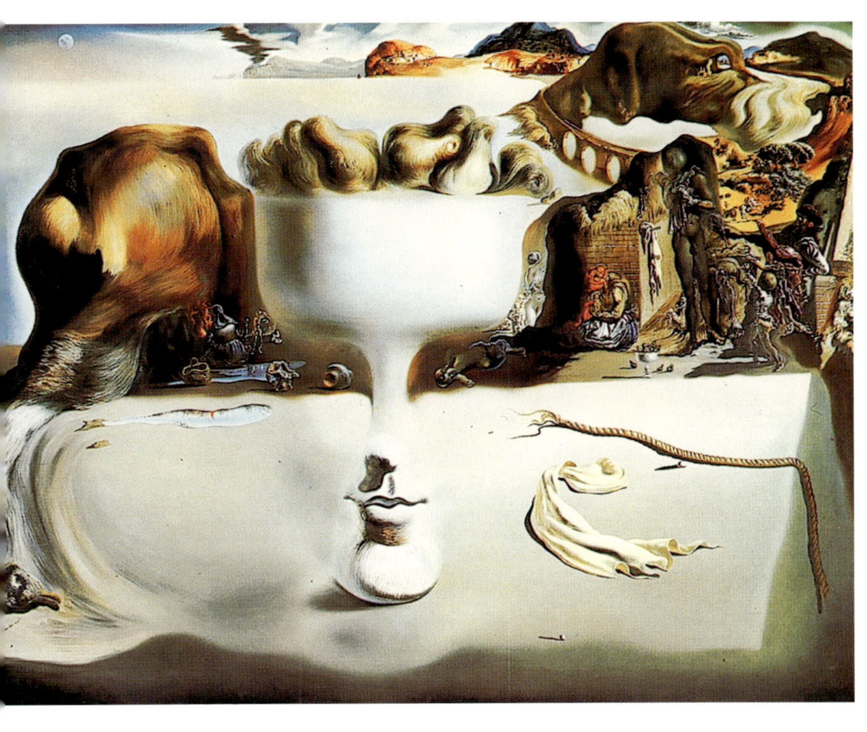

Apparition of Face and Fruit Dish on a Beach · 1938

The Wadsworth Atheneum, Hartford, Connecticut

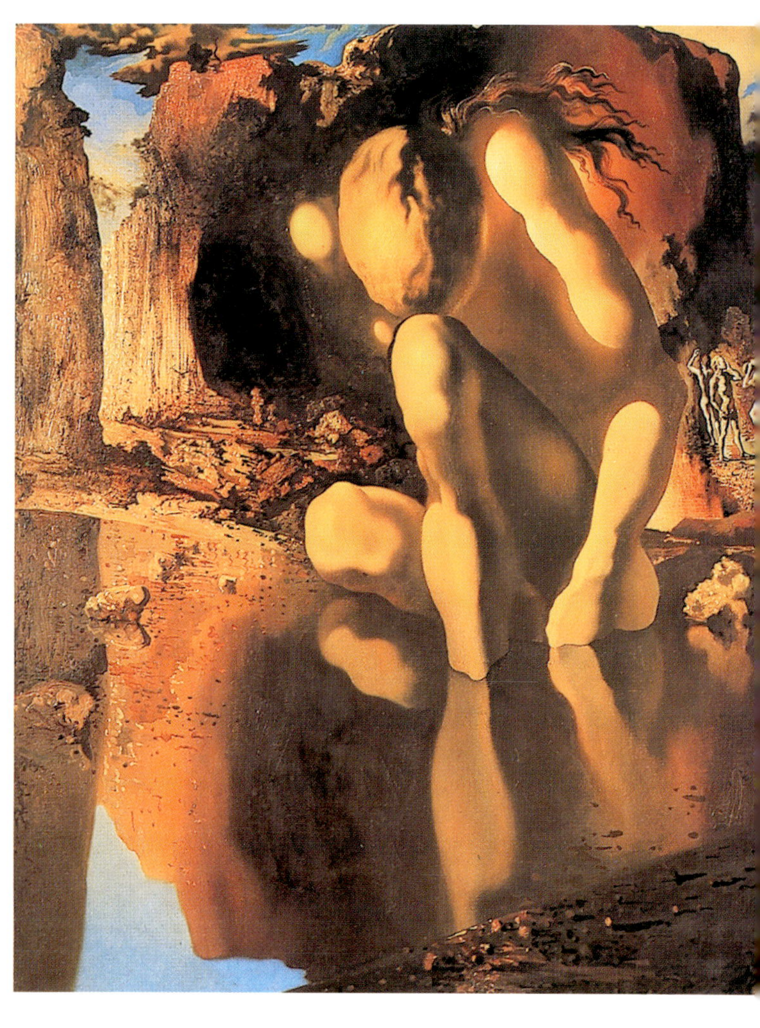

The Metamorphosis of Narcissus · 1937
Tate Gallery, London; formerly Collection Edward James

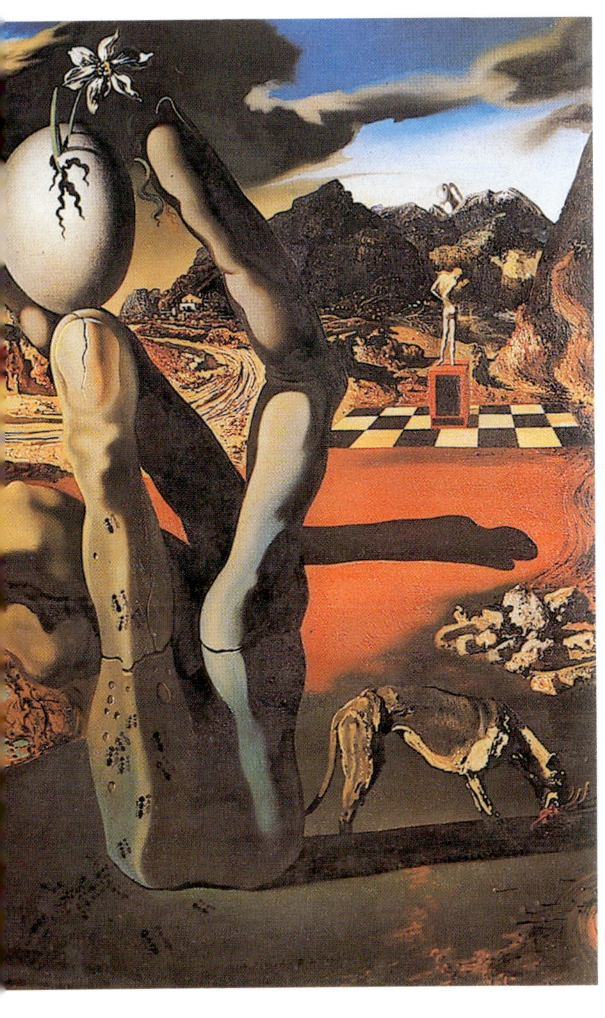

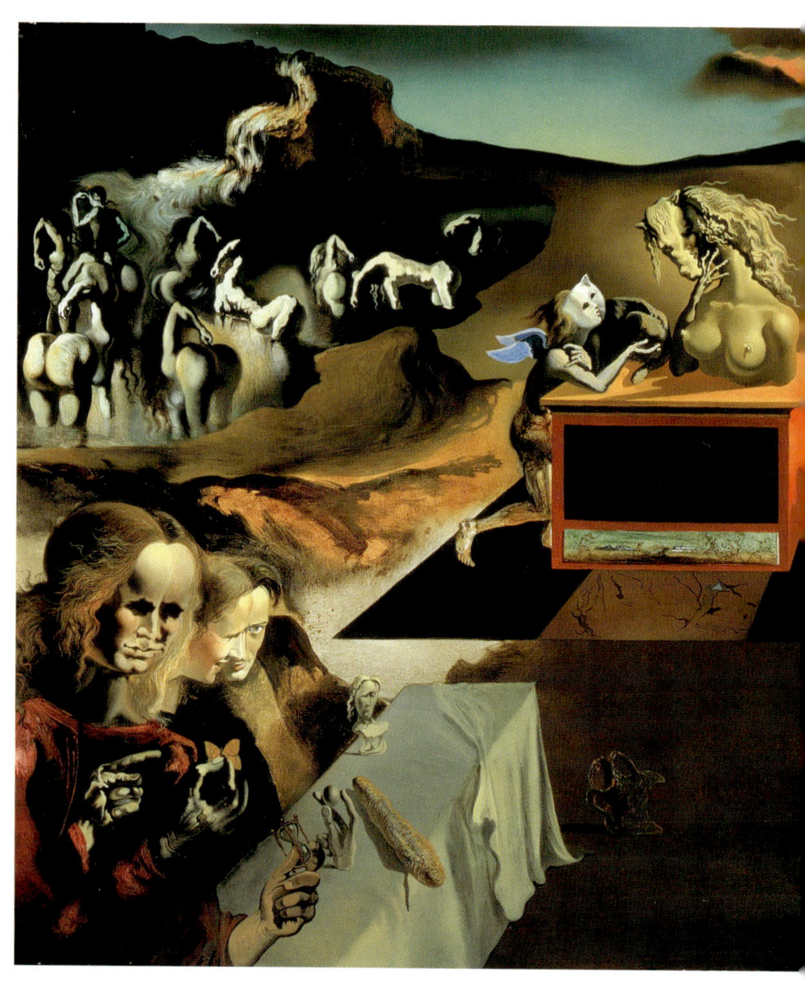

The Invention of the Monster · 1937

The Art Institute of Chicago; Joseph Winterbotham Collection

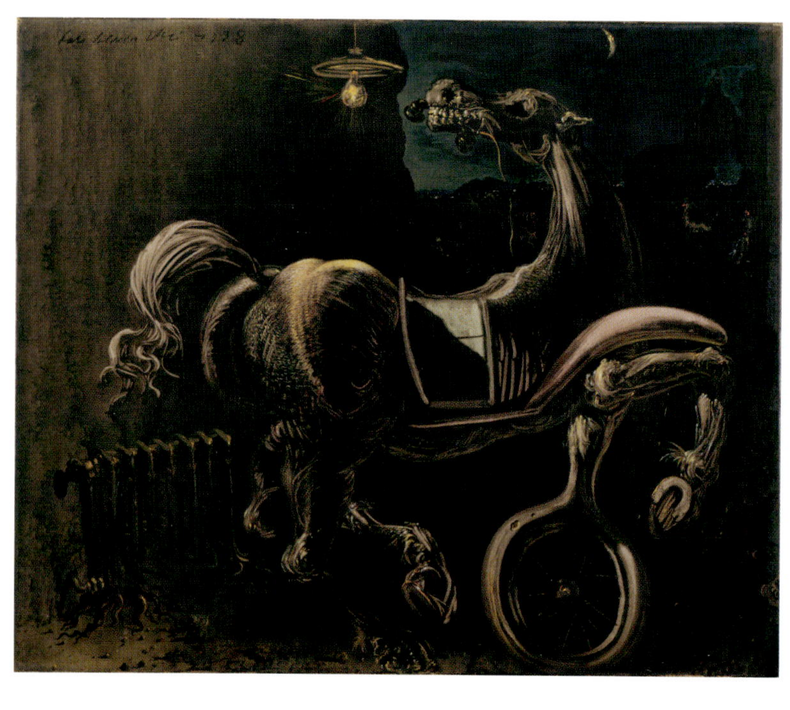

Debris of an Automobile Giving Birth to a Blind Horse Biting a Telephone · 1938
The Museum of Modern Art, New York, gift of James Thrall Soby

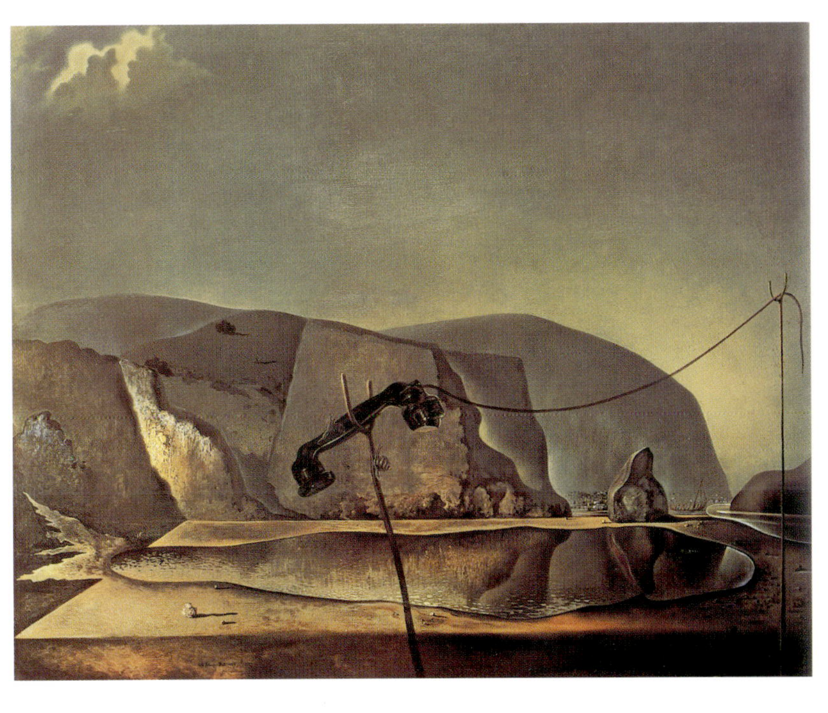

Beach with Telephone · 1938

Tate Gallery, London; formerly Collection Edward James

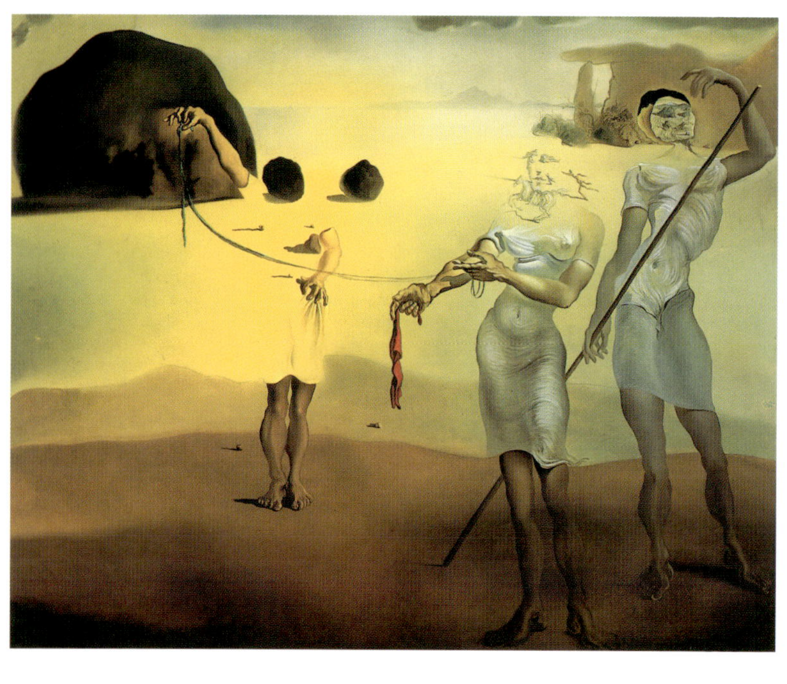

Enchanted Beach with Three Fluid Graces · 1938
The Salvador Dalí Museum, St. Petersburg, Florida,
on loan from the Morse Charitable Trust

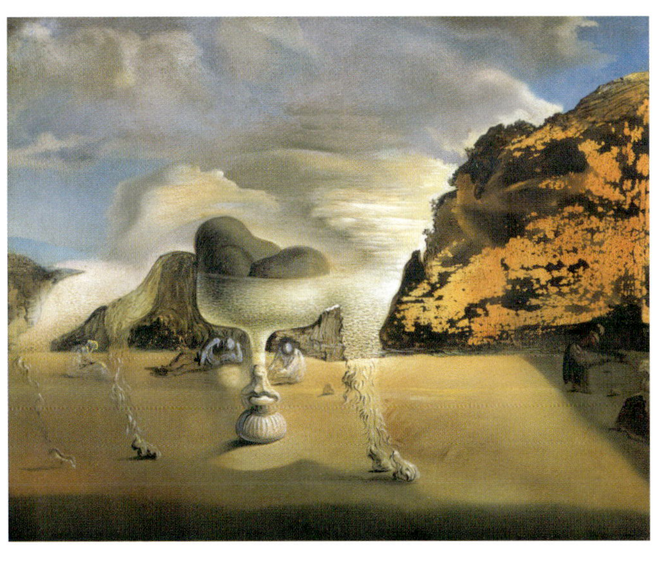

**Invisible Afghan with the Apparition on the Beach of the Face
of García Lorca in the Form of a Fruit Dish with Three Figs · 1938**
Private collection

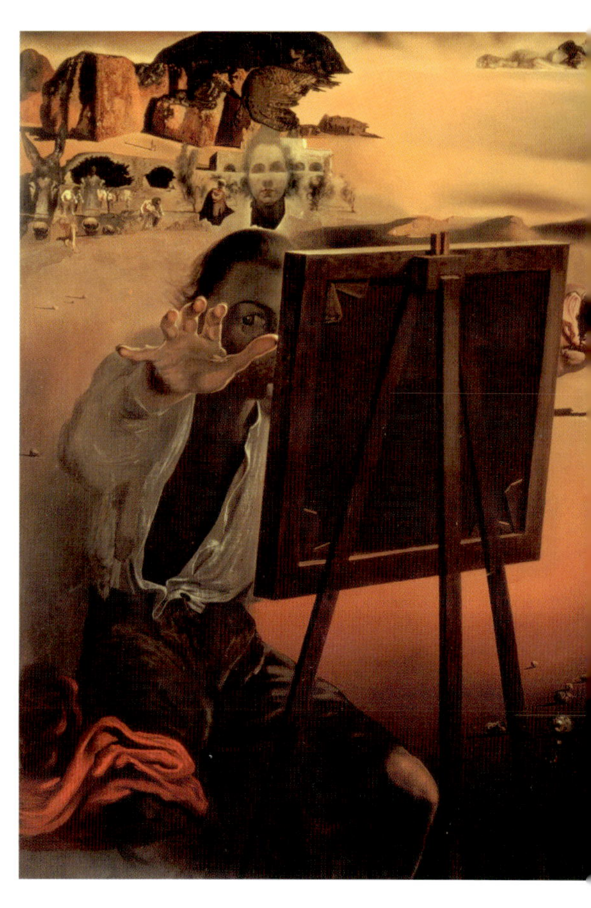

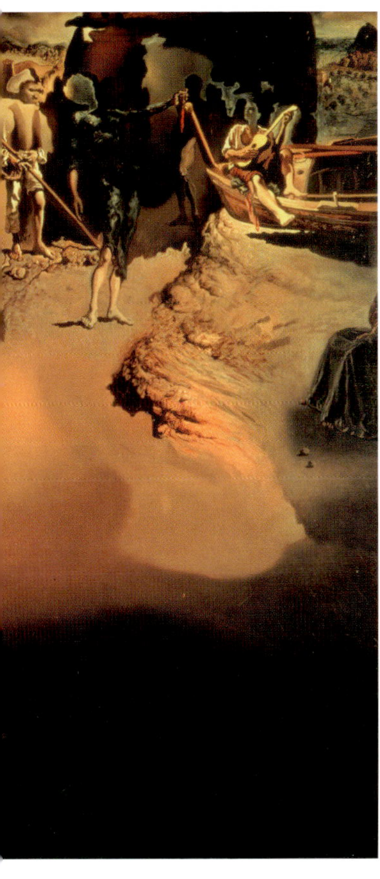

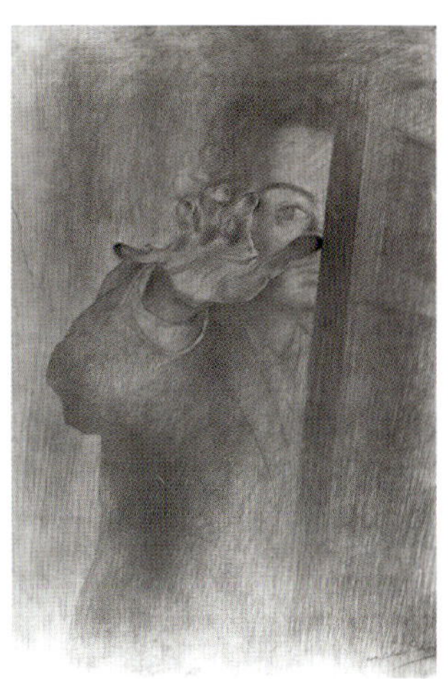

Impressions of Africa · 1938

Museum Boijmans Van Beuningen, Rotterdam; formerly Collection Edward James

Study for the self-portrait in "Impressions of Africa" · 1938

Museum Boijmans Van Beuningen, Rotterdam; formerly Collection Edward James

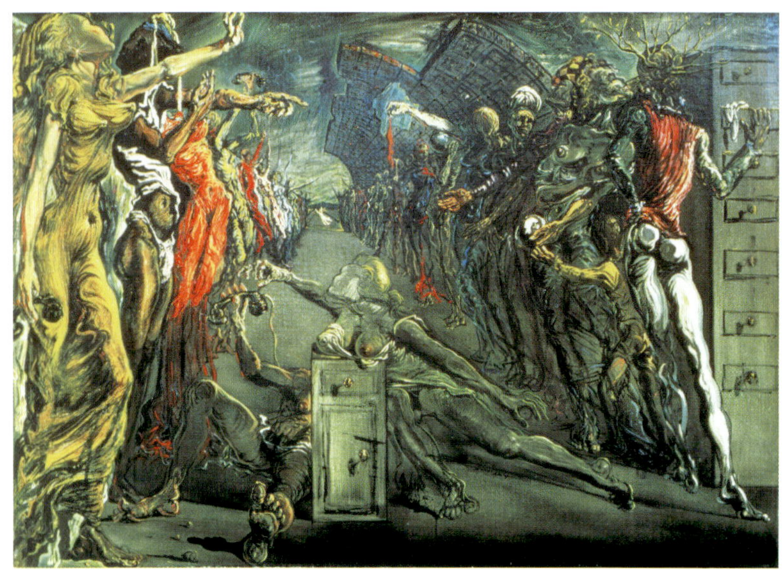

Palladio's Corridor of Dramatic Surprise · 1938
Private collection

> **Spain** · 1938
Museum Boijmans Van Beuningen, Rotterdam; formerly Collection Edward James

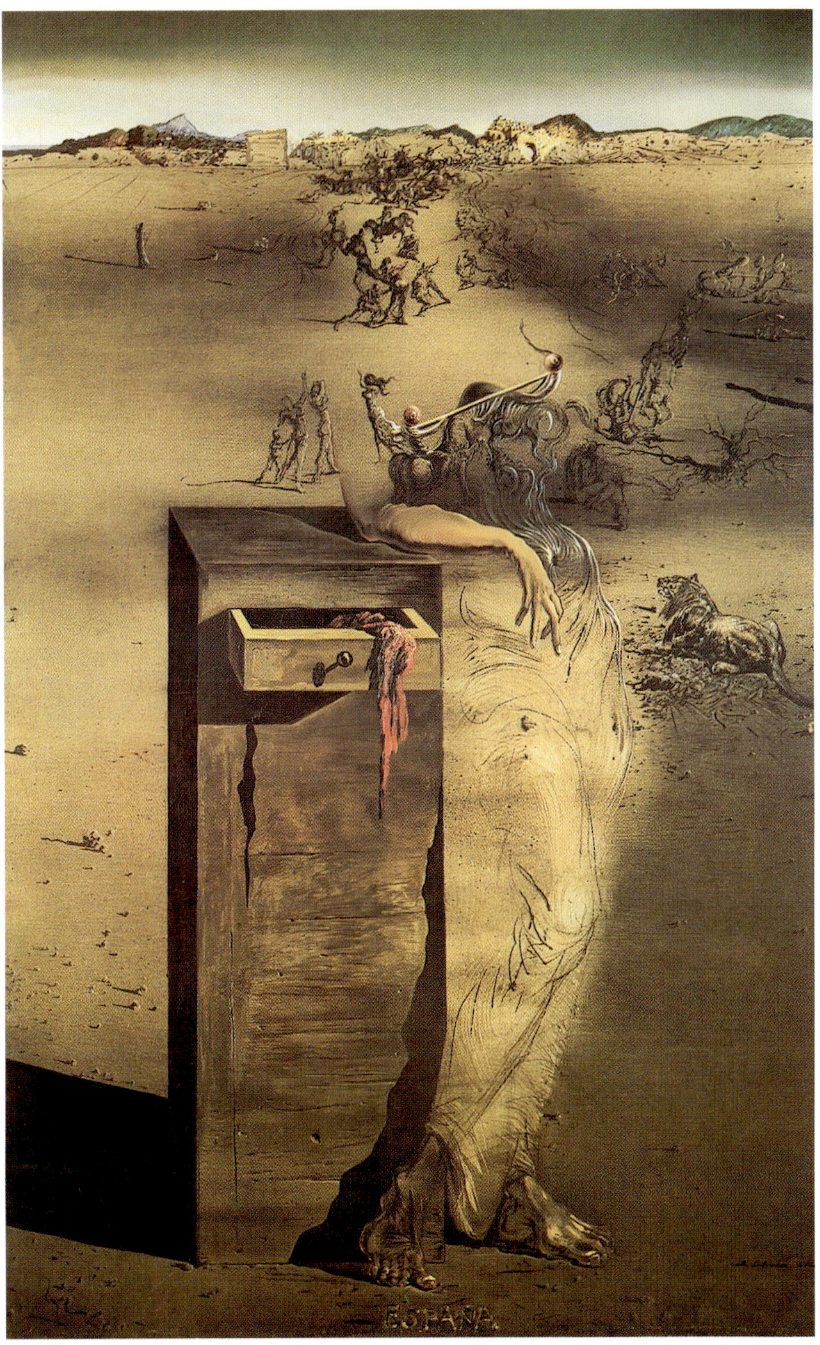
ESPAÑA

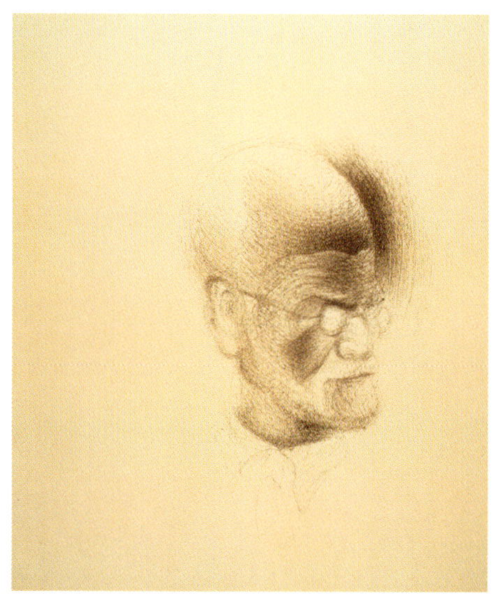

Portrait of Freud · 1938
Freud Museum, London

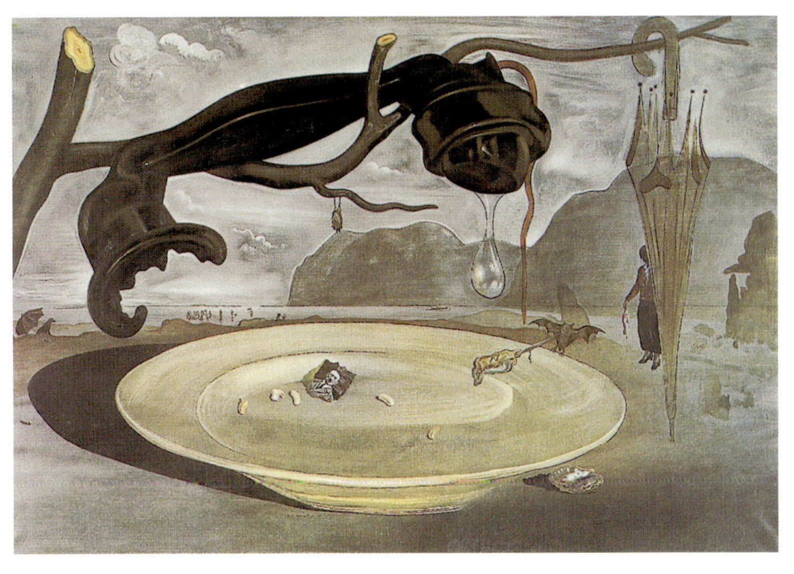

The Enigma of Hitler · c. 1939

Museo Nacional Centro de Arte Reina Sofía, Madrid, gift of Dalí to the Spanish state

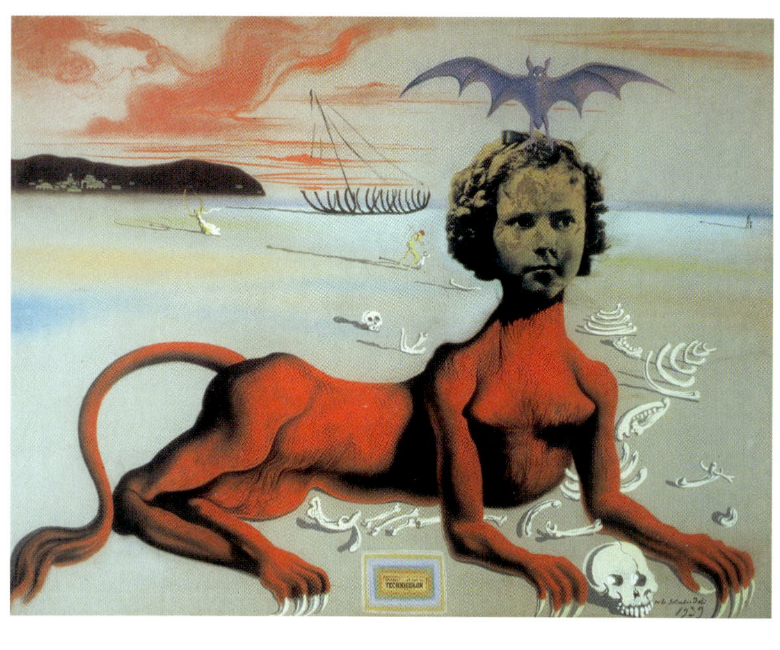

Shirley Temple, the Youngest, Most Sacred Monster of the Cinema in Her Time · 1939

Museum Boijmans Van Beuningen, Rotterdam

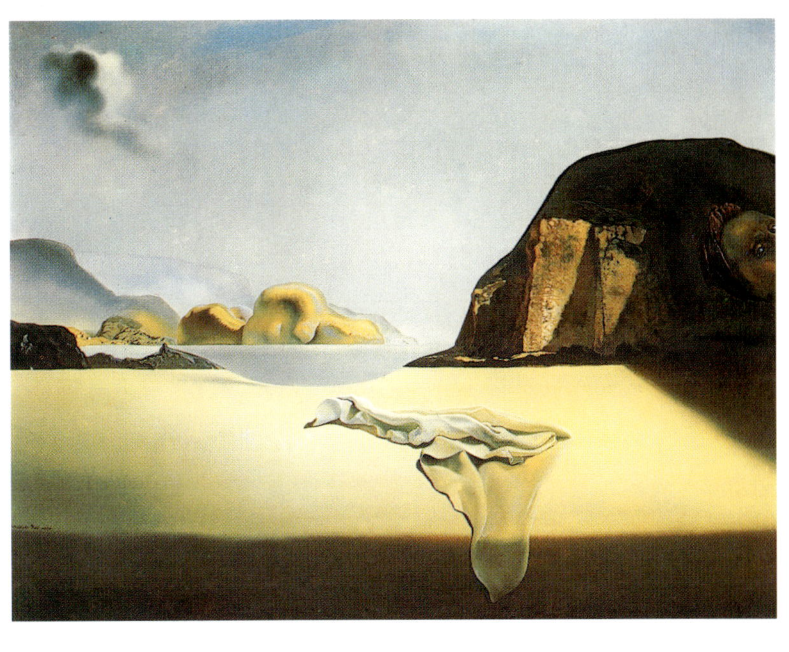

The Transparent Simulacrum of the Feigned Image · 1938

Albright-Knox Art Gallery, Buffalo, New York, A. Conger Goodyear, 1966

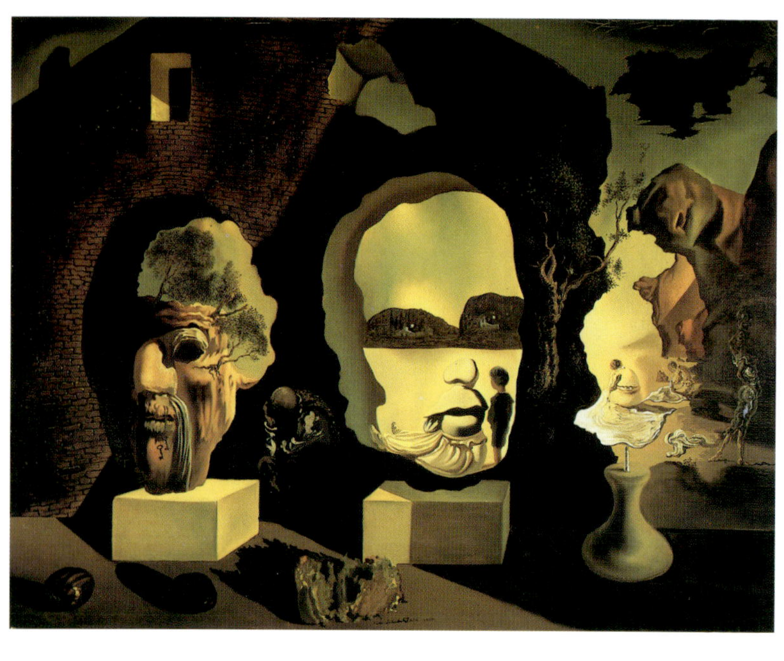

Old Age, Adolescence, Infancy (The Three Ages) · 1940
The Salvador Dalí Museum, St. Petersburg, Florida,
on loan from E. and A. Reynolds Morse

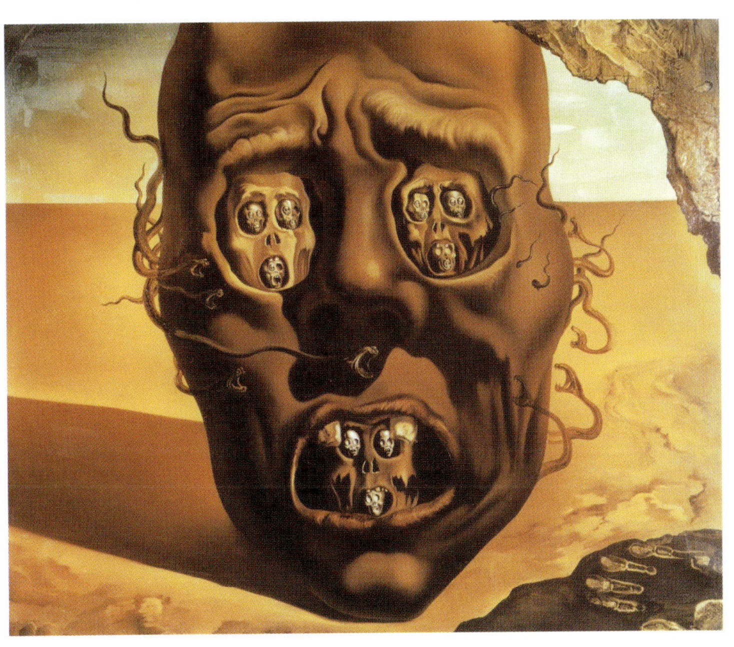

The Face of War · 1940–41

Museum Boijmans Van Beuningen, Rotterdam; formerly Collection André Cauvin

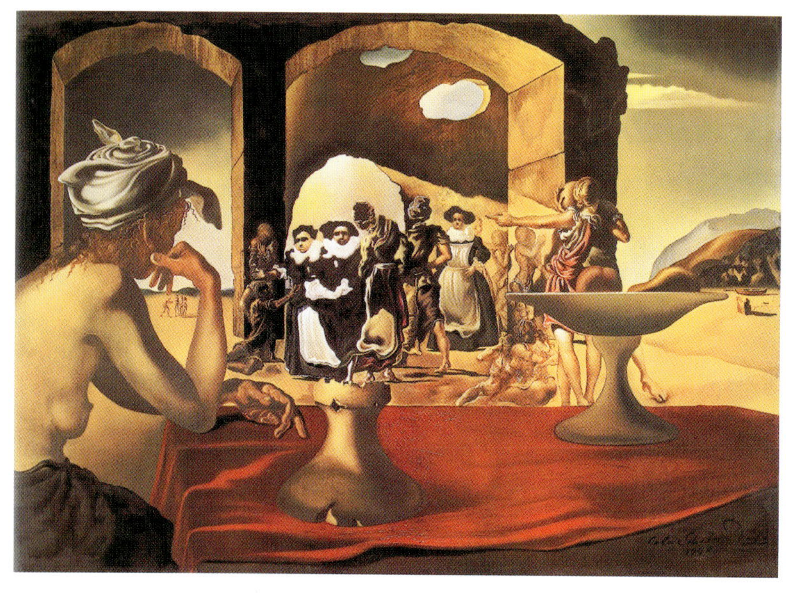

Slave Market with the Disappearing Bust of Voltaire · 1940
The Salvador Dalí Museum, St. Petersburg, Florida,
on loan from the Morse Charitable Trust

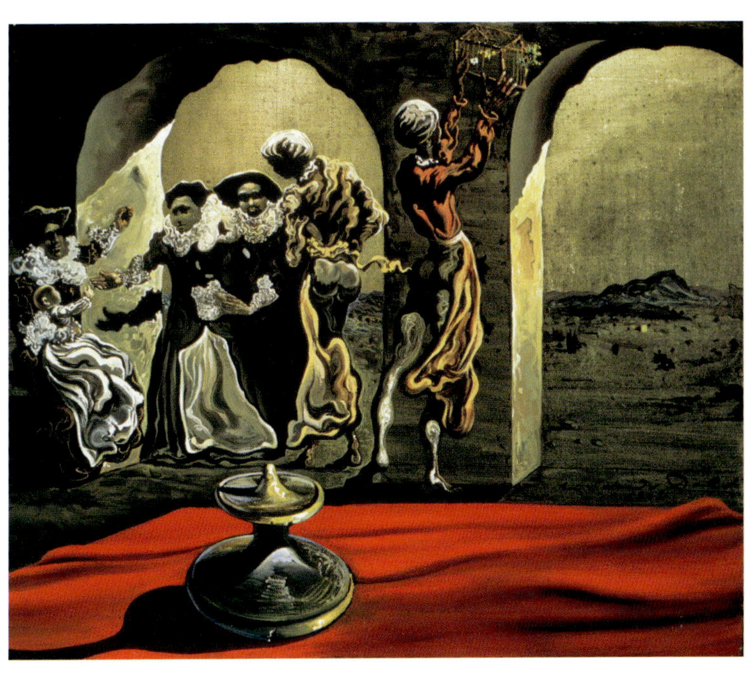

Disappearing Bust of Voltaire · 1941

The Salvador Dalí Museum, St. Petersburg, Florida,
on loan from E. and A. Reynolds Morse

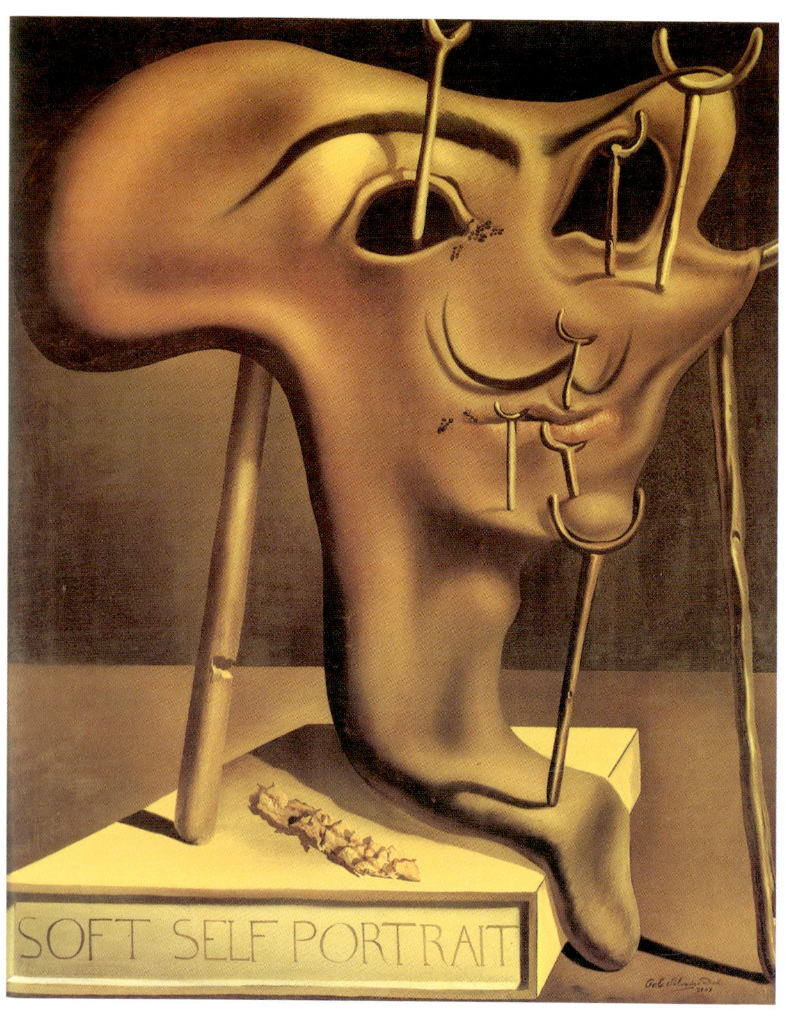

Soft Self-Portrait with Fried Bacon · 1941

Fundación Gala-Salvador Dalí, Figueras

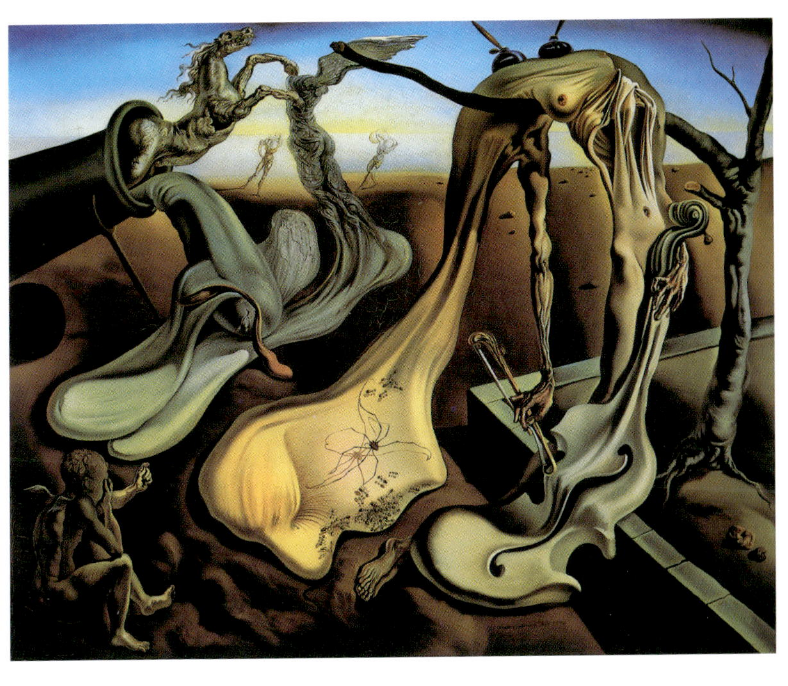

Spider of the Evening . . . Hope! · 1940
The Salvador Dalí Museum, St. Petersburg, Florida,
on loan from the Morse Charitable Trust

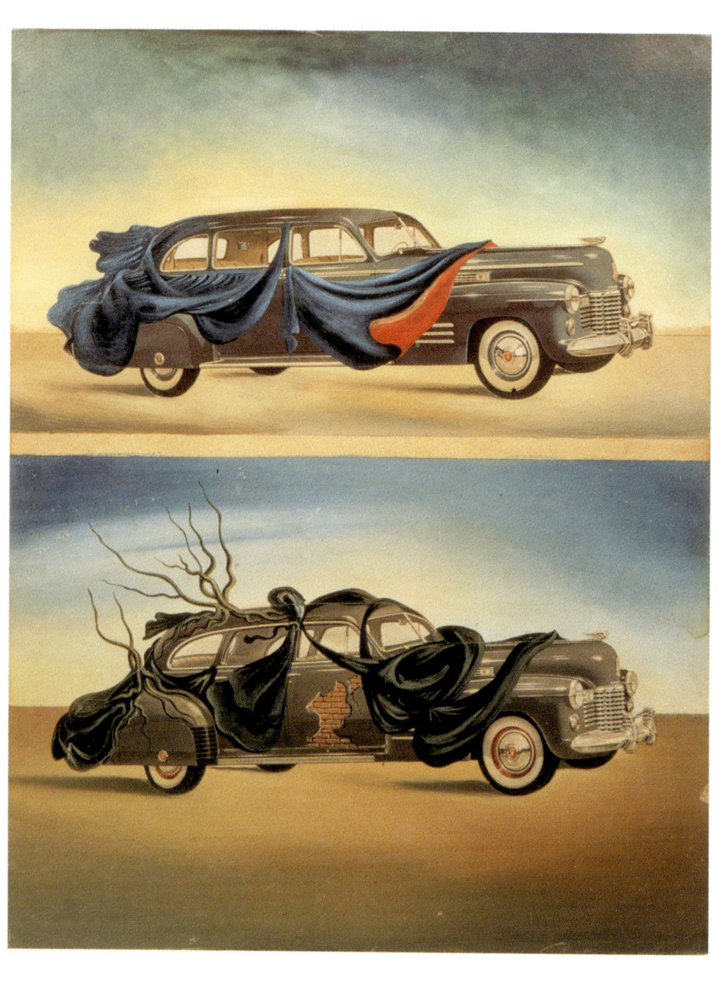

Clothed Automobile (Two Cadillacs) · 1941
Fundación Gala-Salvador Dalí, Figueras

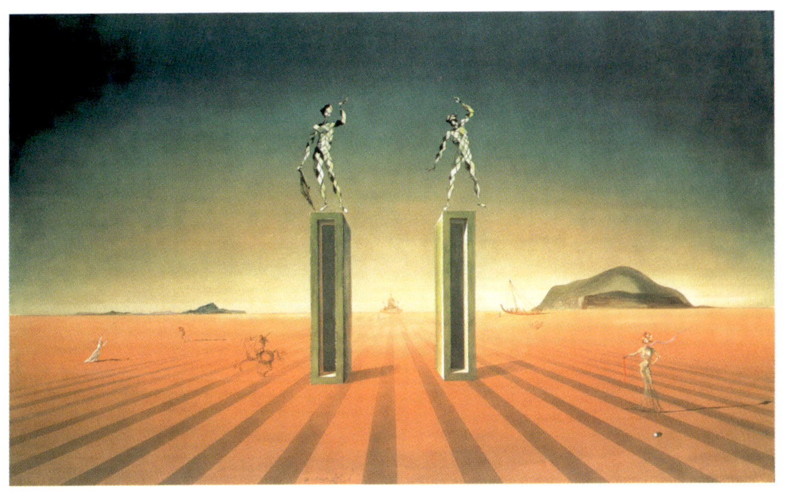

Composition (Two Harlequins) · 1942
Private collection

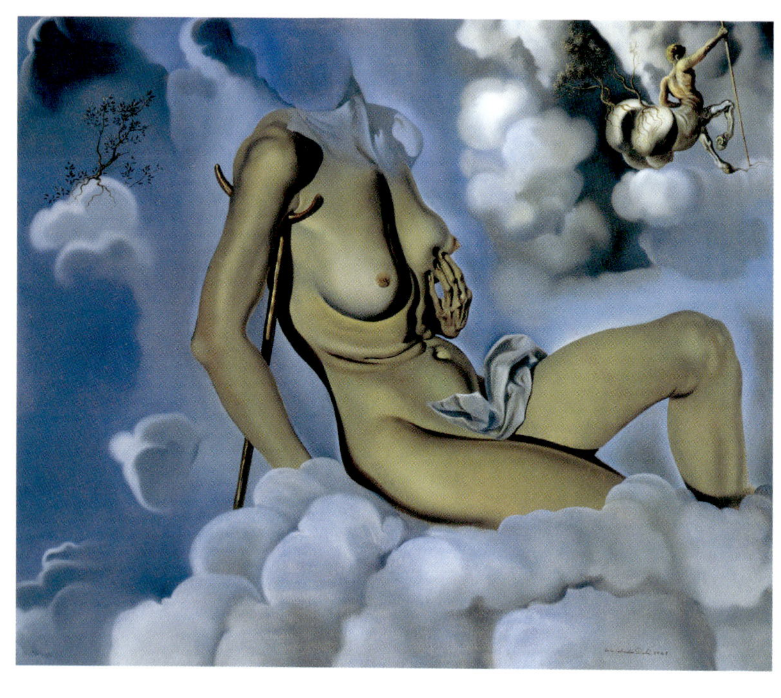

Honey Is Sweeter than Blood · 1941
The Santa Barbara Museum of Art, California,
gift of Mr. and Mrs. Warren Tremaine, 1949

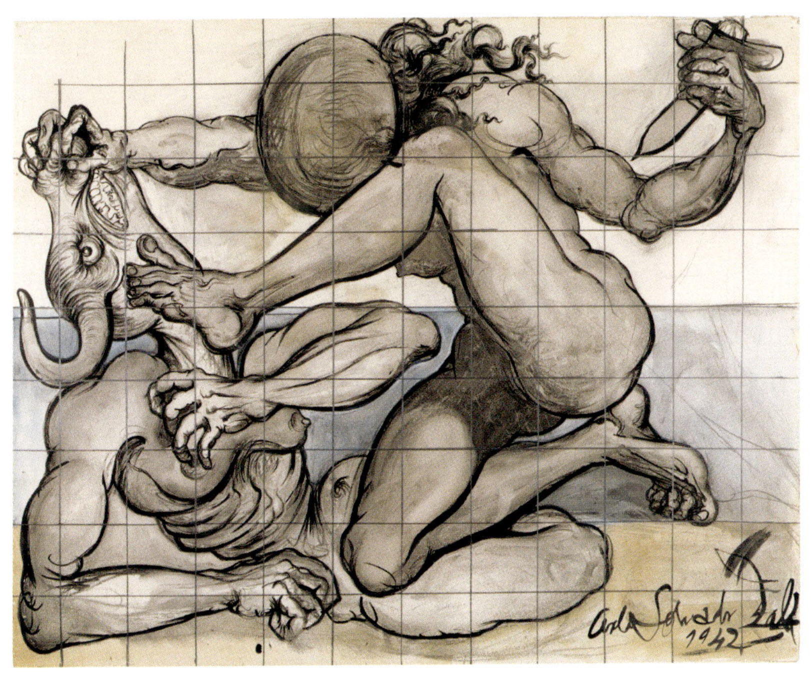

Study for the set of "Labyrinth"—Fighting the Minotaur · 1942
Fundación Gala-Salvador Dalí, Figueras

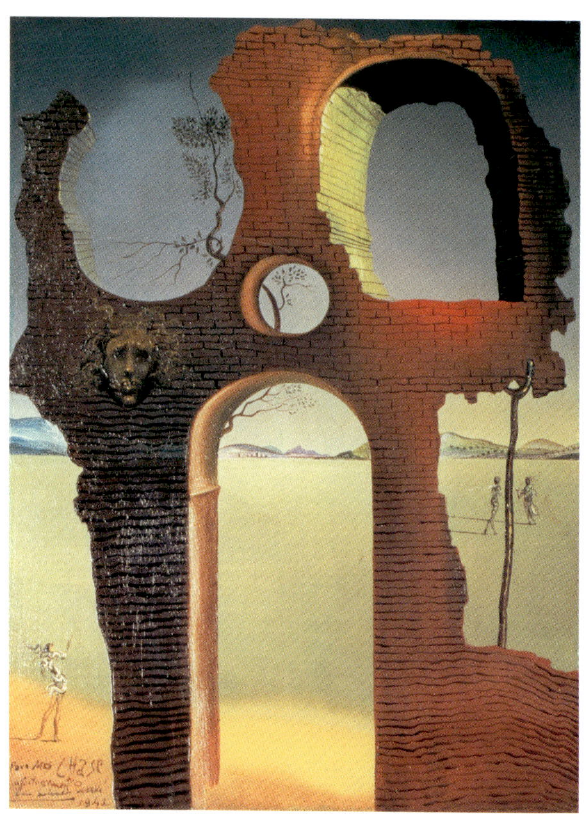

**Ruin with Head of Medusa and Landscape
(Dedicated to Mrs. Chase)** · 1941

Collection Juan Abelló Gallo, Madrid

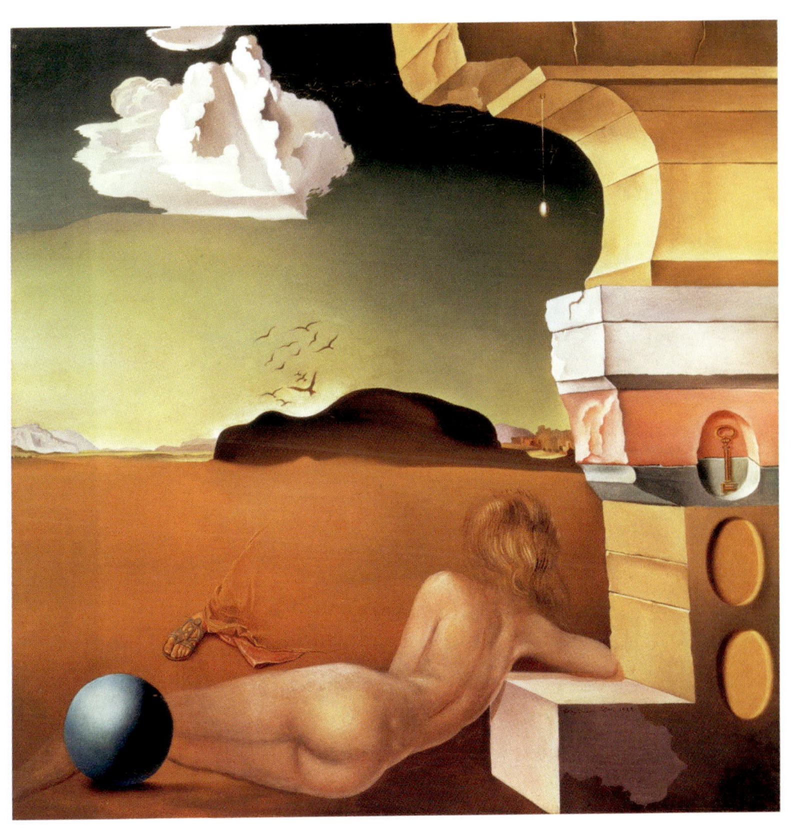

Nude on the Plain of Rosas · 1942

Yokohama Museum of Art; formerly Collection P. de Gavardie

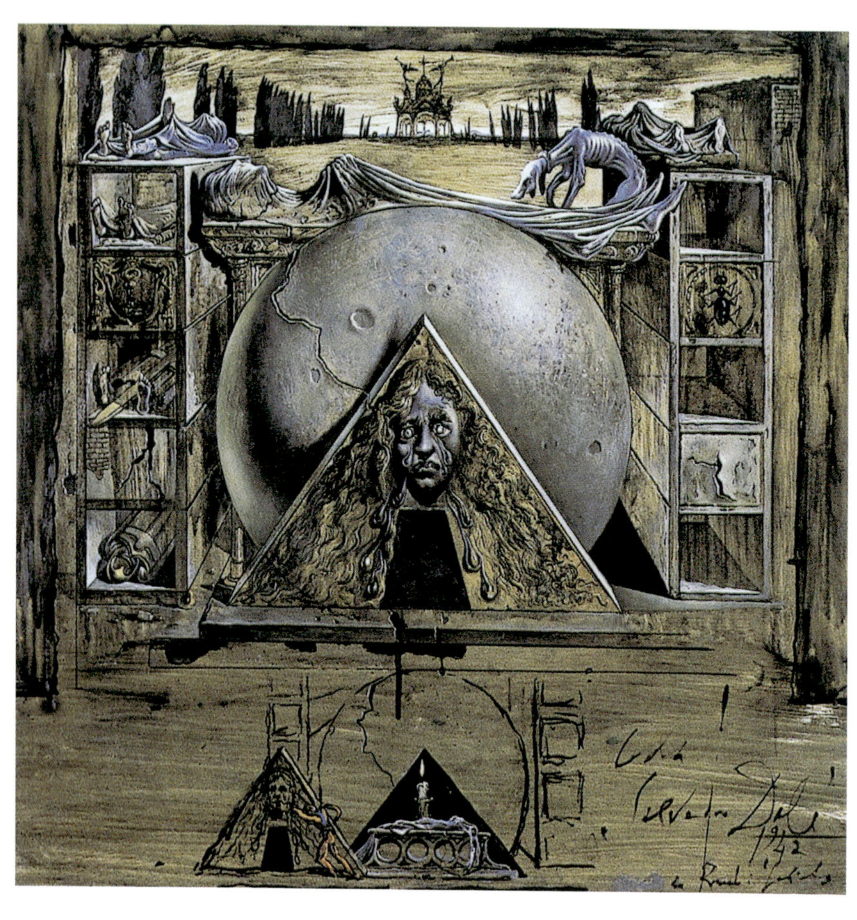

Juliet's Tomb · 1942
Private collection

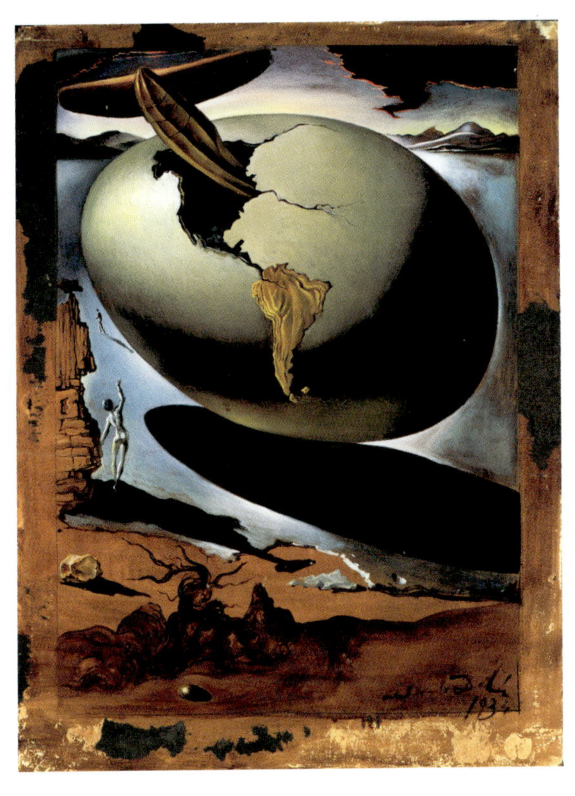

Allegory of an American Christmas · 1943
Private collection

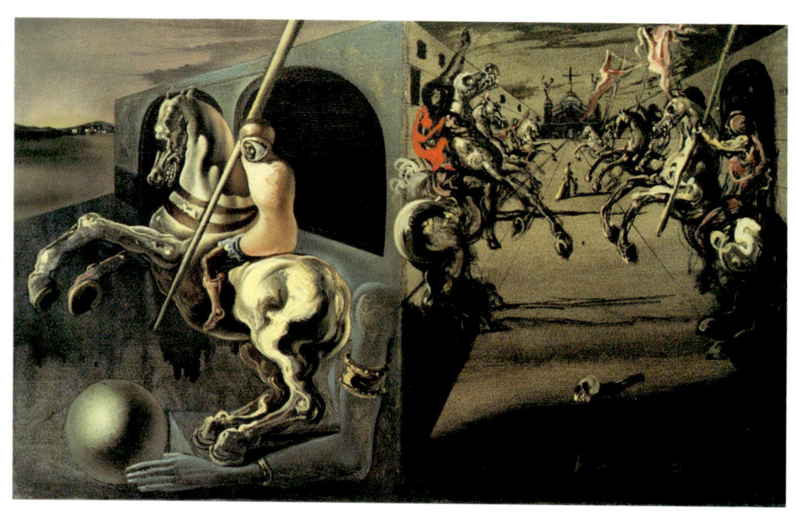

Equestrian Parade · 1942

Private collection

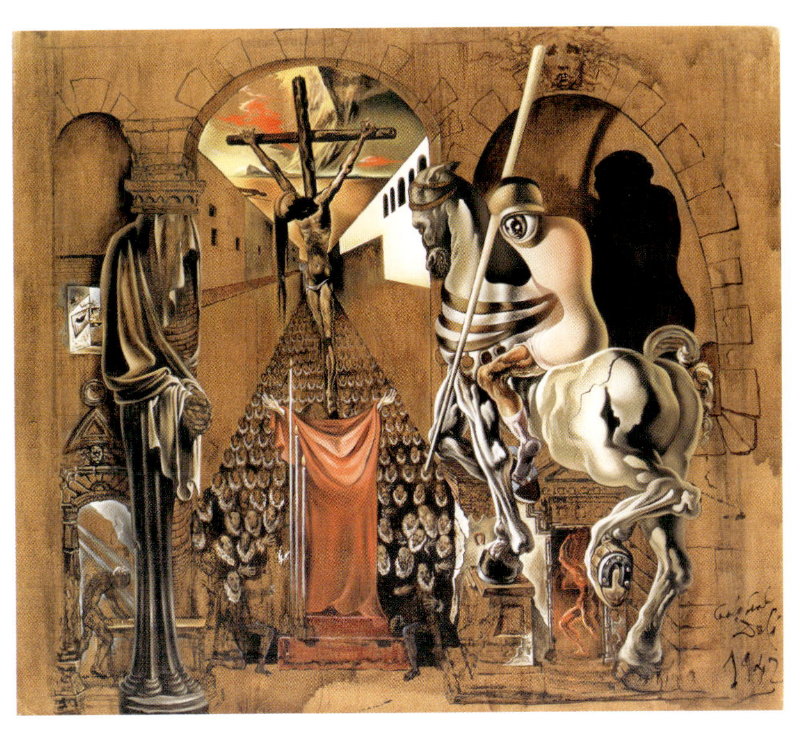

Study for the set of "Romeo and Juliet" · 1942
Private collection

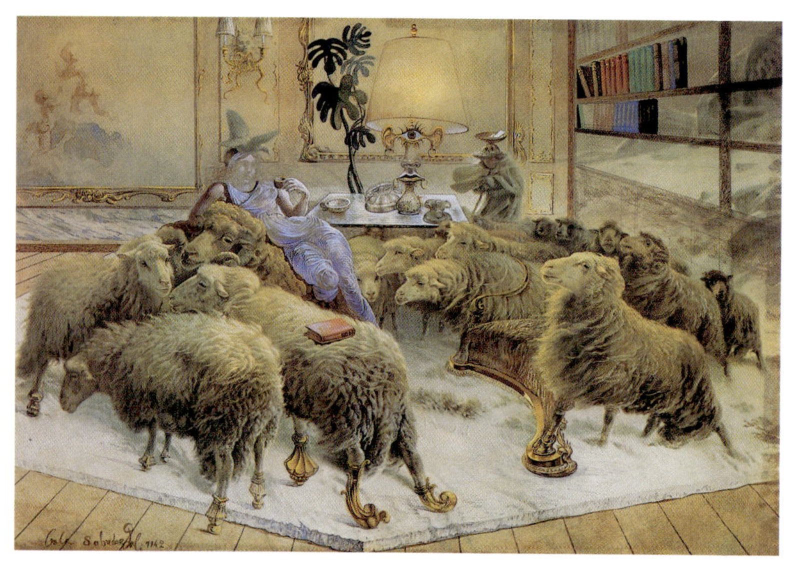

The Sheep (after conversion) · 1942
The Salvador Dalí Museum, St. Petersburg, Florida,
on loan from E. and A. Reynolds Morse

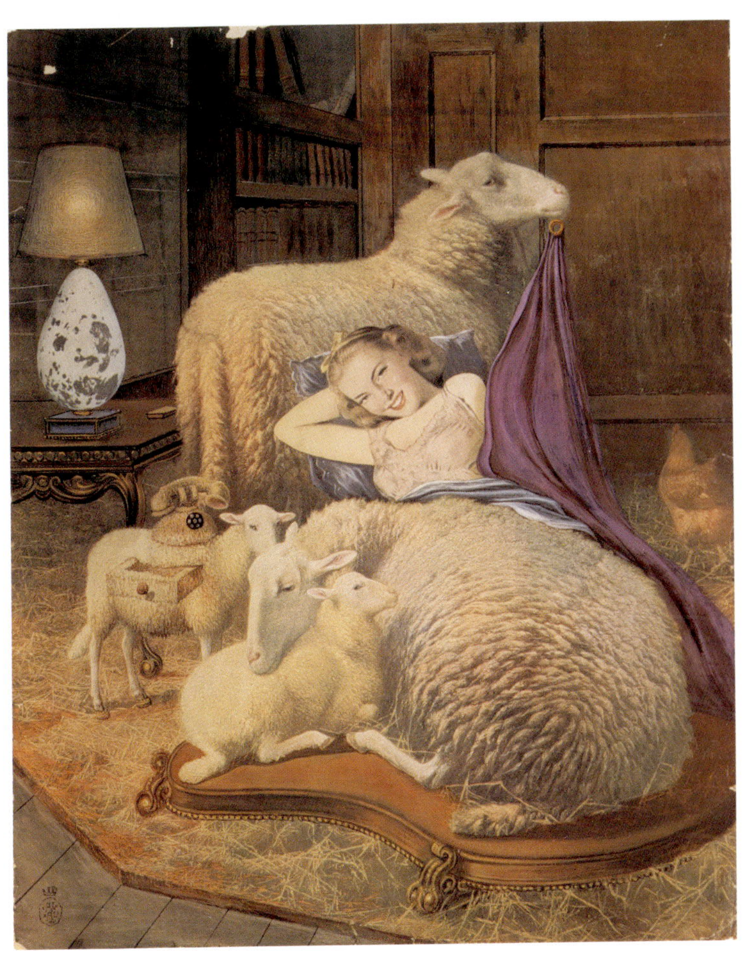

Design for the Interior Decoration of a Stable-Library · 1942

Fundación Gala-Salvador Dalí, Figueras

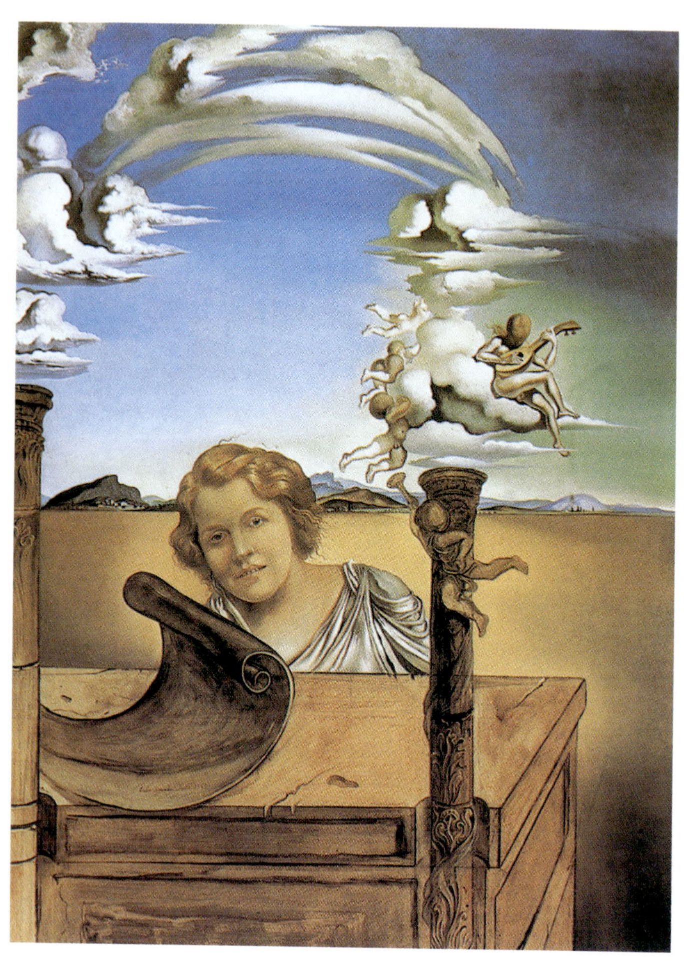

Melancholy—Portrait of Singer Claire Dux · 1942
Private collection

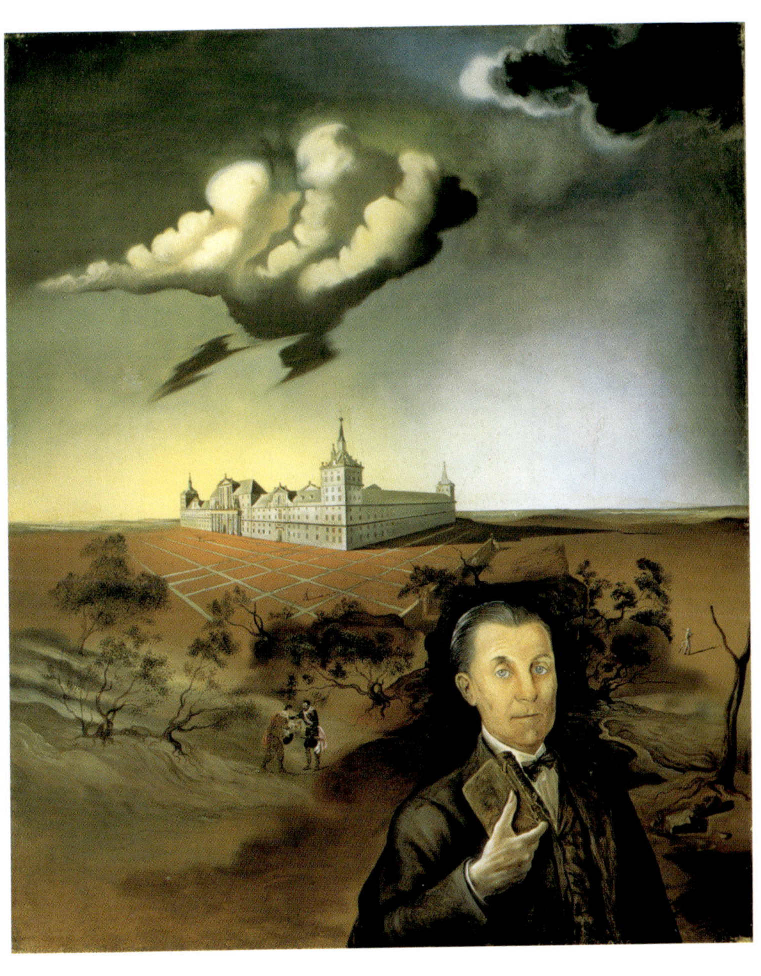

Portrait of Ambassador Cardenas · 1943
Private collection

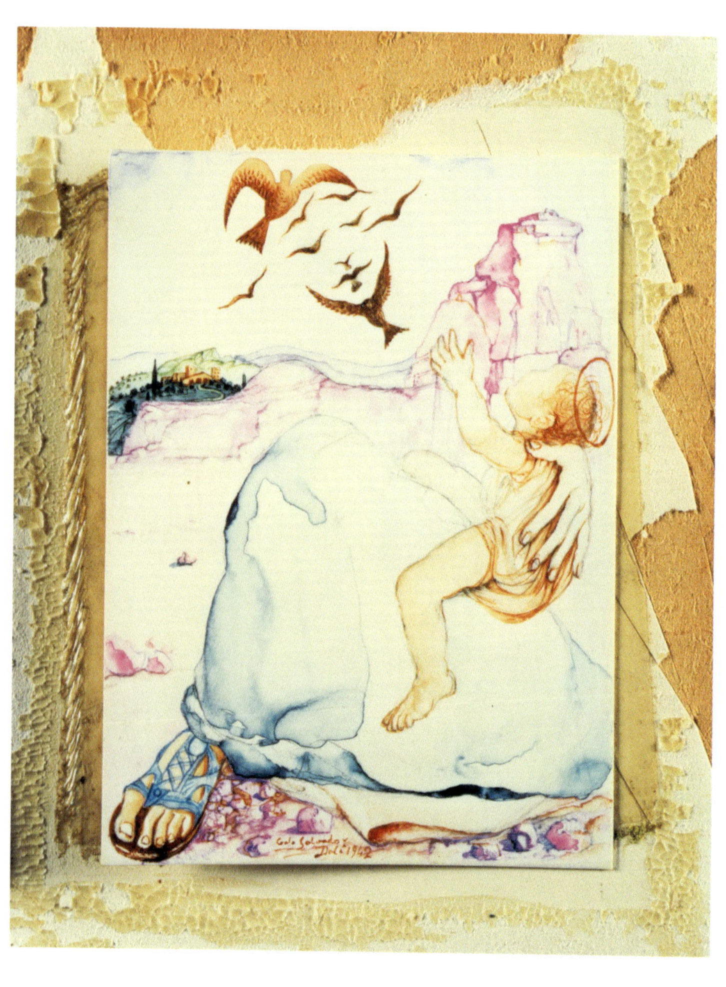

Virgin and Child · 1942
Private collection

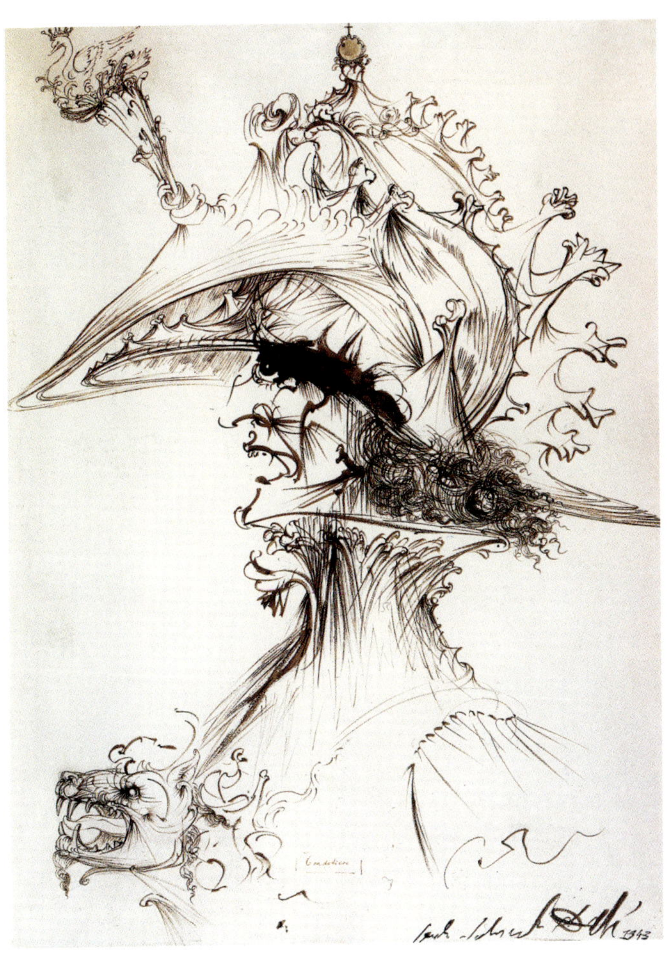

Condottiere (Self-Portrait as Condottiere) · 1943
Private collection

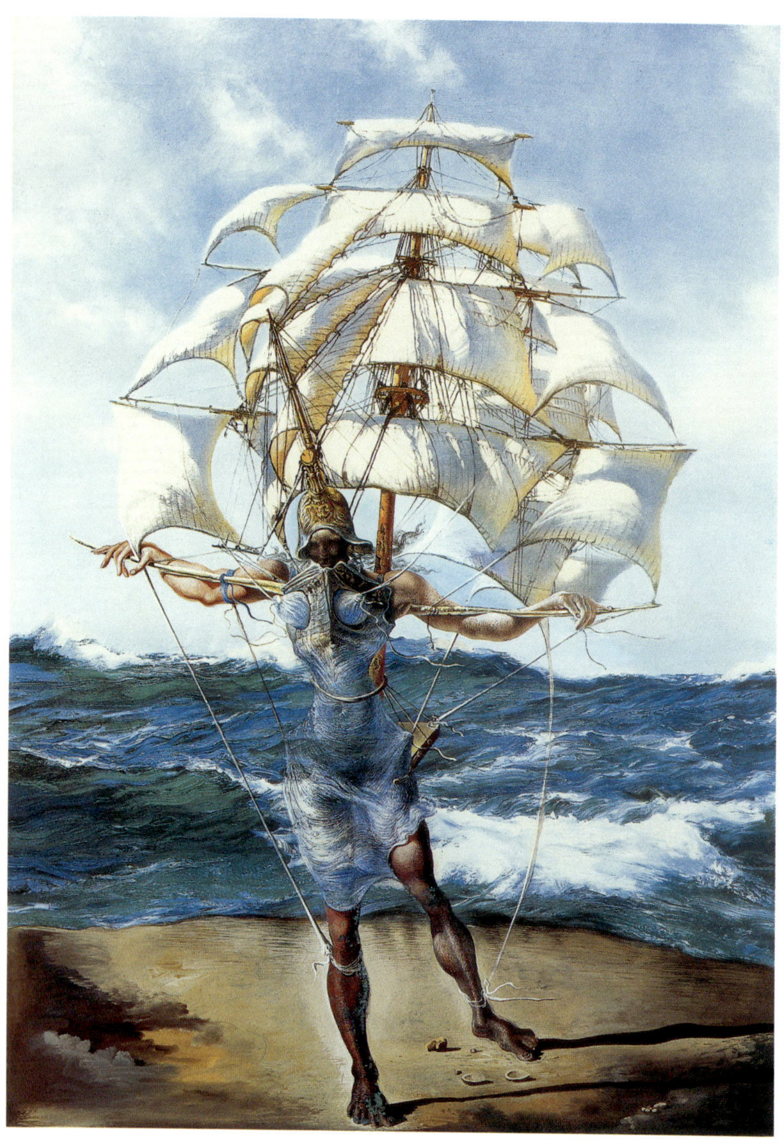

Costume for "Tristan Insane"—The Ship · 1942–43

The Salvador Dalí Museum, St. Petersburg, Florida

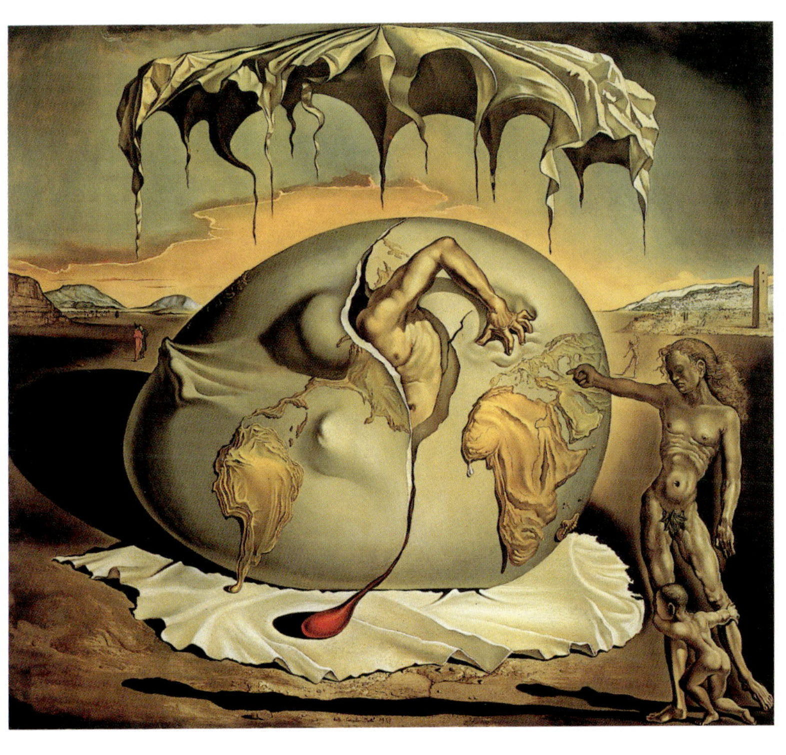

Geopolitical Child Watching the Birth of the New Man · 1943
The Salvador Dalí Museum, St. Petersburg, Florida,
on loan from the Morse Charitable Trust

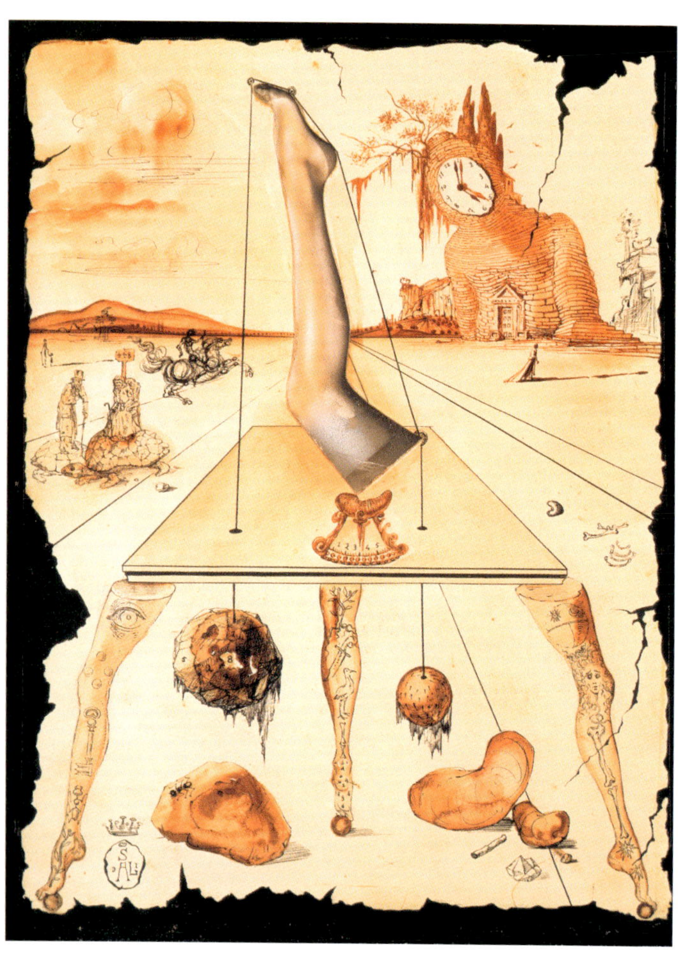

**Leg Composition. Drawing from a series of advertisements
for Bryans Hosiery** · C. 1944
Whereabouts unknown

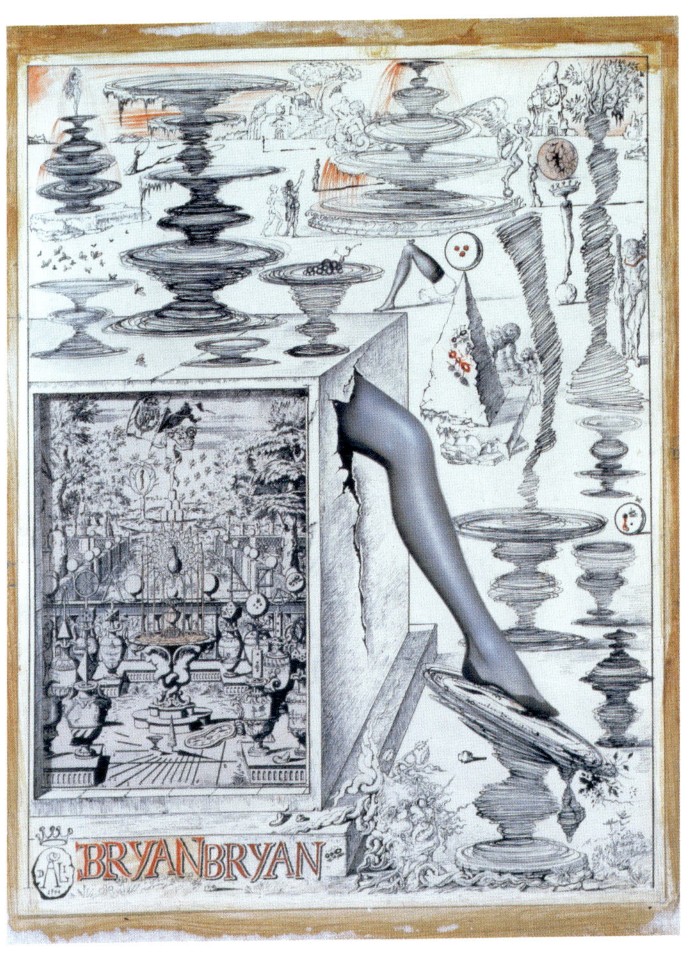

**Leg Composition. Drawing from a series of advertisements
for Bryans Hosiery · c. 1944**
Bonhams, London

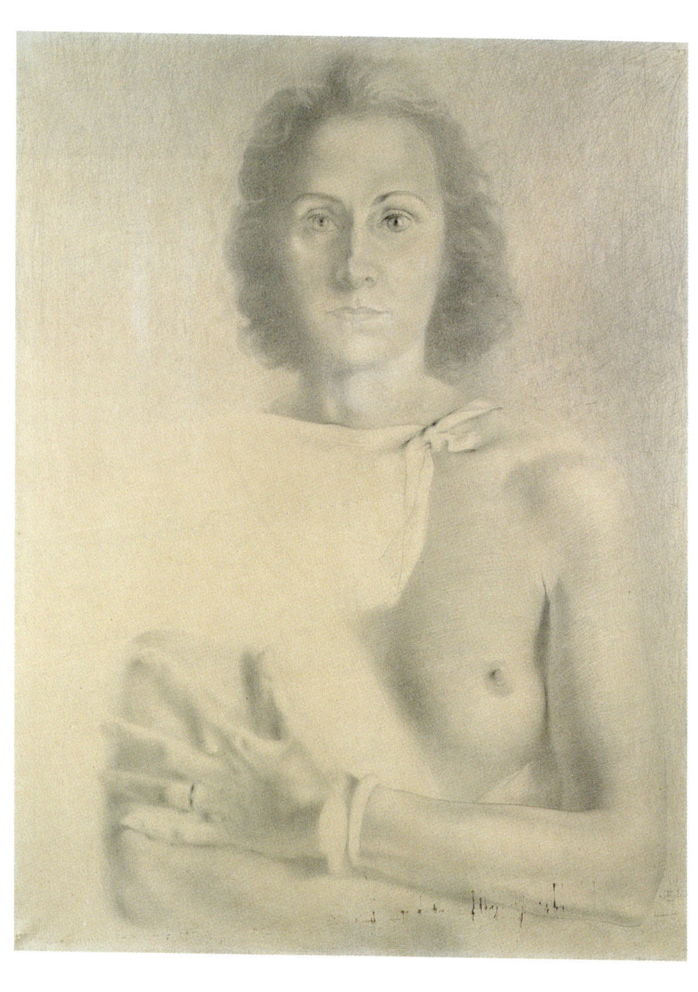

Portrait of Gala · 1941
Museum Boijmans Van Beuningen, Rotterdam,
on loan from the New Trebizond Foundation

244

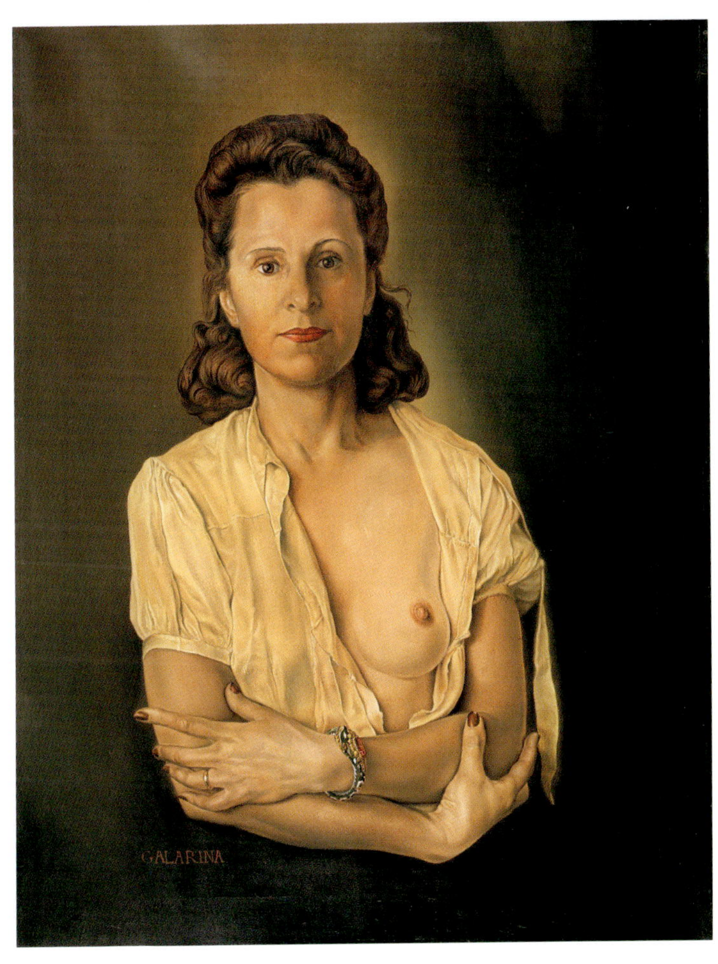

Galarina · 1944–45
Fundación Gala-Salvador Dalí, Figueras, gift of Dalí to the Spanish state

245

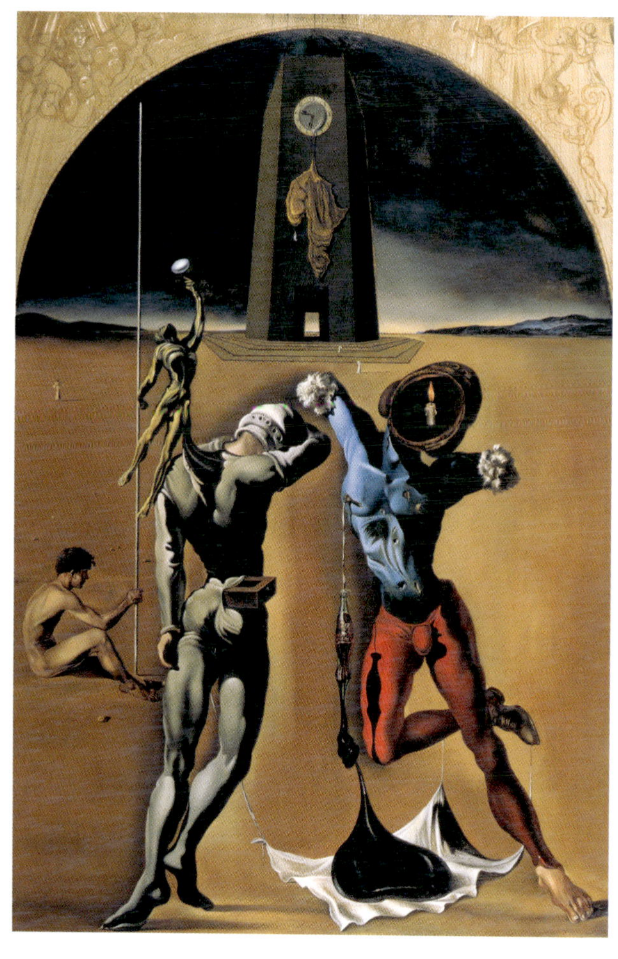

Poetry of America—The Cosmic Athletes · 1943
Fundación Gala-Salvador Dalí, Figueras

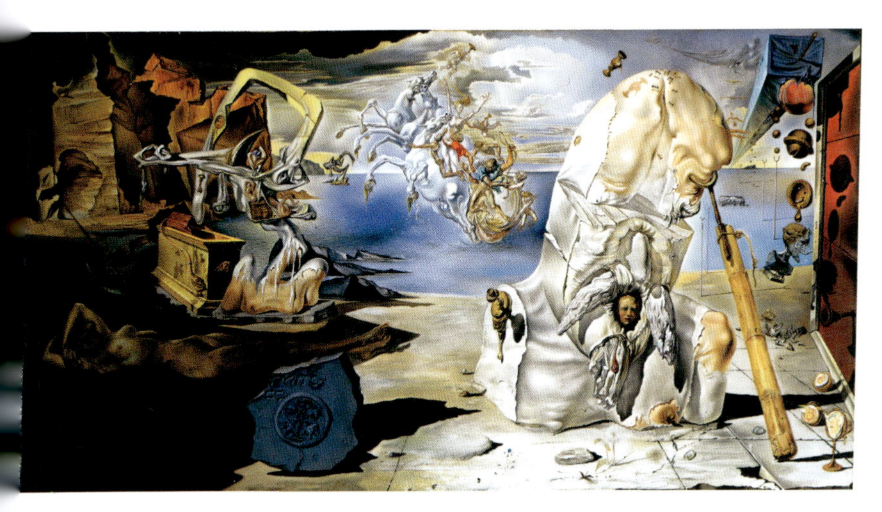

The Apotheosis of Homer · 1944–45

Staatsgalerie Moderner Kunst, Munich; formerly Collection Gonzales Pardo

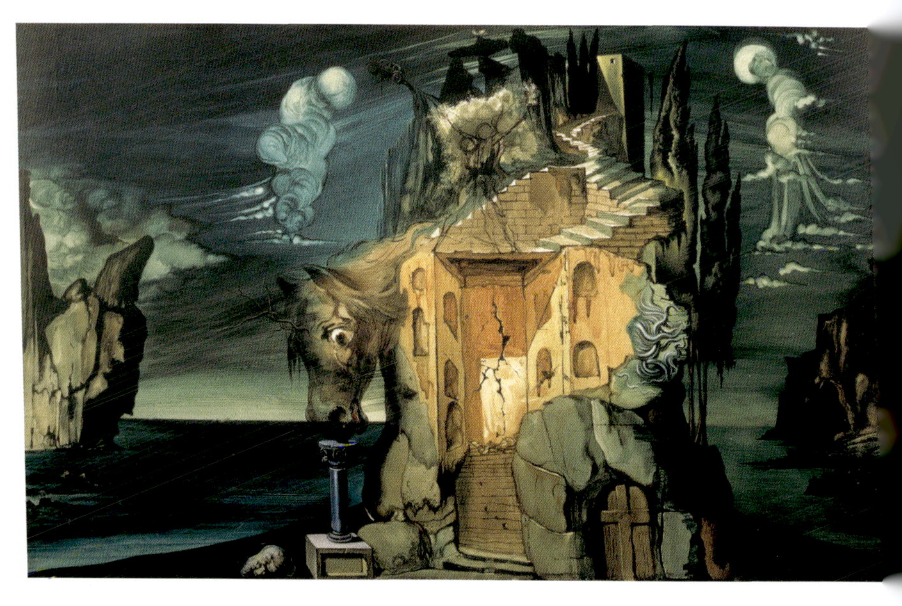

Study for the backdrop of the ballet "Tristan Insane" (Act II) · 1944
Fundación Gala-Salvador Dalí, Figueras

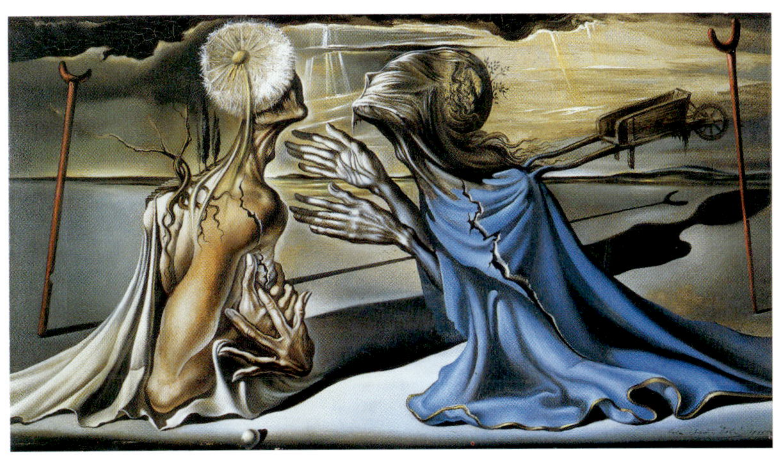

Design for the set of the ballet "Tristan and Isolde" · 1944

Fundación Gala-Salvador Dalí, Figueras

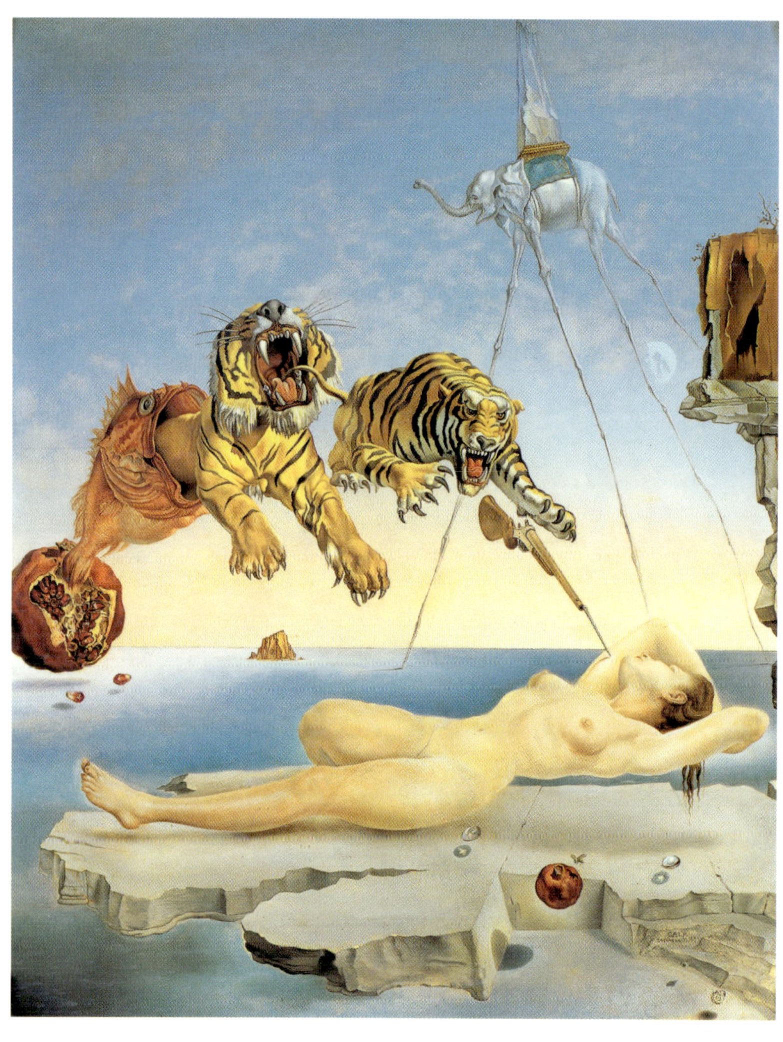

**Dream Caused by the Flight of a Bee around a Pomegranate,
One Second before Awakening** · 1944

Museo Thyssen-Bornemisza, Madrid

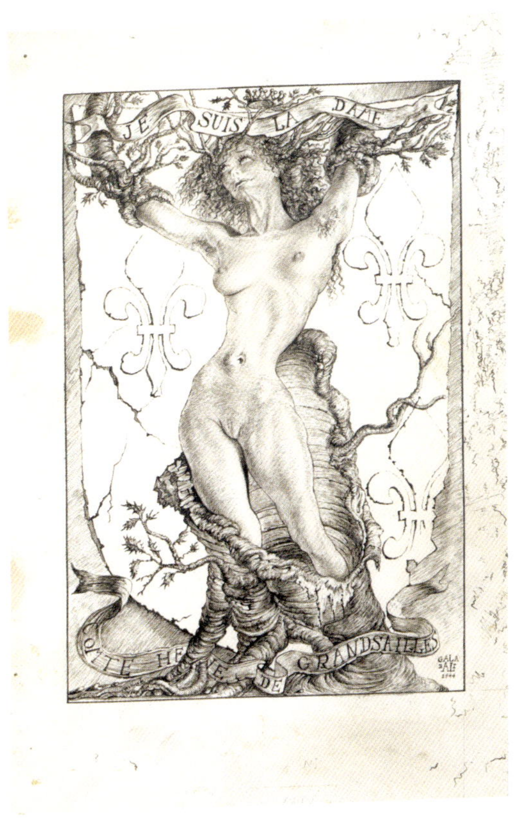

Frontispiece for "Hidden Faces"—I am the Lady · 1944

Gift of Dalí to the Spanish state

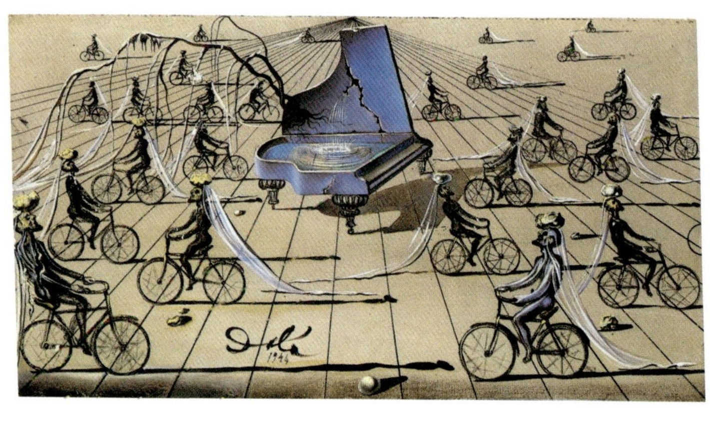

Study for "Colloque sentimental" · 1944
The Salvador Dalí Museum, St. Petersburg, Florida,
on loan from E. and A. Reynolds Morse

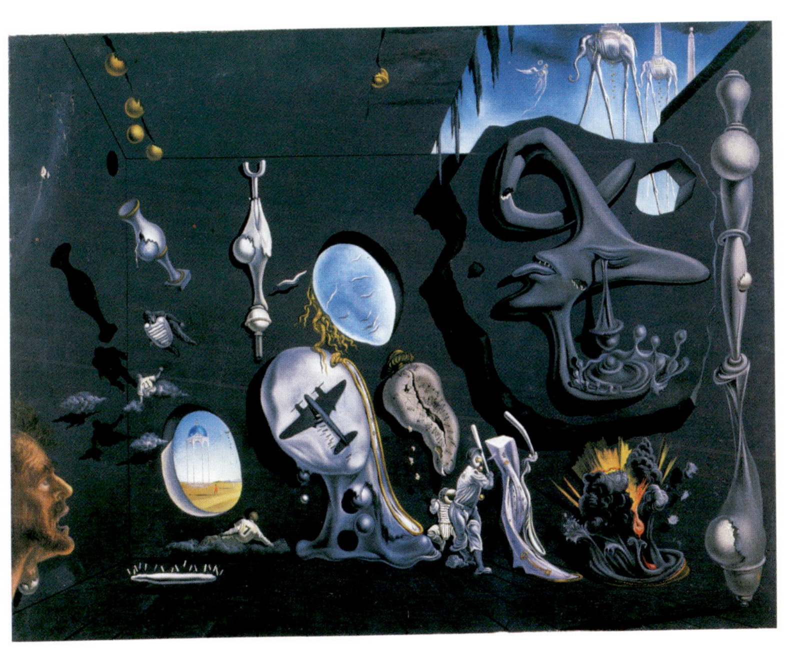

Melancholy Atomic Uranic Idyll · 1945

Museo Nacional Centro de Arte Reina Sofía, Madrid, gift of Dalí to the Spanish state

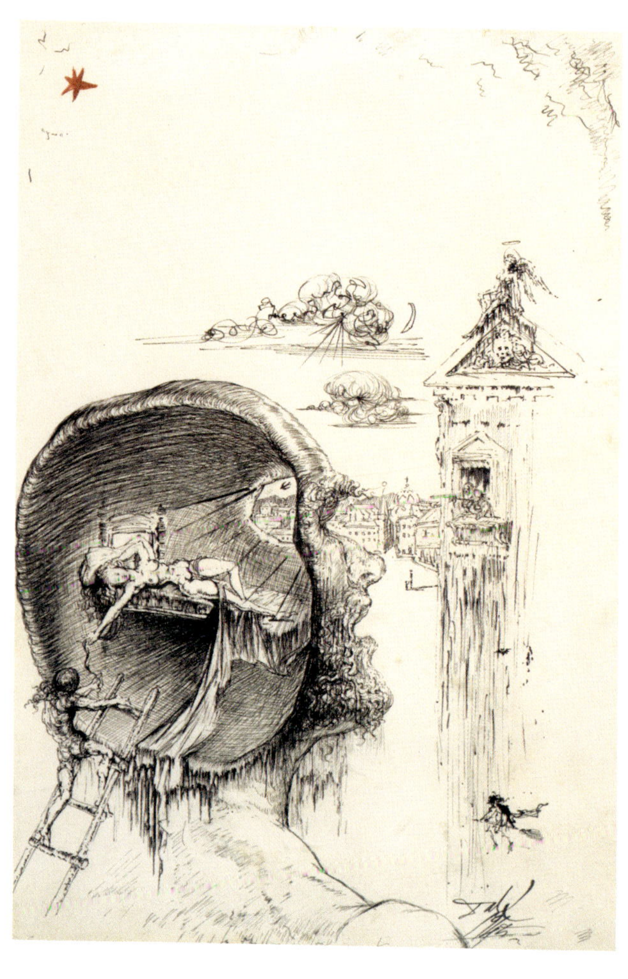

Illustration for "The Autobiography of Benvenuto Cellini" · 1945
Gift of Dalí to the Spanish state

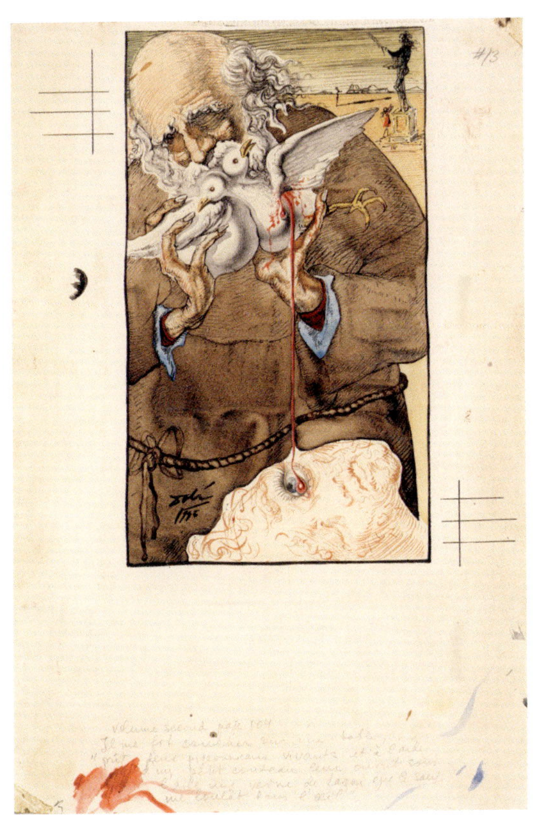

Illustration for "The Autobiography of Benvenuto Cellini" · 1945

Gift of Dalí to the Spanish state

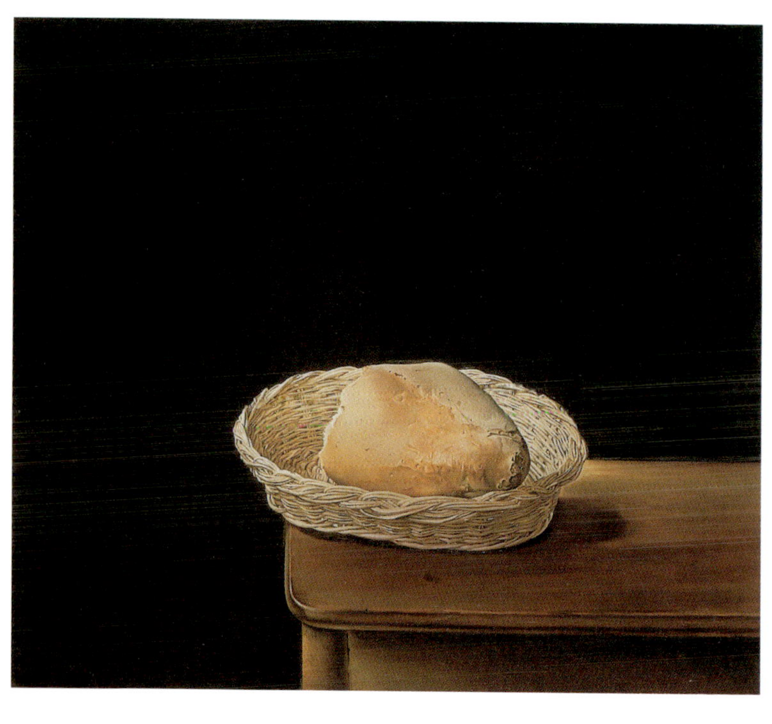

Basket of Bread—Rather Death than Shame · 1945
Fundación Gala-Salvador Dalí, Figueras

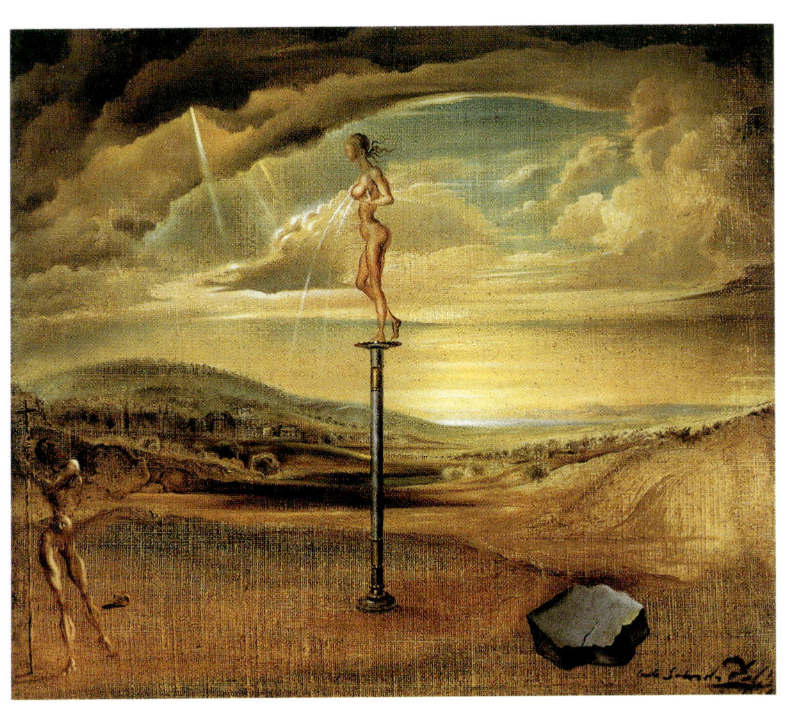

Fountain of Milk Flowing Uselessly on Three Shoes · 1945

The Salvador Dalí Museum, St. Petersburg, Florida,
on loan from E. and A. Reynolds Morse

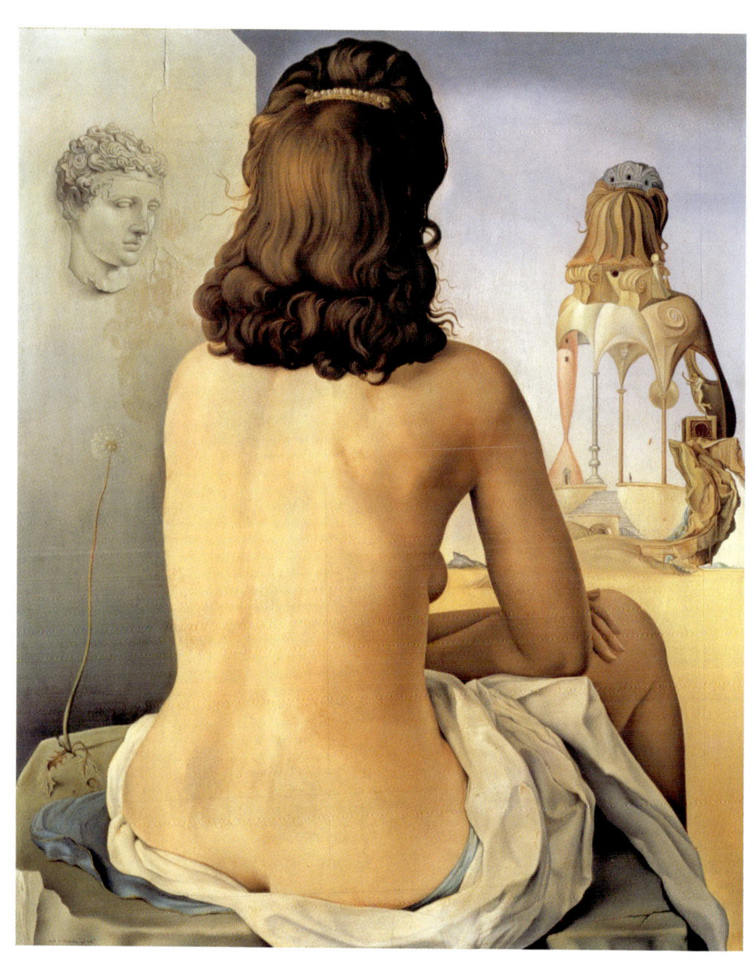

**My Wife, Nude, Contemplating Her Own Flesh Becoming Stairs,
Three Vertebrae of a Column, Sky, and Architecture** · 1945
Collection José Mugrabi, New York

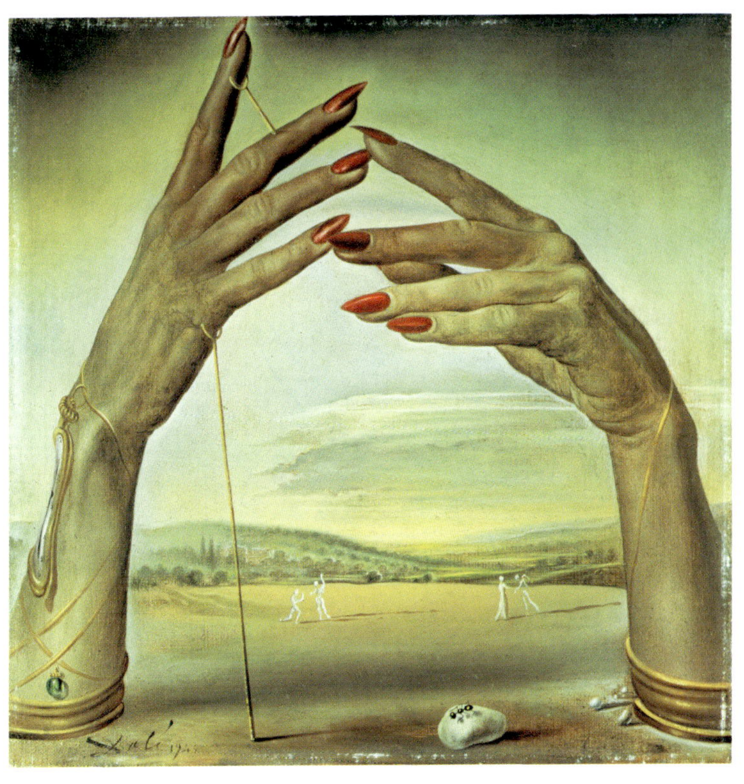

Portrait of a Passionate Woman (The Hands) · 1945
Private collection

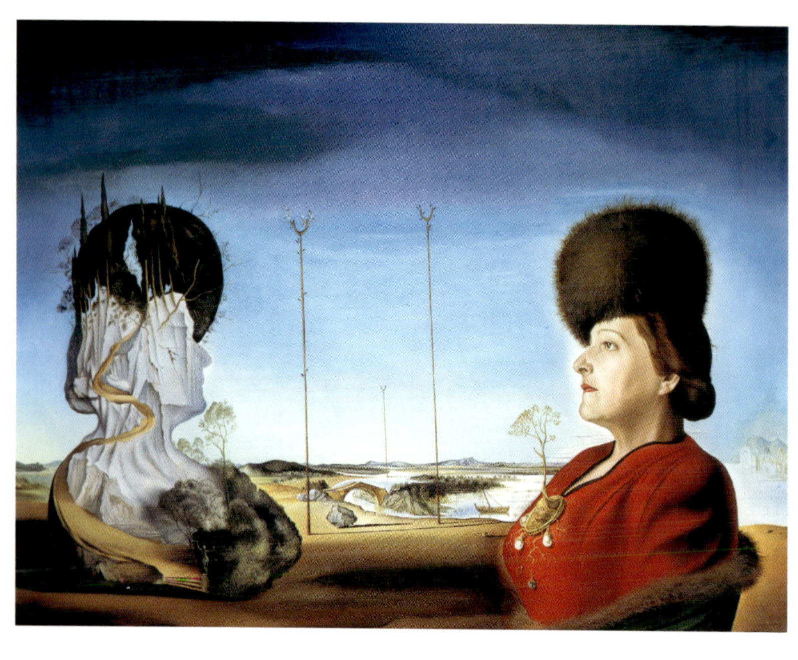

Portrait of Mrs. Isabel Styler-Tas (Melancholia) · 1945
Staatliche Museen zu Berlin – Preußischer Kulturbesitz, Nationalgalerie, Berlin

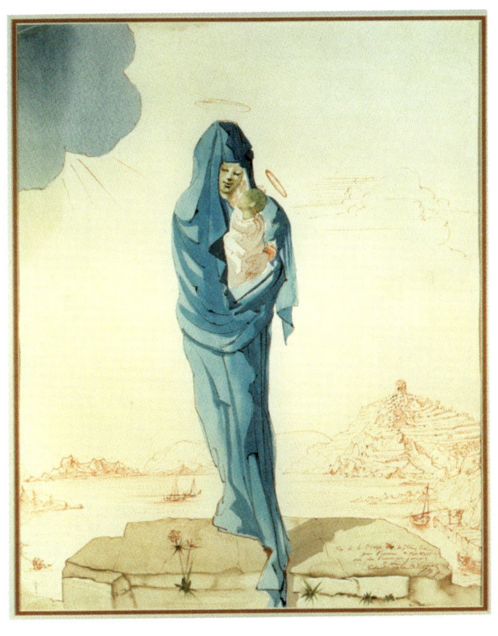

Day of the Virgin · 1947
Private collection

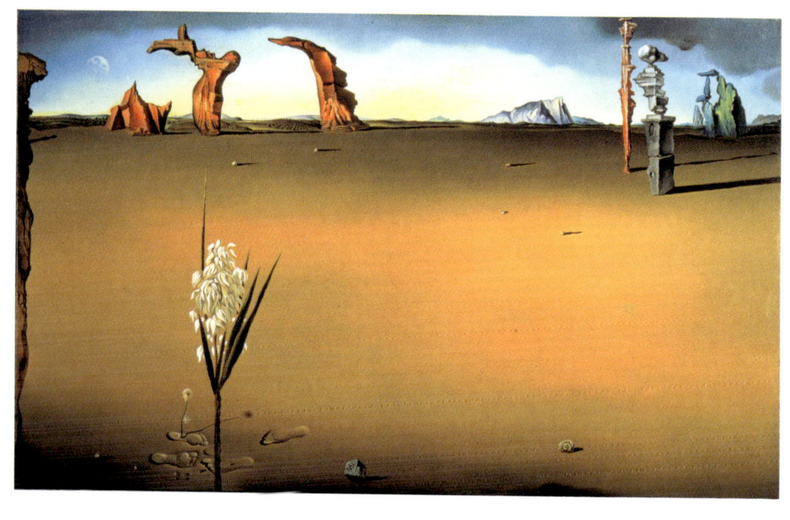

The Invisible Lovers · 1946
Private collection; formerly Christie's, London

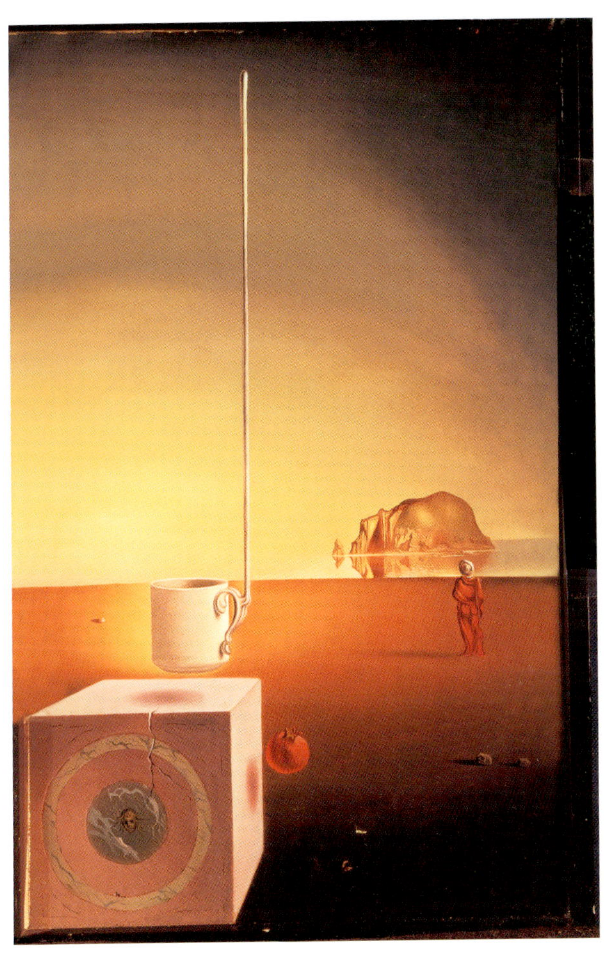

Giant Flying Mocca Cup with an Inexplicable Five-Metre Appendage · c.1946
Private collection, Basel; formerly Collection Marquis Georges de Cuevas

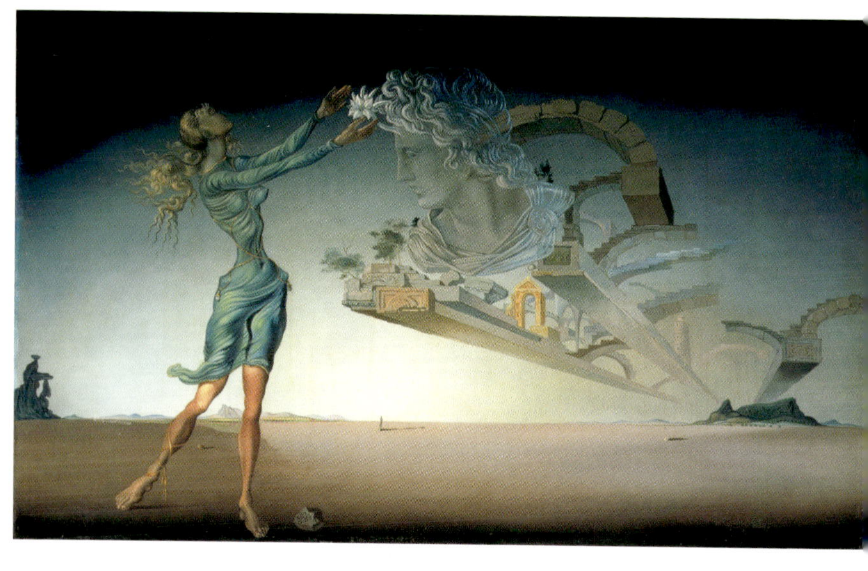

**Desert Trilogy—Apparition of a Woman and Suspended Architecture
in the Desert. For "Desert Flower" perfume** · 1946
Private collection

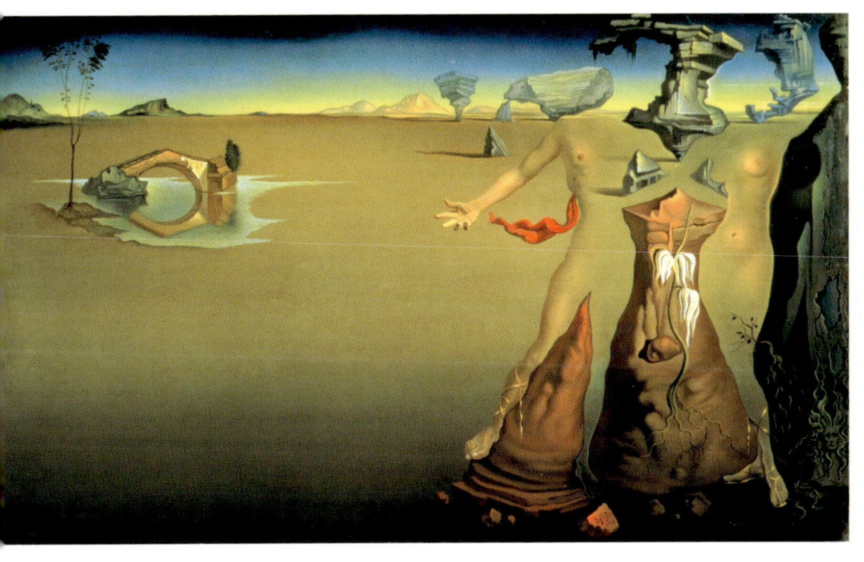

Desert Trilogy—Apparition of a Couple in the Desert.
For "Desert Flower" perfume · 1946
Private collection
> The Temptation of St. Anthony · 1946
Musées Royaux des Beaux-Arts de Belgique, Brussels

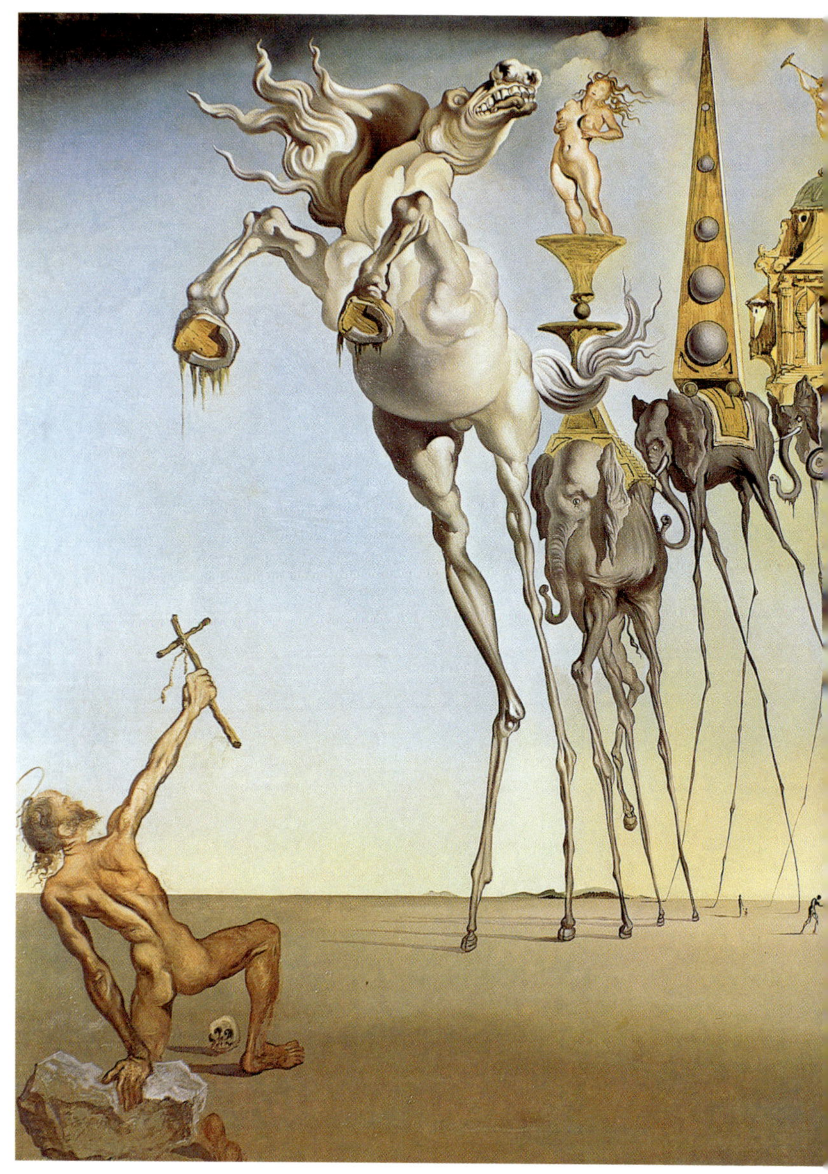

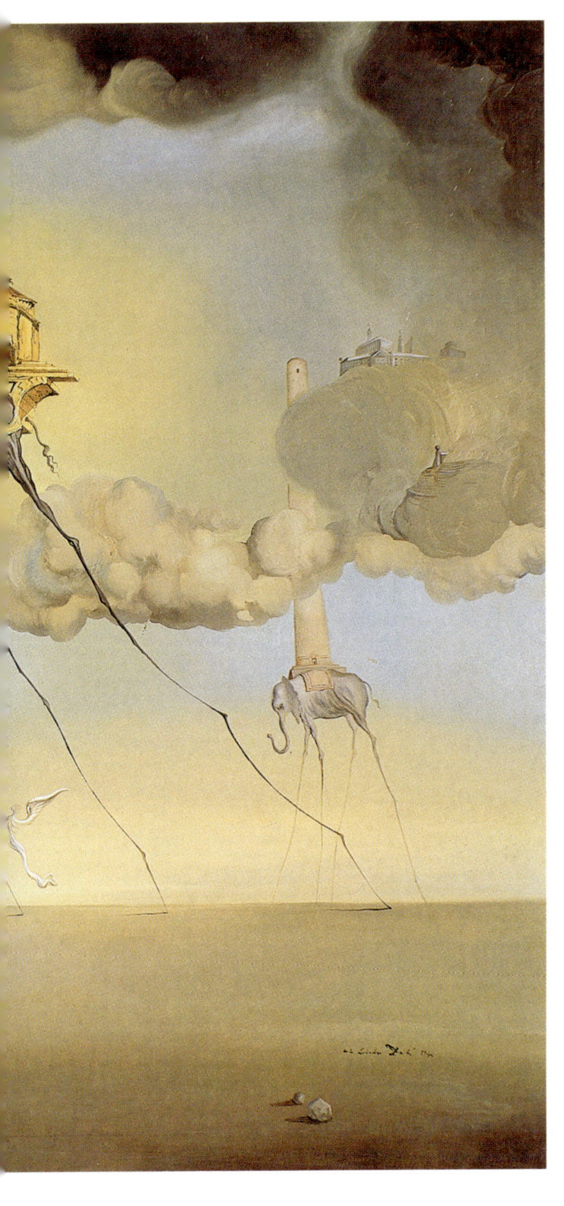

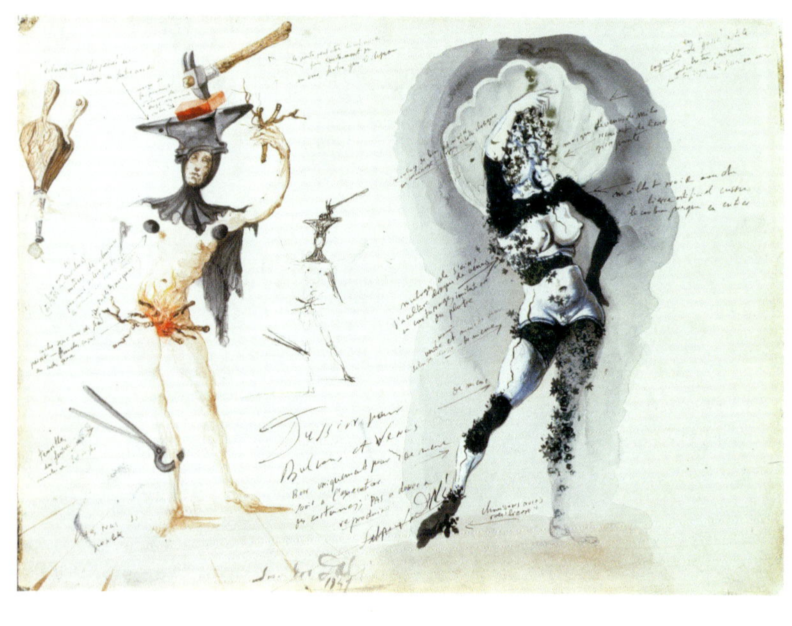

Design for "Vulcan and Venus" · 1947

Bonhams, London

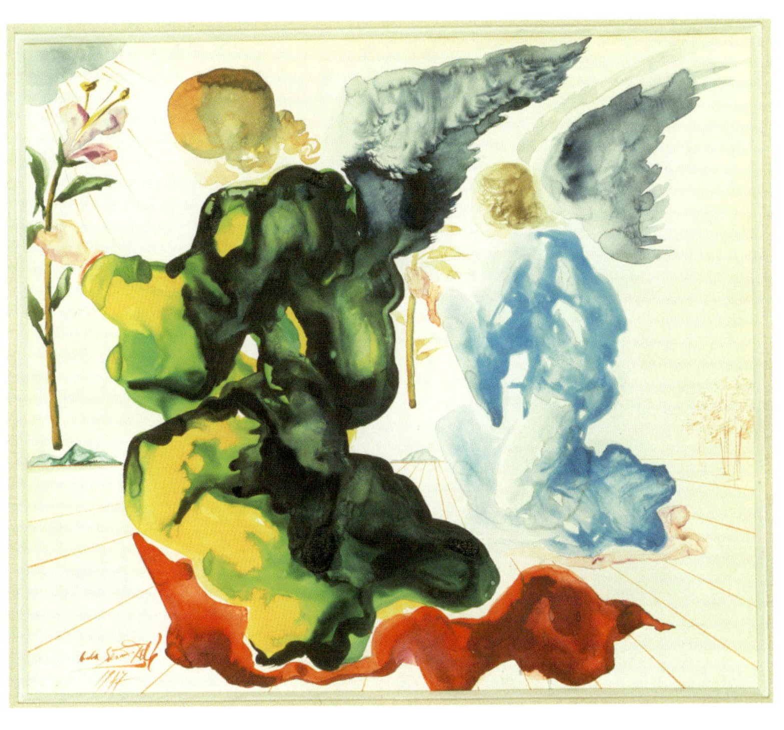

The Annunciation · 1947
Private collection; formerly New York, Harry N. Abrams Collection

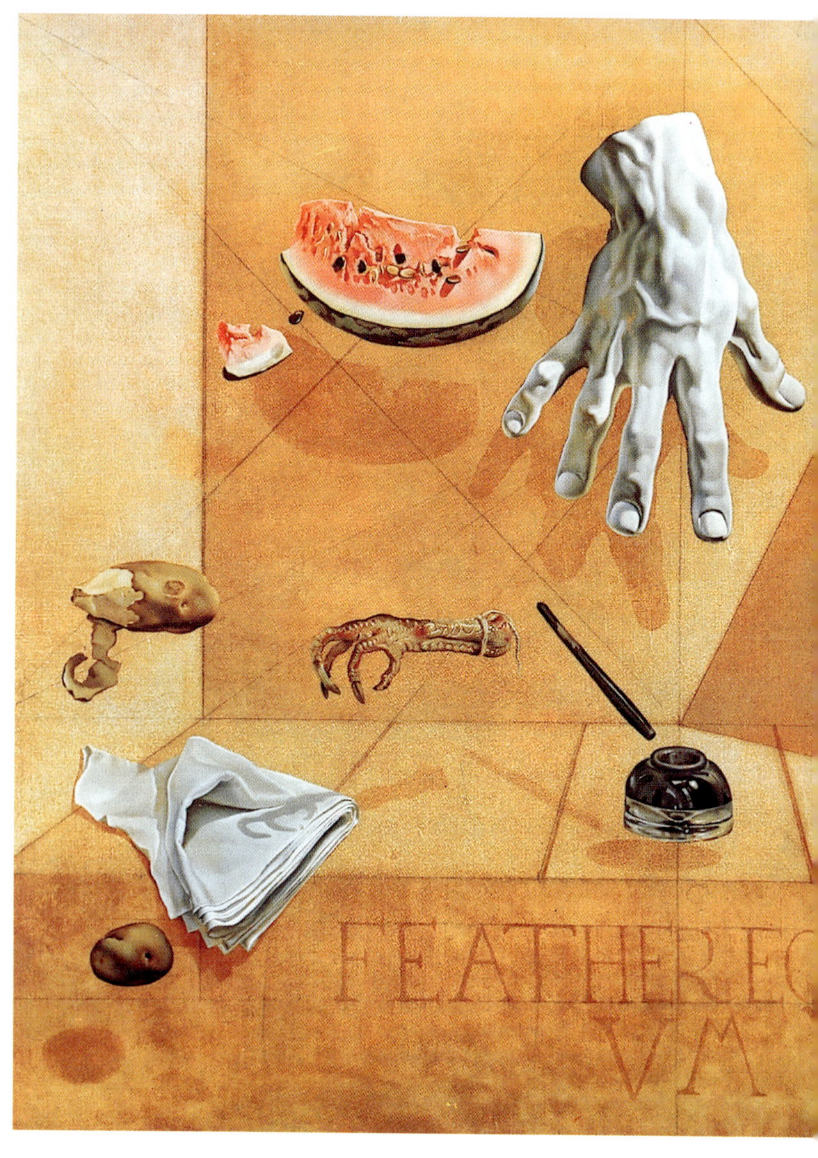

Feather Equilibrium · 1947
Fundación Gala-Salvador Dalí, Figueras, gift of Dalí to the Spanish state

270

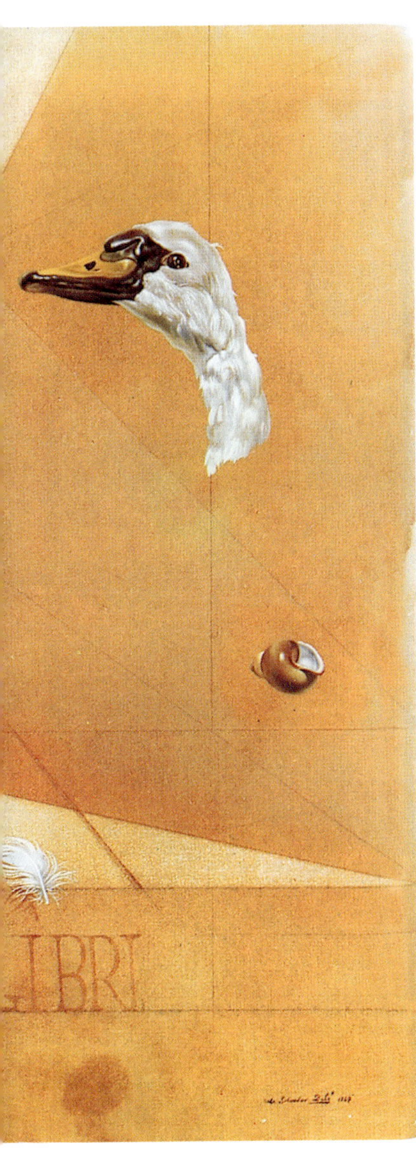
LIBRI

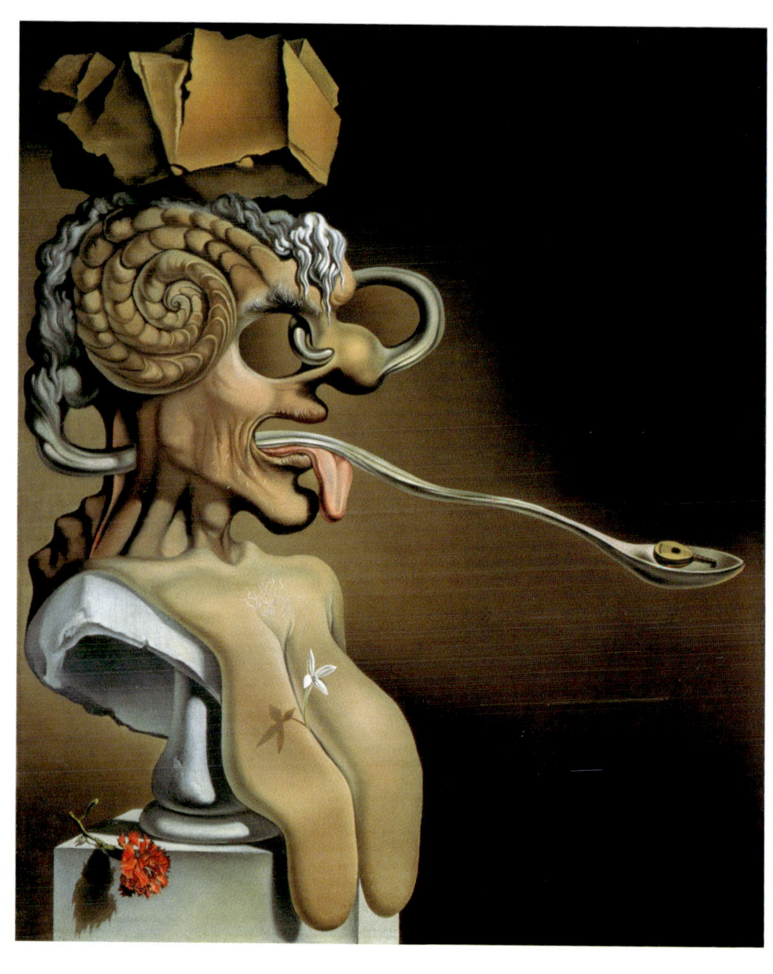

Portrait of Picasso · 1947
Fundación Gala-Salvador Dalí, Figueras

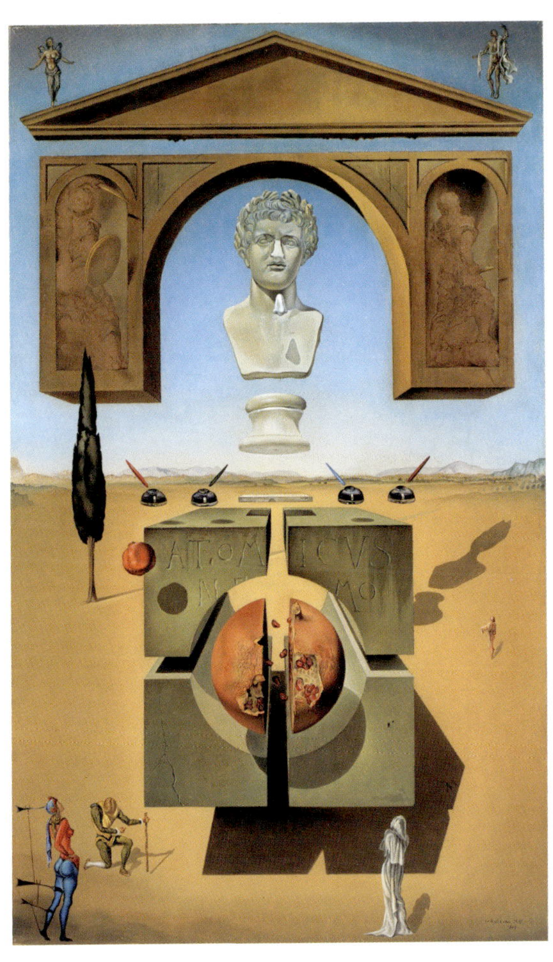

Dematerialization near the Nose of Nero · 1947
Fundación Gala-Salvador Dalí, Figueras, gift of Dalí to the Spanish state

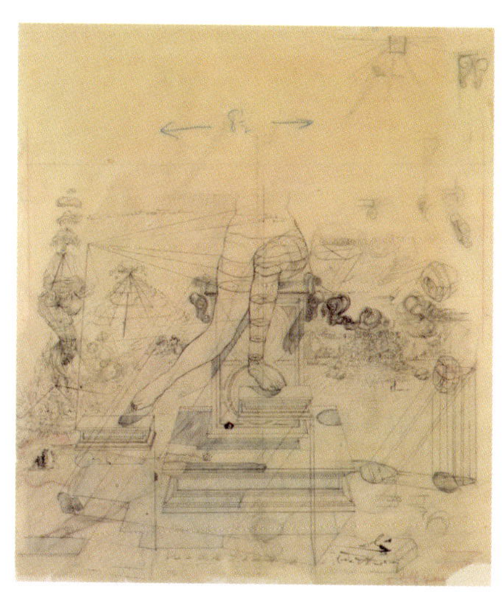

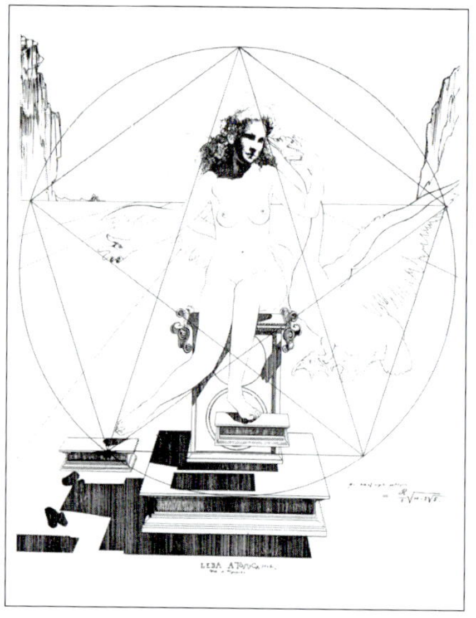

Studies for the Air Centers and Soft Morphologies of "Leda Atomica" · 1947
Fundación Gala-Salvador Dalí, Figueras
Study for "Leda Atomica" · 1947
Private collection

274

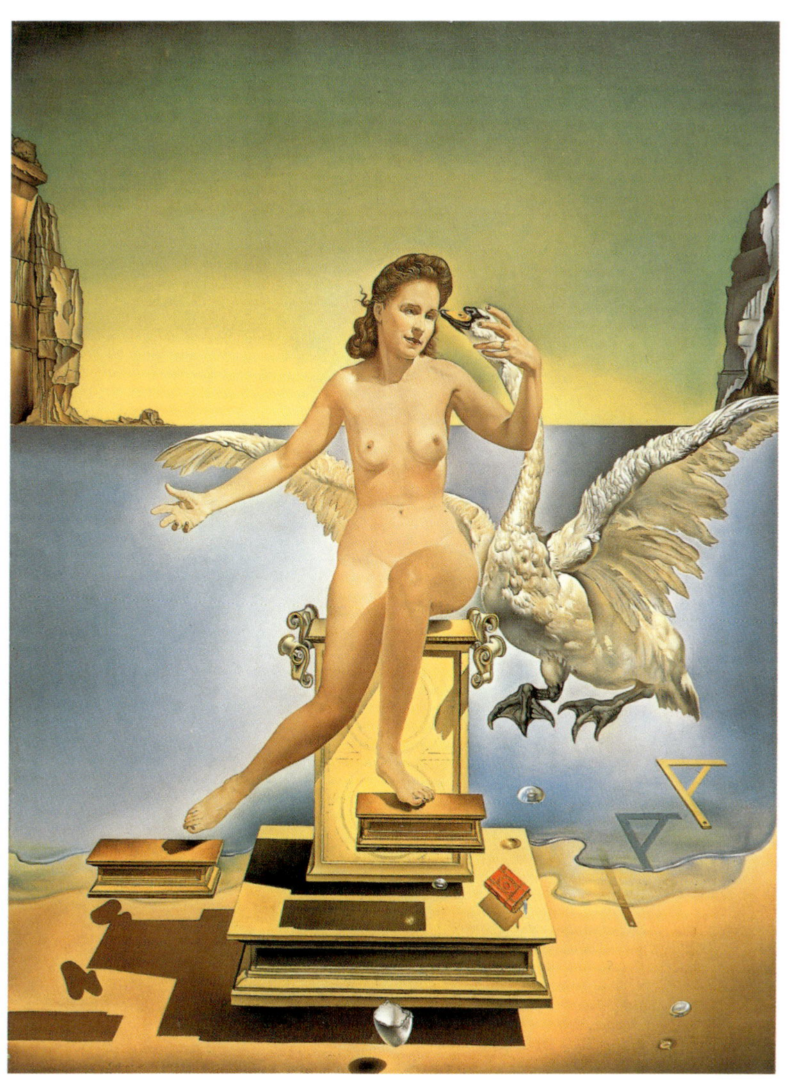

Leda Atomica · 1949
Fundación Gala-Salvador Dalí, Figueras

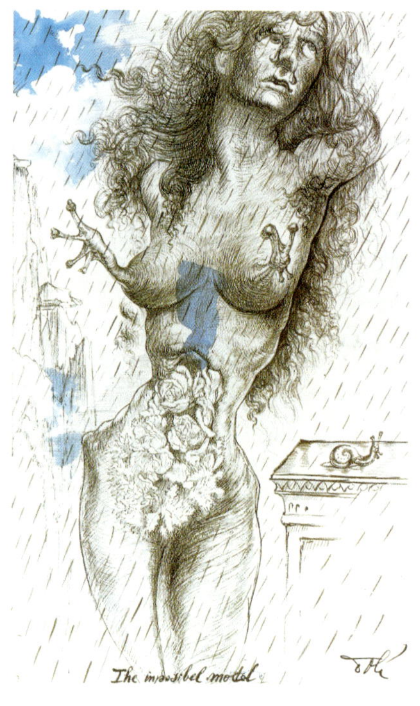

The Impossible Model.
Drawing for "50 Secrets of Magic Craftsmanship" · 1947
Private collection

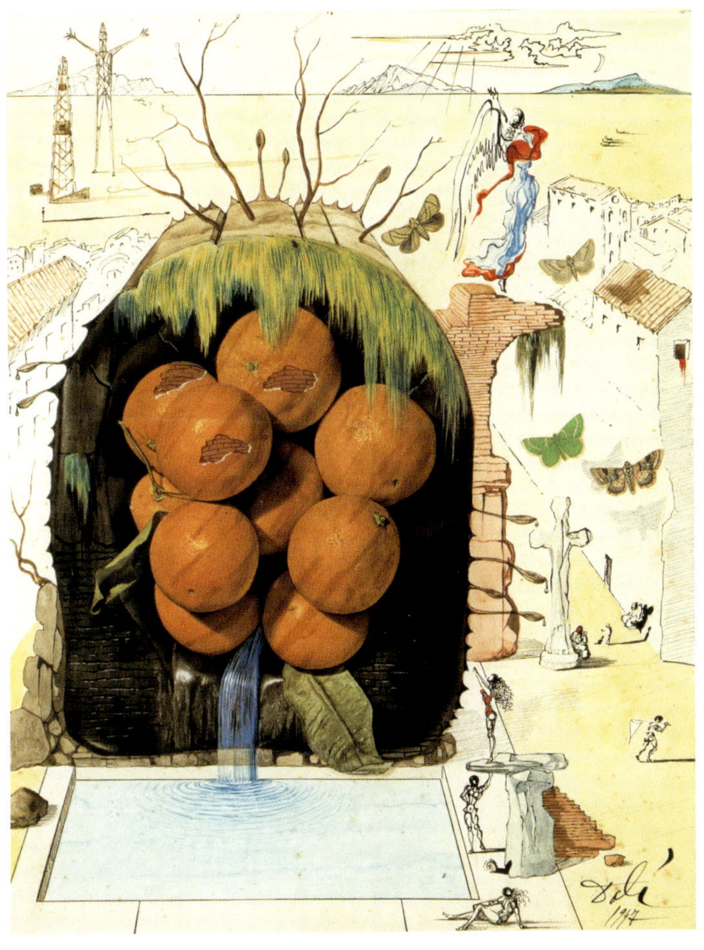

Southern California · 1947
Christie's, New York

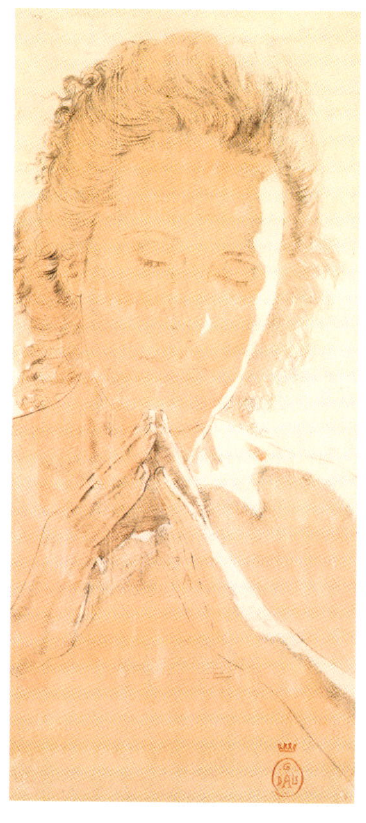

Study for the head of "The Madonna of Port Lligat" · 1950
The Salvador Dalí Museum, St. Petersburg, Florida,
on loan from E. and A. Reynolds Morse

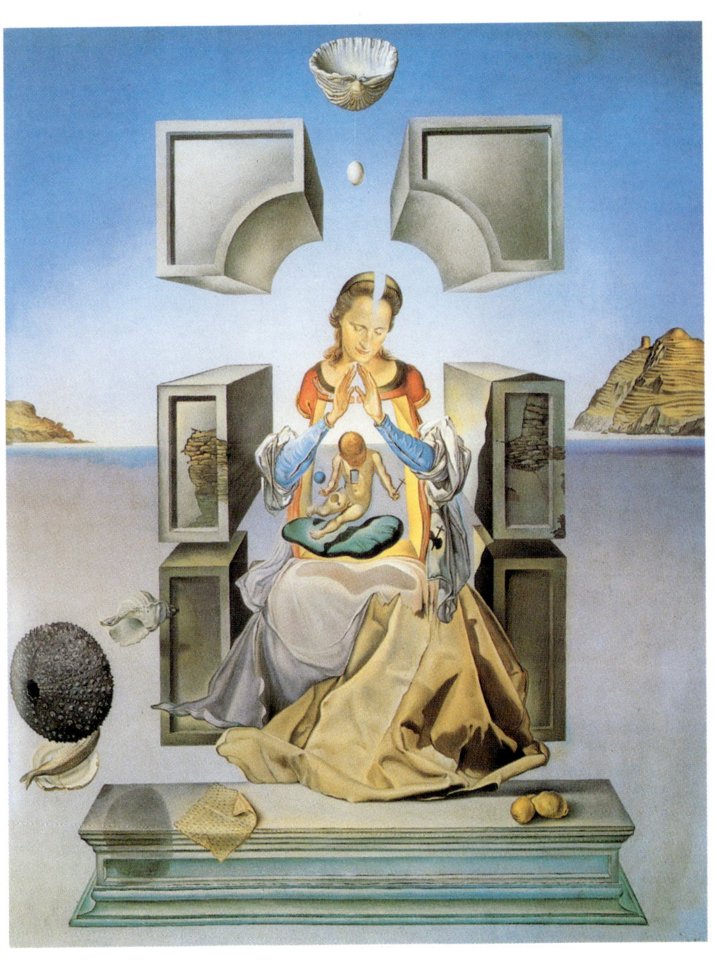

The Madonna of Port Lligat (first version) · 1949
Marquette University, Haggerty Museum of Art, Milwaukee,
gift of Mr. and Mrs. Ira Haupt, 1959

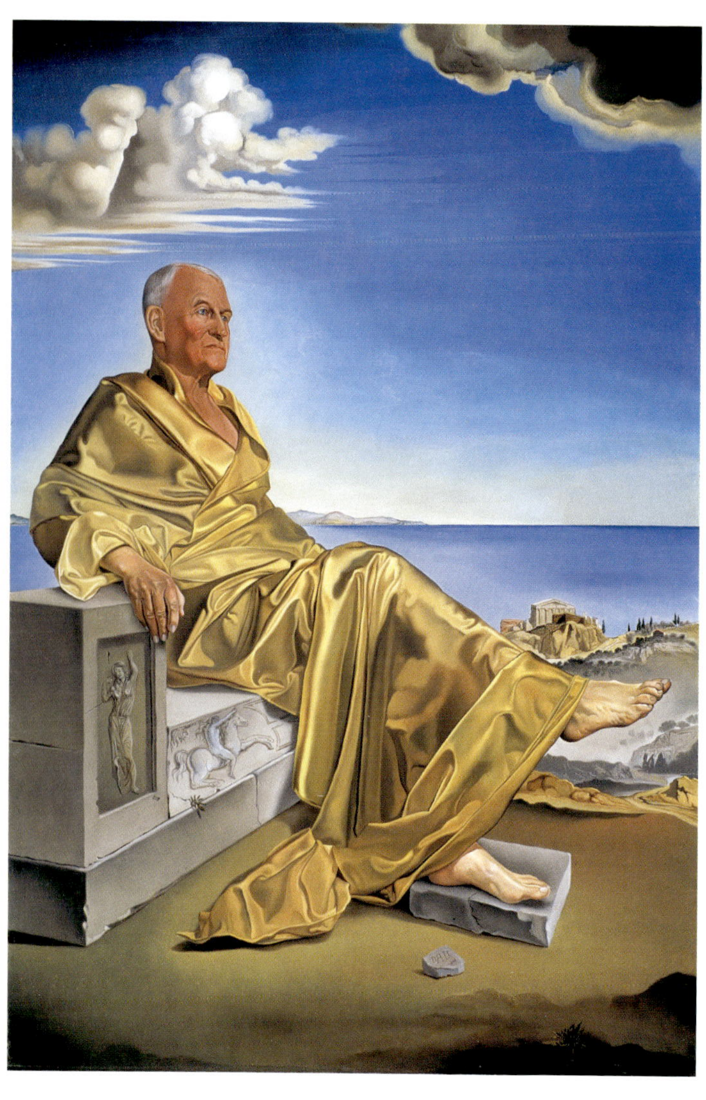

"La Turbie"—Sir James Dunn Seated · 1949
Beaverbrook Art Gallery, Fredericton, New Brunswick

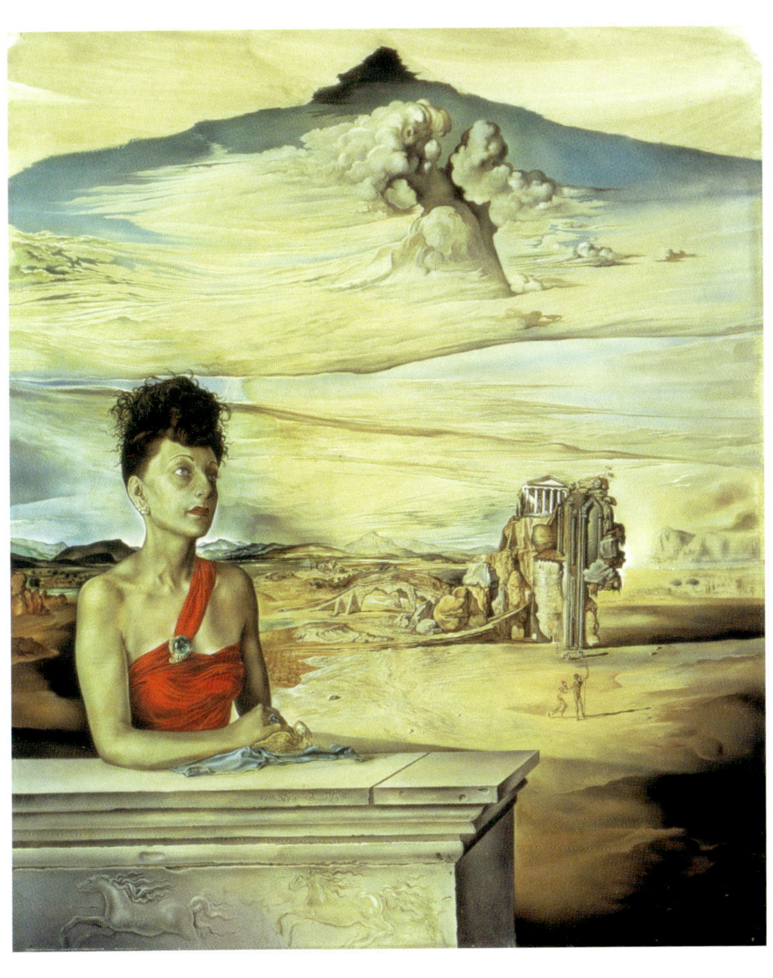

Portrait of Mrs. Jack Warner · 1951

Private collection

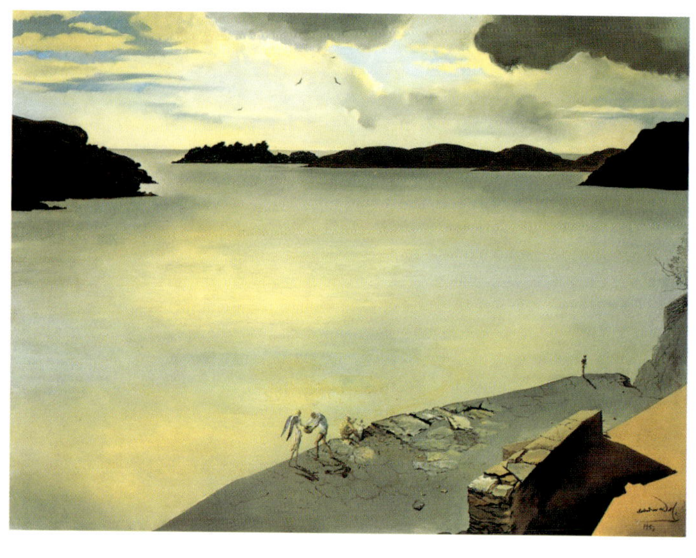

Landscape at Port Lligat · 1950
The Salvador Dalí Museum, St. Petersburg, Florida,
on loan from E. and A. Reynolds Morse

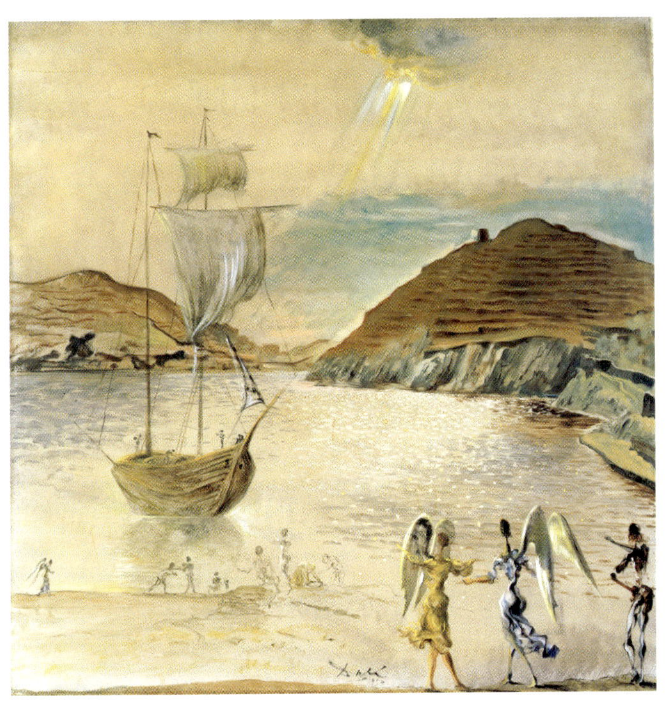

Landscape of Port Lligat with Homely Angels and Fishermen · 1950
Private collection

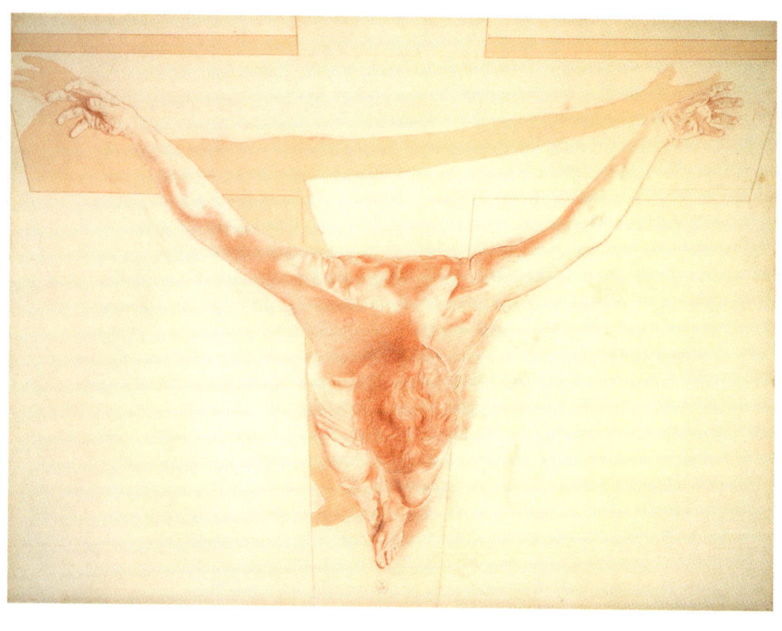

Christ in Perspective. Study for "Christ of St. John of the Cross" · 1950
The Salvador Dalí Museum, St. Petersburg, Florida
> **Christ of St. John of the Cross** · 1951
St. Mungo Museum of Religious Life and Art, Glasgow

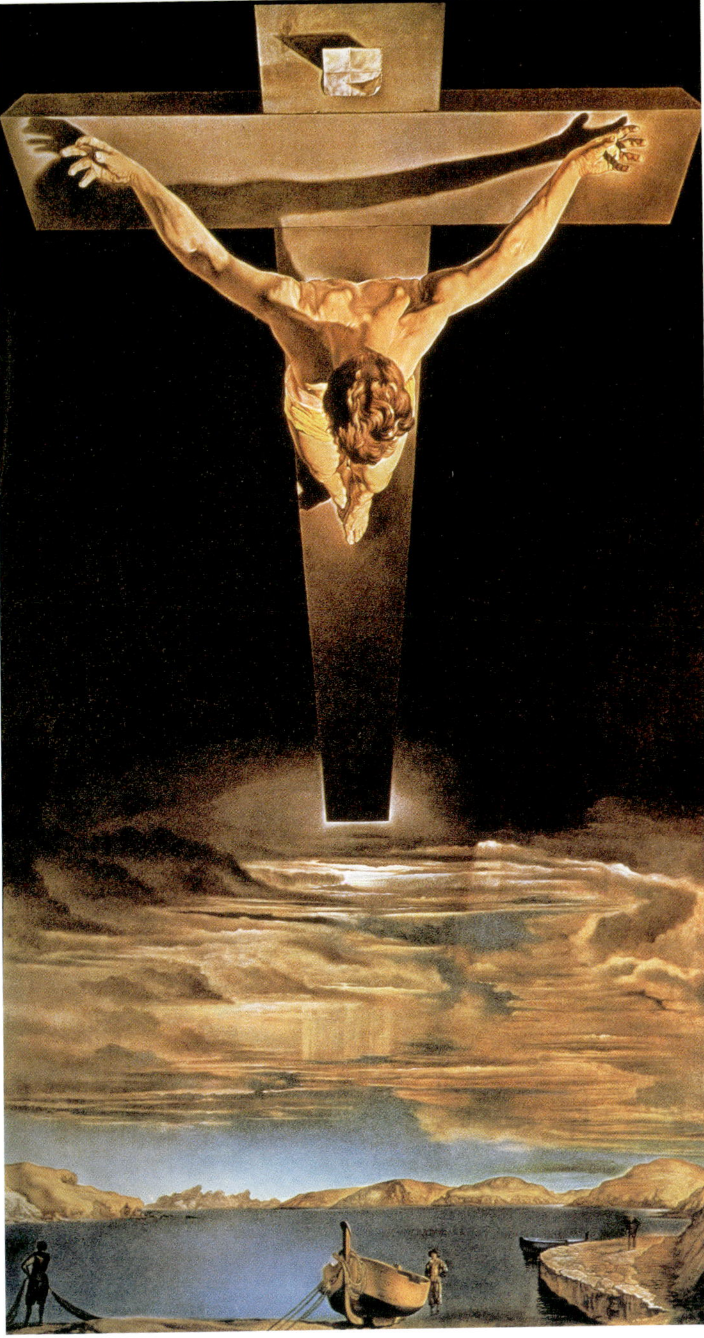

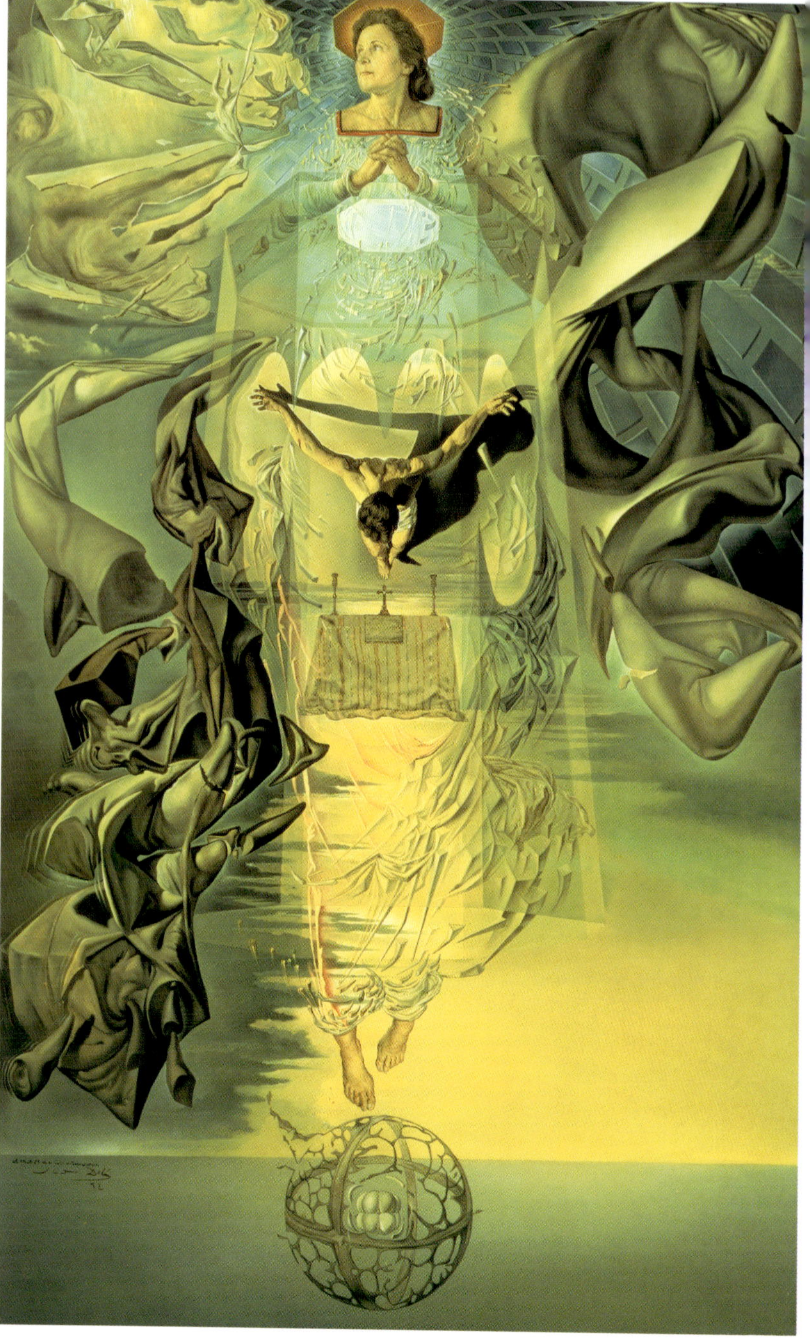

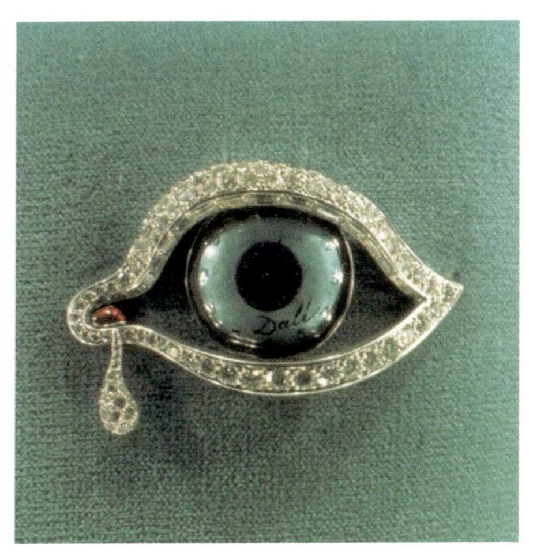

The Eye of Time · 1949
Whereabouts unknown
< **Assumpta corpuscularia lapislazulina** · 1952
Collection John Theodoracopoulos

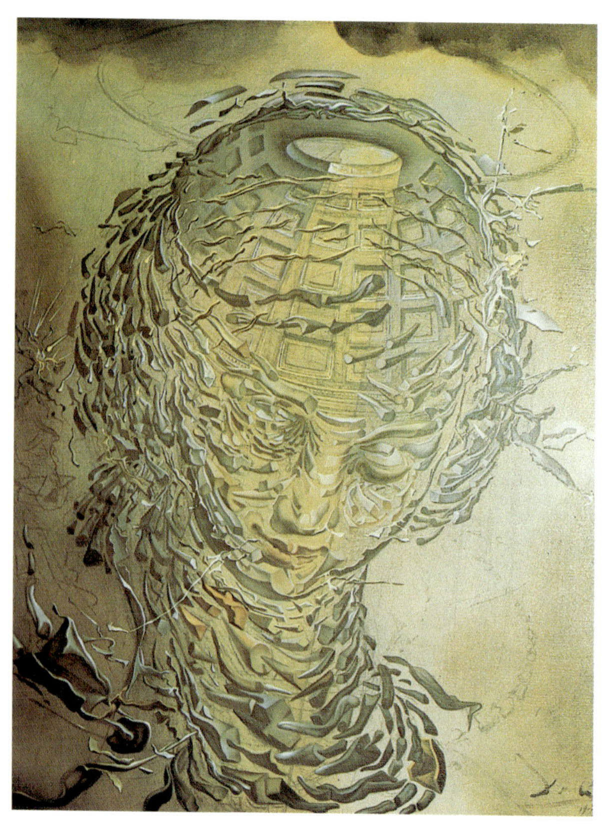

Raphaelesque Head, Exploded · 1951
Scottish National Gallery of Modern Art, Edinburgh, on permanent loan
from Miss Stead-Ellis, Somerset

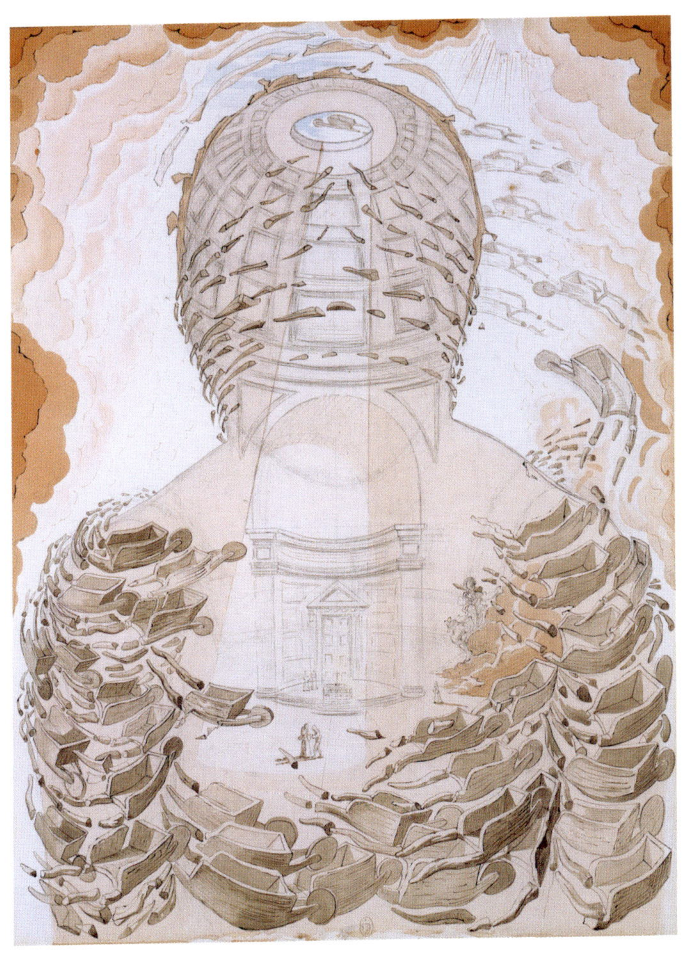

The Wheelbarrows (Cupola Consisting of Twisted Carts) · 1951
The Salvador Dalí Museum, St. Petersburg, Florida;
formerly Collection E. and A. Reynolds Morse

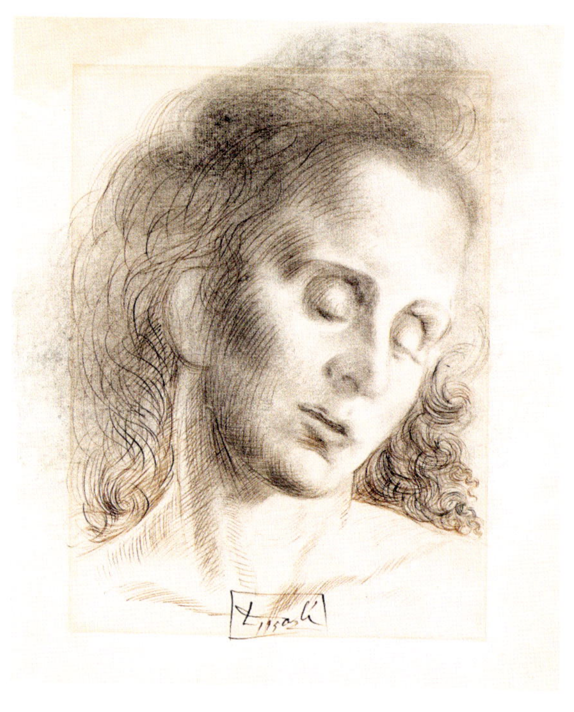

Gala Placida · 1952
University of Arizona Museum of Art, The Edward Joseph Gallagher III
Memorial Collection, Tucson

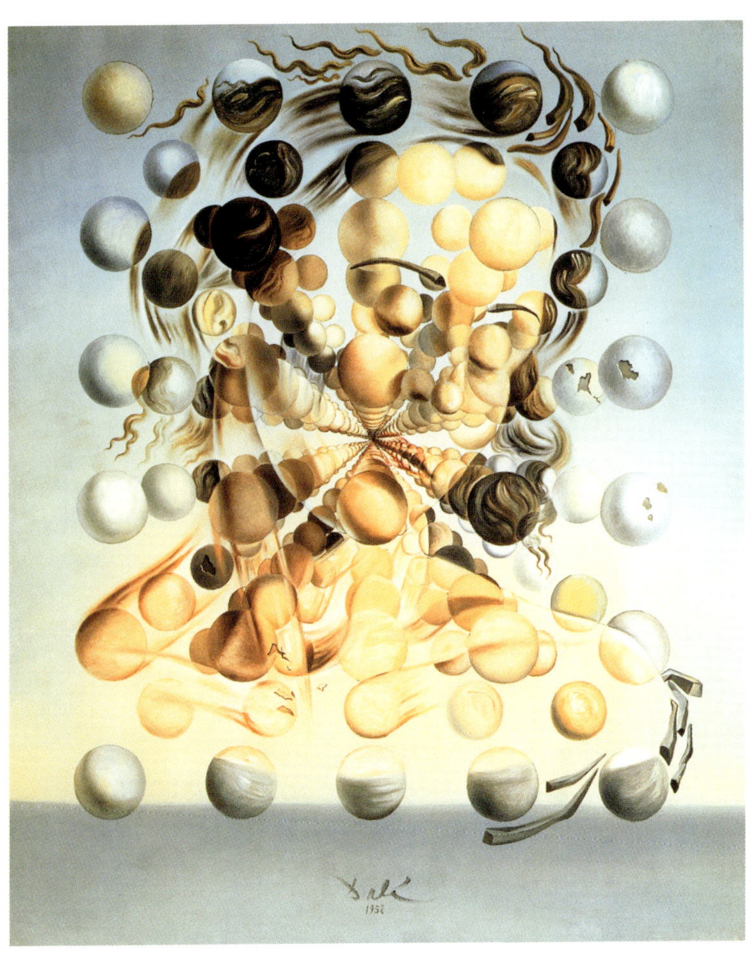

Galatea of the Spheres · 1952
Fundación Gala-Salvador Dalí, Figueras

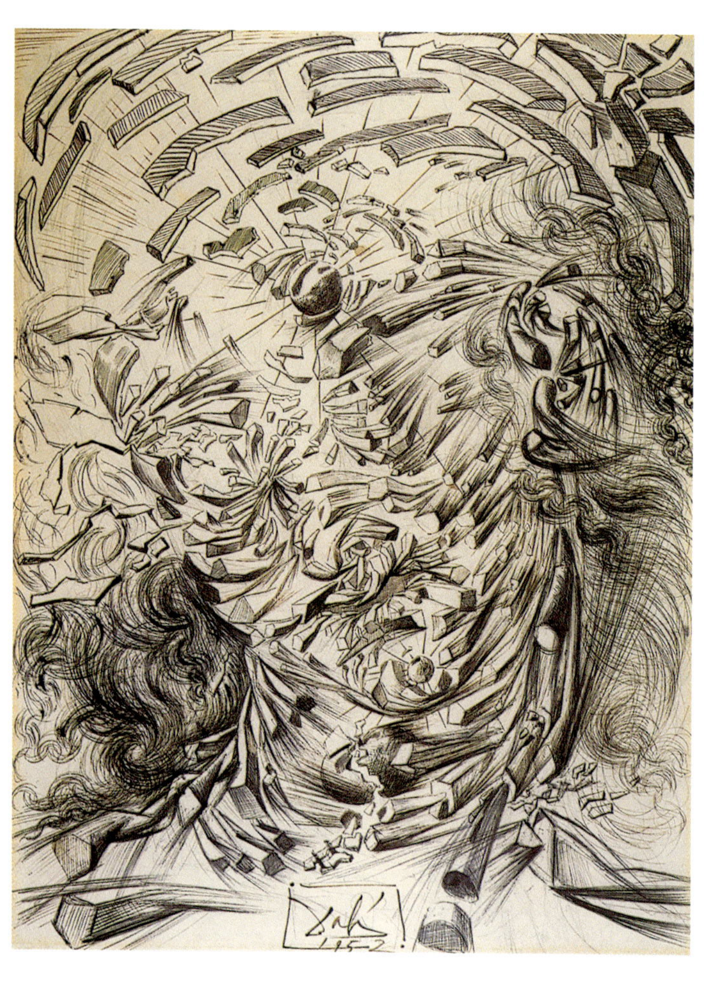

Nuclear Head of an Angel · 1952
Private collection

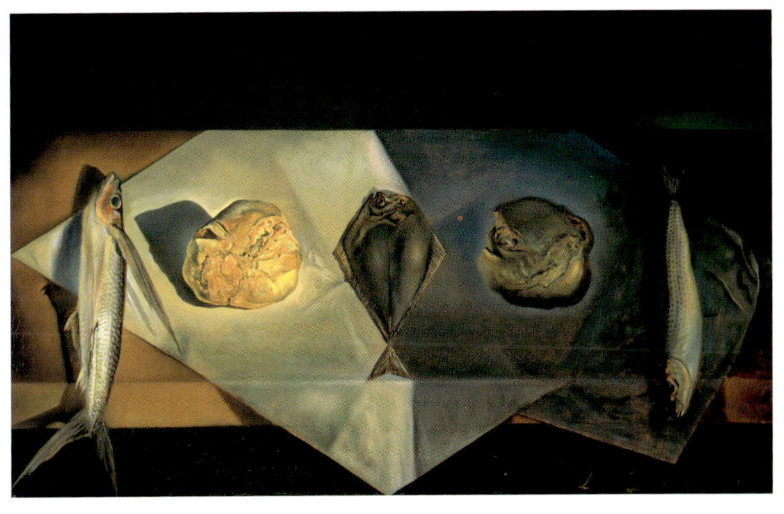

Eucharistic Still Life · 1952
The Salvador Dalí Museum, St. Petersburg, Florida,
on loan from E. and A. Reynolds Morse

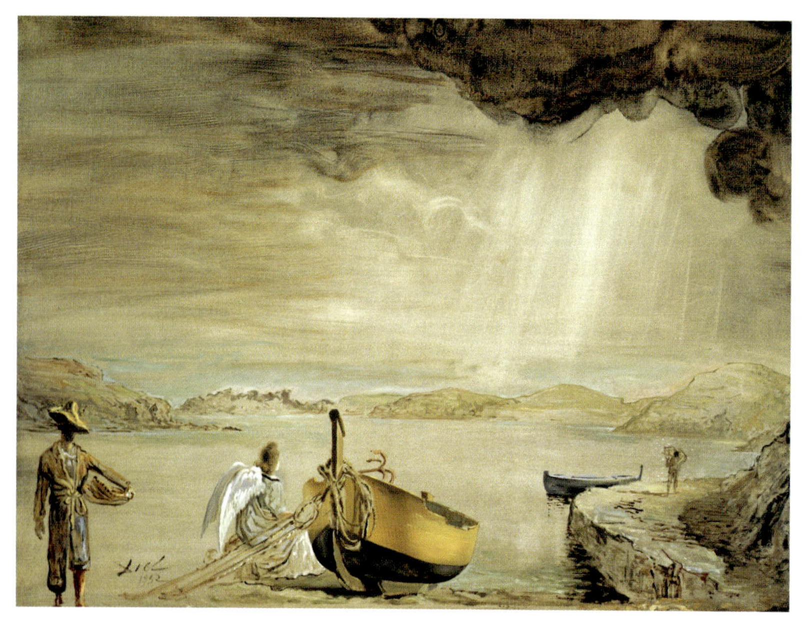

The Angel of Port Lligat · 1952
The Salvador Dalí Museum, St. Petersburg, Florida,
on loan from E. and A. Reynolds Morse

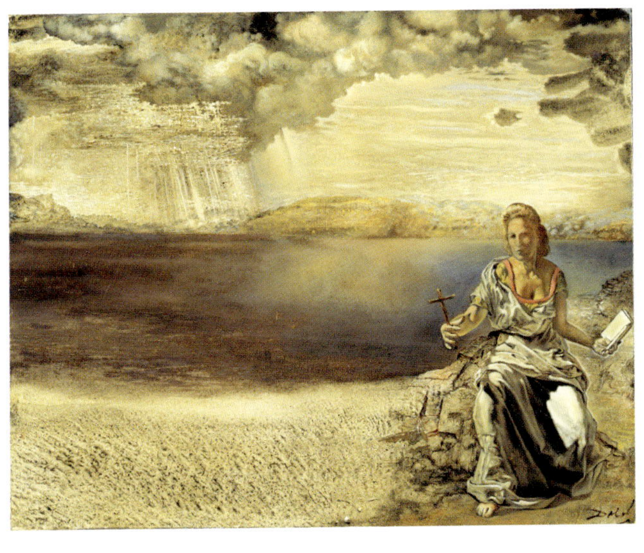

St. Helen of Port Lligat · 1956
The Salvador Dalí Museum, St. Petersburg, Florida,
on loan from E. and A. Reynolds Morse

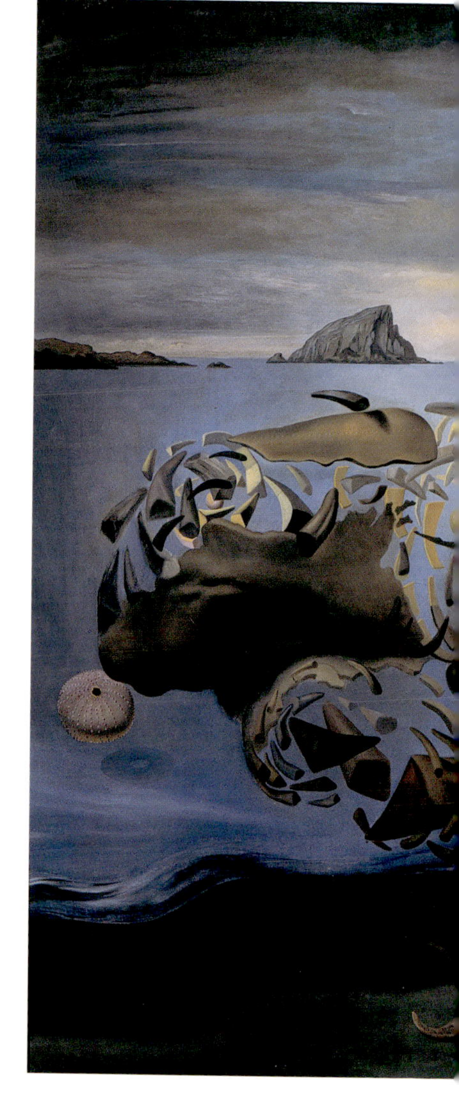

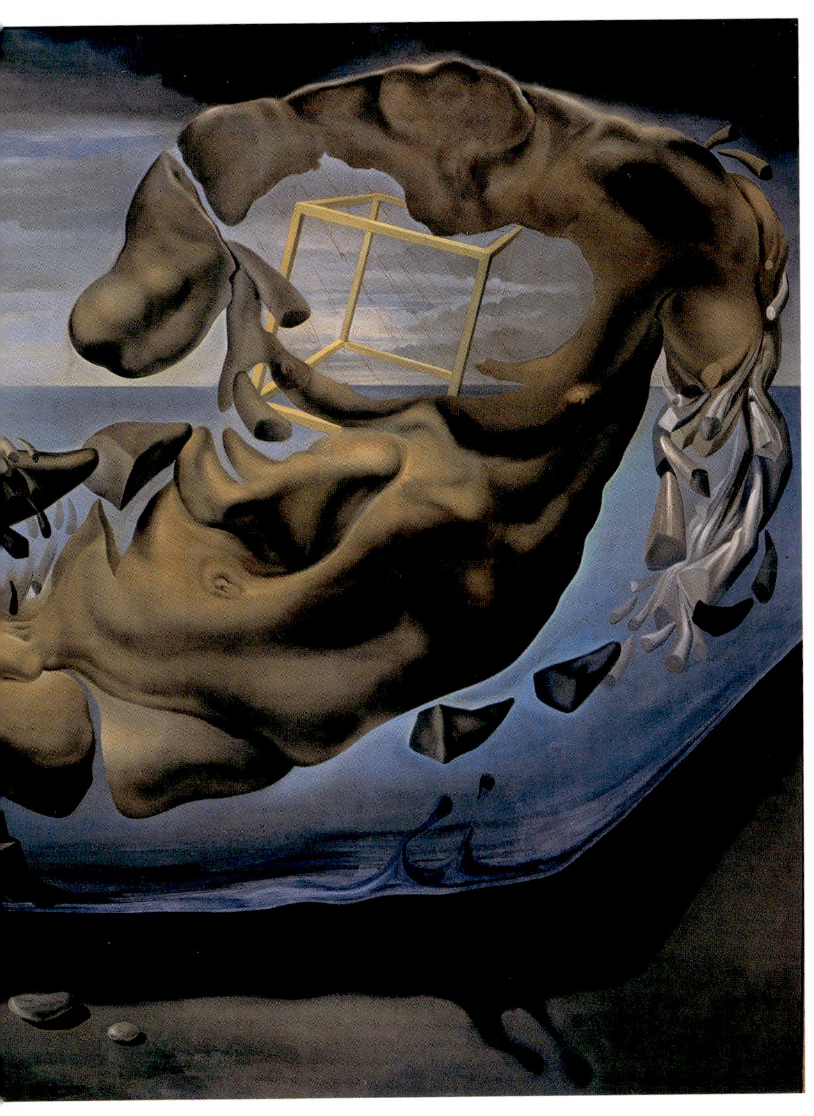

Rhinocerotic Disintegration of Illissus of Phidias · 1954
Fundación Gala-Salvador Dalí, Figueras, gift of Dalí to the Spanish state

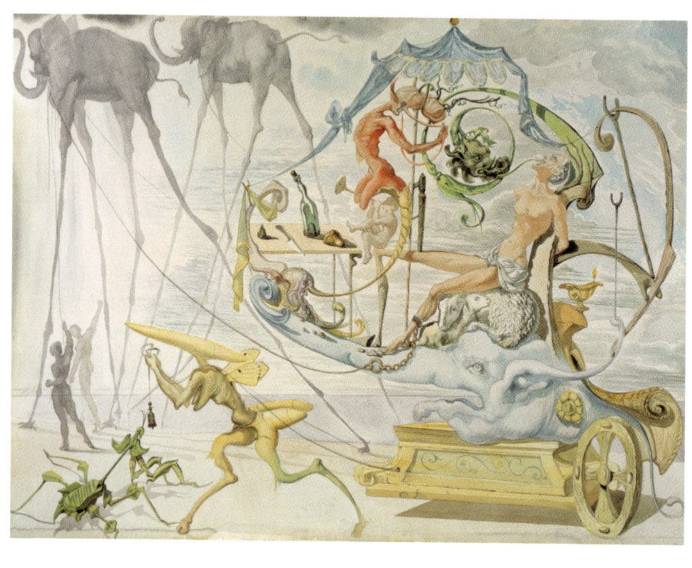

The Grape Pickers: Bacchus' Chariot (The Triumph of Dionysus) · 1953
Gift of Dalí to the Spanish state
> **Corpus Hypercubus (Crucifixion)** · 1954
The Metropolitan Museum of Art, New York, gift of Chester Dale

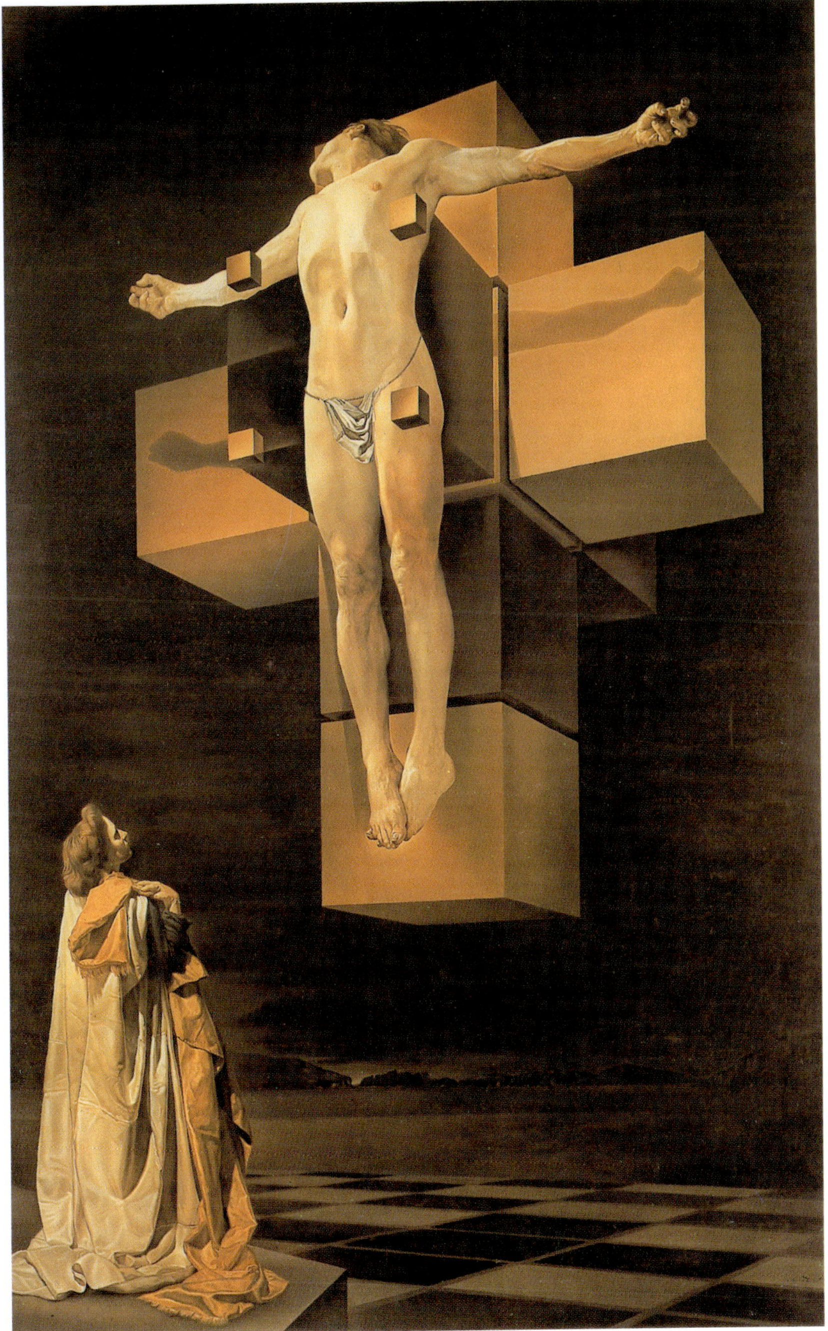

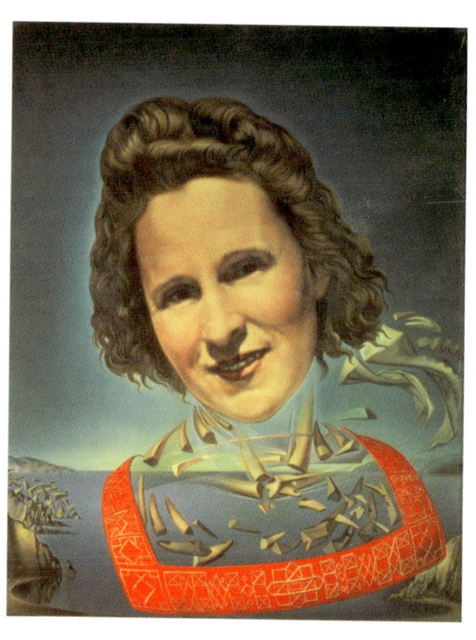

Portrait of Gala with Rhinocerotic Symptoms · 1954
Private collection

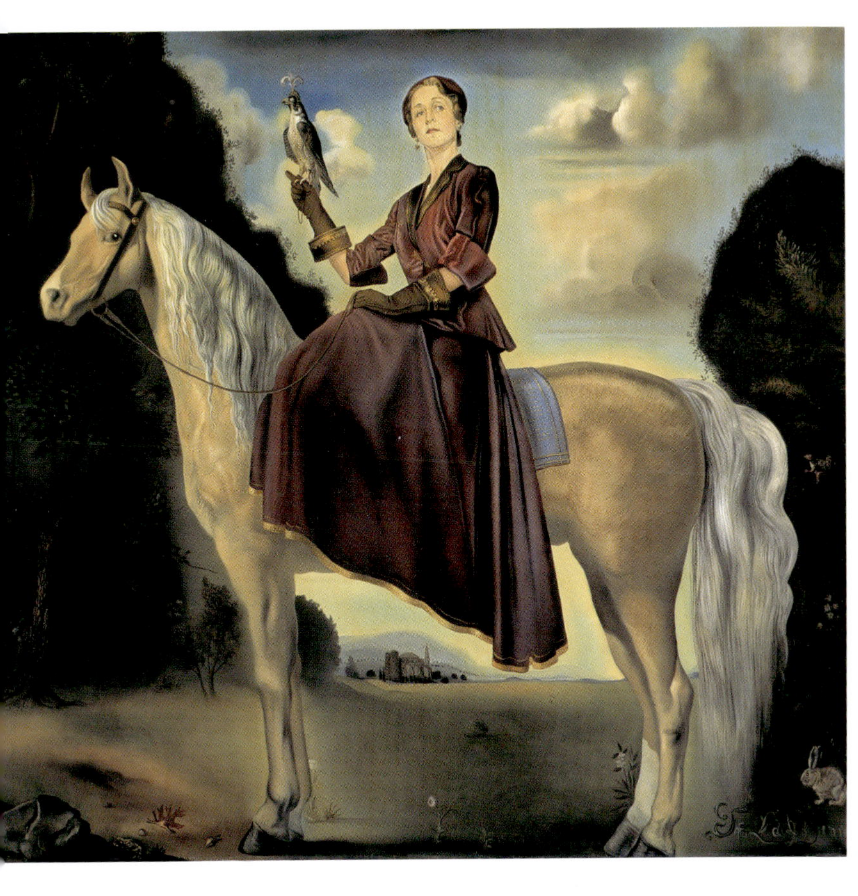

Equestrian Fantasy (Portrait of Lady Dunn-Beaverbrook) · 1954

Beaverbrook Art Gallery, Fredericton, New Brunswick

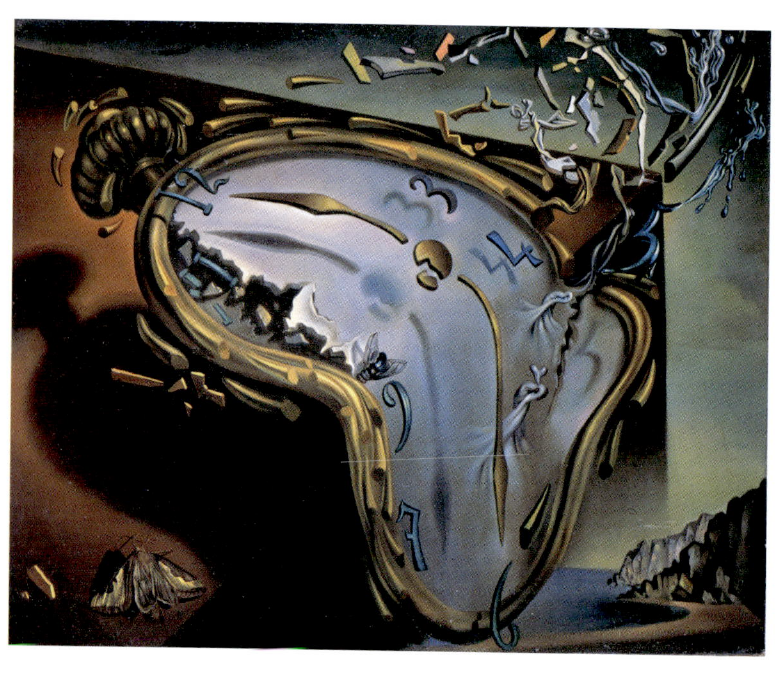

Soft Watch at the Moment of First Explosion · 1954
Private collection

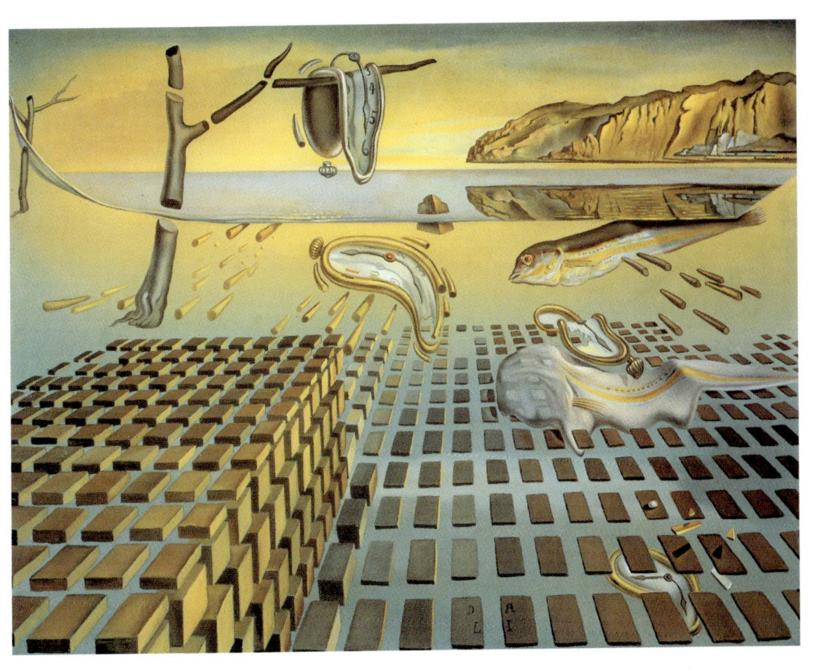

The Disintegration of the Persistence of Memory · 1952–54
The Salvador Dalí Museum, St. Petersburg, Florida,
on loan from E. and A. Reynolds Morse

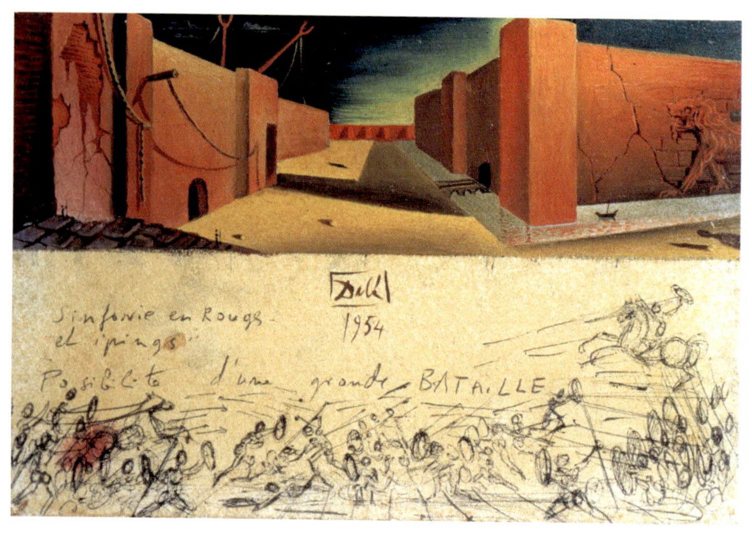

Symphony in Red · 1954
Private collection

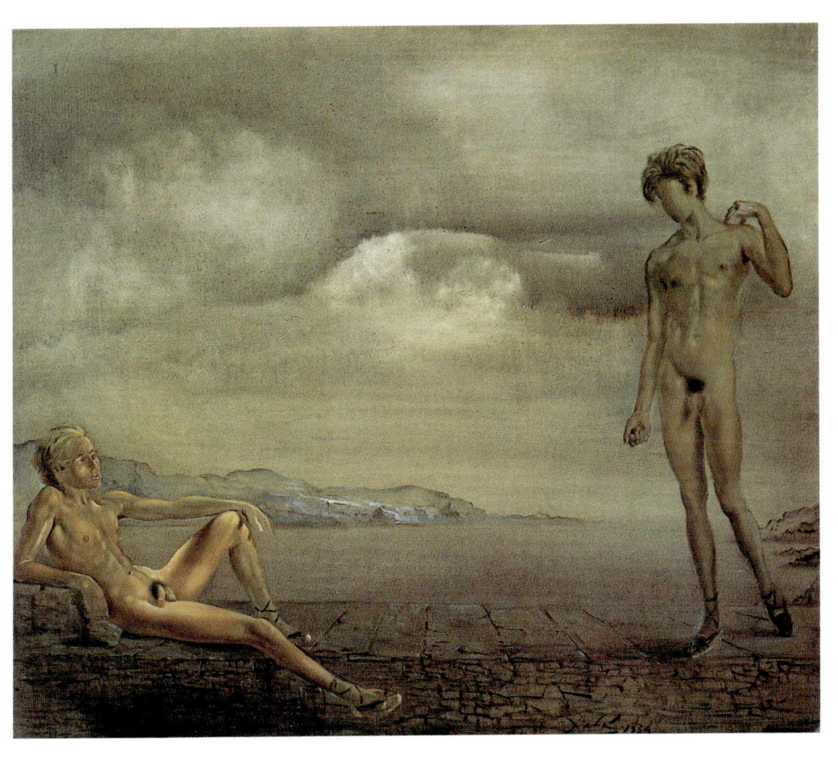

Two Adolescents · 1954
The Salvador Dalí Museum, St. Petersburg, Florida,
on loan from E. and A. Reynolds Morse

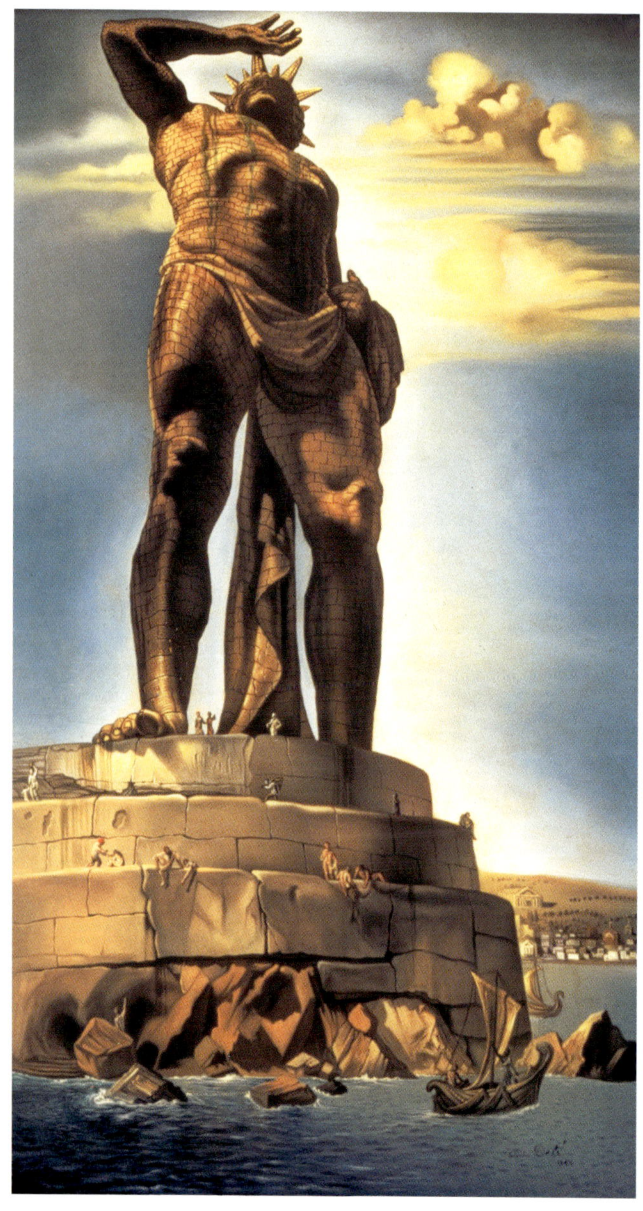

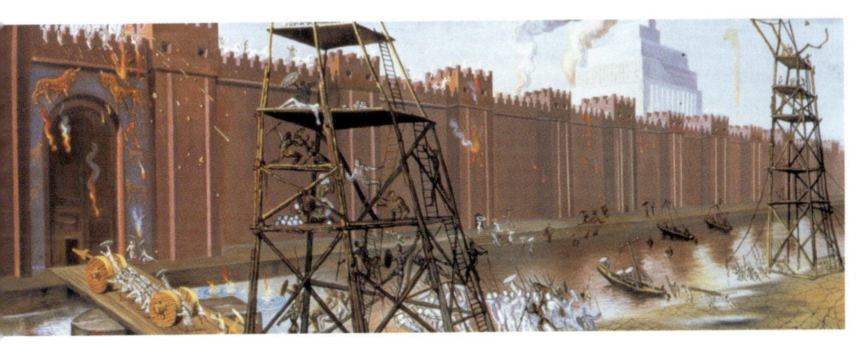

The Walls of Babylon · 1954
Private collection
< **The Colossus of Rhodes** · 1954
Kunstmuseum Bern

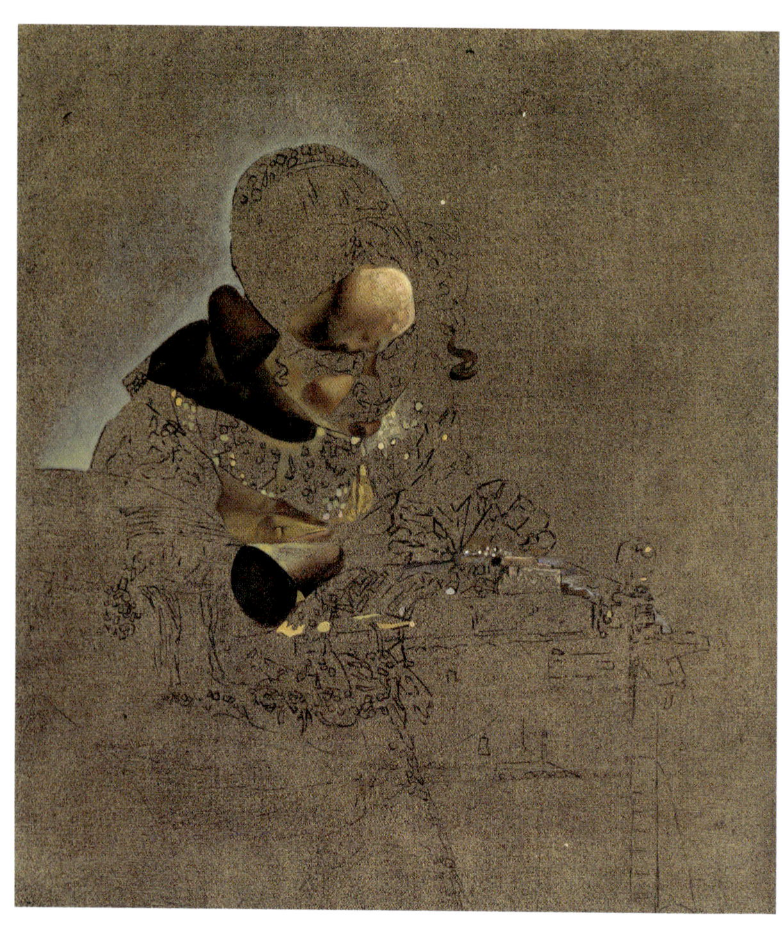

Study for Rhinocerotic Portrait of The Lacemaker of Vermeer · 1955
Gift of Dalí to the Spanish state

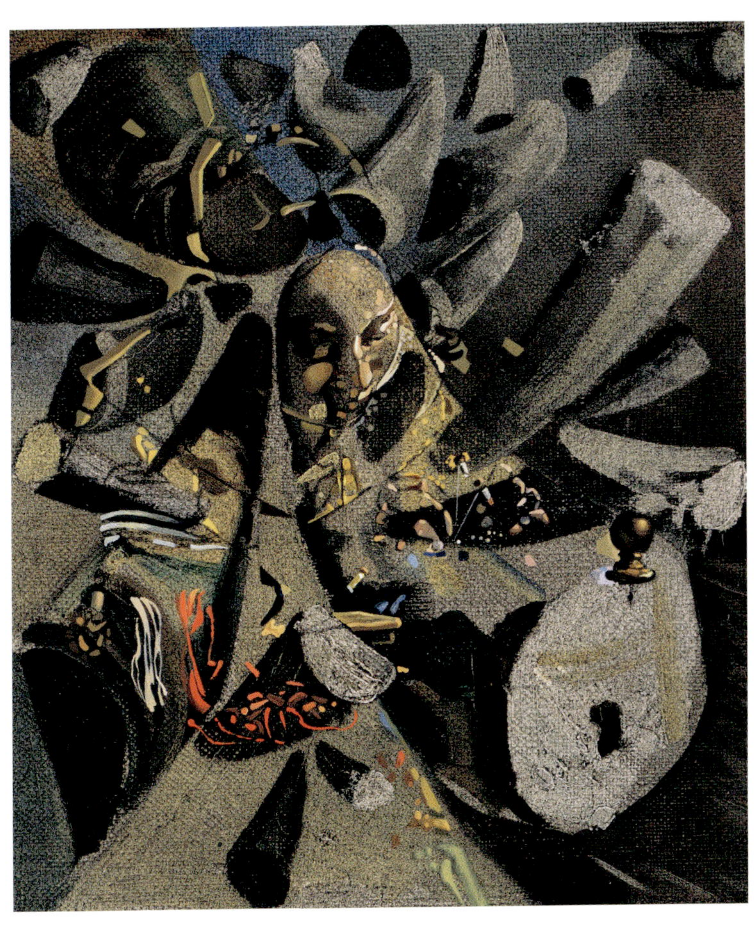

Paranoiac-Critical Painting of Vermeer's "Lacemaker" · 1955

The Solomon R. Guggenheim Museum, New York, Anonymous gift

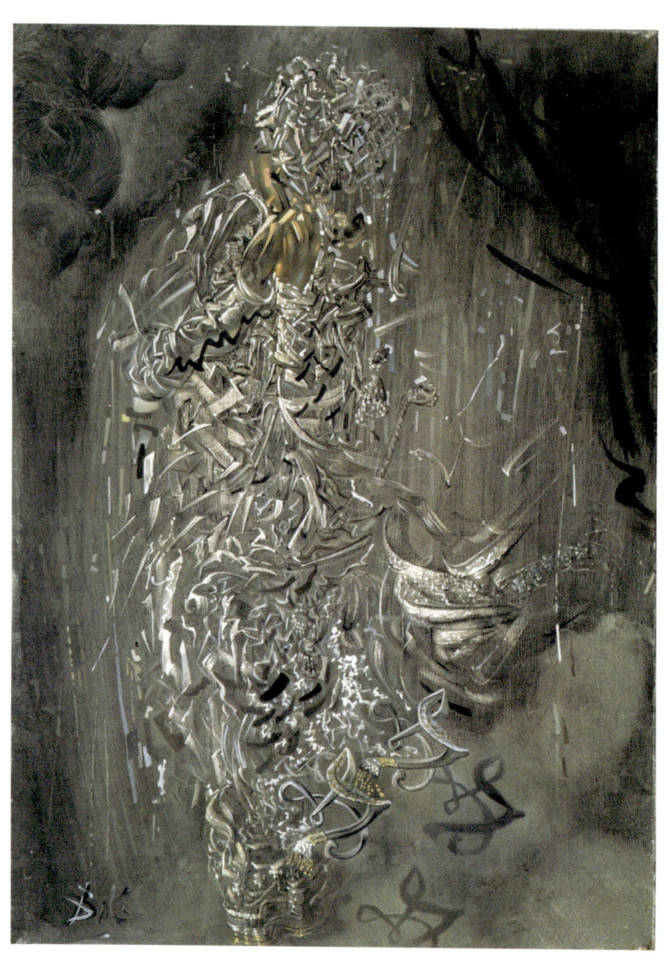

Saint Surrounded by Three Pi-Mesons · 1956
Fundación Gala-Salvador Dalí, Figueras

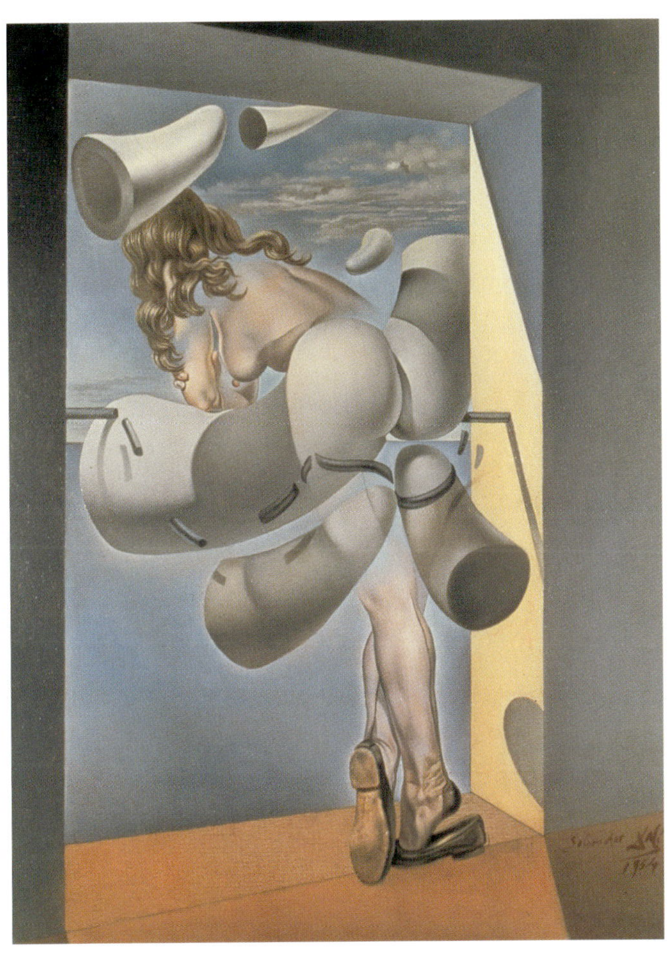

Young Virgin Auto-Sodomized by Her Own Chastity · 1954
Playboy Collection, Los Angeles

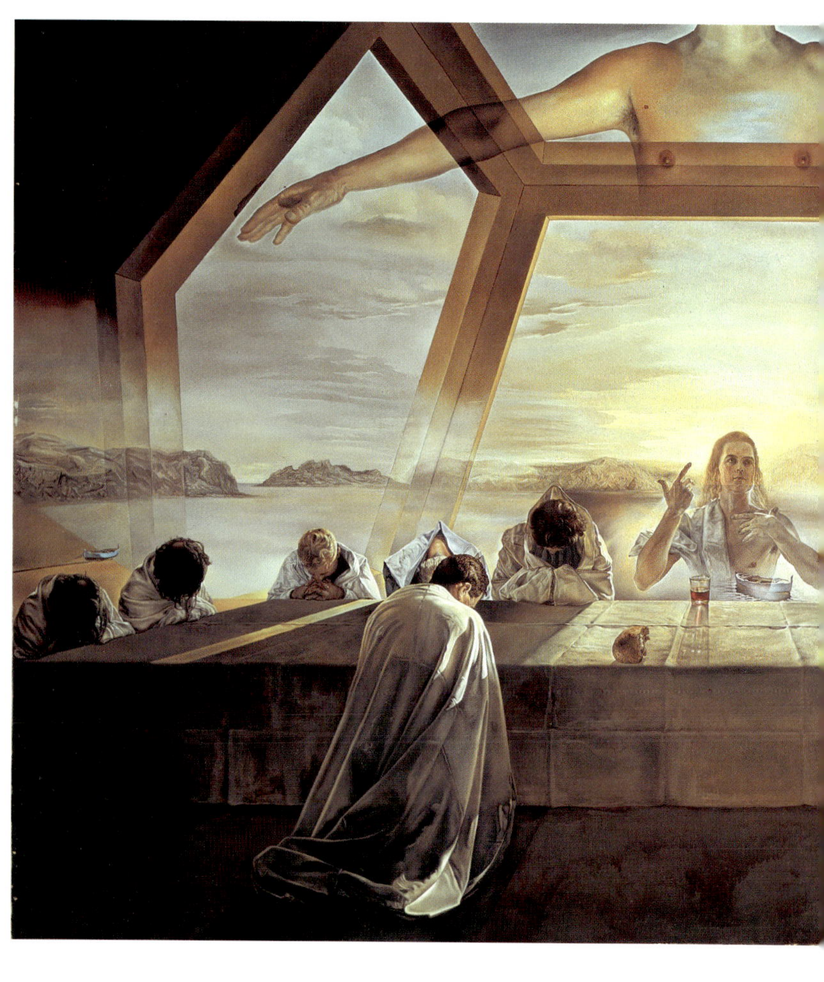

The Last Supper · 1955

National Gallery of Art, Washington, D.C., Chester Dale Collection

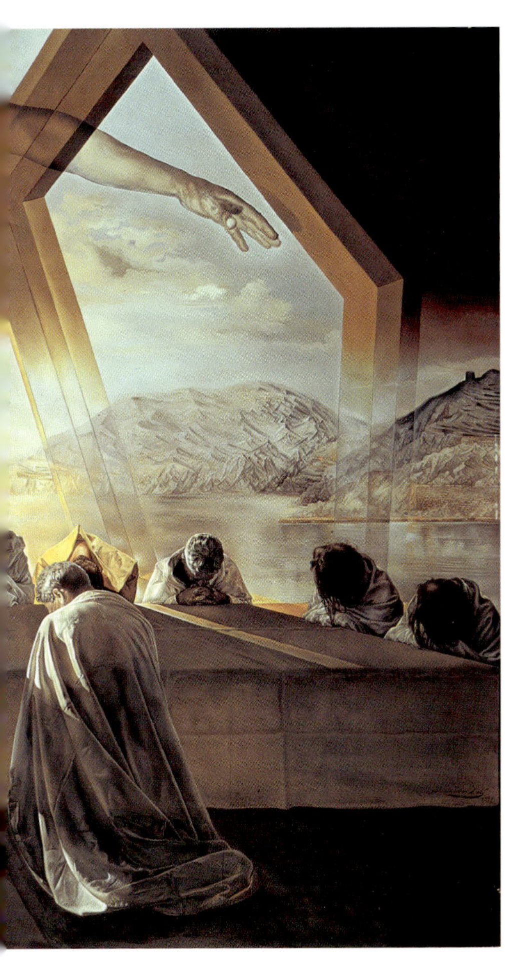

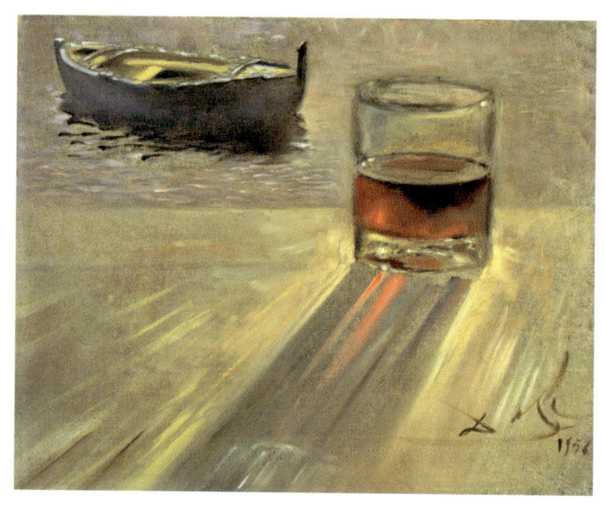

Wine Glass and Boat · 1956
Private collection; formerly New York, Carstairs Gallery

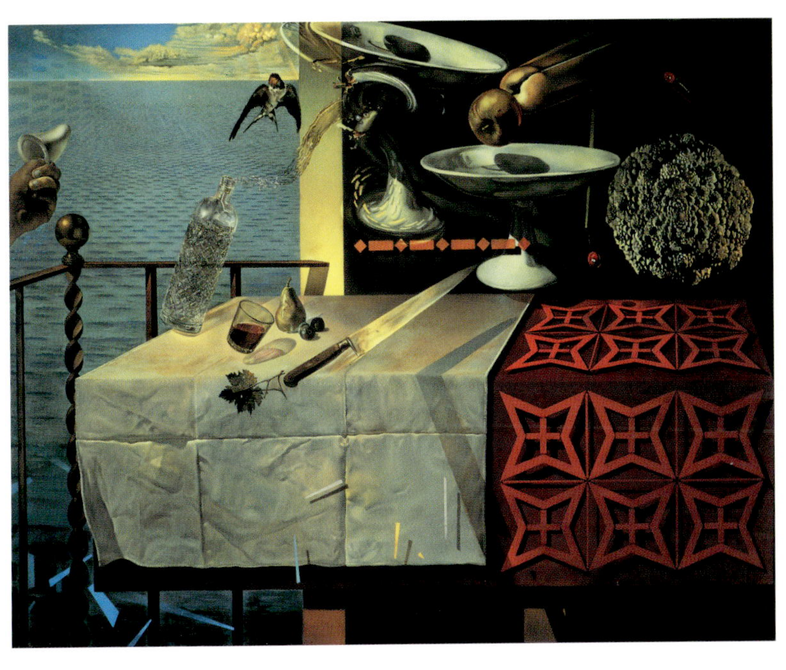

Still Life—Fast Moving · 1956
The Salvador Dalí Museum, St. Petersburg, Florida,
on loan from E. and A. Reynolds Morse

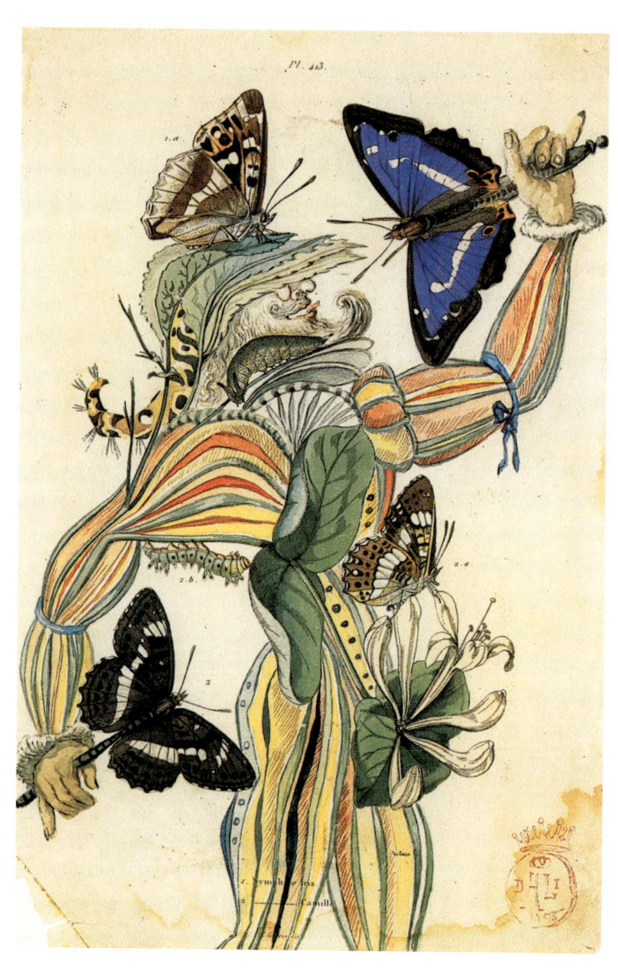

Illustration for "Trois papillons" · 1955
The Salvador Dalí Museum, St. Petersburg, Florida,
on loan from E. and A. Reynolds Morse

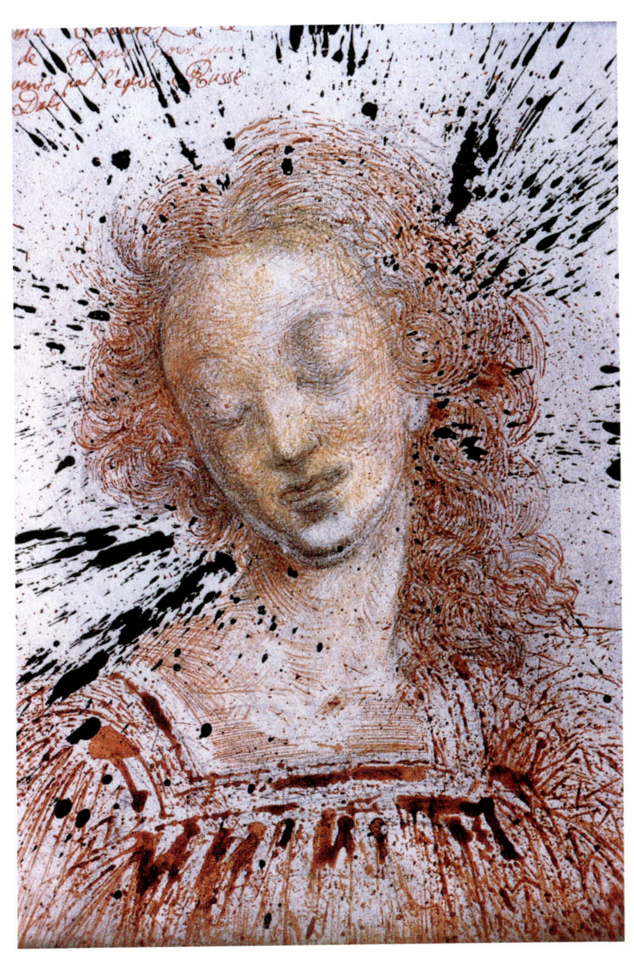

St. John · 1957
Private collection

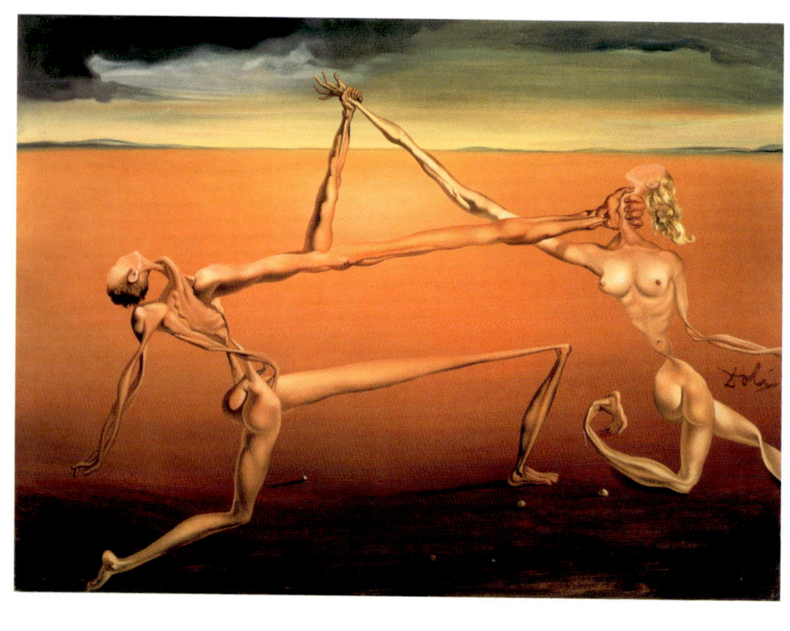

Dance—The Seven Arts · 1957

Private collection; formerly Billy Rose Collection

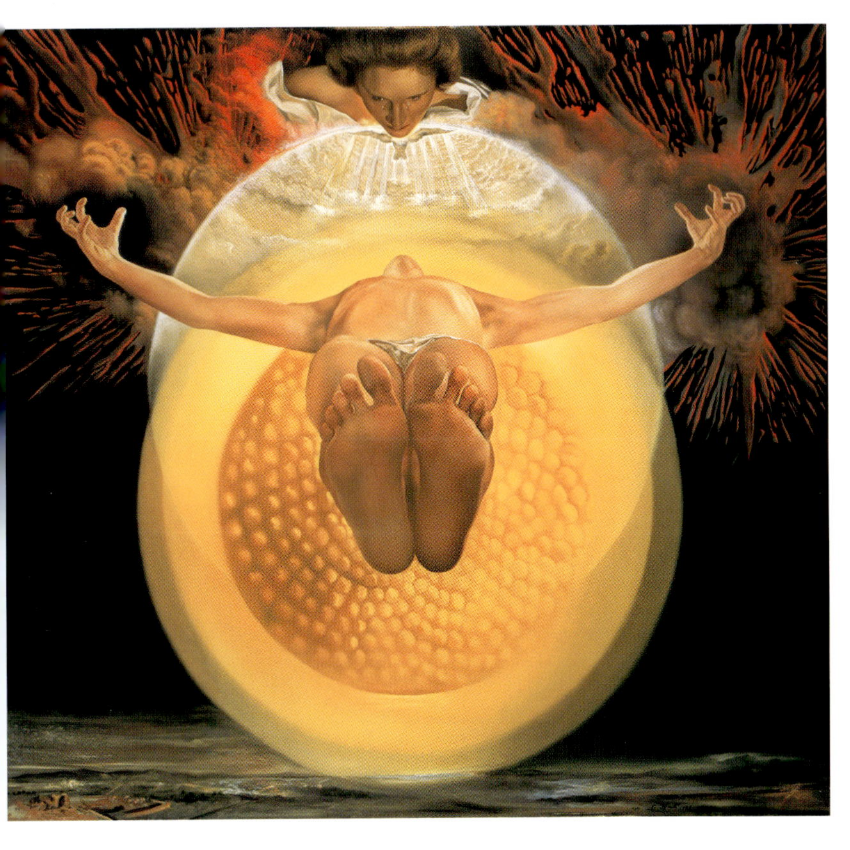

Ascension · 1958

Private collection

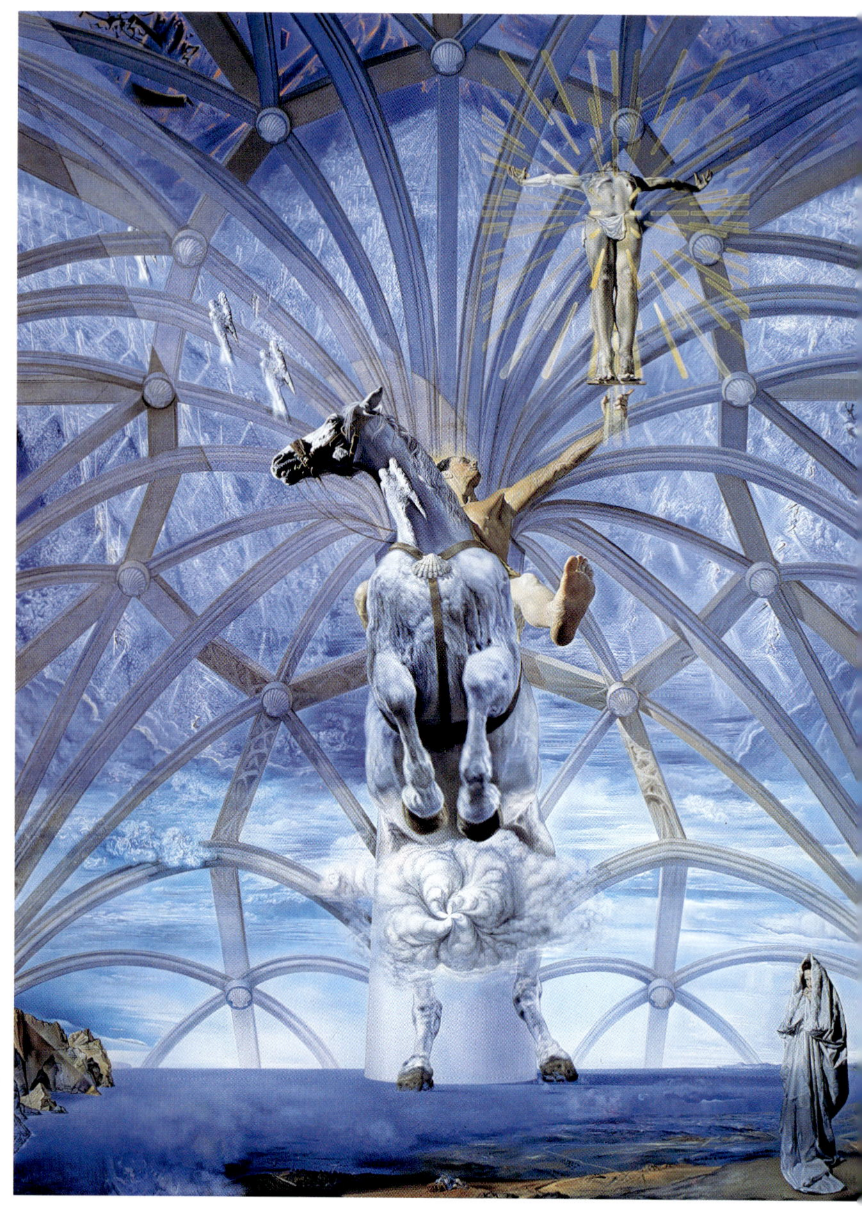

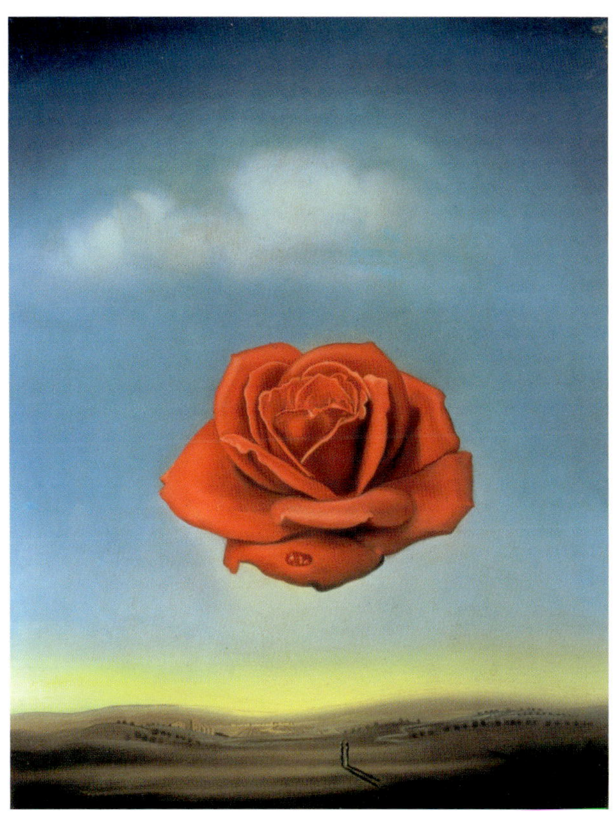

Meditative Rose · 1958
Private collection; formerly New York, Arnold Grand Collection
‹ **St. James of Compostela** · 1957
Beaverbrook Art Gallery, Fredericton, New Brunswick

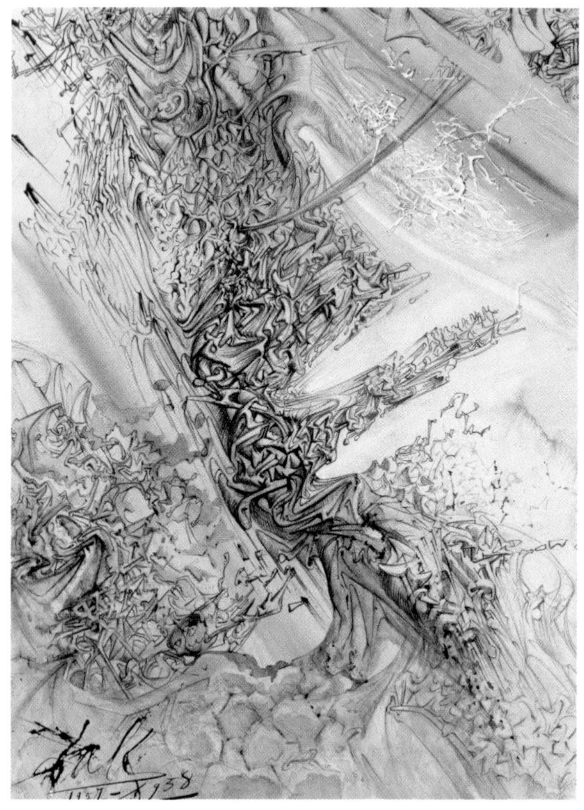

Pi-Mesonic Angel · 1958
The Salvador Dalí Museum, St. Petersburg, Florida,
on loan from E. and A. Reynolds Morse
> **Velázquez Painting the Infanta Margarita
with the Lights and Shadows of His Own Glory** · 1958
The Salvador Dalí Museum, St. Petersburg, Florida,
on loan from E. and A. Reynolds Morse

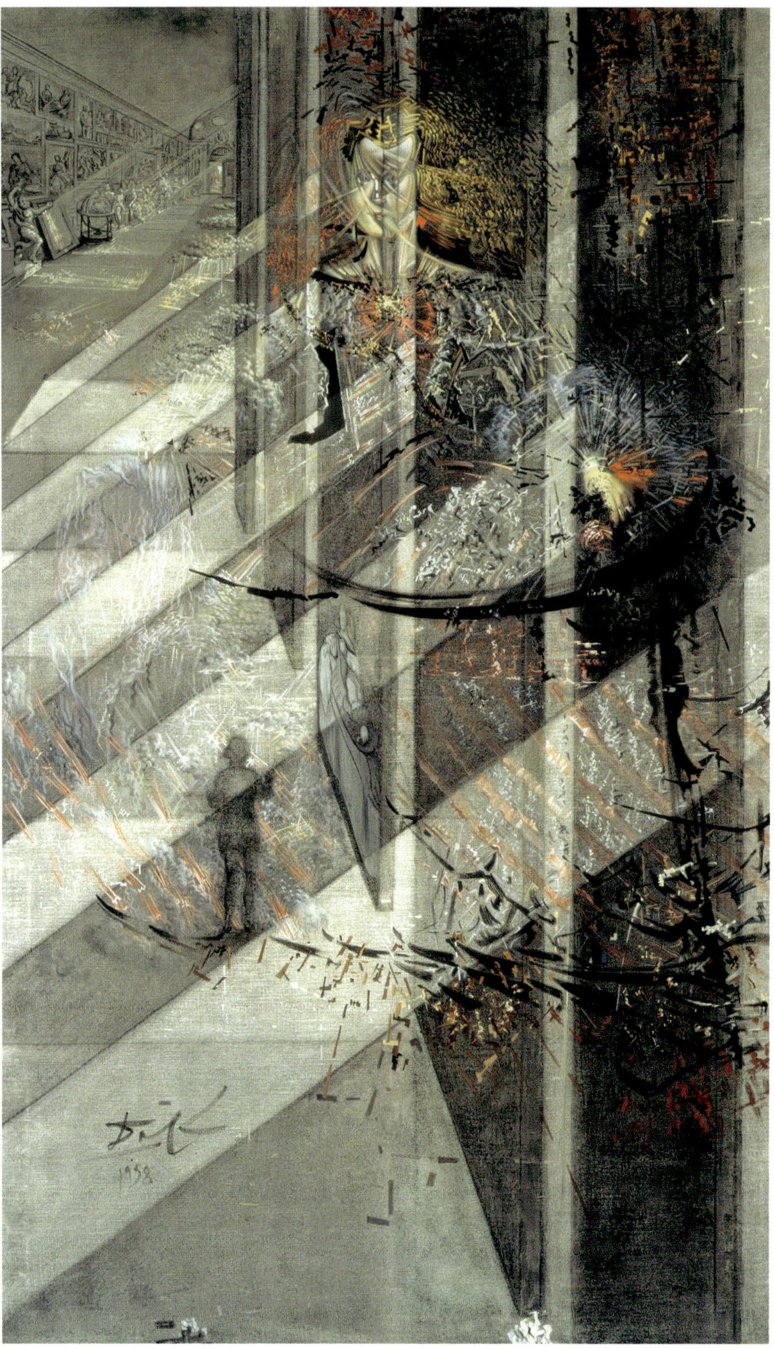

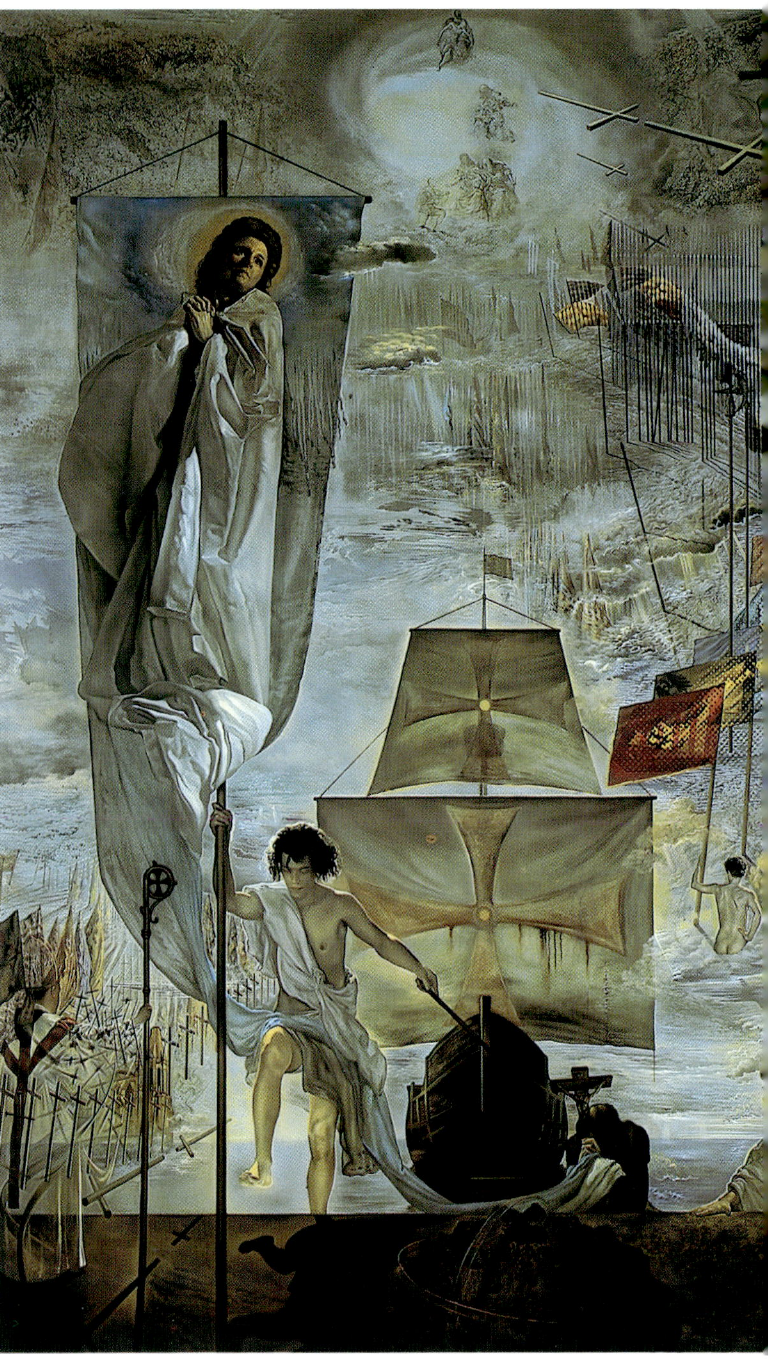

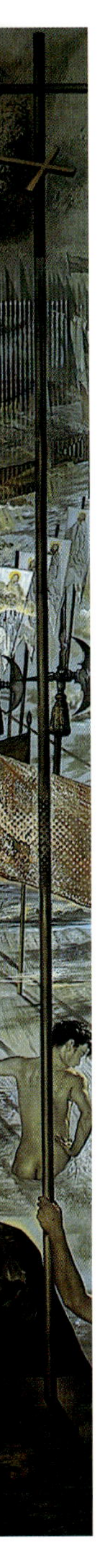

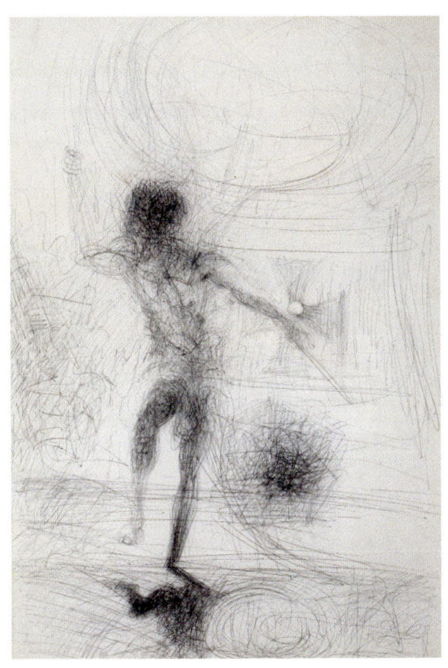

Study for
"The Discovery of America by Christopher Columbus" · 1958
Gift of Dalí to the Spanish state
< **The Discovery of America by Christopher Columbus**
(The Dream of Christopher Columbus) · 1958–59
The Salvador Dalí Museum, St. Petersburg, Florida,
on loan from the Morse Charitable Trust

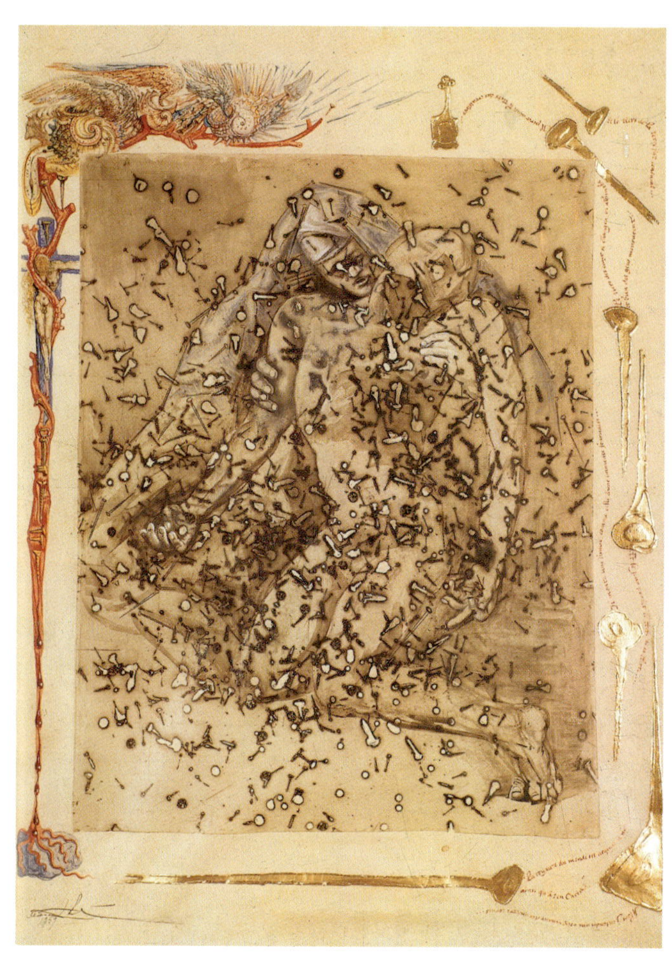

Pietà from "The Apocalypse of St. John" · 1959
Private collection

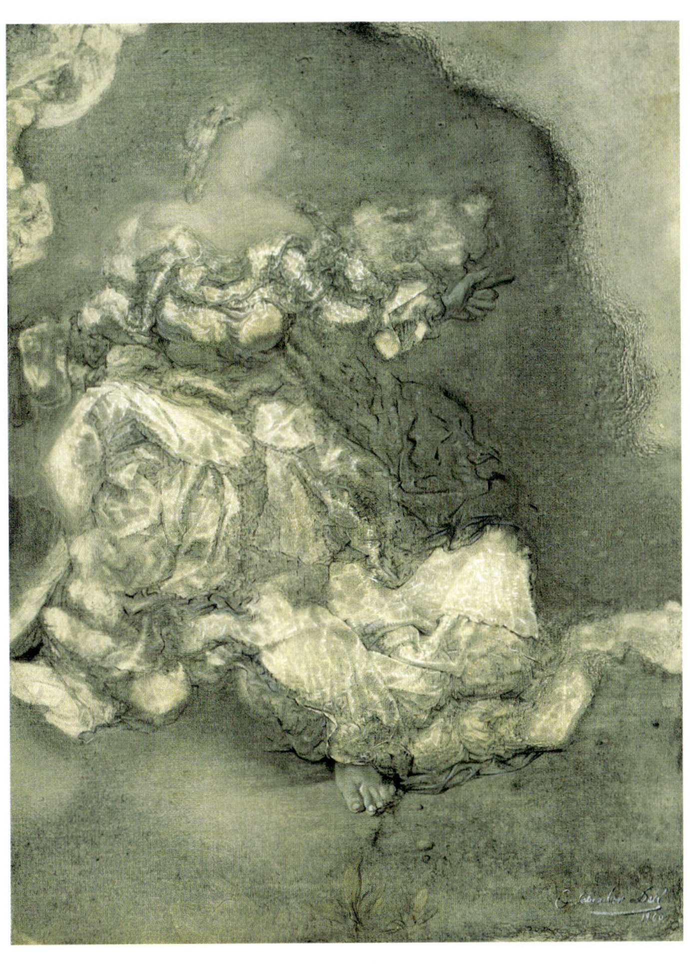

Beatrice · 1960
The Salvador Dalí Museum, St. Petersburg, Florida,
on loan from E. and A. Reynolds Morse

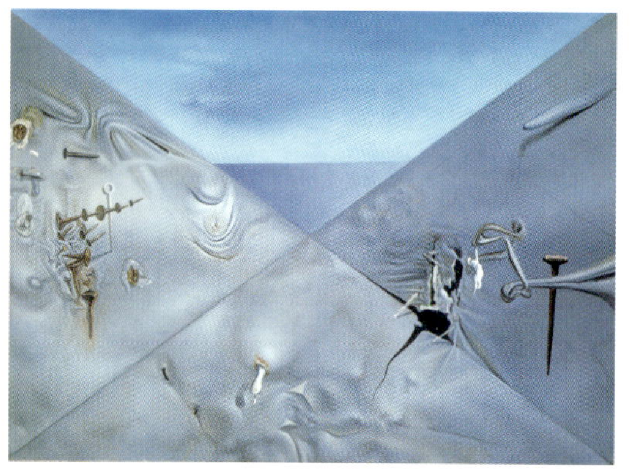
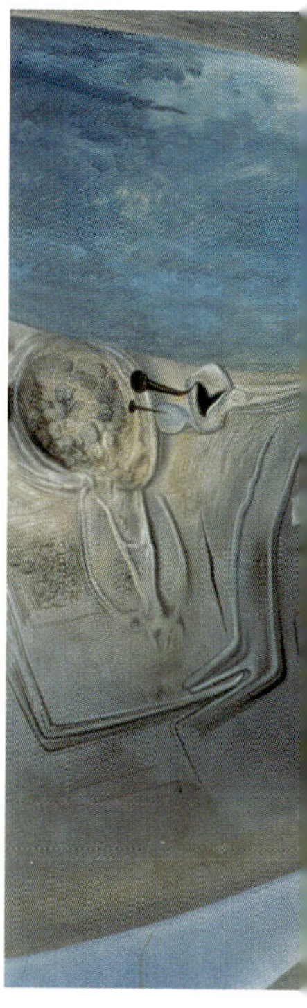

Hyperxiological Sky · 1960
Private collection

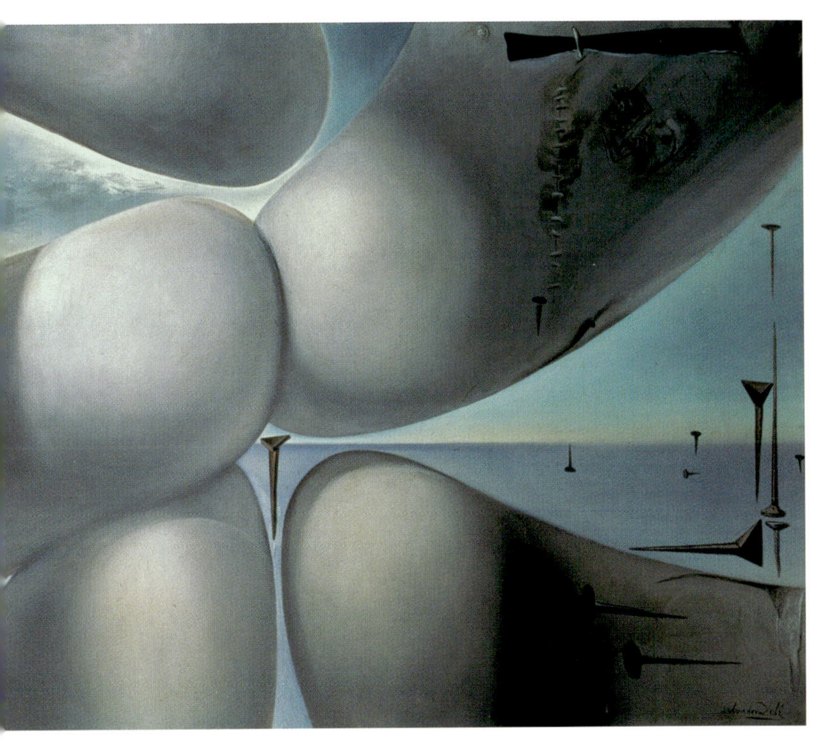

Continuum of the Four Buttocks · 1960

Generalitat de Catalunya, Departament de Cultura, Barcelona, gift of the artist, 1980

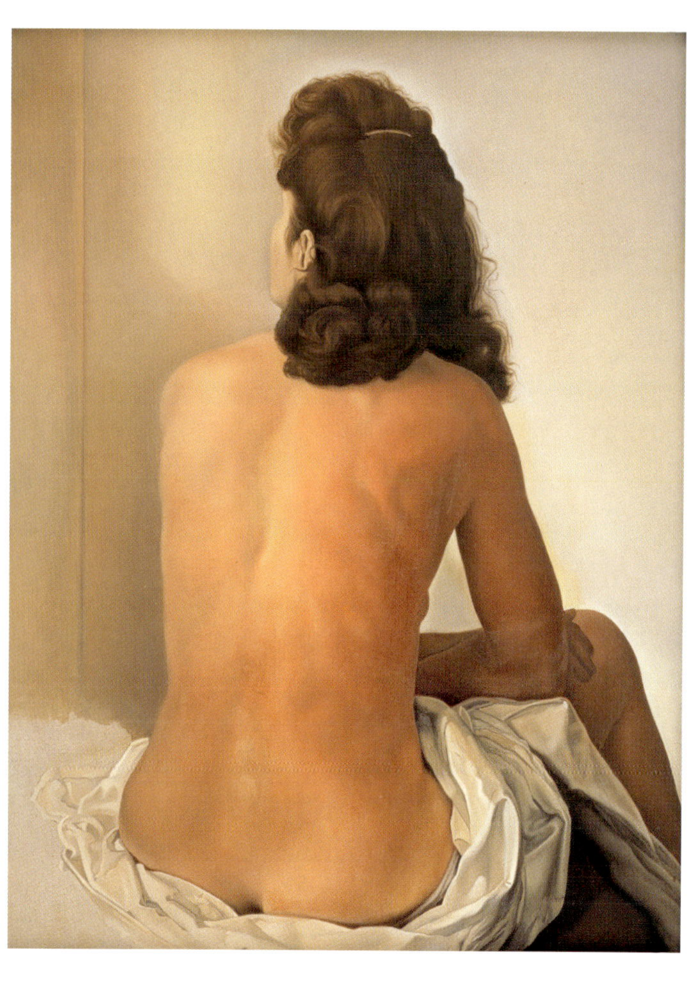

Gala Nude Seen from behind Watching an Invisible Mirror · 1960
Fundación Gala-Salvador Dalí, Figueras

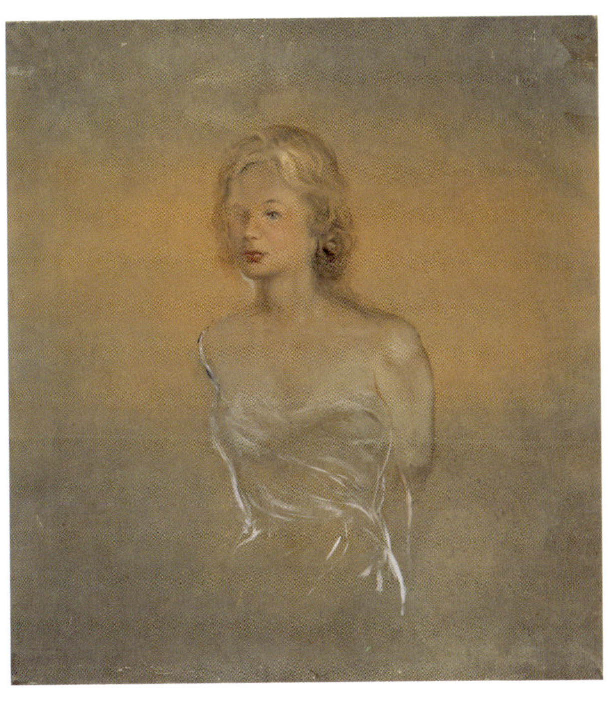

Portrait of "Bobo" Rockefeller (unfinished) · 1960

Fundación Gala-Salvador Dalí, Figueras, gift of Dalí to the Spanish state

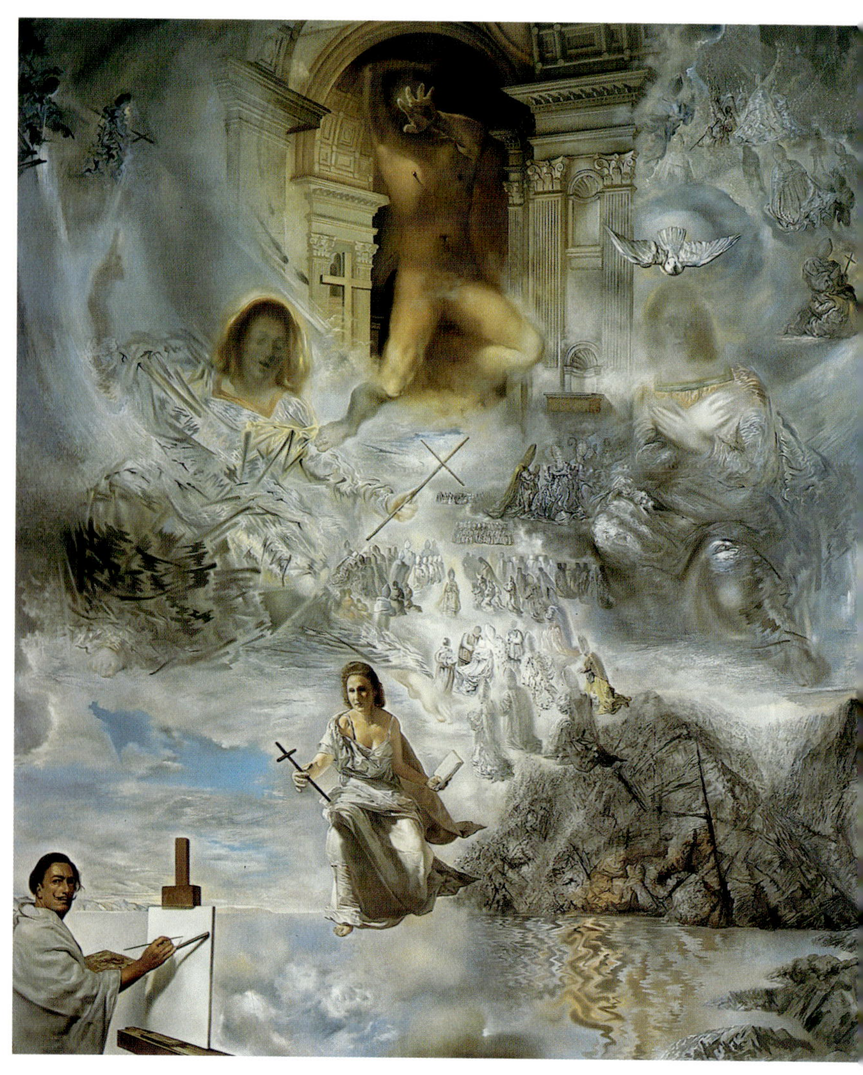

The Ecumenical Council · 1960
The Salvador Dalí Museum, St. Petersburg, Florida,
on loan from the Morse Charitable Trust

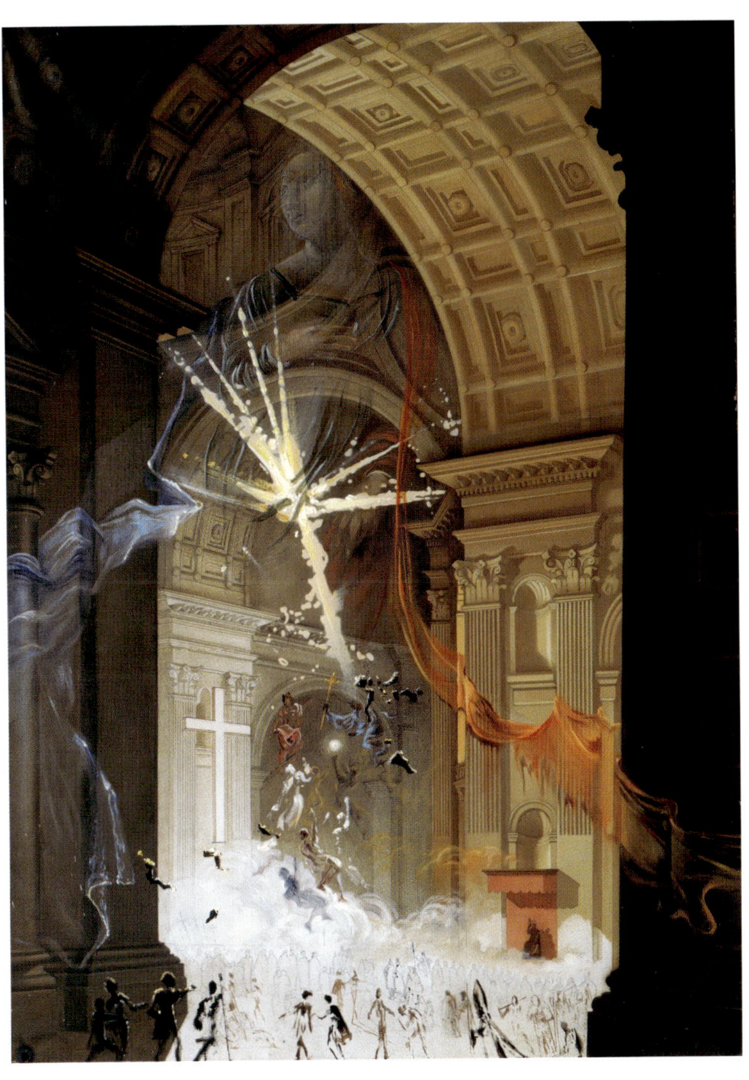

**St. Peter's in Rome (Explosion of Mystical Faith
in the Midst of a Cathedral)** · 1960–74
Fundación Gala-Salvador Dalí, Figueras

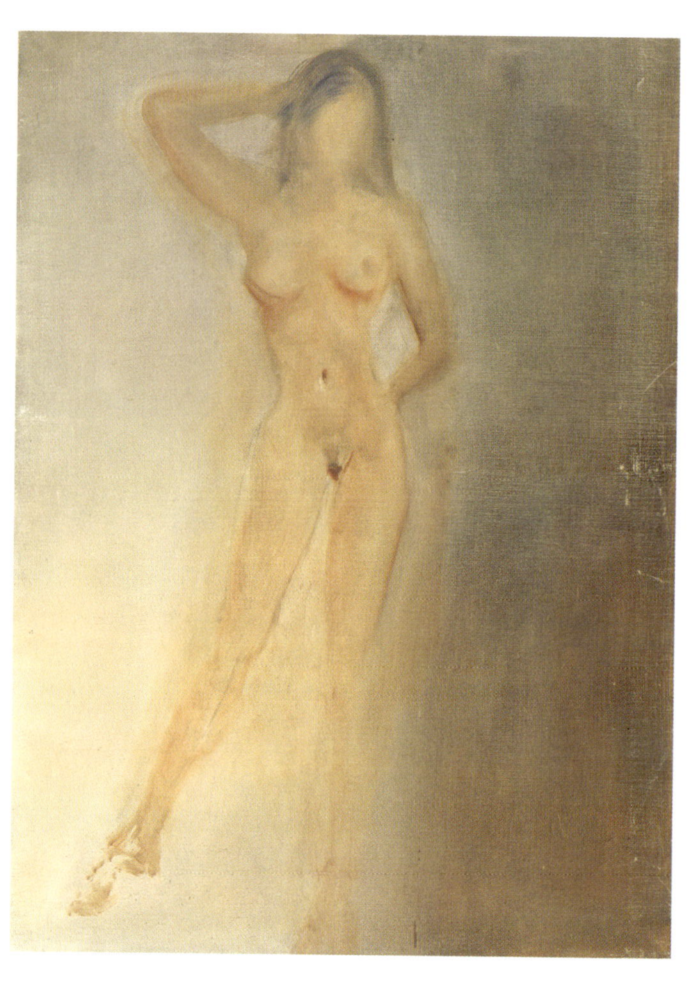

Study of a Female Nude · c. 1962

Fundación Gala-Salvador Dalí, Figueras, gift of Dalí to the Spanish state

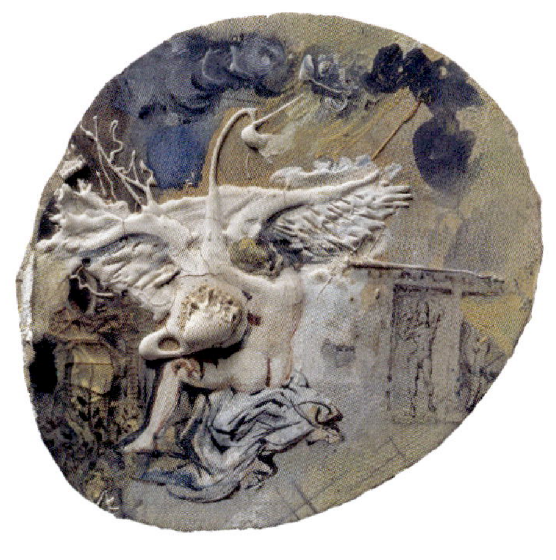

Leda and the Swan · 1961
Fundación Gala-Salvador Dalí, Figueras, gift of Dalí to the Spanish state

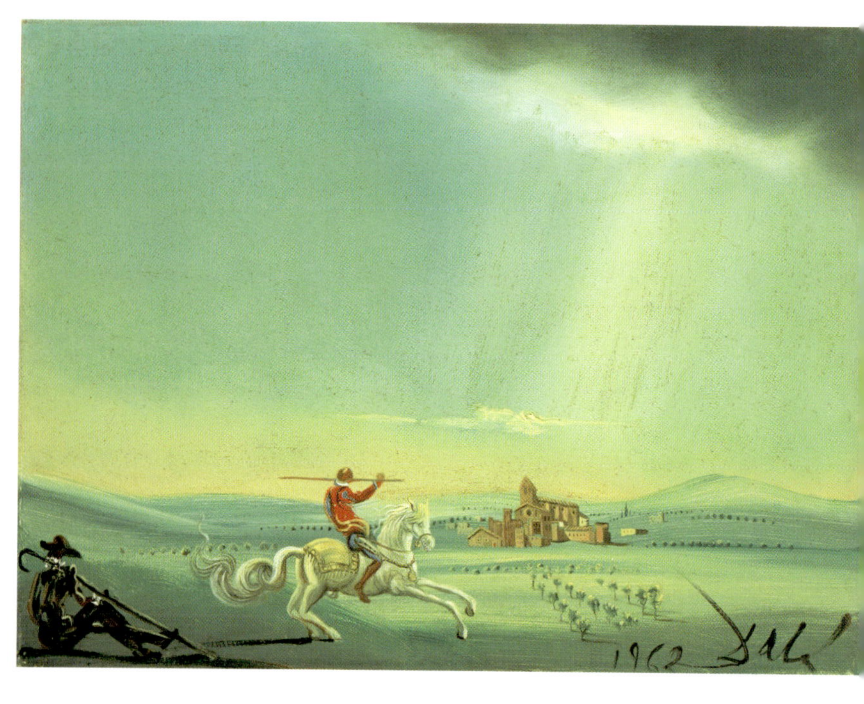

St. George and the Dragon · 1962
Private collection

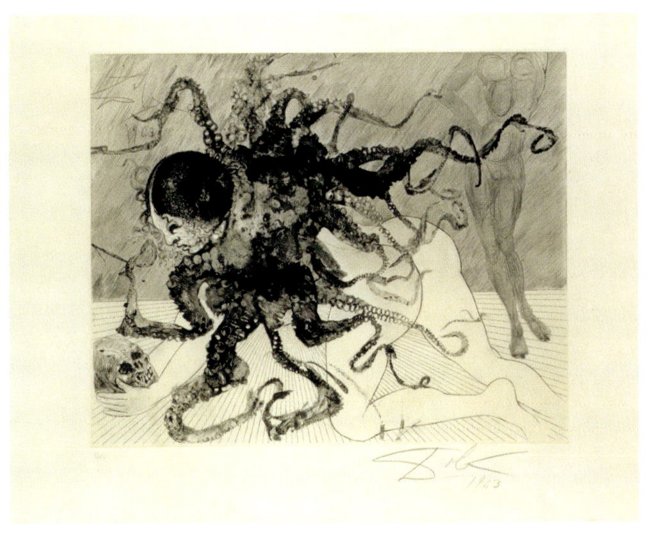

Medusa · 1963
Phillips, The International Fine Art Auctioneers

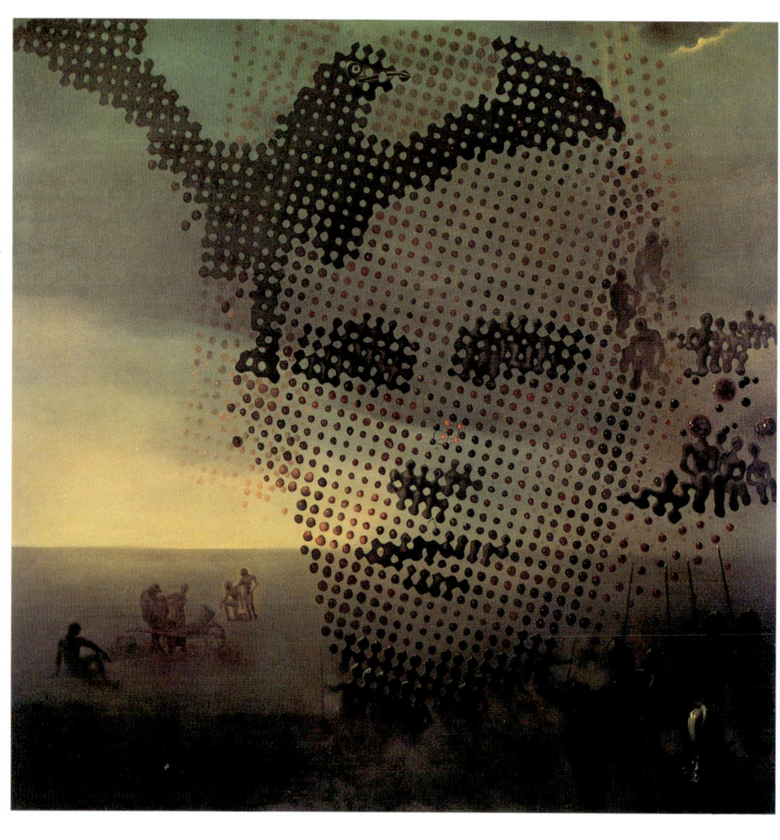

Portrait of My Dead Brother · 1963
Private collection, Switzerland
> **Homage to John F. Kennedy** · 1963
Phillips, The International Fine Art Auctioneers

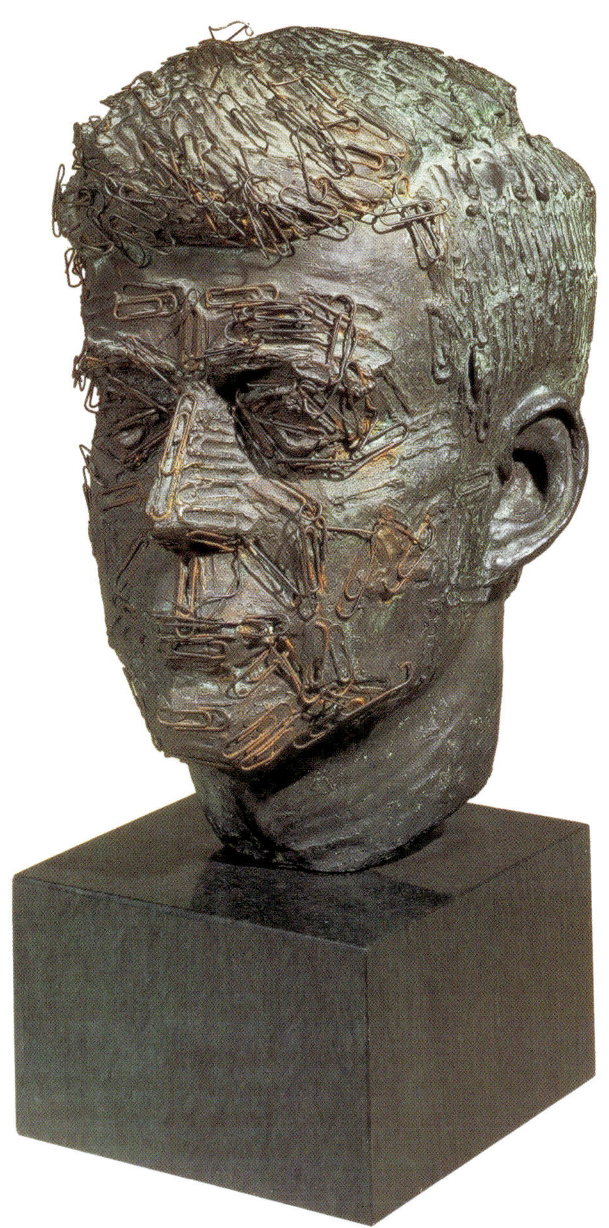

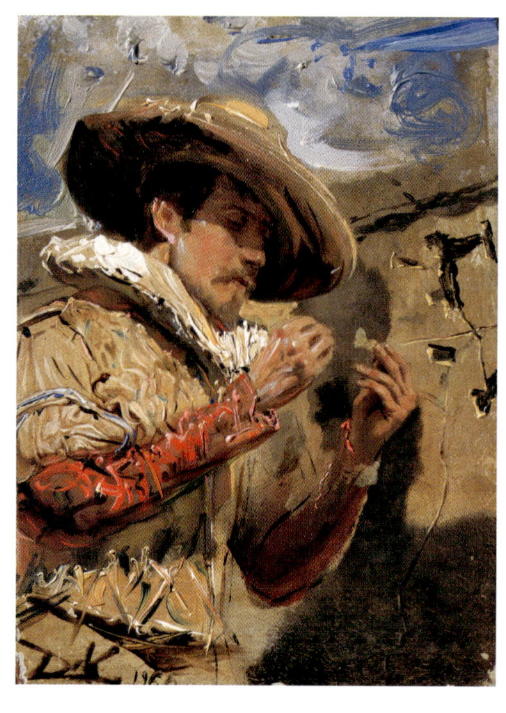

Disguised Personage Pinning a Butterfly · 1965
Fundación Gala-Salvador Dalí, Figueras, gift of Dalí to the Spanish state

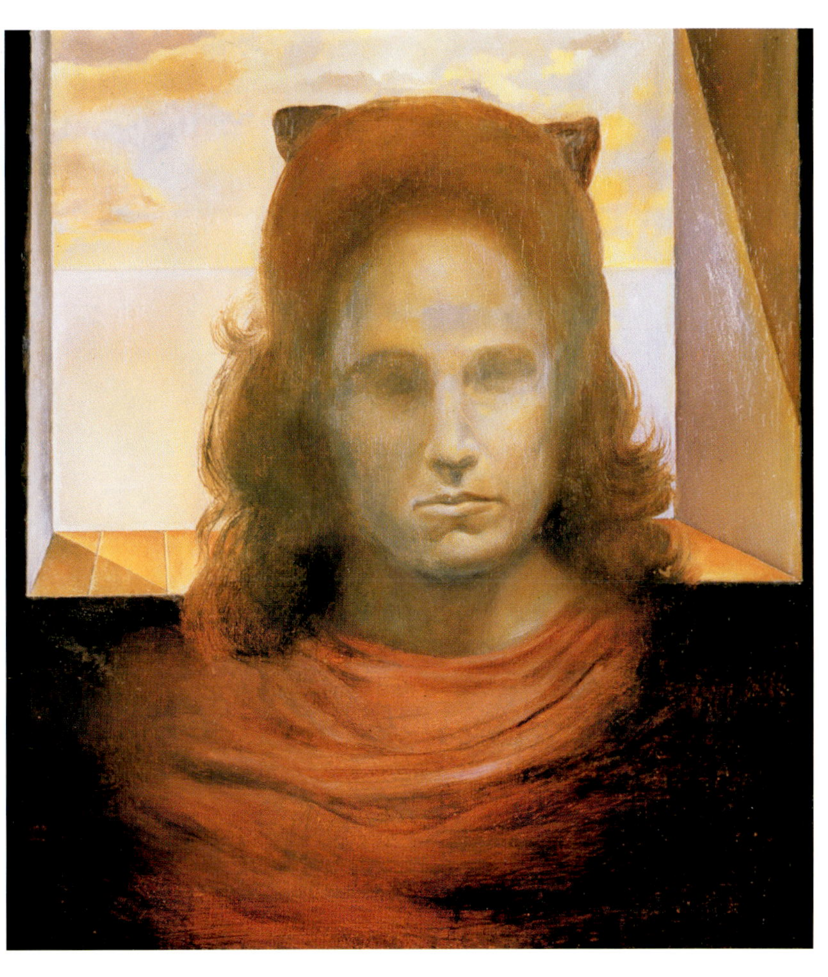

Portrait of Gala (Gala against the Light) · 1965
Museo Nacional Centro de Arte Reina Sofía, Madrid, gift of Dalí to the Spanish state

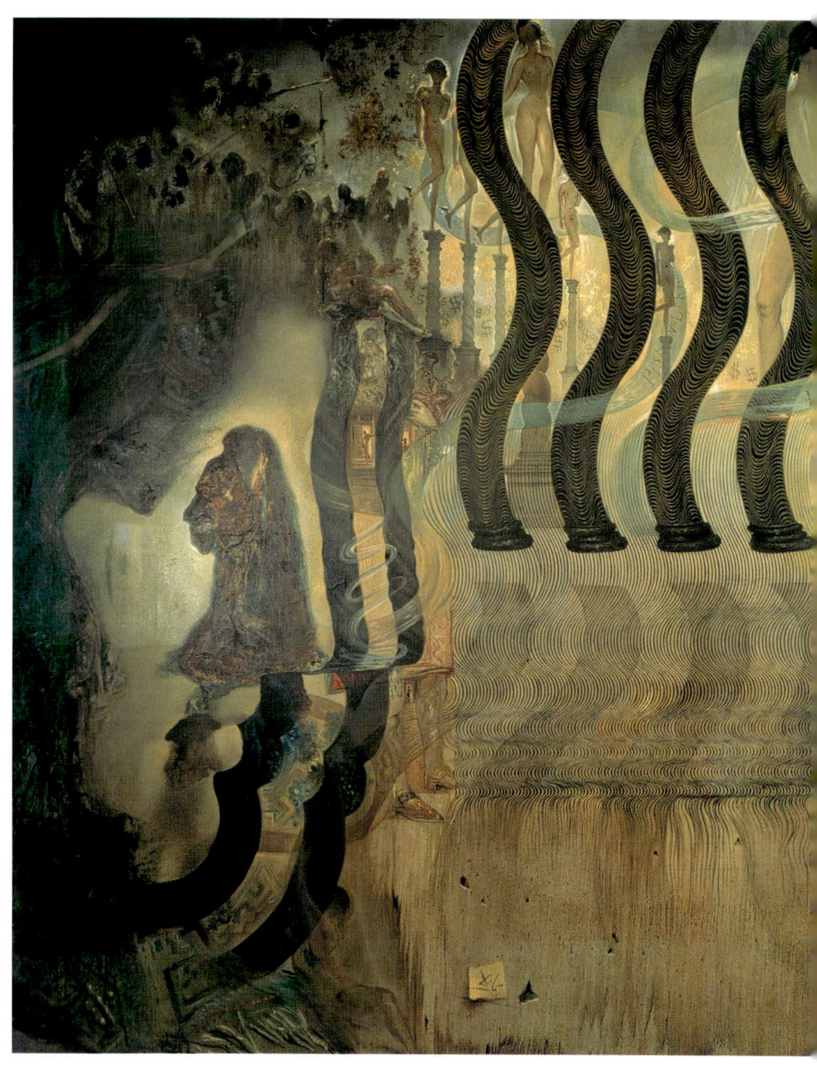

The Apotheosis of the Dollar
(Salvador Dalí in the Act of Painting Gala in the Apotheosis of the Dollar . . .) · 1965
Fundación Gala-Salvador Dalí, Figueras;
formerly Museo Perrot-Moore, Cadaqués

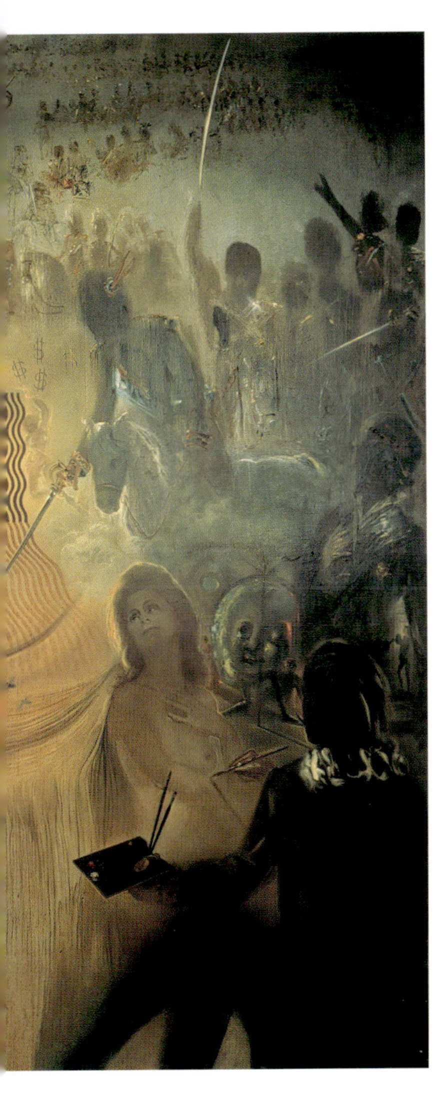

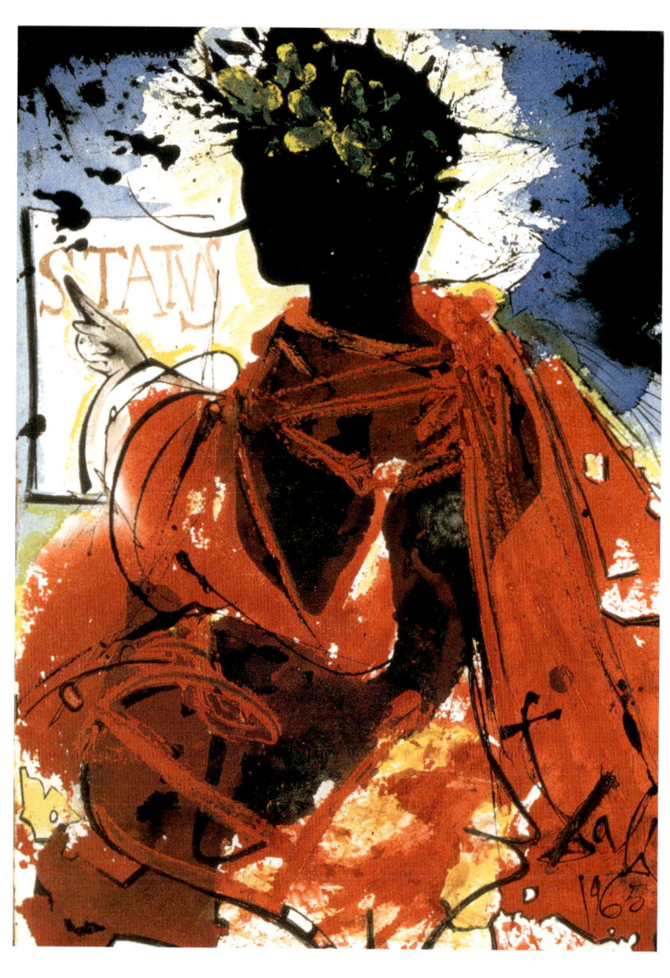

Status, Roman Emperor · 1965
Christie's, New York

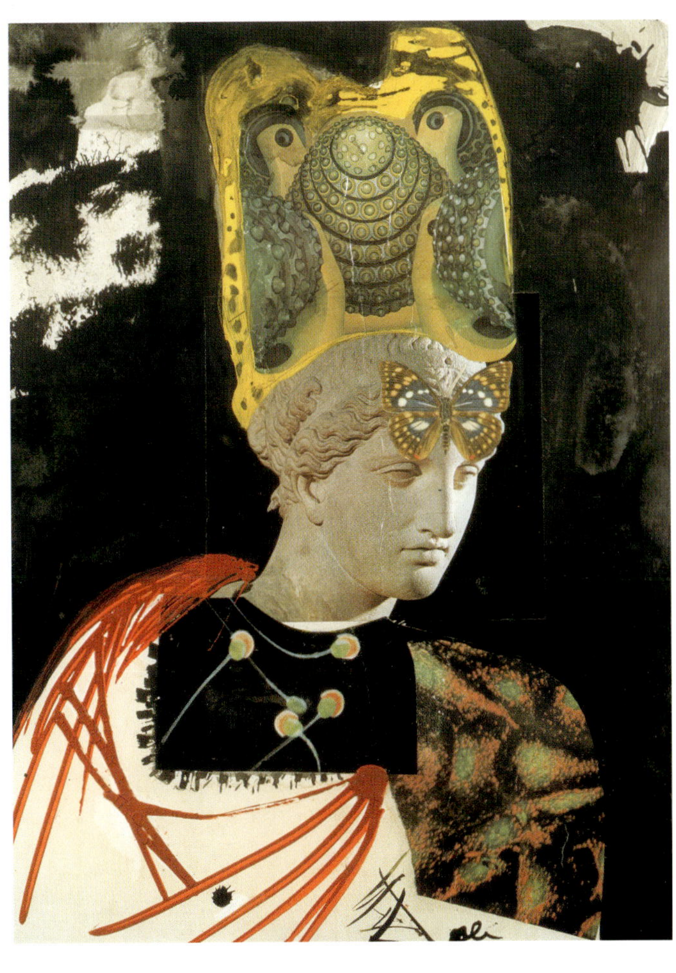

Mad Mad Mad Minerva. Illustration for "Memories of Surrealism" · c. 1968
Galerie Kalb, Vienna

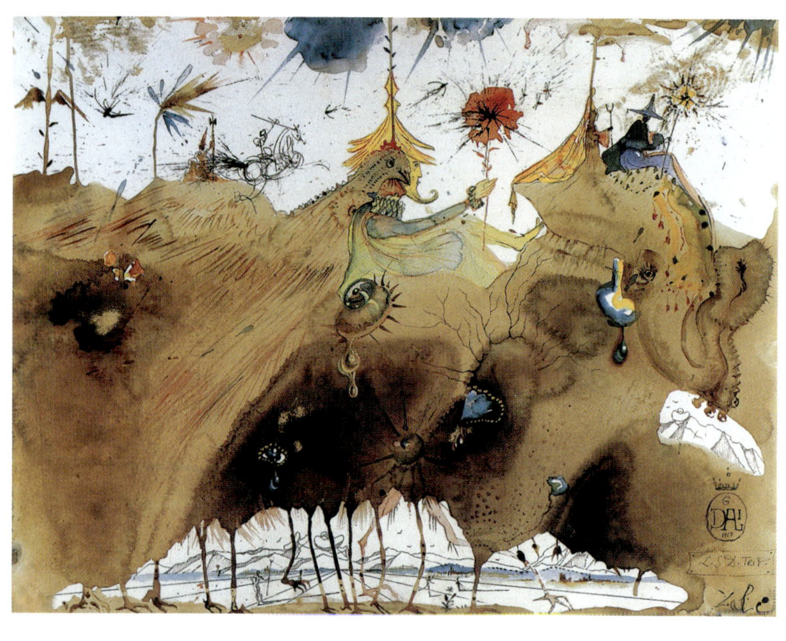

The Mountains of Cape Creus on the March (LSD Trip) · 1967

Fondation Paul Ricard, Ile de Bendor

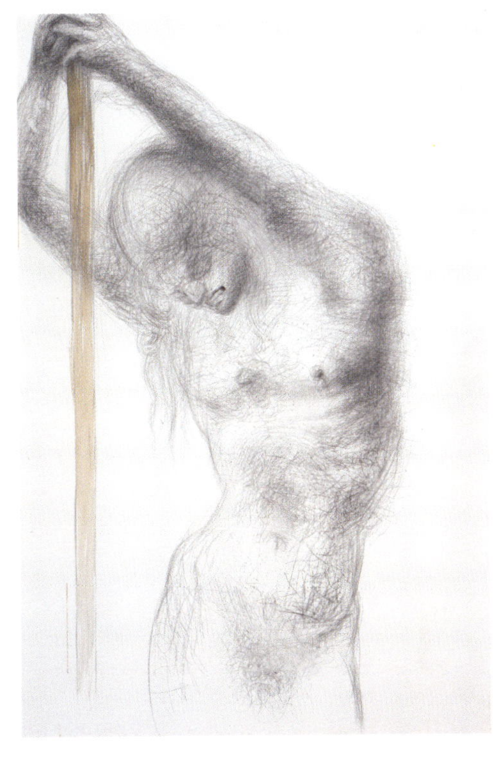

Large Figure for "Tuna Fishing" · c. 1966–67
Gift of Dalí to the Spanish state
> **Tuna Fishing** · c. 1966–67
Fondation Paul Ricard, Ile de Bendor

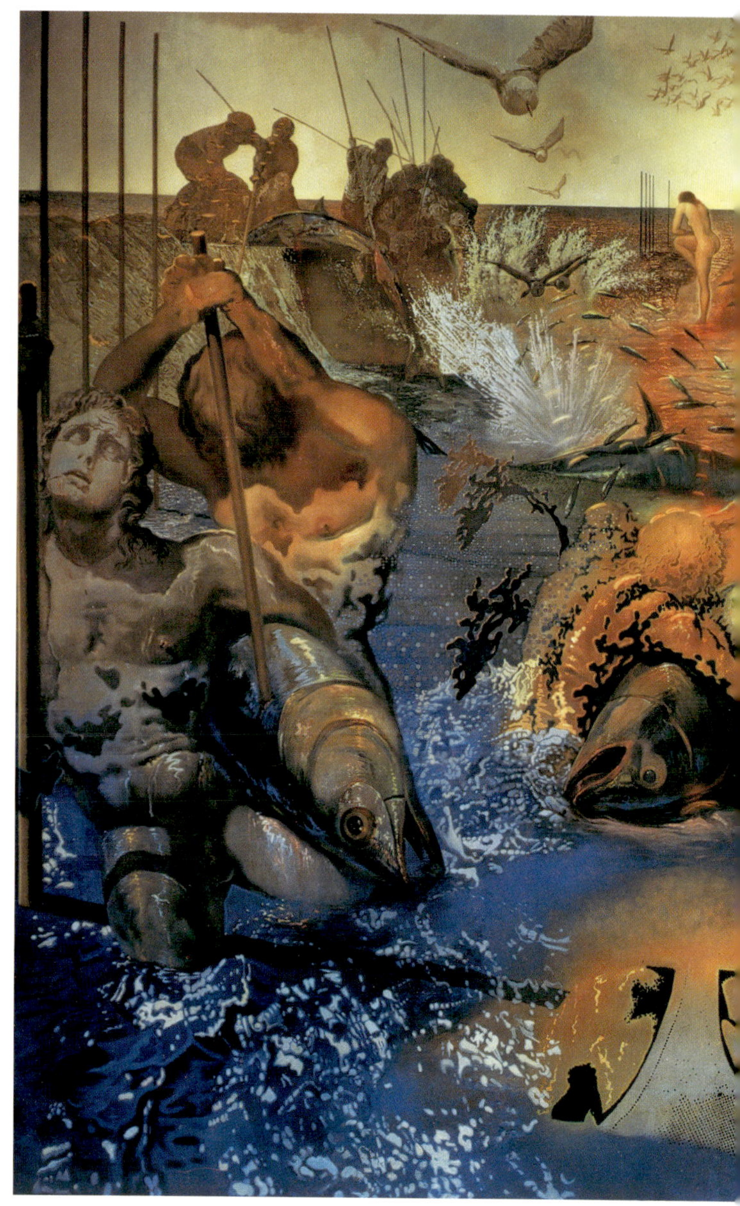

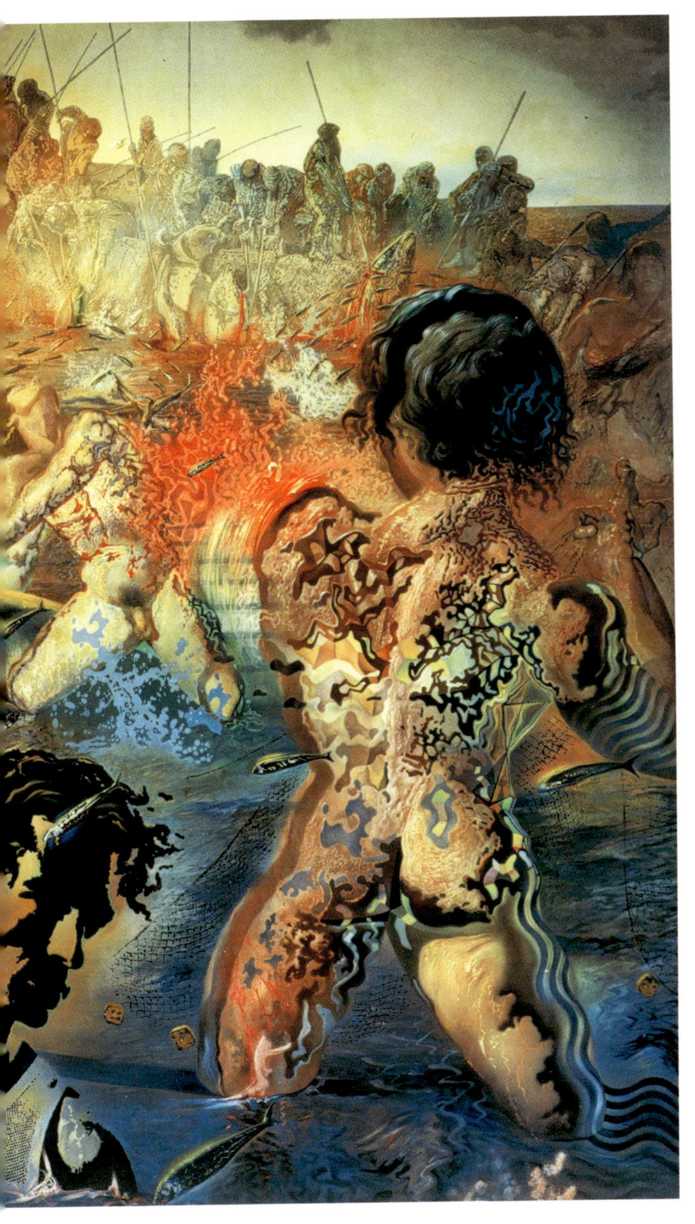

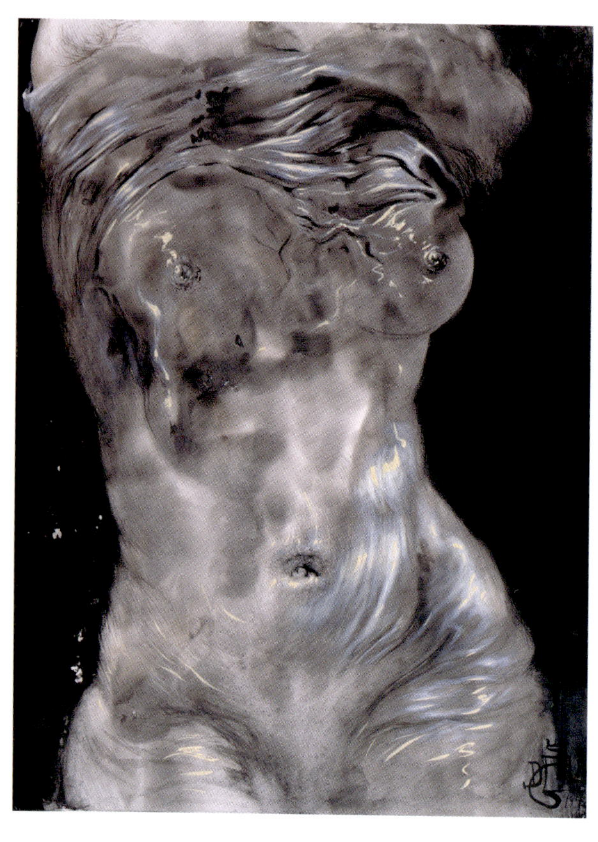

Sfumato · 1972
Fundación Gala-Salvador Dalí, Figueras

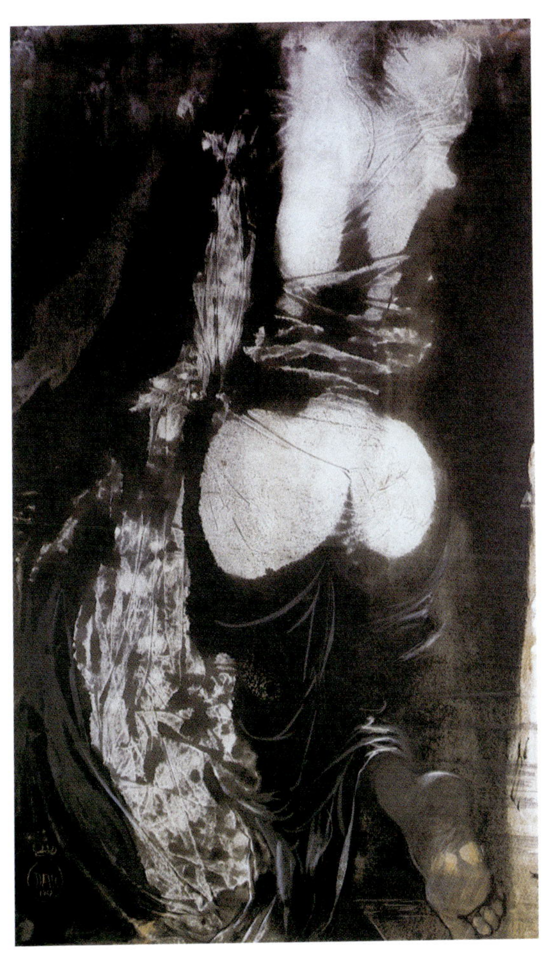

Figure Climbing a Stair · 1967
Private collection

351

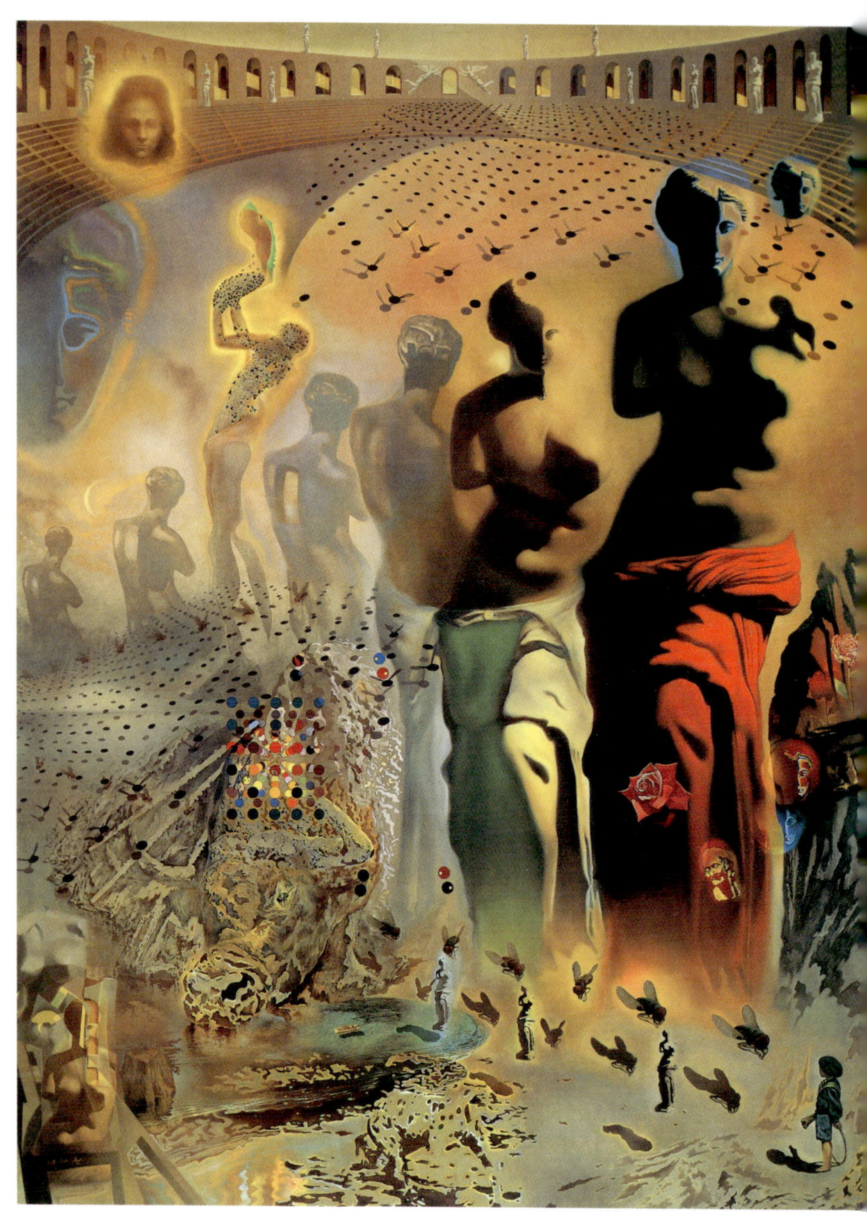

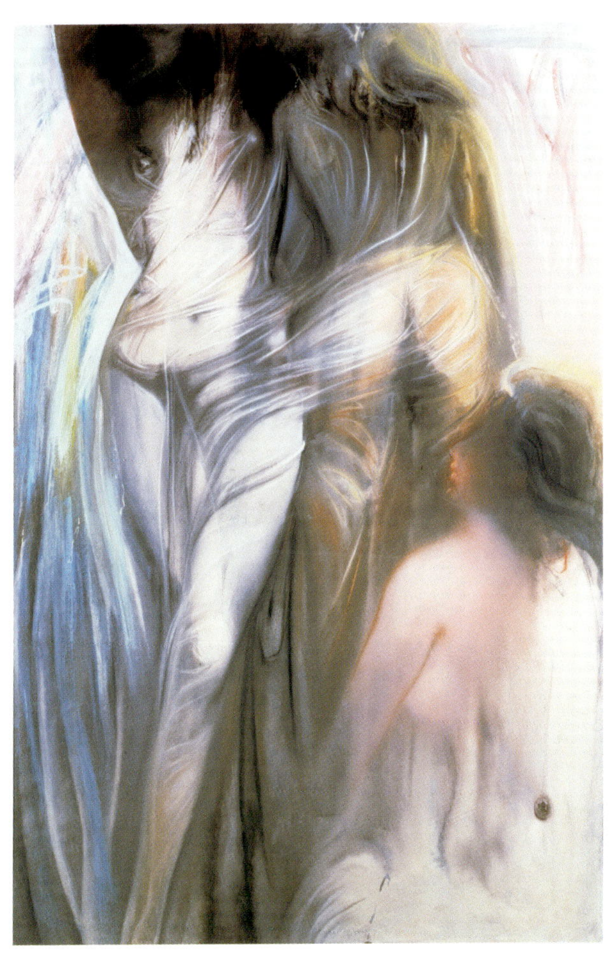

Female Trio · 1970
Christie's, London
‹ **Hallucinogenic Toreador** · 1968–70
The Salvador Dalí Museum, St. Petersburg, Florida,
on loan from the Morse Charitable Trust

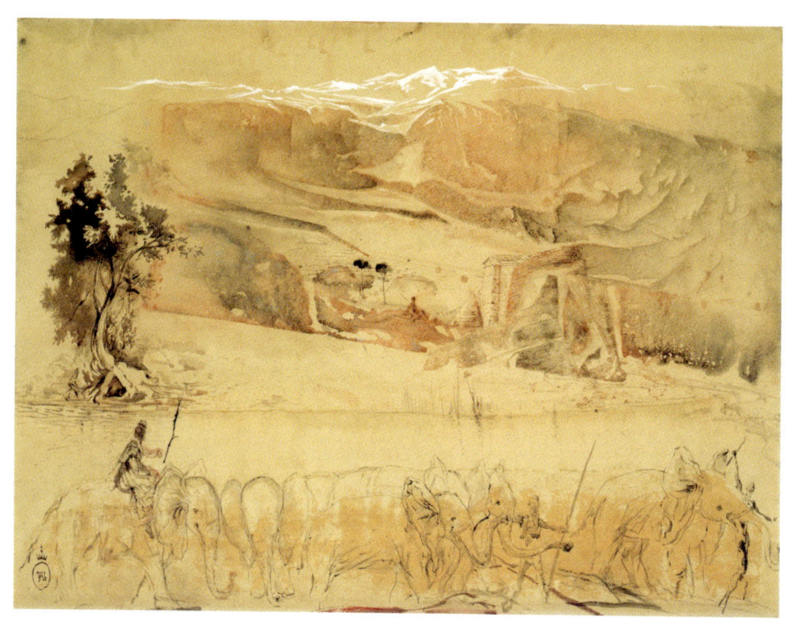

Hannibal Crossing the Alps · 1970
The Salvador Dalí Museum, St. Petersburg, Florida,
on loan from E. and A. Reynolds Morse

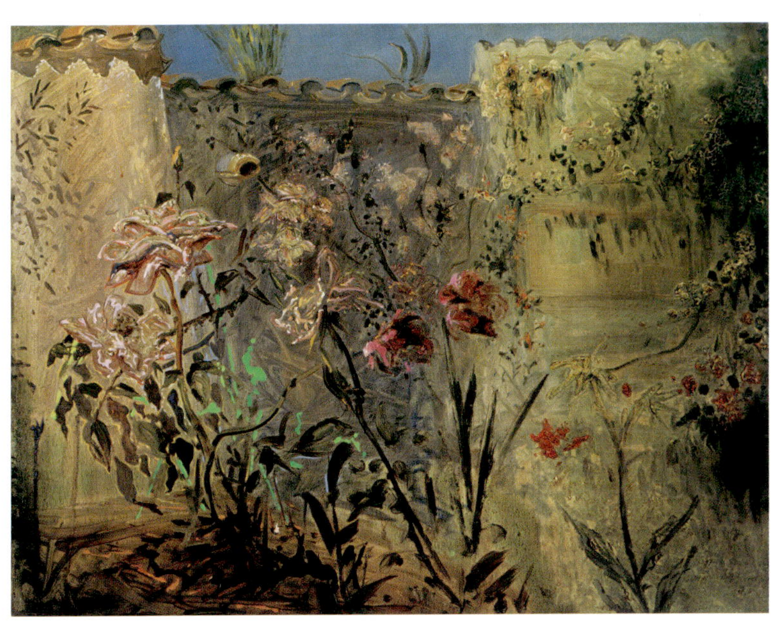

The Patio of Port Lligat · 1968
Fundación Gala-Salvador Dalí, Figueras, gift of Dalí to the Spanish state

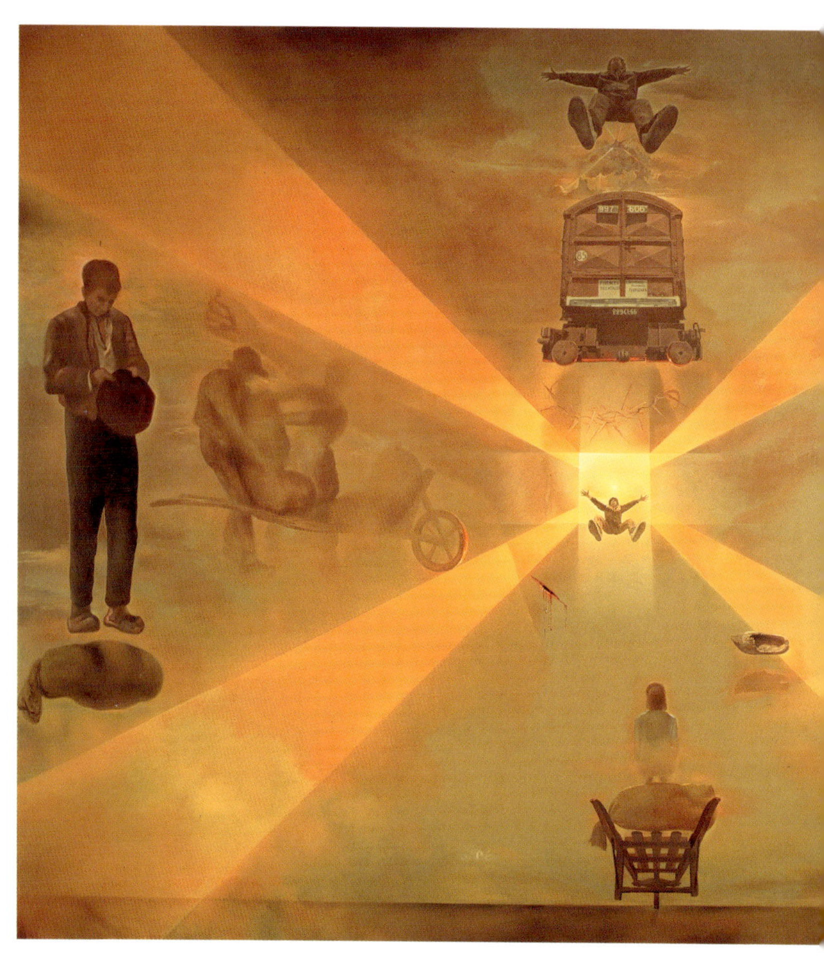

The Railway Station at Perpignan · 1965
Museum Ludwig, Cologne

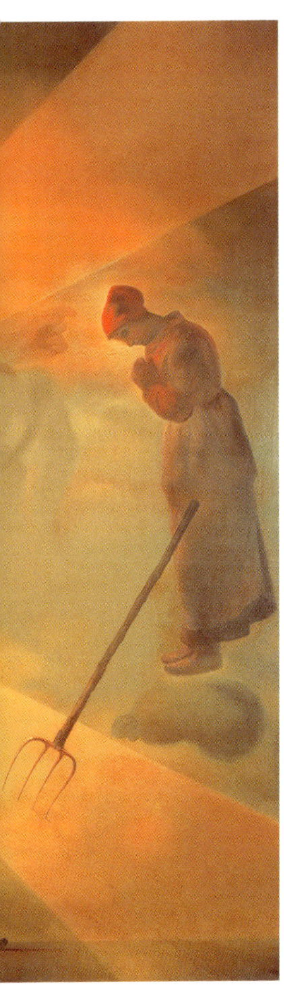

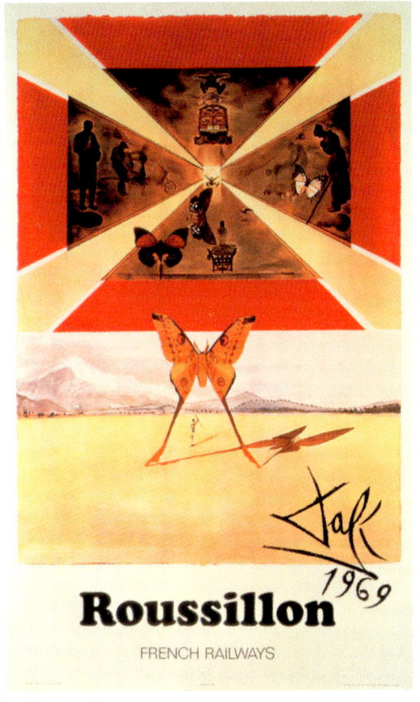

Roussillon—French Railways. Poster · 1969
Lords Gallery, London

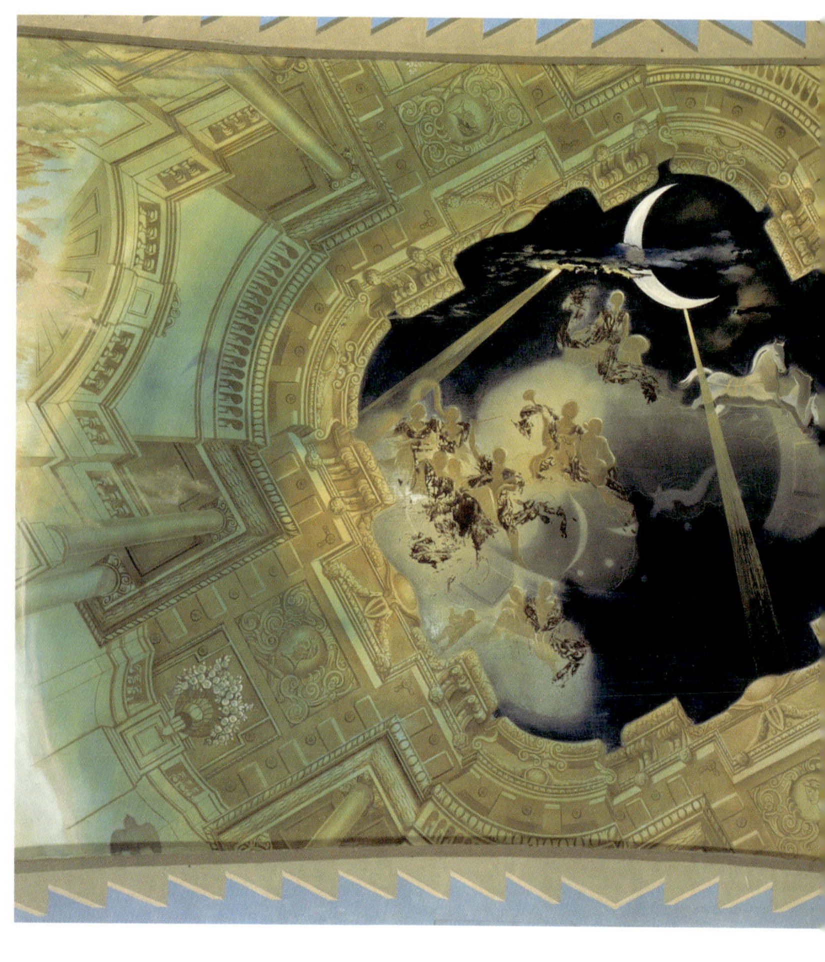

Ceiling of the hall of Gala's castle at Púbol · 1971
Gift of Dalí to the Spanish state

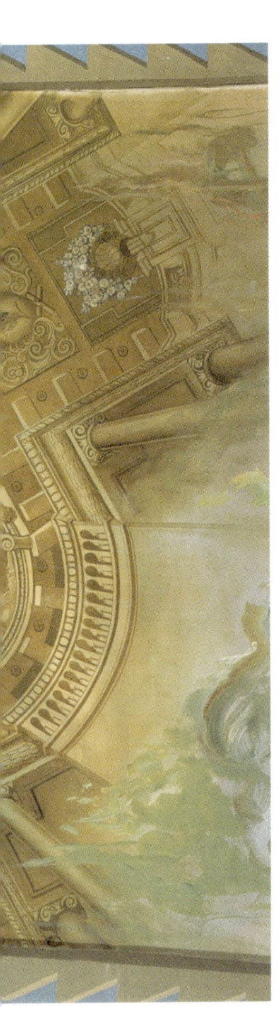

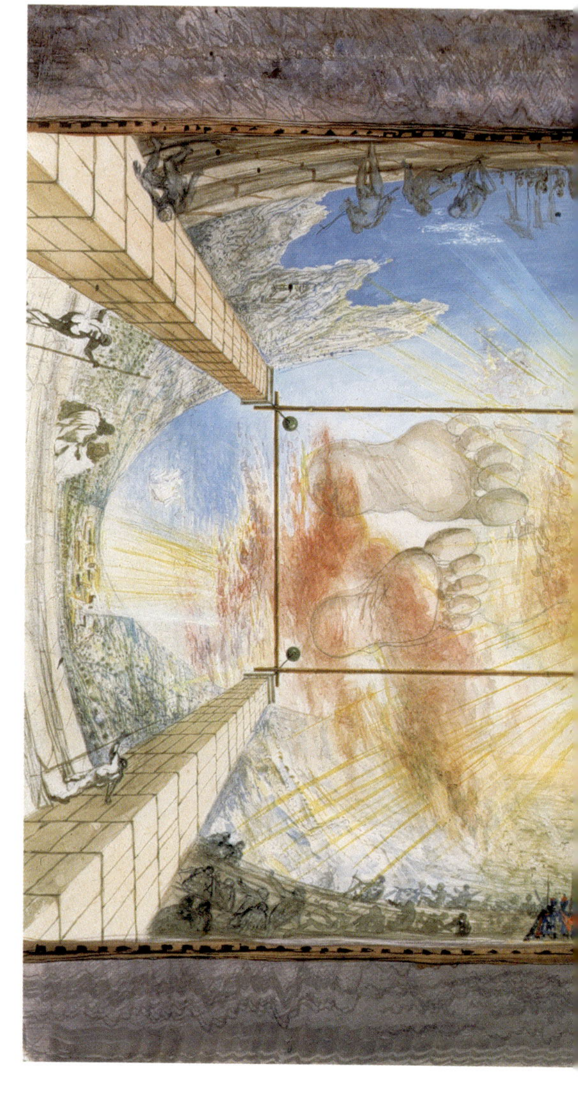

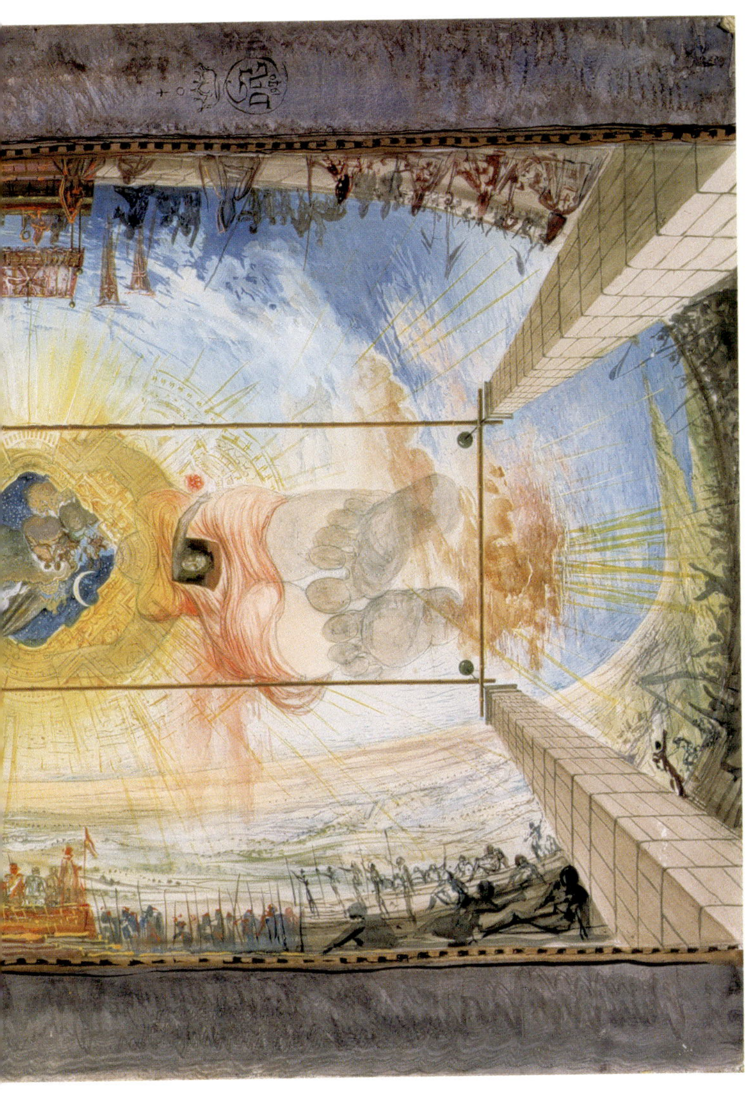

Sketch for a ceiling of the Teatro Museo Dalí · 1970
Fundación Gala-Salvador Dalí, Figueras

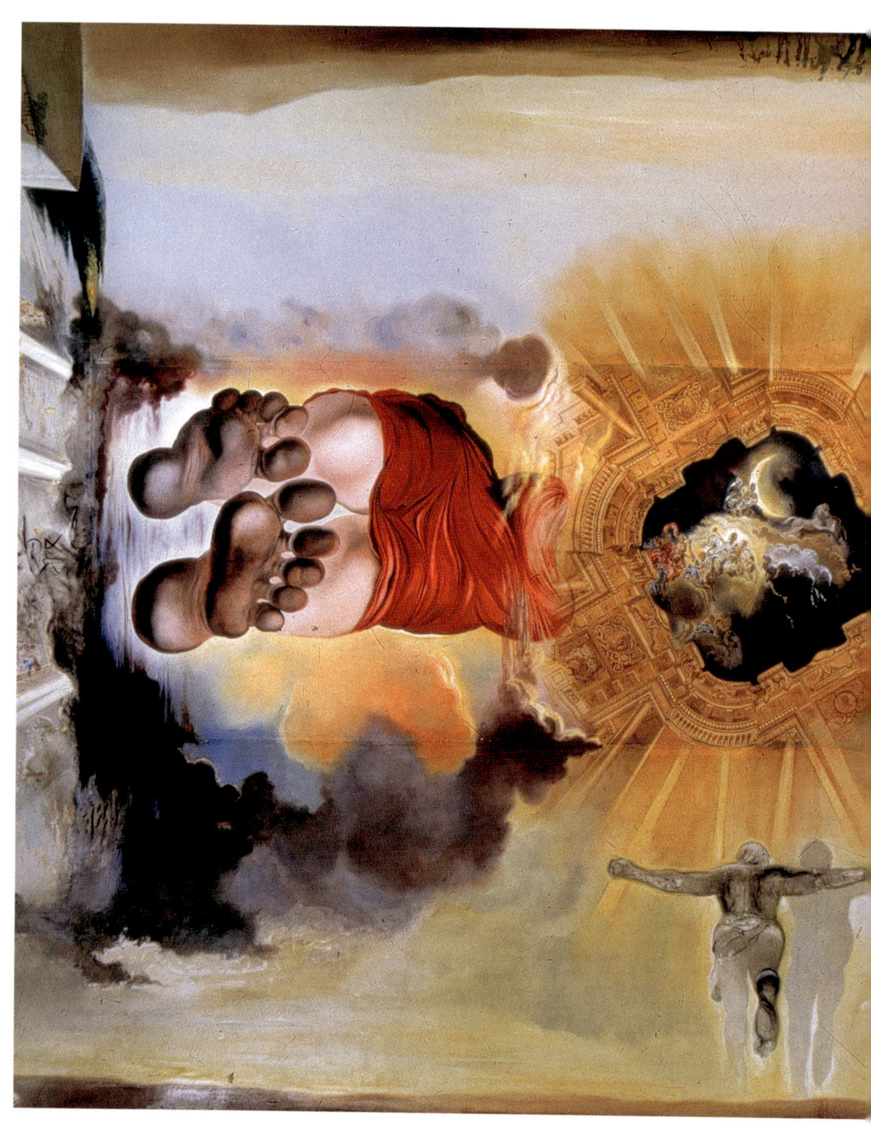

Palace of the Winds · 1972
Fundación Gala-Salvador Dalí, Figueras

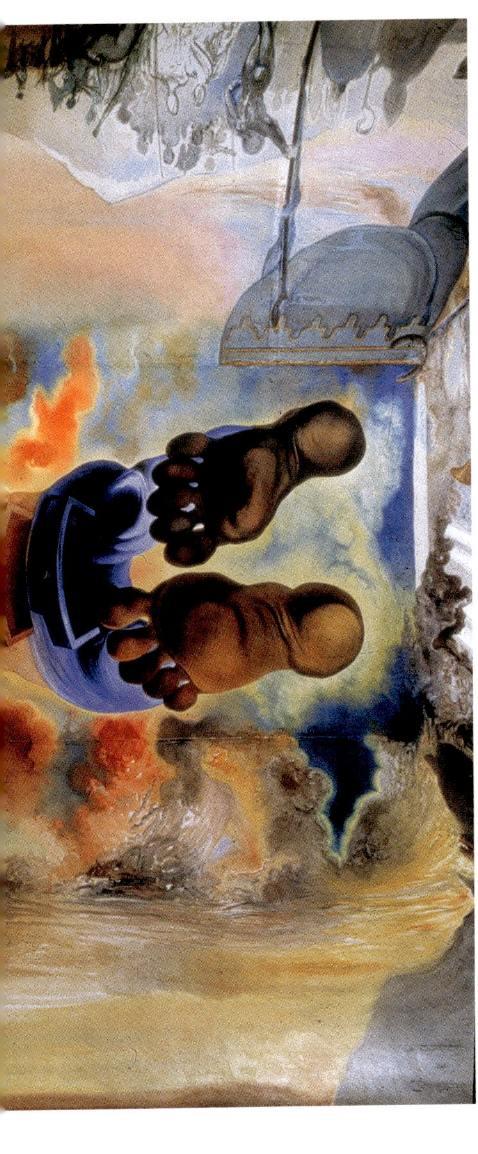

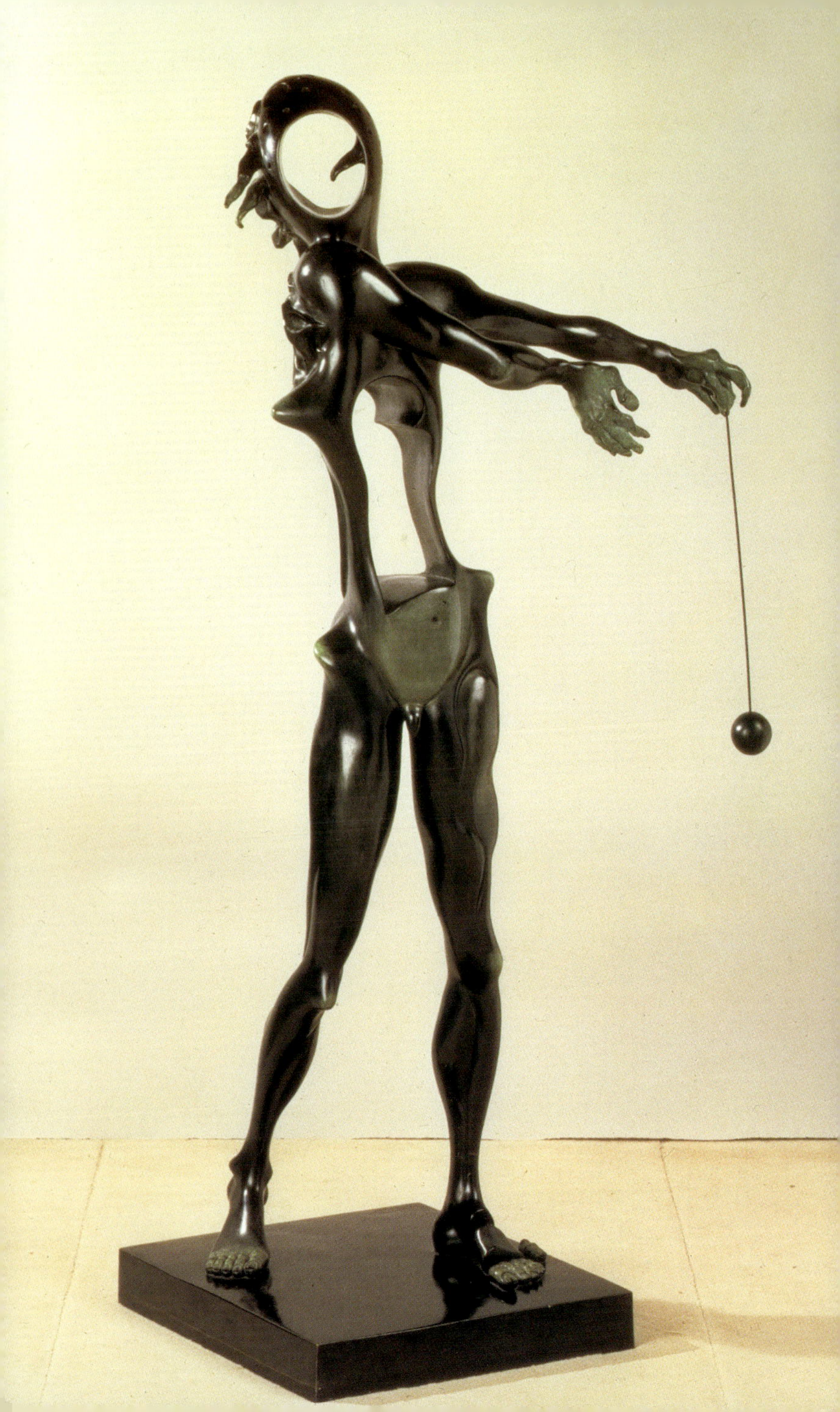

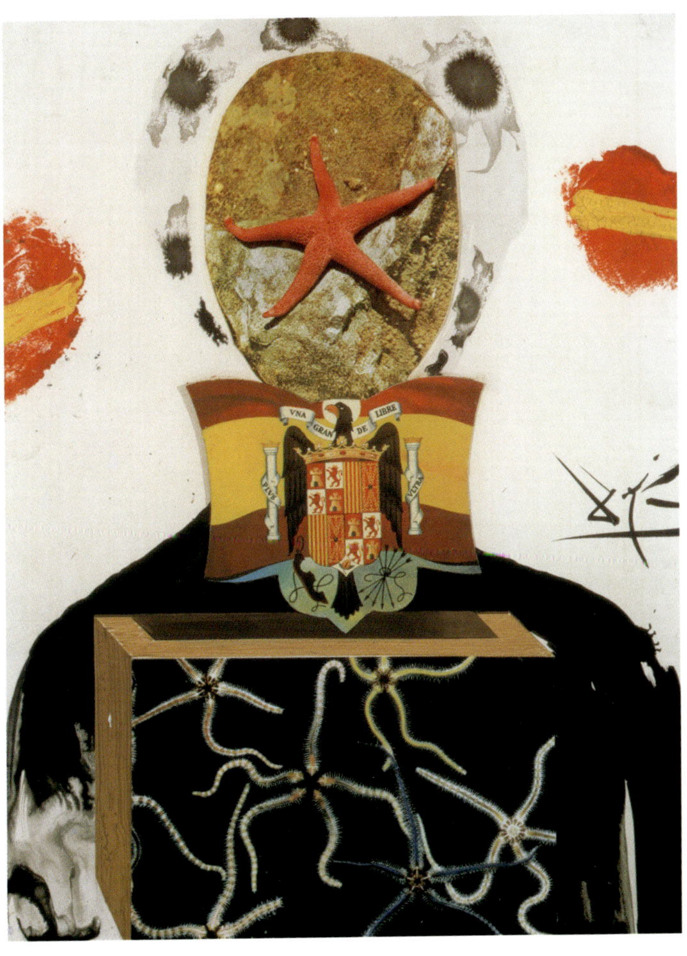

Figure with Flag. Illustration for "Memories of Surrealism" · C. 1971
Private collection
‹ **Homage to Newton** · 1969
Plaza Dalí, Madrid

365

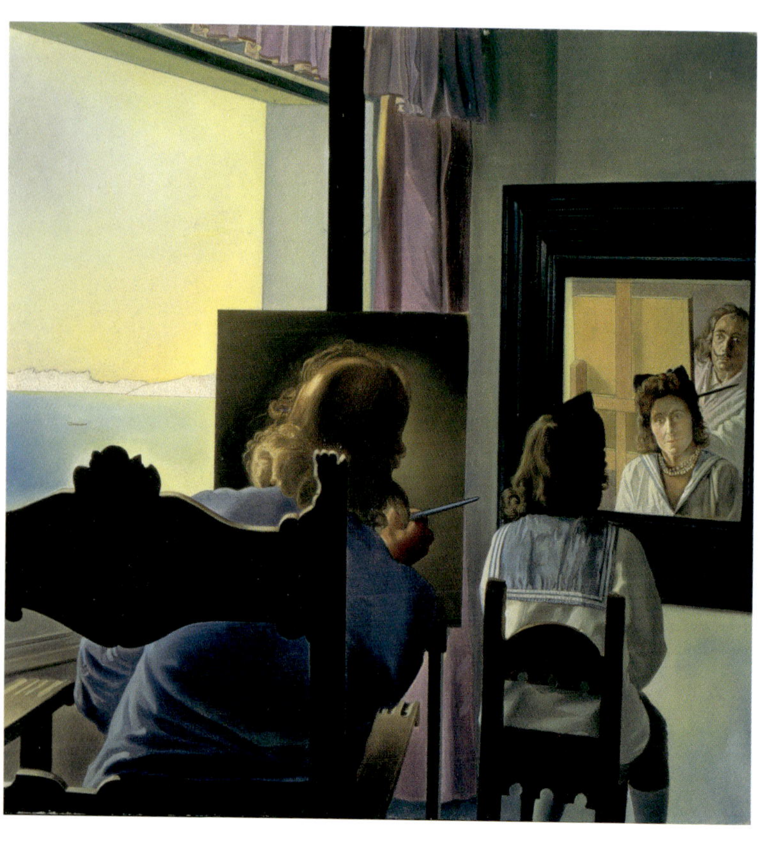

Dalí from the Back Painting Gala from the Back Eternalized by Six Virtual Corneas Provisionally Reflected in Six Real Mirrors (unfinished) · c. 1972–73
Fundación Gala-Salvador Dalí, Figueras

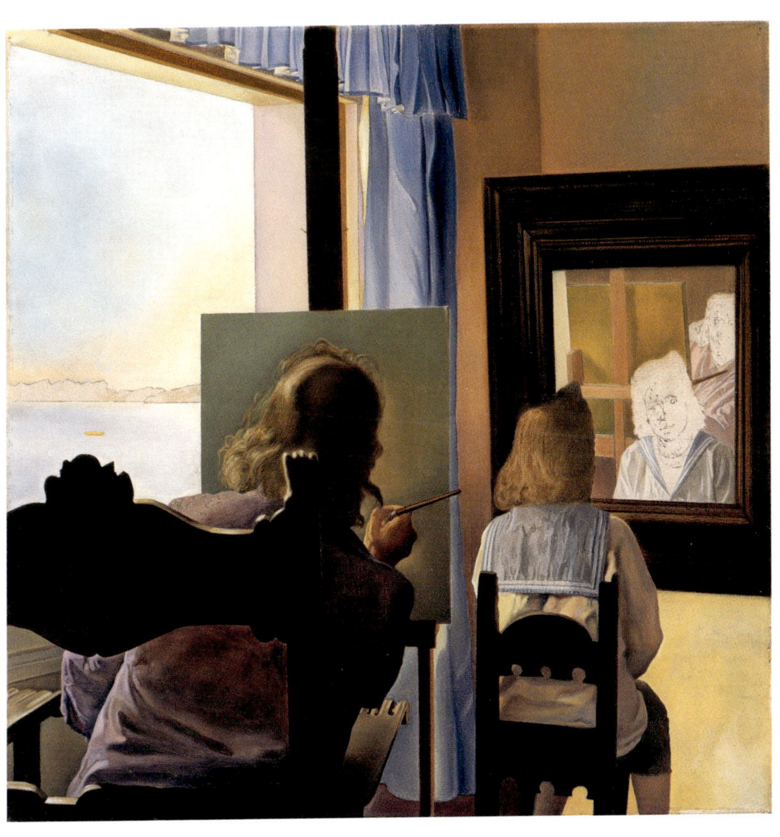

Dalí from the Back Painting Gala from the Back Eternalized by Six Virtual Corneas Provisionally Reflected in Six Real Mirrors (unfinished) · C. 1972–73

Fundación Gala-Salvador Dalí, Figueras

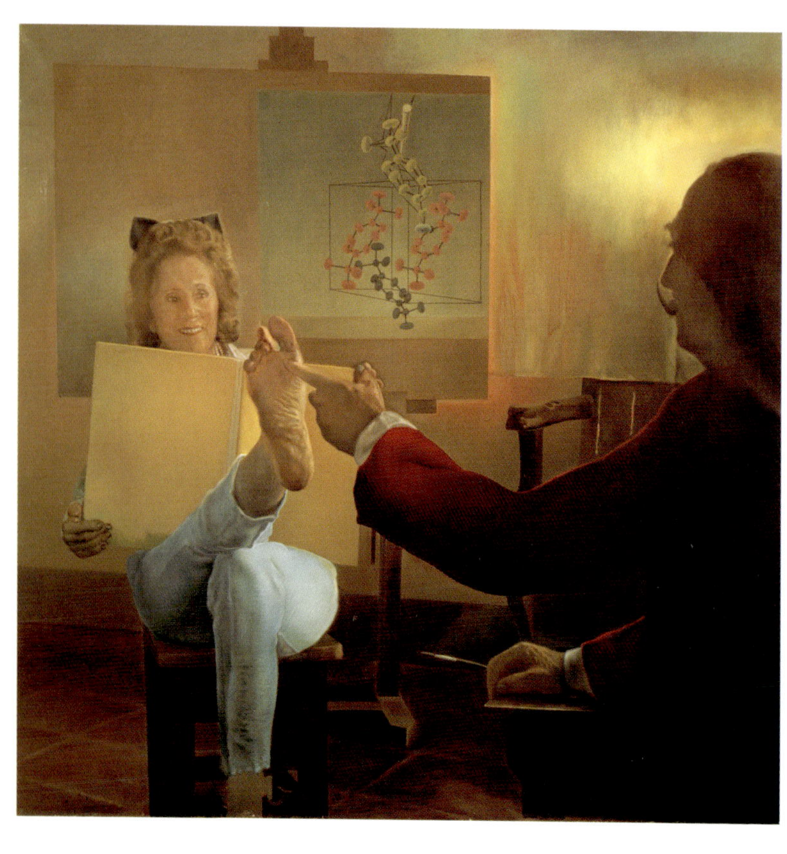

Gala's Foot (Stereoscopic work; left component) · 1973
Fundación Gala-Salvador Dalí, Figueras

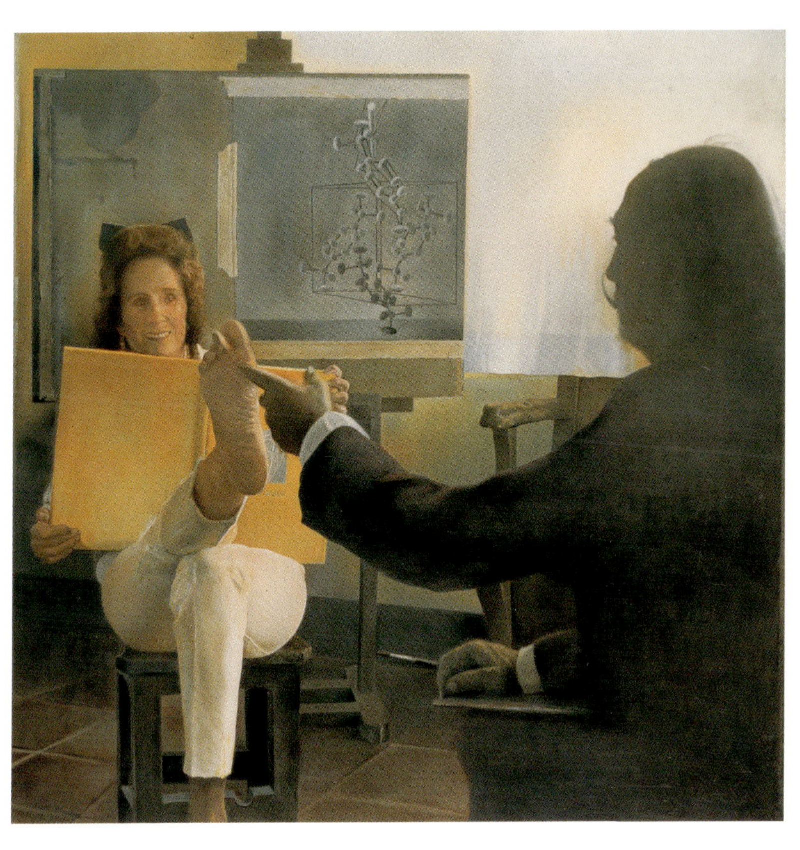

Gala's Foot (Stereoscopic work; right component) · 1973
Fundación Gala-Salvador Dalí, Figueras

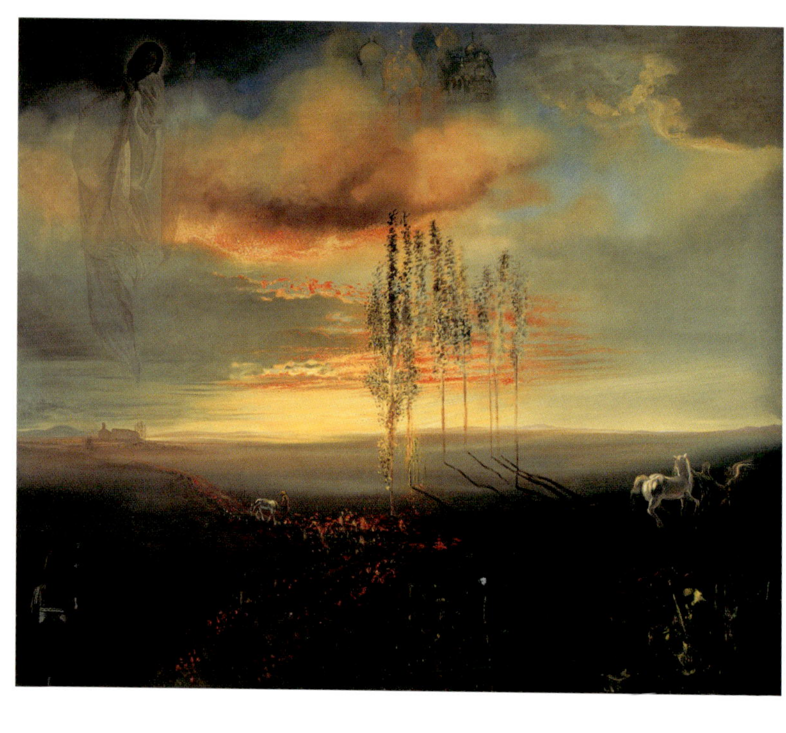

The Way to Púbol · 1973

Gift of Dalí to the Spanish state

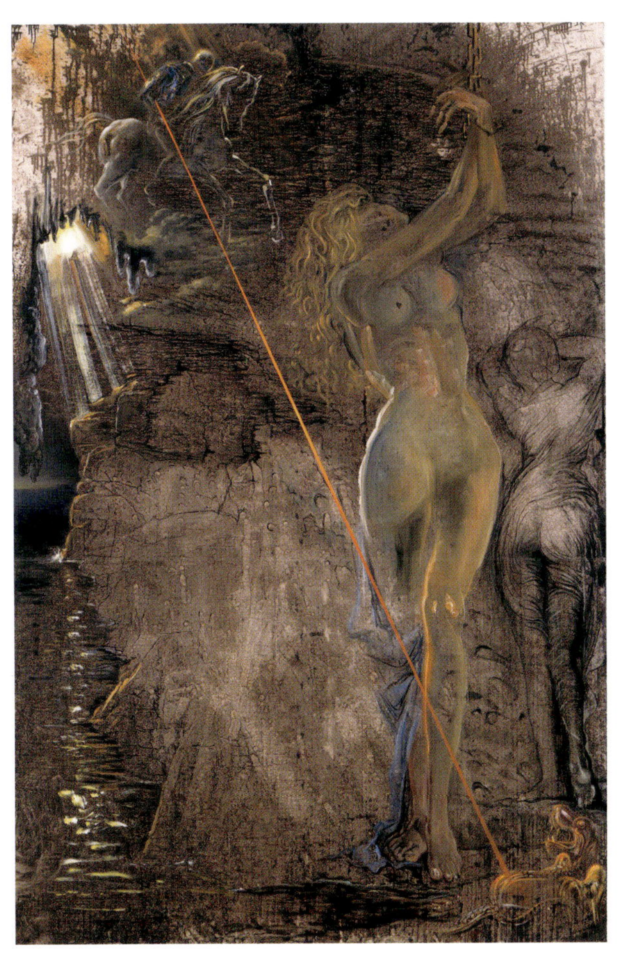

Roger Freeing Angelica (St. George and the Damsel) · 1970–74
Fundación Gala-Salvador Dalí, Figueras

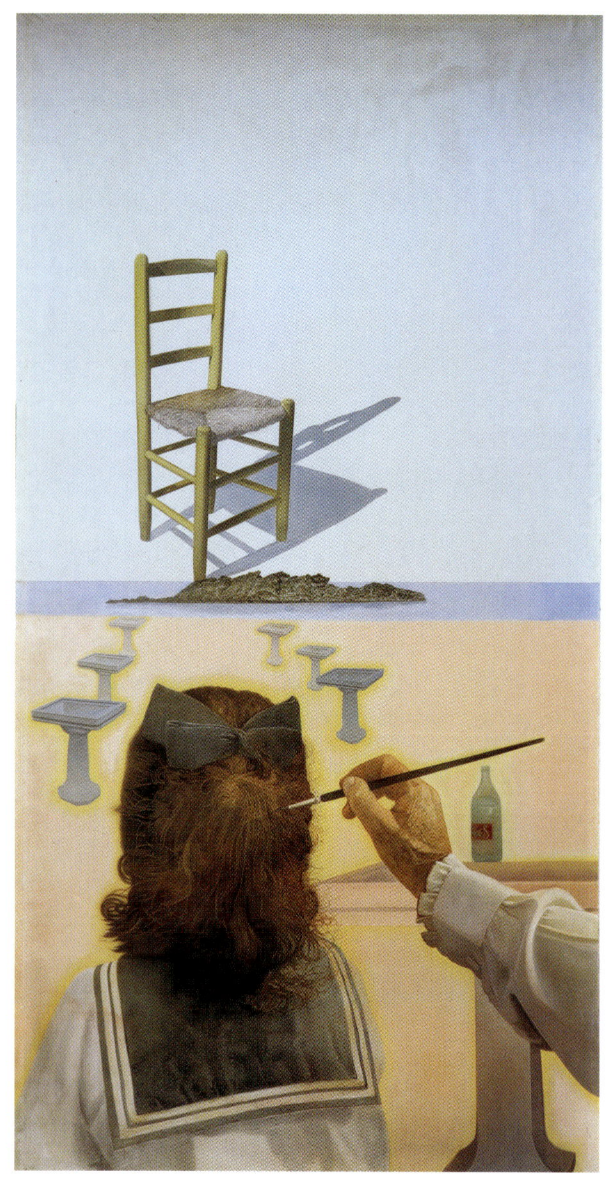

The Chair (Stereoscopic work; left component) · 1975
Fundación Gala-Salvador Dalí, Figueras

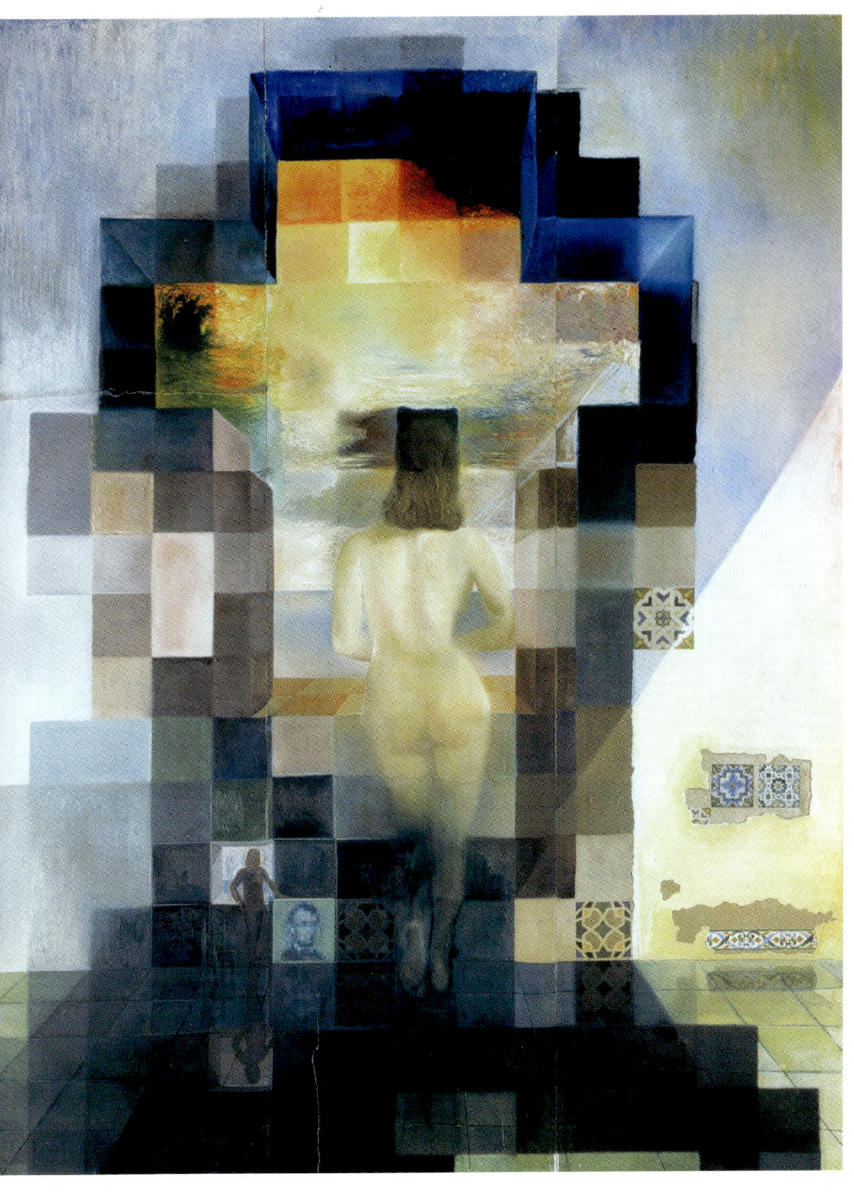

**Gala Contemplating the Mediterranean Sea which at Twenty Meters Becomes
the Portrait of Abraham Lincoln—Homage to Rothko (first version)** · c. 1974–75

Fundación Gala-Salvador Dalí, Figueras

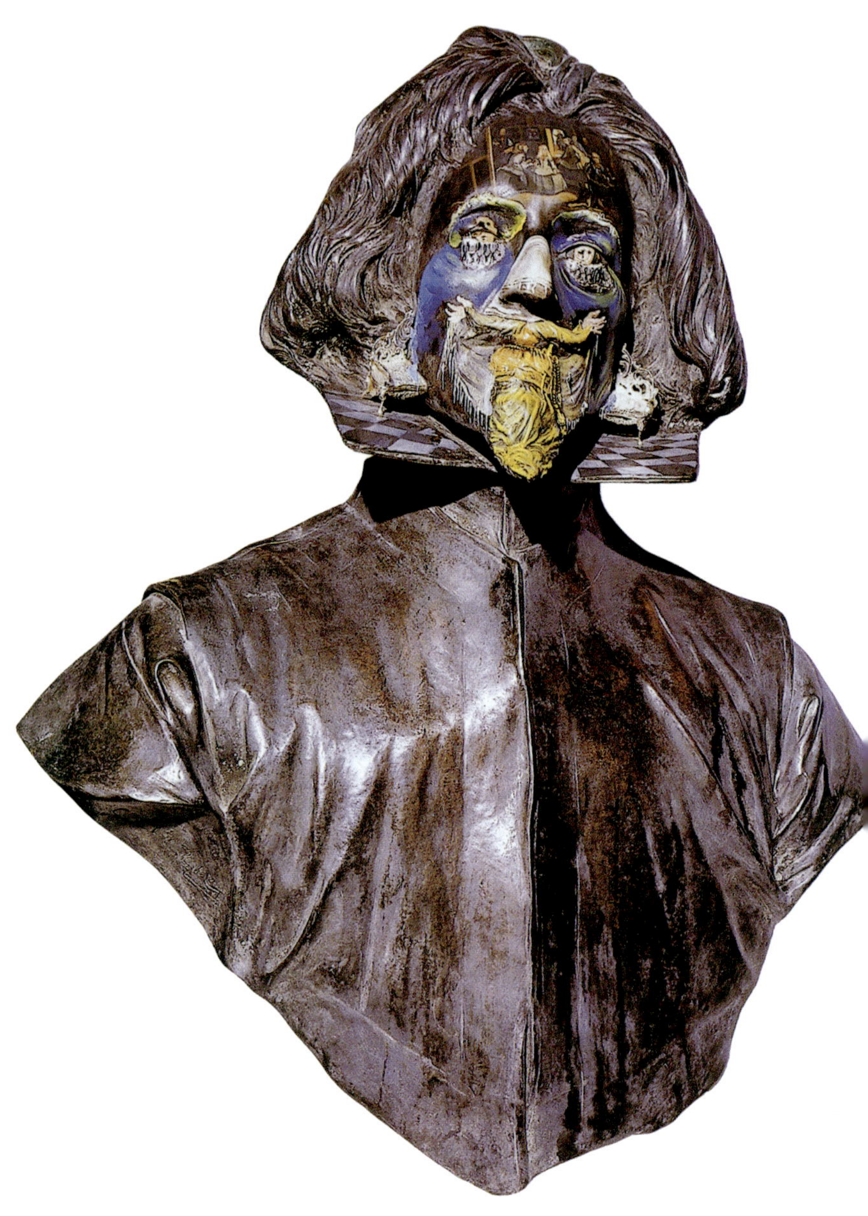

Bust of Velázquez Turning into Three Figures Conversing · 1974
Fundación Gala-Salvador Dalí, Figueras

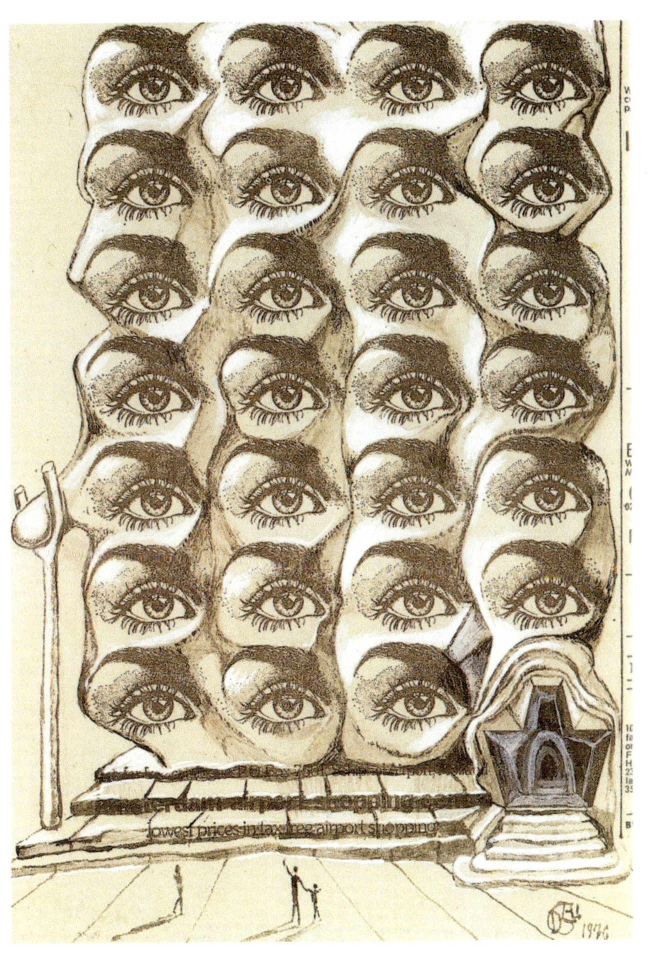

Architectural Project · 1976
Private collection

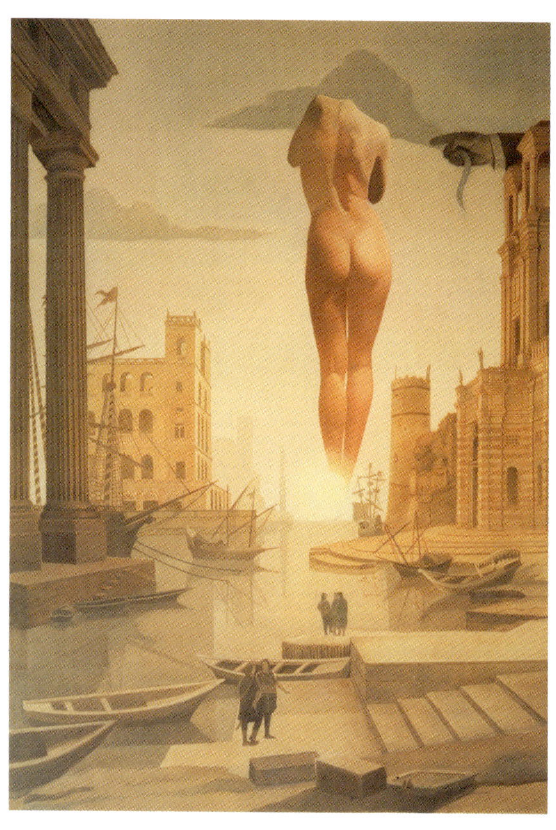

Dalí's Hand Drawing Back the Golden Fleece in the Form of a Cloud to Show Gala, Completely Nude, the Dawn, Very, Very Far Away Behind the Sun (Stereoscopic work; left component) · 1977

Fundación Gala-Salvador Dalí, Figueras, gift of Dalí to the Spanish state

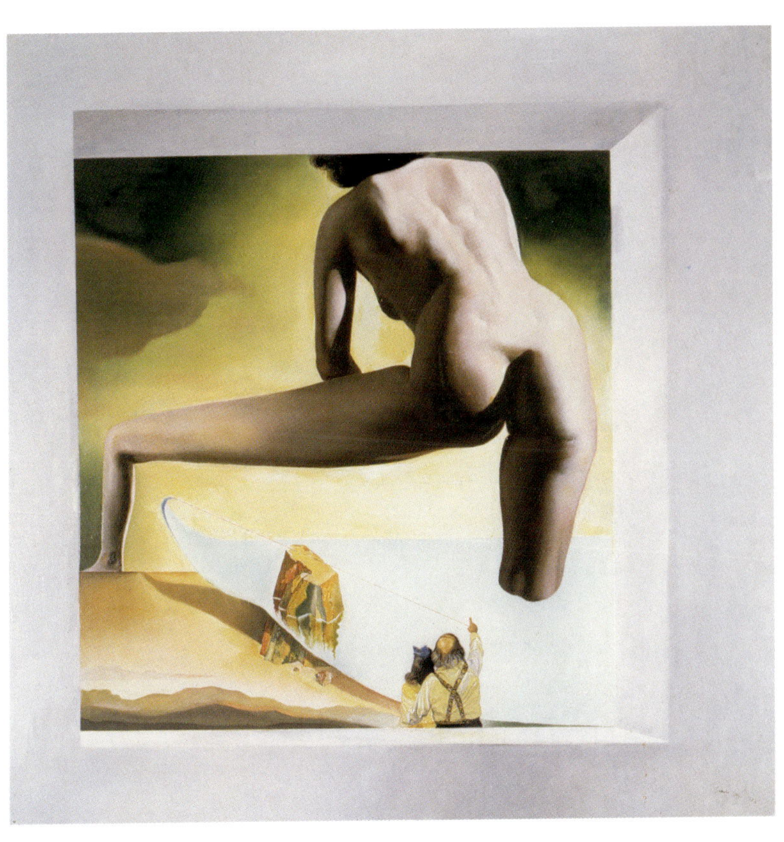

**Dalí Lifting the Skin of the Mediterranean Sea to Show Gala the Birth of Venus
(Stereoscopic work; right component)** · 1977
Fundación Gala-Salvador Dalí, Figueras

Cybernetic Odalisque—Homage to Bela Julesz · 1978
Fundación Gala-Salvador Dalí, Figueras, gift of Dalí to the Spanish state

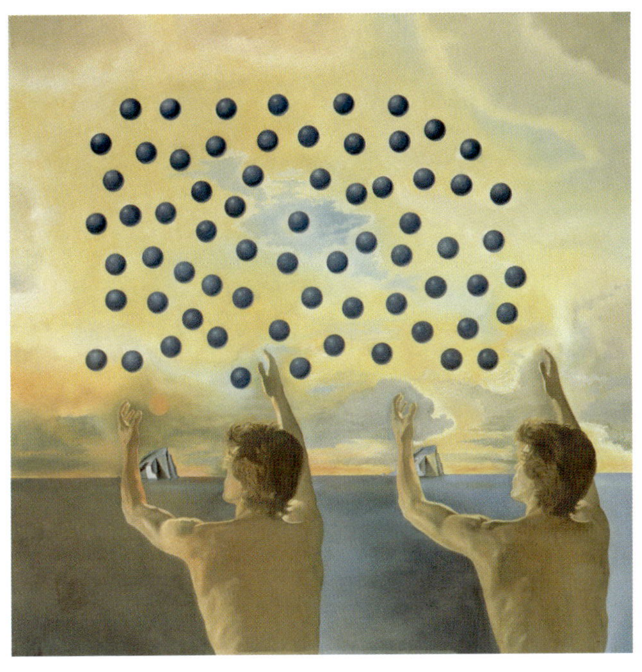

The Harmony of the Spheres · 1978
Fundación Gala-Salvador Dalí, Figueras, gift of Dalí to the Spanish state

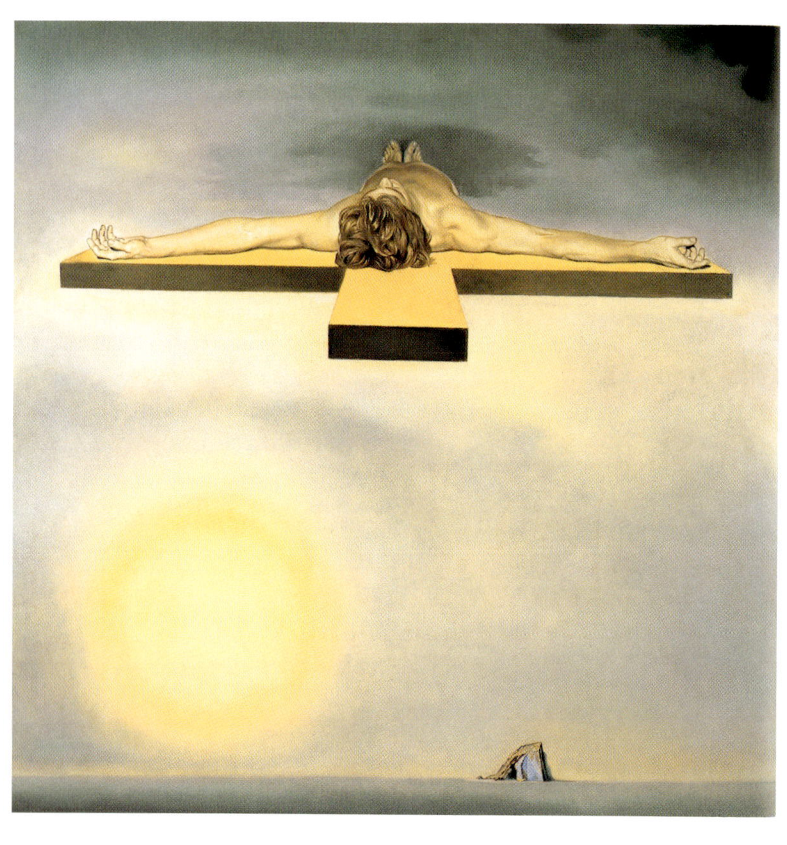

Gala's Christ (Stereoscopic work; left component) · 1978
Private collection

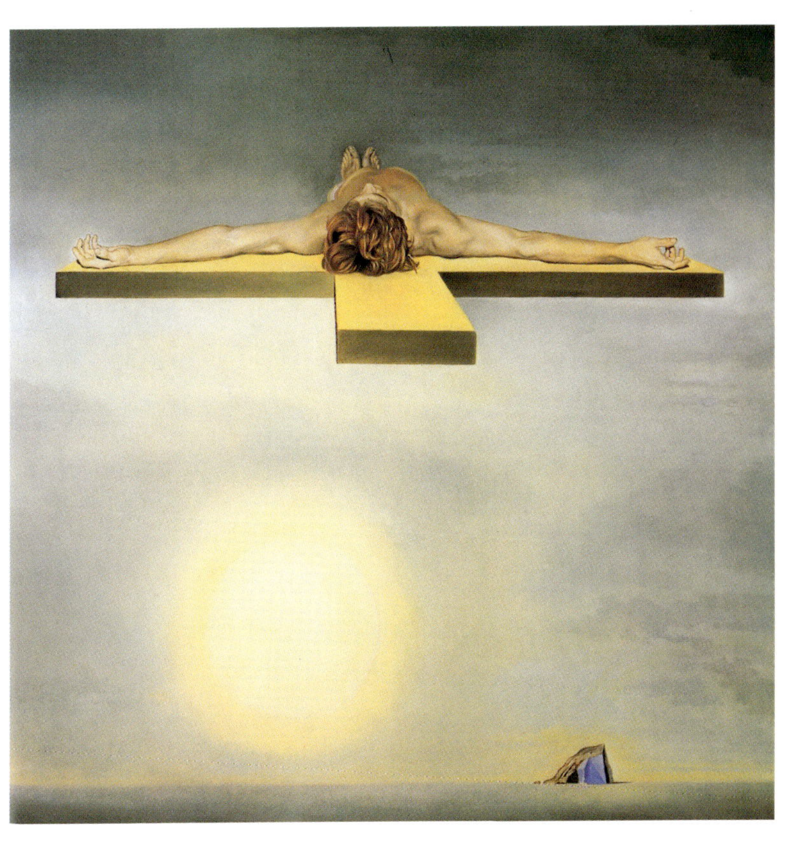

Gala's Christ (Stereoscopic work; right component) · 1978
Private collection

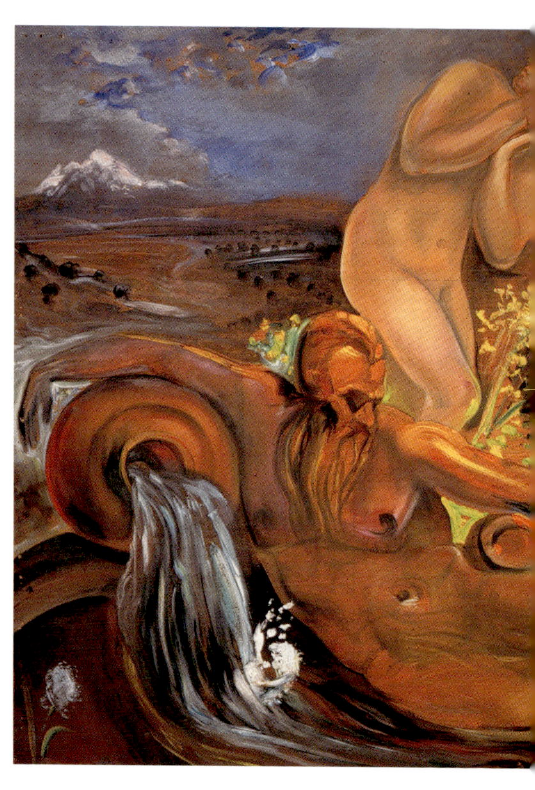

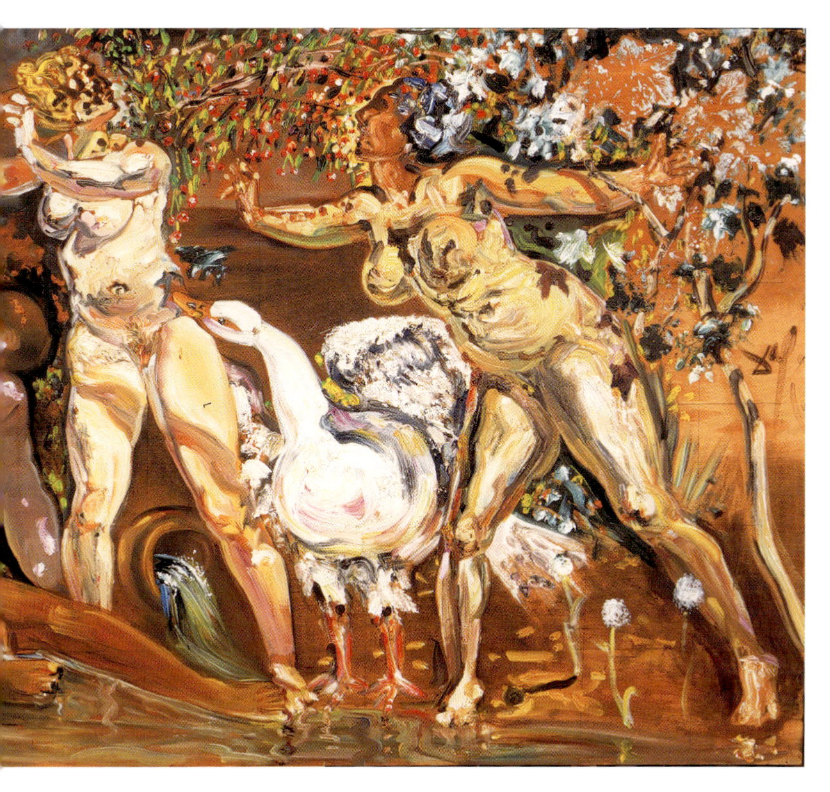

Allegory of Spring · 1978

Fundación Gala-Salvador Dalí, Figueras

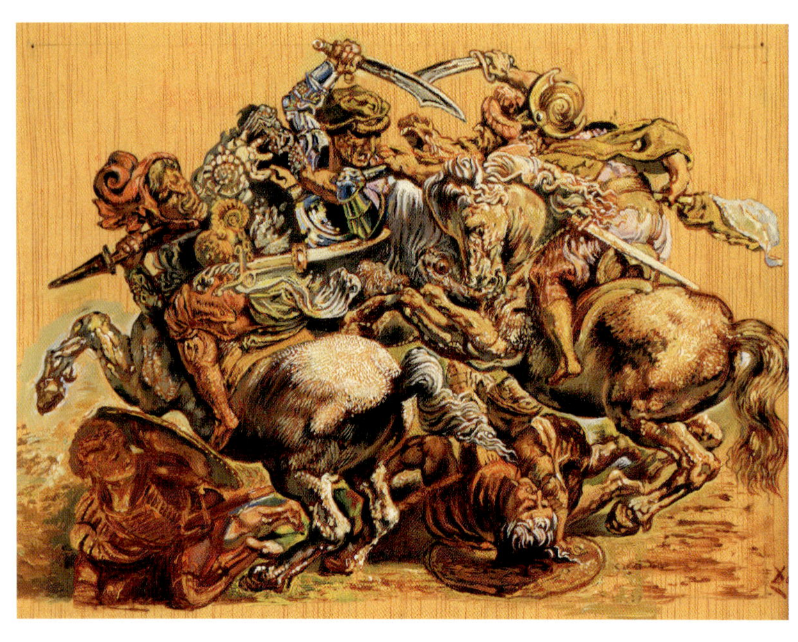

Copy of a Rubens Copy of a Leonardo · 1979
Fundación Gala-Salvador Dalí, Figueras, gift of Dalí to the Spanish state

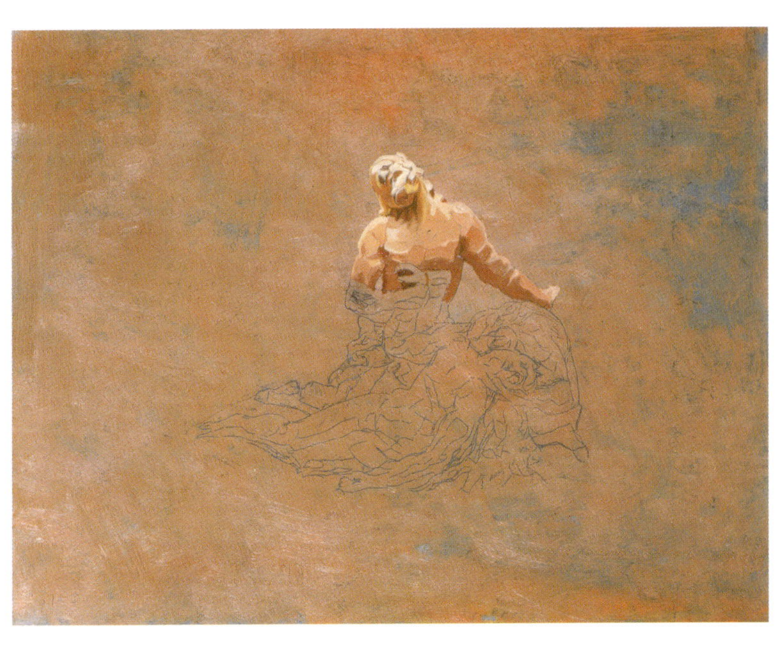

Study for "Compianto Diabele" by Canova (unfinished) · c. 1979

Museo Nacional Centro de Arte Reina Sofía, Madrid, gift of Dalí to the Spanish state

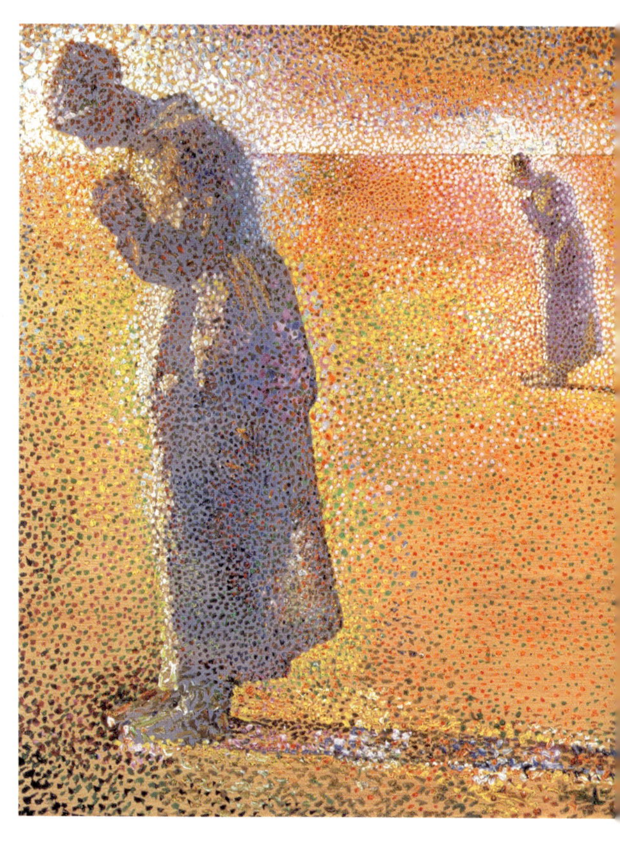

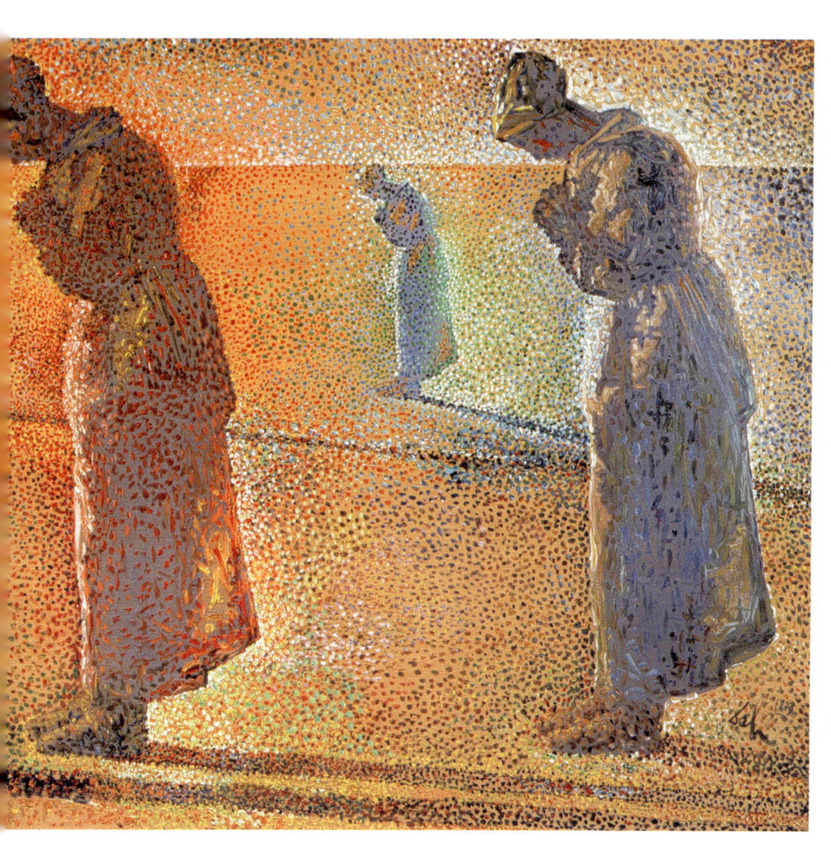

Dawn, Noon, Sunset, and Twilight · 1979
Fundación Gala-Salvador Dalí, Figueras

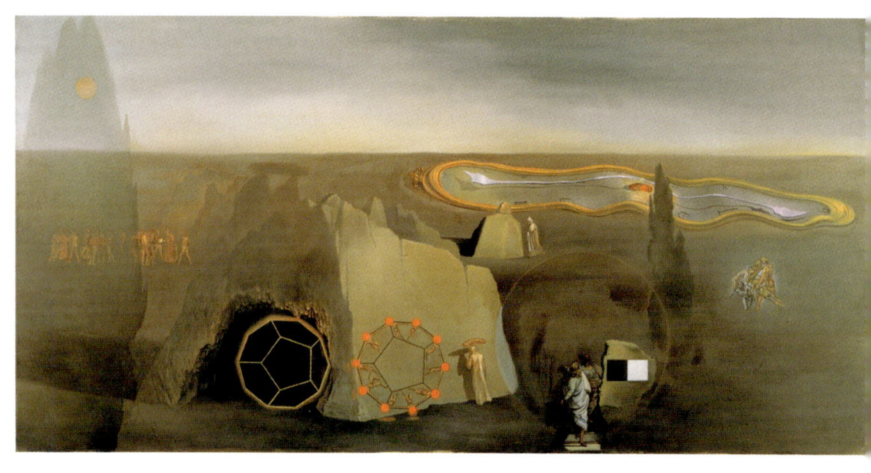

Searching for the Fourth Dimension · 1979
Fundación Gala-Salvador Dalí, Figueras, gift of Dalí to the Spanish state

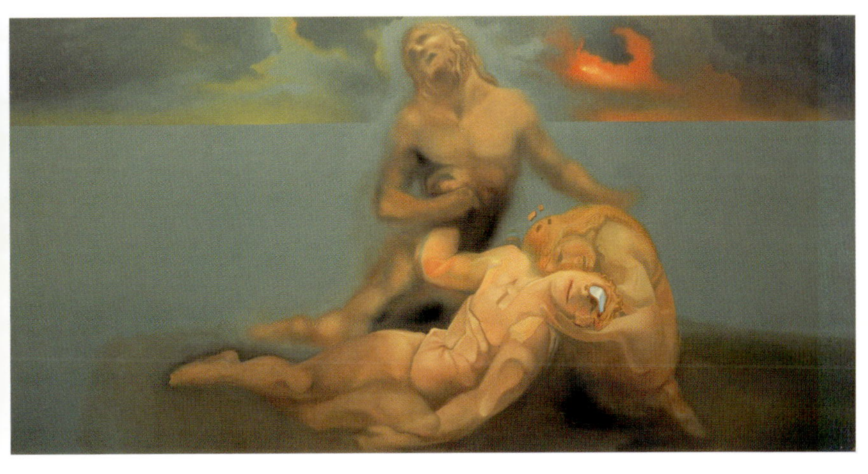

**A Soft Watch Put in the Appropriate Place to Cause a Young Ephebe to Die
and Be Resuscitated by Excess of Satisfaction (unfinished)** · 1979

Fundación Gala-Salvador Dalí, Figueras, gift of Dalí to the Spanish state

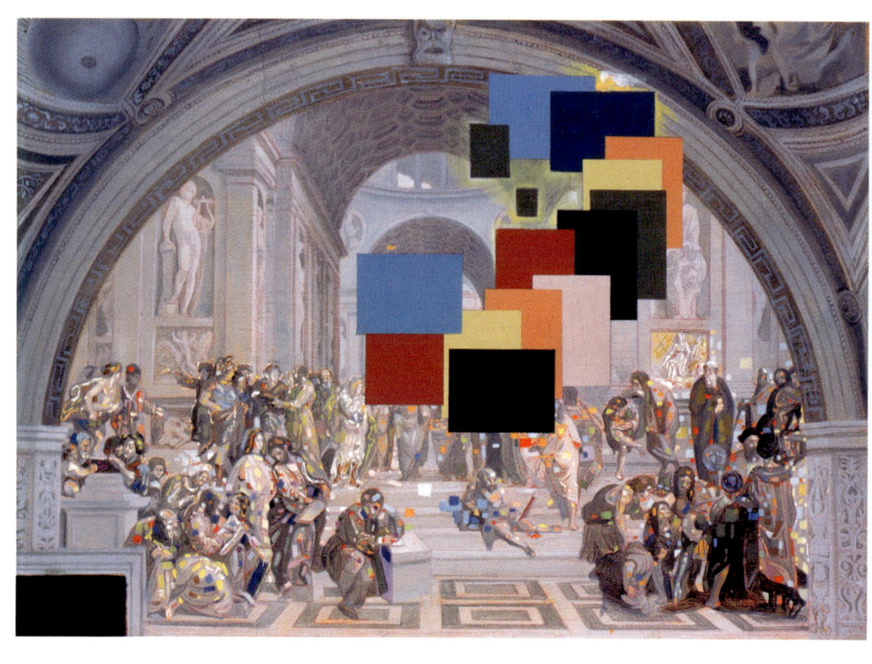

**Athens Is Burning!—The School of Athens and the Fire in the Borgo
(Stereoscopic work; left component)** · 1979–80
Fundación Gala-Salvador Dalí, Figueras

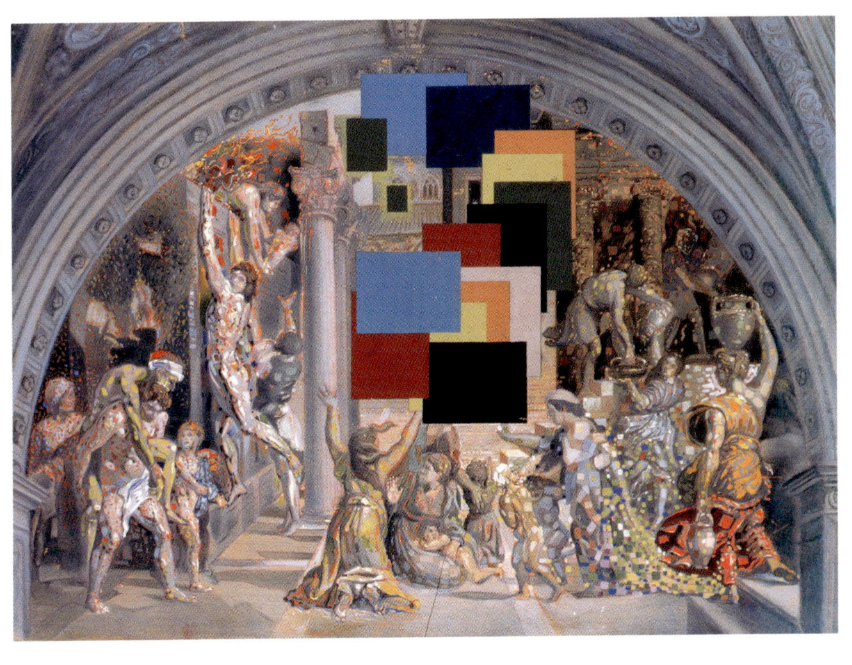

**Athens Is Burning!—The School of Athens and the Fire in the Borgo
(Stereoscopic work; right component)** · 1979–80
Fundación Gala-Salvador Dalí, Figueras

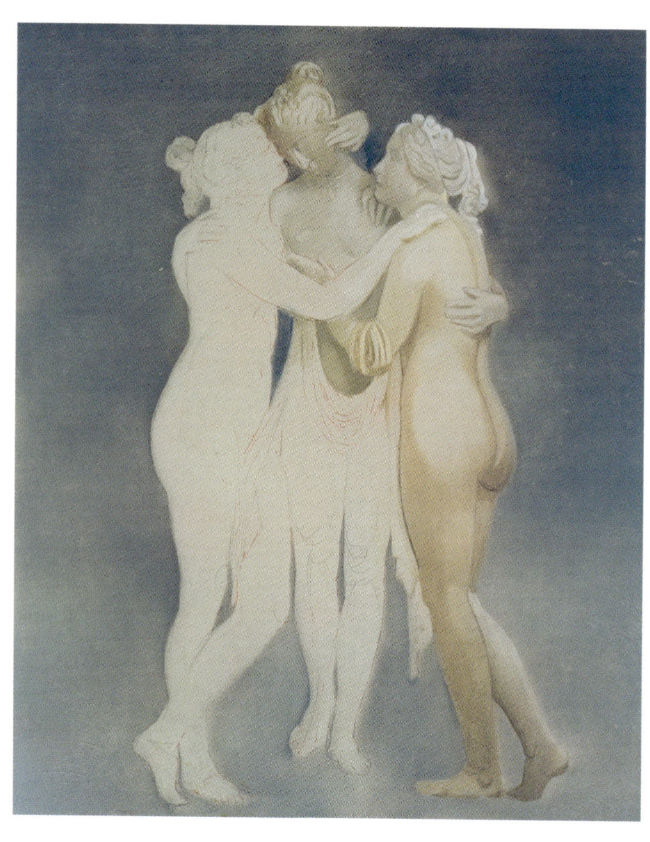

Untitled—After Canova's "Three Graces" · 1979
Fundación Gala-Salvador Dalí, Figueras, gift of Dalí to the Spanish state
> **Woman in Flames** · 1980
Phillips, The International Fine Art Auctioneers

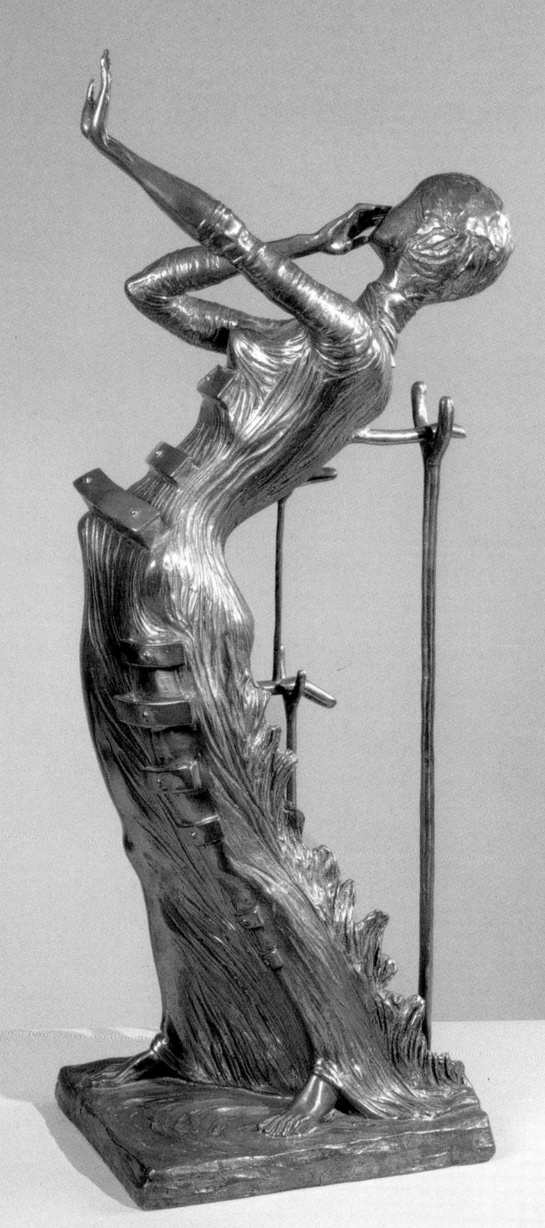

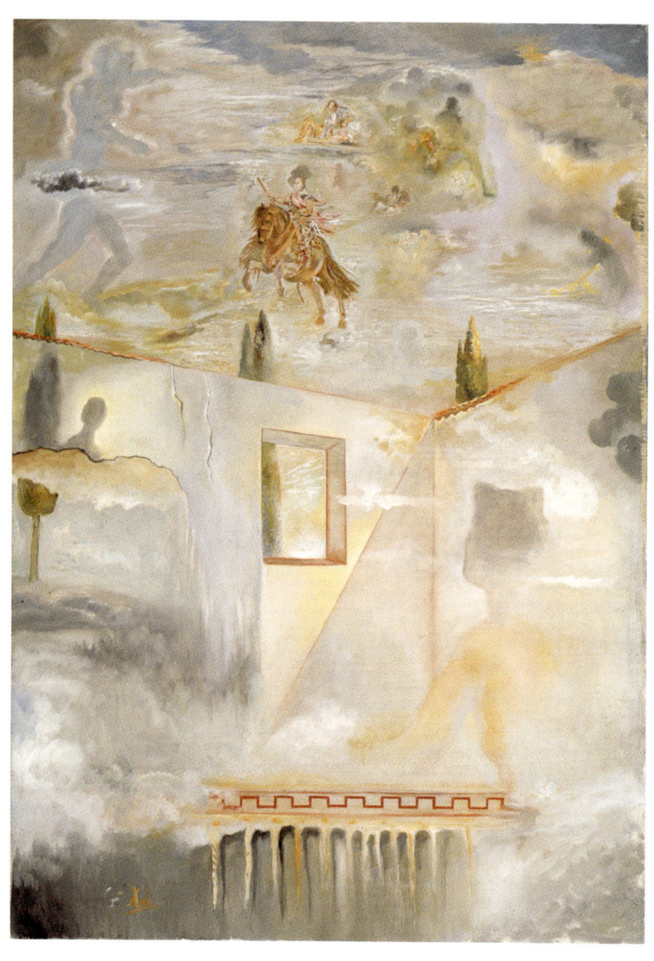

Gala in a Patio Watching the Sky, Where the Equestrian Figure of Prince Baltasar Carlos and Several Constellations (All) Appear, after Velázquez · 1981

Fundación Gala-Salvador Dalí, Figueras,
gift of Dalí to the Spanish state

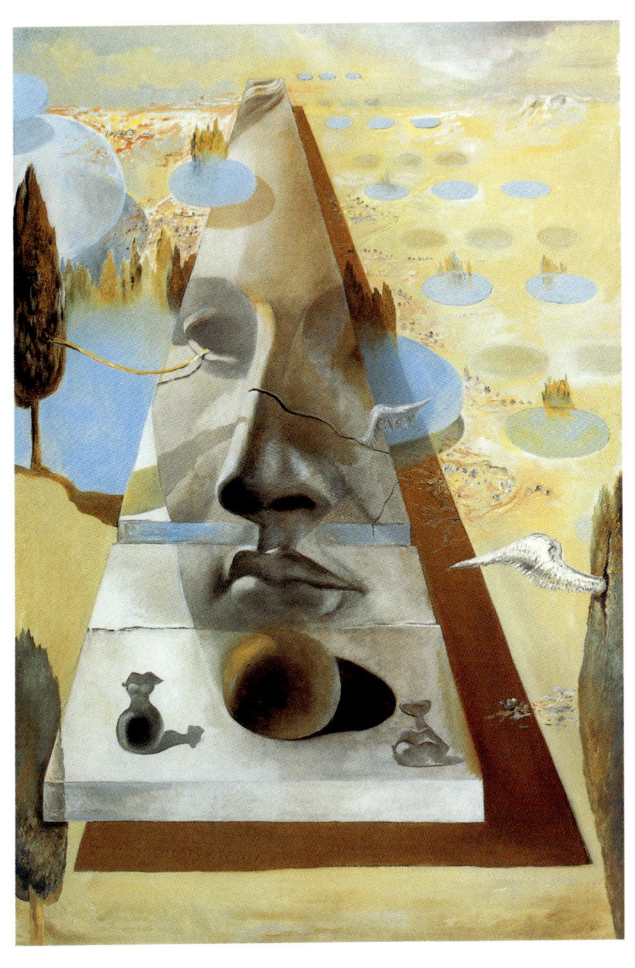

Apparition of the Visage of Aphrodite of Cnidos in a Landscape · 1981
Fundación Gala-Salvador Dalí, Figueras,
gift of Dalí to the Spanish state

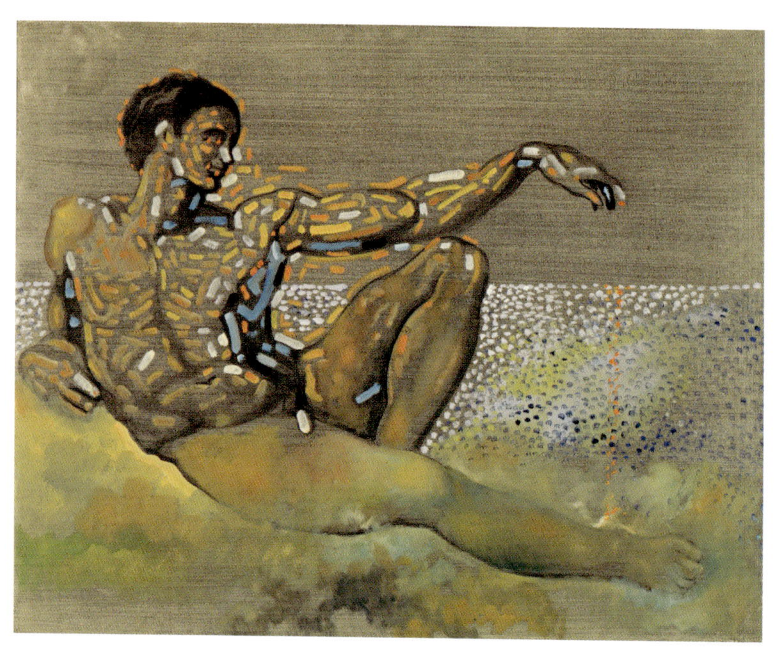

**Figure Inspired by Michelangelo's Adam on the Ceiling
of the Sistine Chapel, Rome** · 1982

Fundación Gala-Salvador Dalí, Figueras, gift of Dalí to the Spanish state

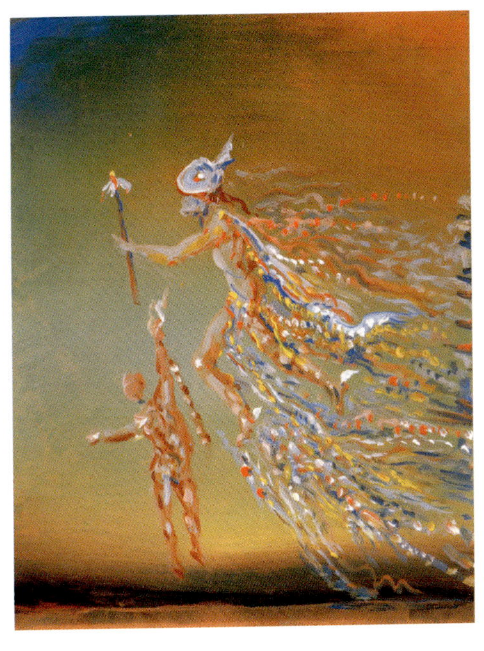

Hermes · 1981
Museo Nacional Centro de Arte Reina Sofía, Madrid,
gift of Dalí to the Spanish state

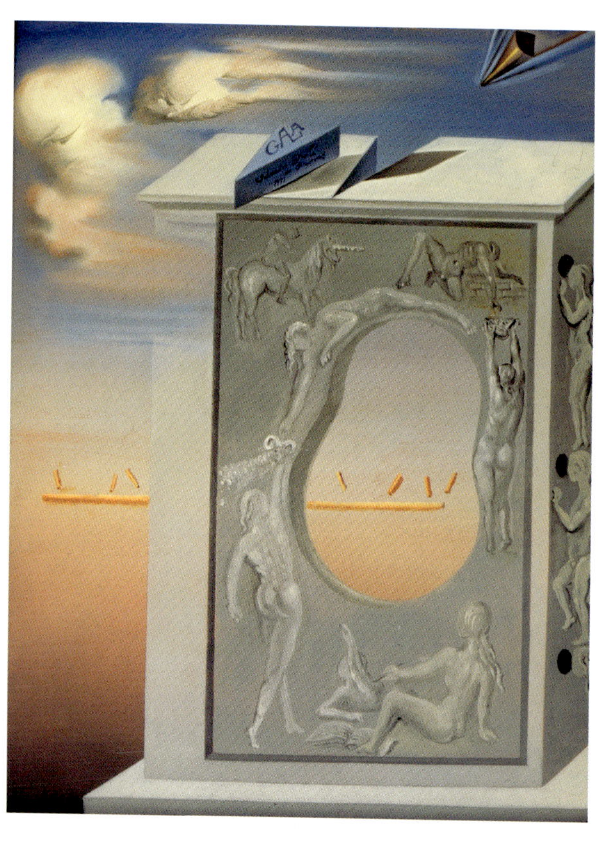

The Tower of Enigmas. Project for the cover of "Vogue" · 1971–81
Fundación Gala-Salvador Dalí, Figueras, gift of Dalí to the Spanish state

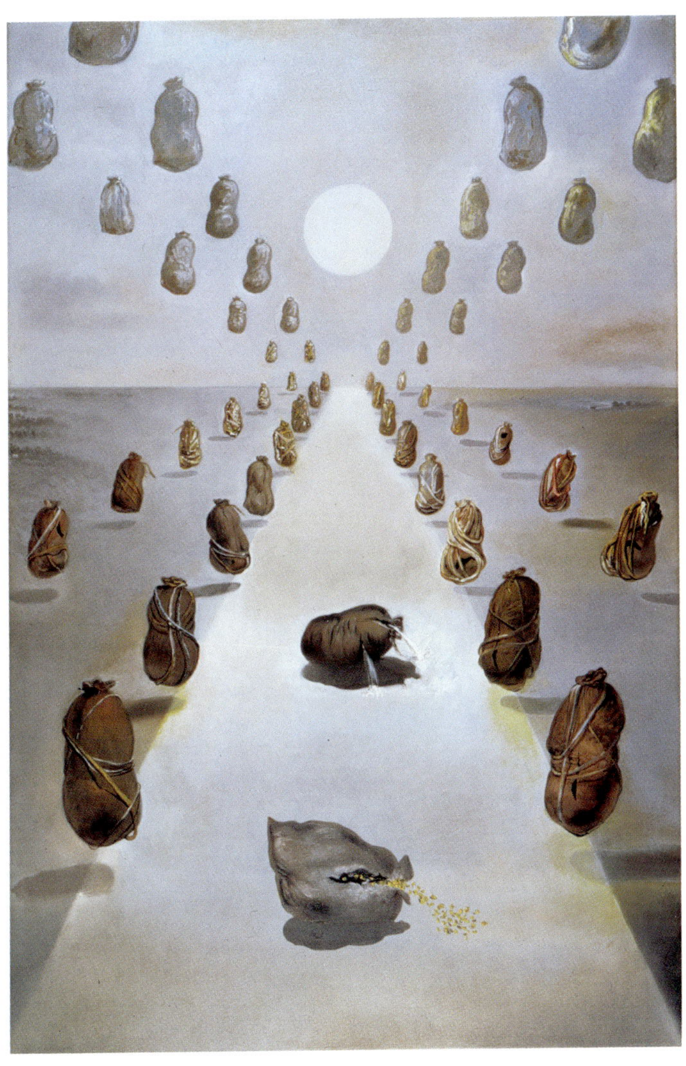

The Path of Enigmas (second version) · 1981
Fundación Gala-Salvador Dalí, Figueras

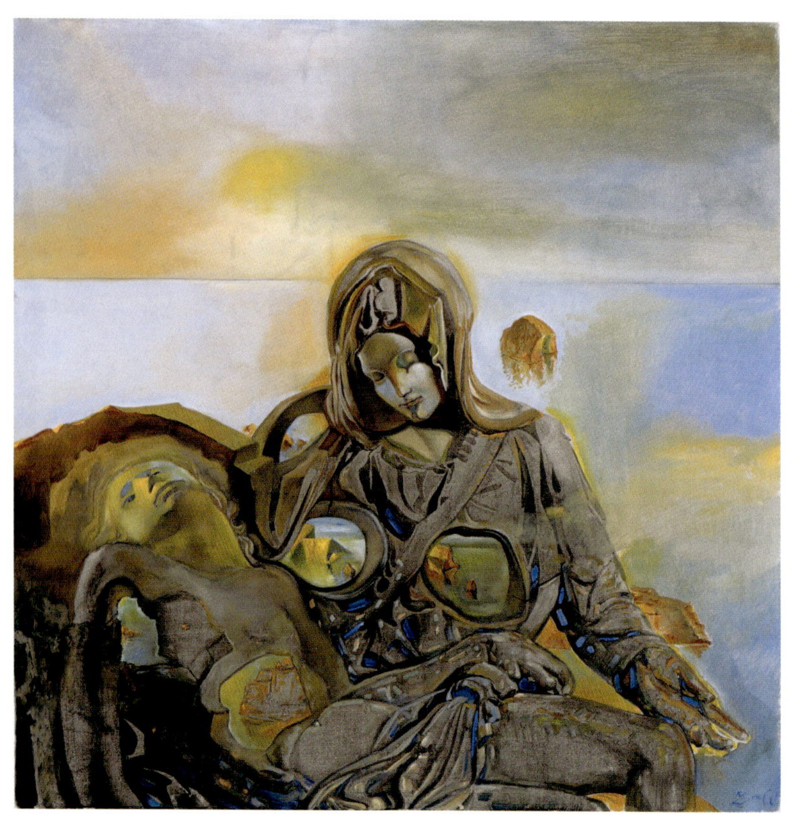

Geological Echo (Pietà) · 1982
Fundación Gala-Salvador Dalí, Figueras

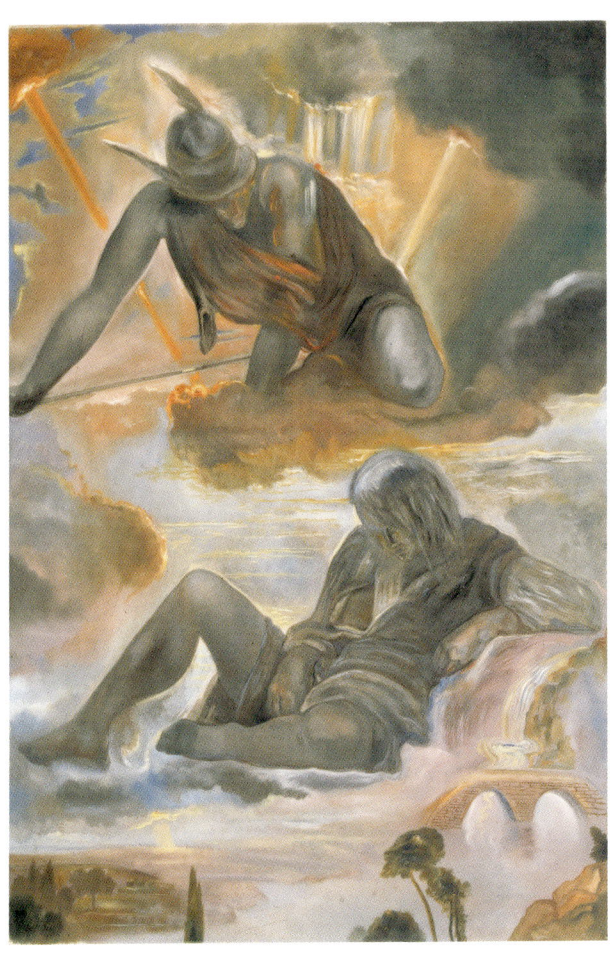

**Mercury and Argos
(after "Mercury and Argos" by Velázquez,
Museo del Prado) · 1981**

Fundación Gala-Salvador Dalí, Figueras, gift of Dalí to the Spanish state

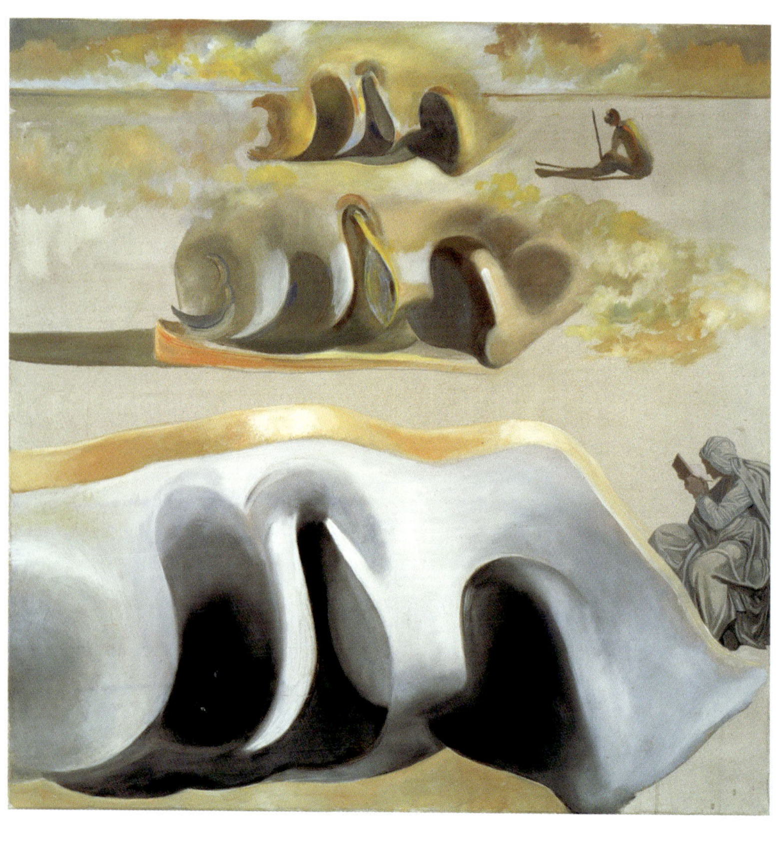

The Three Glorious Enigmas of Gala (second version) · 1982

Fundación Gala-Salvador Dalí, Figueras, gift of Dalí to the Spanish state

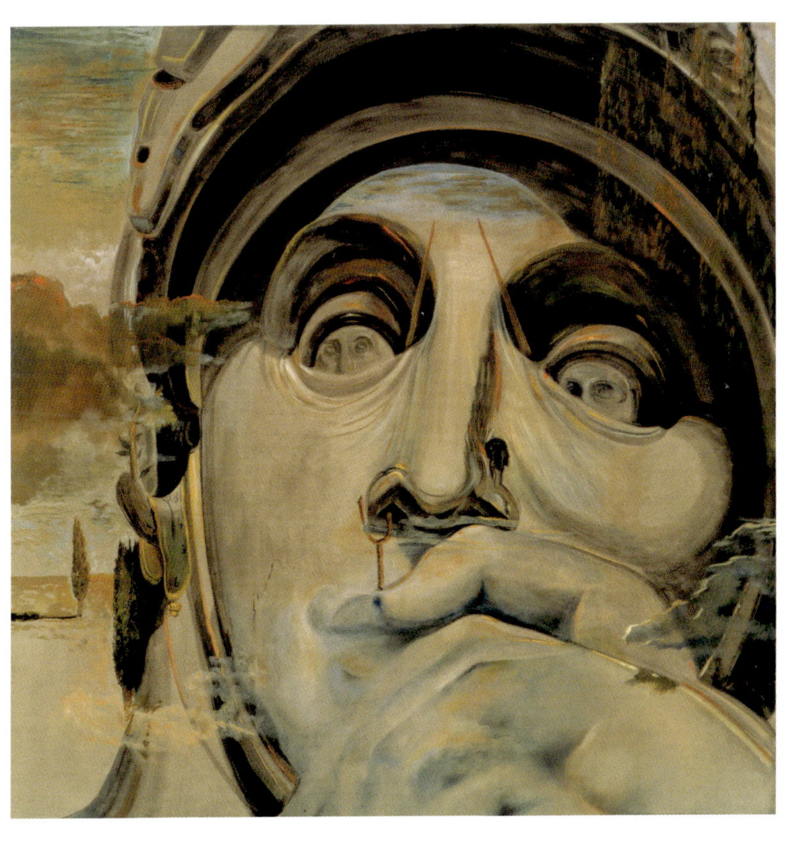

Warrior · 1982
Fundación Gala-Salvador Dalí, Figueras, gift of Dalí to the Spanish state

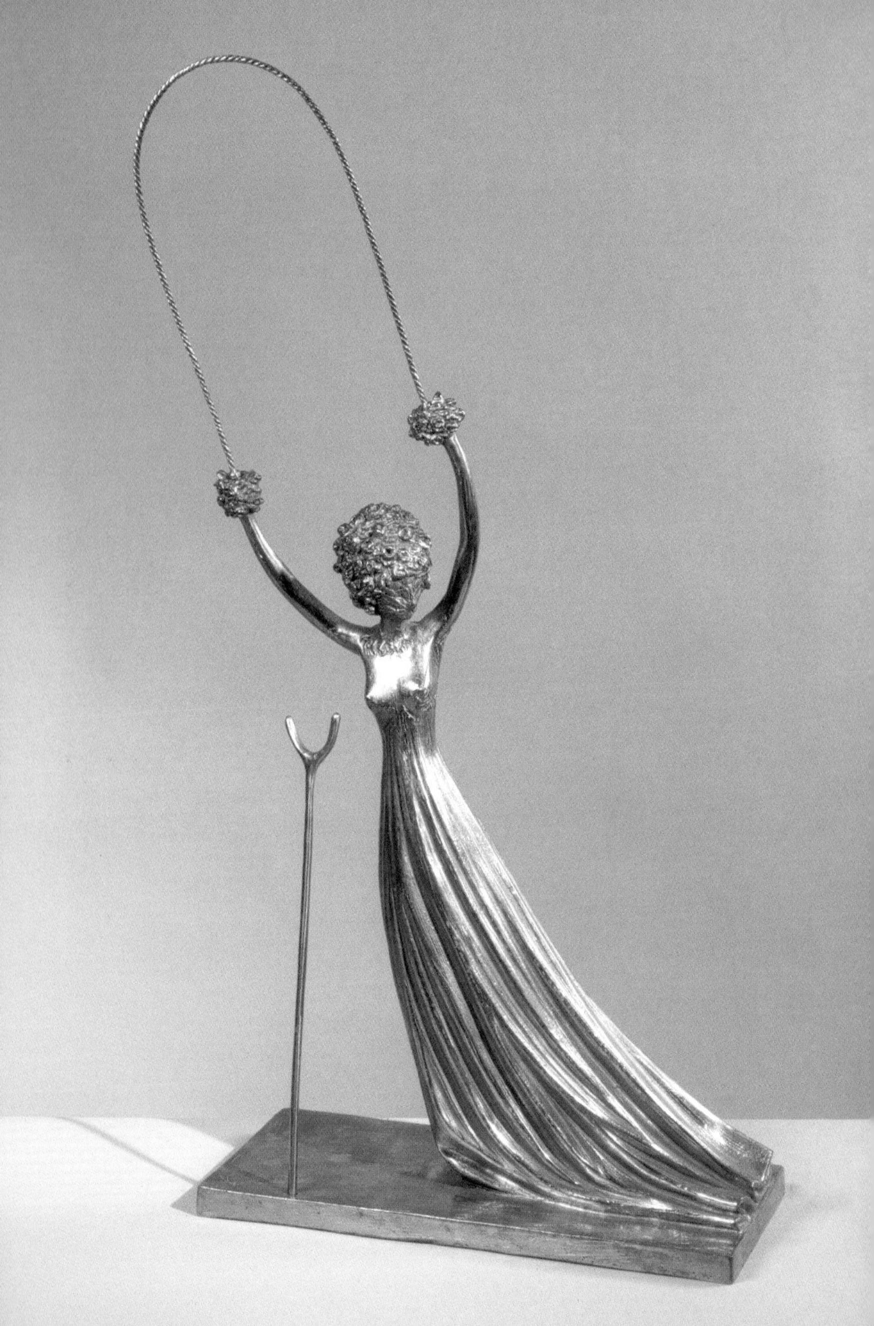

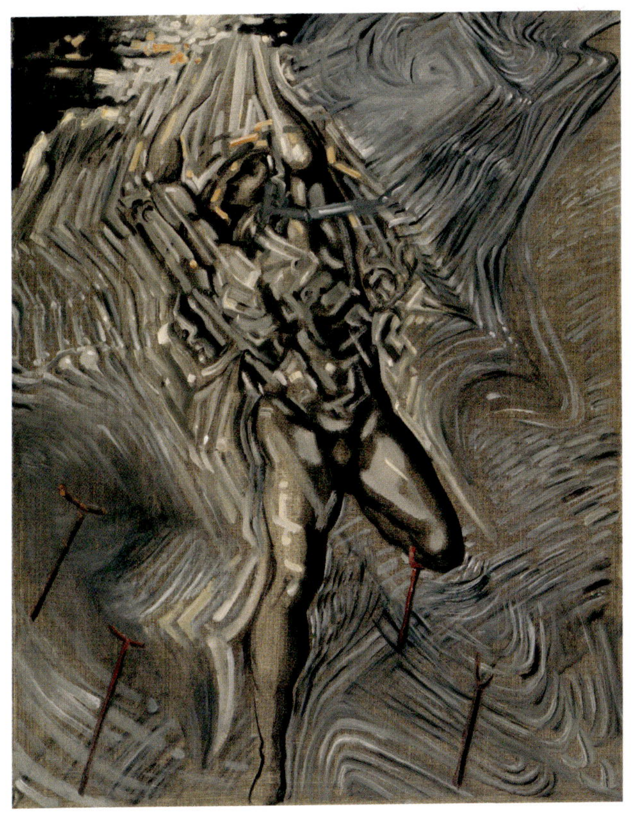

Martyr—Inspired by the Sufferings of Dalí in His Illness · 1982
Fundación Gala-Salvador Dalí, Figueras, gift of Dalí to the Spanish state
‹ **Alice in the Land of Wonder** · 1984
Phillips, The International Fine Art Auctioneers

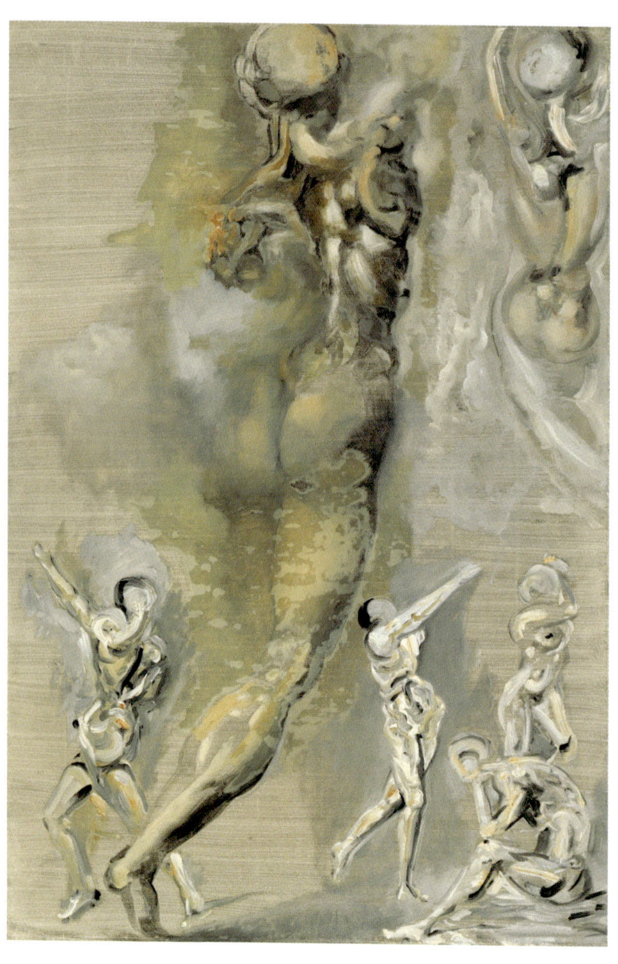

Untitled (Nude Figures after Michelangelo) · 1982
Fundación Gala-Salvador Dalí, Figueras,
gift of Dalí to the Spanish state

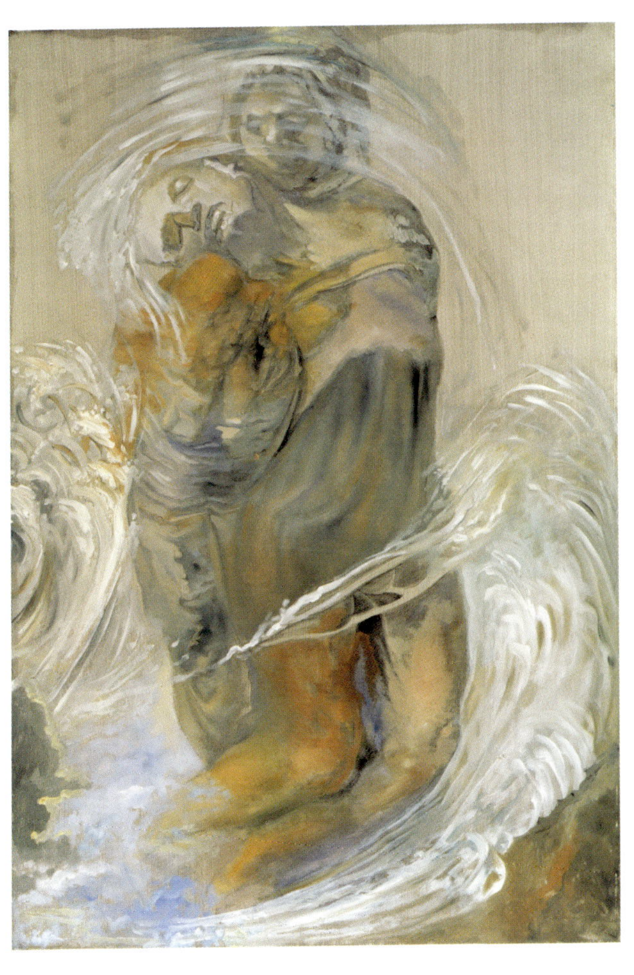

Pietà · 1982
Fundación Gala-Salvador Dalí, Figueras,
gift of Dalí to the Spanish state

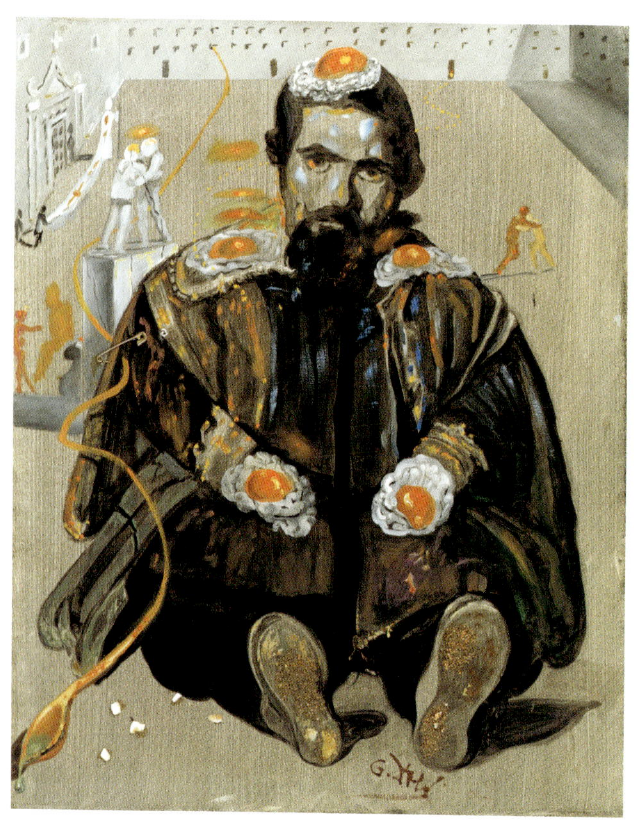

**Velázquez Dying behind the Window
on the Left Side out of which a Spoon Projects** · 1982
Fundación Gala-Salvador Dalí, Figueras, gift of Dalí to the Spanish state

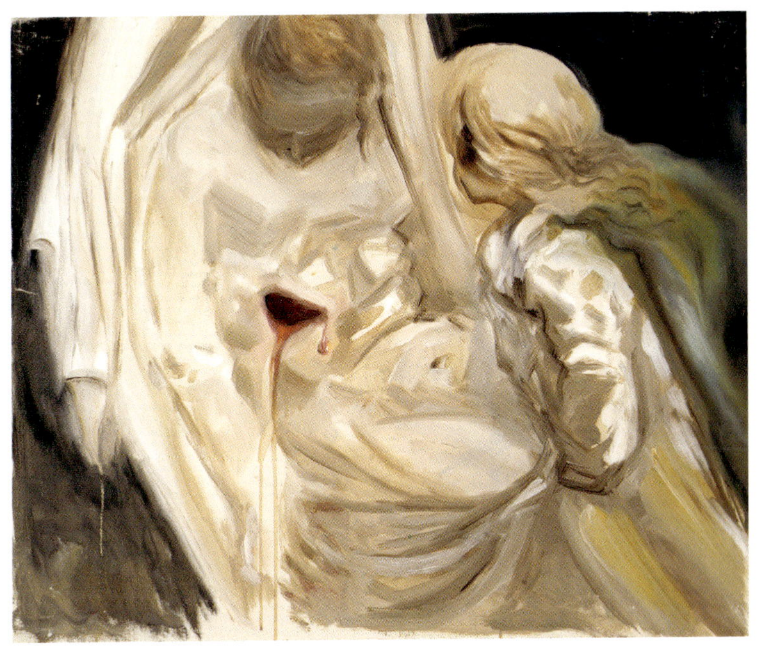

Pietà · 1983
Fundación Gala-Salvador Dalí, Figueras,
gift of Dalí to the Spanish state

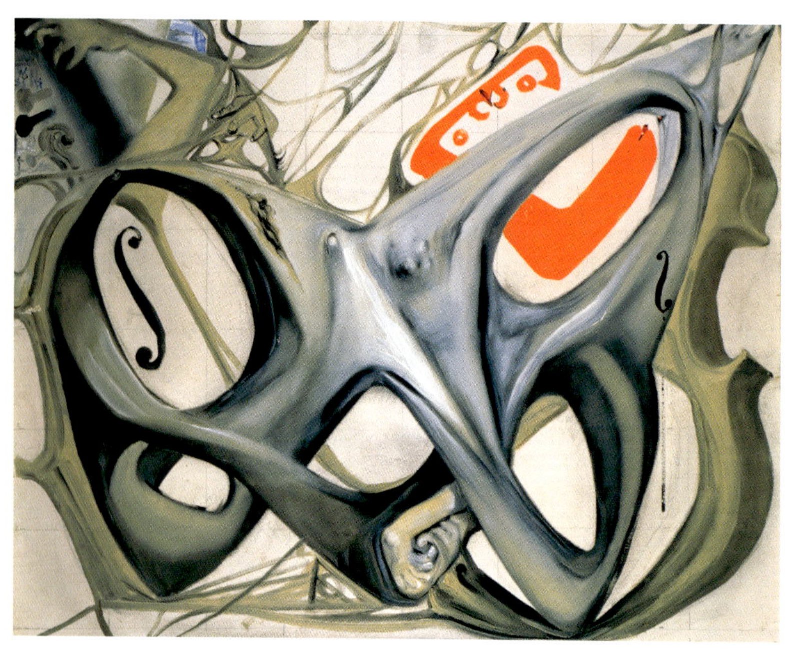

Topological Contortion of a Female Figure Becoming a Cello · 1983
Museo Nacional Centro de Arte Reina Sofía, Madrid, gift of Dalí to the Spanish state

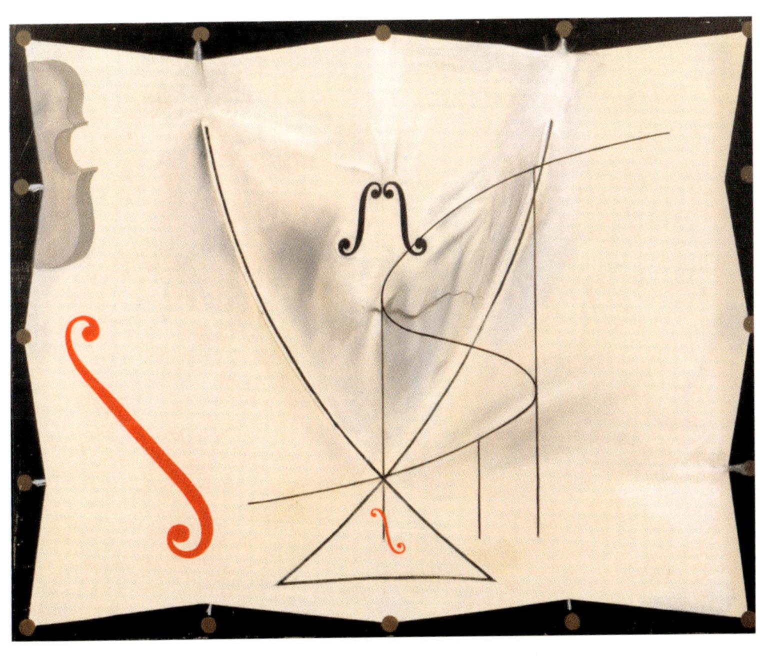

The Swallow's Tail—Series on Catastrophes · 1983
Fundación Gala-Salvador Dalí, Figueras, gift of Dalí to the Spanish state

Biographical Chronology

1904 Salvador Felipe Jacinto Dalí y Domenech is born in Figueras near Gerona (Catalonia, Spain). His father is the 40-year-old notary Salvador Dalí y Cusí, his mother the 30-year-old Felipa Domenech. Dalí spends his childhood years in Figueras, Barcelona, and Cadaqués, where his parents own a summer house. His drawing skills become apparent from a very early age. **1918** Dalí has his first exhibition at the municipal theater in Figueras, which is later to become his own museum, the Teatro Museo Dalí (1974). **1919** Dalí publishes an arts chronicle in the local magazine *Studium*, writing on painters he admires: Michelangelo, El Greco, Velázquez, Dürer, Goya, and Leonardo da Vinci. **1920** Dalí paints landscapes in and near Cadaqués and portraits of the cellist Ricardo Pichot and of his father (pp. 16, 17, 19). **1921** Dalí's mother dies in February. Around this time he starts exploring his potential as a dandy; he paints several self-portraits (pp. 20, 21). He studies the Old Masters in the Prado and is accepted at the Academia de San Fernando, Madrid, in October. In the student residence where he lives, he makes friends with the poet Federico García Lorca and the filmmaker Luis Buñuel. **1922–24** Dalí is coming to terms with the major Modernist movements. His work shows influences of Picasso and Cubism, Purism, and Italian "Pittura Metafisica." In 1923 he is suspended for a year from the Academy for subversive behavior. Arrested for disturbance of the peace and political agitation against the dictatorship of Primo de Rivera, who had seized power that year, he is detained for a month at Figueras and Gerona. He paints *Self-Portrait with "L'Humanité"*; *Cubist Self-Portrait* (1923, pp. 31, 30) and portraits of Buñuel and his sister Ana María (1924, p. 37). **1925** Dalí spends the holidays at Cadaqués with Lorca. He starts studying the work of Sigmund Freud. In November his first solo exhibition at the Galerie Dalmau in Barcelona (17 paintings and 5 drawings) is noticed by Pablo Picasso and Joan Miró. Further portraits of his sister Ana María (*Seated Girl from the Back*; *Figure at a Window*; pp. 42, 45) and of his father (pp. 40, 41). **1926** Dalí travels to Paris for the first time; there he meets Picasso in April. In October he is permanently expelled from the Academia de San Fernando. Lorca's poem "Ode to Salvador Dalí" is published in *Revista de Occidente* (April). December–January: second one-man show at the Galerie Dalmau. **1927** Between February and October Dalí completes his military service. He designs sets and costumes for Lorca's drama *Mariana Pineda* (premiere in Barcelona, June); their friendship deepens. Dalí begins to contribute texts to the Catalan review *L'Amic de les Arts* (until 1929). He spends the summer in Cadaqués with Lorca. First Surrealist works: *Honey is Sweeter than Blood*; *Apparatus and Hand*; *Little Cinders* (pp. 56, 57, 64). **1928** Dalí publishes *Manifeste groc* (*The Yellow Manifesto*) with Lluis Montanyá and Sebastiá Gasch. *Basket of Bread* and *Seated Girl from the Back* (pp. 44, 42) are among his first works that are exhibited in the USA (Carnegie Institute, Pittsburgh). **1929** With Buñuel in Paris he shoots *Un Chien andalou* (*An Andalusian Dog*), the film that makes them famous overnight and marks their acceptance into the ranks of the Paris Surrealists. *L'Amic de les Arts* No. 31 (March) contains several contributions by Dalí, including an interview with Buñuel. Gala and Paul Eluard, René and Georgette Magritte, and his new dealer Camille Goemans visit him at Cadaqués in the summer. Dalí's first meeting with Gala, the "muse of the Surrealists," is the beginning of their lifelong companionship. Their relationship leads to a break with his father. November: first one-man show in Paris at Goemans's gallery. Paintings such as *The Great Masturbator*; *The Lugubrious Game*; *The Enigma of Desire*; *Illuminated Pleasures*; *Portrait of Paul Eluard*; *Accommodations of Desire* (pp. 87, 89, 86, 80, 83, 79) show a new confidence after the stylistic vagaries of the preceding years. **1930** Successful exhibitions in Paris and the sale of some of his major works to the Surrealists and their circle (the Vicomte de Noailles purchases *The Lugubrious Game*, p. 89) enable Dalí to buy a fisherman's house at Port Lligat near Cadaqués. There he henceforth spends several months each year with Gala. He begins to develop his paranoiac-critical method, an attempt at "the critical and systematic objectification of delirious associations and interpretations," based on the ability to perceive different images within a given configuration, which results in his famous "double images" (*The Invisible Man*; *Invisible Sleeping Woman, Horse, Lion*; pp. 85, 90). The first public showing of *L'Age d'Or* (*The Golden Age*), his second film with Luis Buñuel, ends in turmoil. He participates in the first Surrealist exhibition in the USA at the Wadsworth Atheneum, Hartford, Connecticut. **1931** Dalí's first one-man show at the Pierre Colle Gallery, Paris, with whom the artist had concluded a contract after the closure of Goemans's gallery in 1930, includes *Invisible Sleeping Woman, Horse, Lion* (1930); *William Tell*; and *The Persistence of Memory* (*Soft Watches*) (pp. 90, 99, 110). **1932** Dalí is represented in the Surrealist exhibition at the Julien Levy Gallery, New York. Second one-man show at Pierre Colle's. **1933** The newly established group of collectors "Zodiac" begins to buy Dalí's work on a regular basis. Dalí participates in the exhibition of Surrealist objects at Pierre Colle's. A one-man show in June includes several works on what is to become a recurrent theme in his oeuvre, Jean-François Millet's *The Angelus*. First solo exhibition at the Julien Levy Gallery, New York. Dalí publishes an article on "edible beauty" and Art Nouveau architecture in *Minotaure* magazine. Surrealist object: *Retrospective Bust of a Woman* (p. 123). **1934** The exhibition of *The Enigma of William Tell* (p. 132) at the Salon des Indépendants, which represents Lenin kneeling with a flaccid, elongated buttock supported with a crutch, very nearly leads to a break with André Breton and the Surrealists. First one-man show in London at the Zwemmer Gallery. November: Dalí makes a first trip to the USA on the occasion of his successful solo exhibitions at the Julien Levy Gallery, New York, and Wadsworth Atheneum, Hartford, Connecticut. **1935** Dalí gives a lecture on Surrealism at the Museum of Modern Art, New York. Financial arrangement with the English collector and supporter of the Surrealists Edward James, who purchases his most important works (until 1939). **1936** During a lecture at the International Exhibition of Surrealism in London, delivered in diving suit and helmet, Dalí narrowly escapes suffocating. His exhibition at Julien Levy's, New York, arouses much interest. *Soft Construction with Boiled Beans—Premonition of Civil War* (p. 177) precedes the actual outbreak of Civil War in Spain (July 1936) by a few months. Dalí is featured on the cover of *Time* magazine's December issue. *The Great Paranoiac; The Anthropomorphic Cabinet; A Couple with Their Heads Full of Clouds; Mae West's Face which May Be Used as a Surrealist Apartment* (pp. 185, 182–83, 164–65, 152); objects: *Lobster Telephone* (p. 169); *Mae West's Lips Sofa* (1936–37; p. 187) **1937** Dalí meets Harpo Marx in Hollywood and together they work on a screenplay for a Marx Brothers film of which only a few drawings and notes survive. He spends several months at Edward James's house in Italy to avoid the Spanish Civil War. His comments on Hitler are condemned by Breton and the Surrealists. *The Burning Giraffe; The Metamorphosis of Narcissus; Sleep* (pp. 189, 202, 196). **1938** January: Dalí participates in the Surrealist exhibition in Paris. In July he visits Sigmund Freud in London. *Impressions of Africa; Spain* (pp. 210, 213). **1939** The conflict with the Surrealists over Dalí's political attitude, among other things, which had been building up since the mid-1930s, has by now become irreparable. (Dalí is henceforth dubbed anagrammatically "Avida Dollars" by André Breton.) The ballet *Bacchanale* (choreography by Leonide Massine; libretto and set design by Dalí) premieres at the Metropolitan Opera in New York. Dalí's solo exhibition at Julien Levy's excites much attention: he sells 21 pictures to private collectors for $25,000. On the outbreak of the Second World War Dalí and Gala move to Arcachon on the Atlantic coast. **1940** After the invasion of France, Dalí and Gala flee to the USA, via Spain (where he visits his father for the first time since the rupture some ten years before). They settle in Hampton, Virginia. They remain in exile in the USA until 1948, during which years Dalí designs numerous advertisements. *Slave Market with the Disappearing Bust of Voltaire* (p. 220). **1941** Exhibition at the Julien Levy Gallery. November: first retrospective at the Museum of Modern Art, New York. Dalí designs his first jewels in collaboration with the Duke of Verdura. *Soft Self-Portrait with Fried Bacon* (p. 222). **1942** Dalí's autobiography, *The Secret Life of Salvador Dalí*, finished in 1941, is published in New York. **1943** He exhibits a series of portraits of American celebrities at Knoedler's, New York. **1944** George Orwell reviews *The Secret Life of Salvador Dalí* ("Benefit of Clergy: Some Notes on Salvador Dalí": "So long as you can paint well enough to pass the test, all shall be forgiven you."). **1945** Exhibition of recent works at the Bignou Gallery, New York. **1946** Dalí is invited by Alfred Hitchcock to design the dream sequence for *Spellbound*, the first Hollywood film in which psychoanalysis is taken seriously. Walt Disney approaches Dalí to design a cartoon, but the plans for "Destino," as it was going to be called, come to nothing. Dalí completes *The Temptation of St. Anthony* (p. 266). **1947** Second show at the Bignou Gallery. First studies for *Leda Atomica* (p. 274). **1948** The Dalís return to Europe. *Fifty Secrets of Magic Craftsmanship* is published in New York, where from now on Dalí spends several weeks each winter. **1949–50** Dalí designs theater productions by Peter Brook (*Salomé*) and Luchino Visconti (*As You Like It*) in London and Rome, respectively. He finishes *Leda Atomica* (p. 275) the two versions of *The Madonna of Port Lligat*, the smaller version of which he offers to the pope, by whom he is received in audience. **1951** Dalí's publication of *The Mystical Manifesto* marks the beginning of his "particle period." The Dalís attend the ball organized in Venice by the Spanish millionaire Charles de Beistegui dressed as giants by Christian Dior. **1952** Dalí lectures throughout the USA on "nuclear mysticism." Controversy over the acquisition of Dalí's *Christ of St. John of the Cross* (1951; p. 285) by the Glasgow Art Museum (the painting is now in the St. Mungo Museum of Religious Life and Art). Dalí exhibits six paintings in the Carstairs Gallery in New York, including *Assumpta corpuscularia lapislazulina* (p. 286). **1954** Large retrospective exhibition in Rome, with later venues in Venice and Milan. *Young Virgin Auto-Sodomized by Her Own Chastity; Corpus Hypercubus (Crucifixion)* (p. 311, 299) **1955** Lecture at the Sorbonne on Vermeer's *Lacemaker* and the rhinoceros: "Aspects phénoménologiques de la méthode paranoïaque-critique" (Phenomenological aspects of the paranoiac-critical method). **1956** Exhibition at the National Gallery of Art, Washington, D.C., of works from the Chester Dale Collection, including *The Last Supper* of 1955 (p. 312). June: private audience with General Franco at the Bardo Palace, Madrid. **1957** Projects for a film on Don Quixote with Walt Disney and for a night club at Acapulco are never realized. Publication of Dalí monograph by Michel Tapié. **1958** Dalí marries Gala in a religious ceremony in Spain. Exhibition of atomic "anti-matter" paintings at Carstairs Gallery, New York. *The Discovery of America by Christopher Columbus* (1958–59; p. 324). **1959** Audience with Pope John XXIII. Lectures in Paris and London (Planetarium). **1960** The Surrealists protest against Dalí's inclusion in the Surrealist exhibition at the d'Arcy Galleries, New York. Dalí continues his series of large-format mystical works with *The Ecumenical Council* (p. 332). **1961** Premiere in Venice of *Ballet of Gala* (choreography by Maurice Béjart; libretto and set design by Dalí). **1962** Publication of Robert Descharnes's monograph *Dalí de Gala*. **1963** Exhibition of his most recent works at Knoedler's, New York. Publication of Dalí's *Tragic Myth of Millet's Angelus*. He completes the painting *Portrait of My Dead Brother* (p. 338). **1964** Dalí is awarded the Grand Cross of Isabella the Catholic, the highest Spanish decoration. Major retrospective exhibition in Japan. His *Journal d'un génie* is published in Paris (*Journal of a Genius*, New York 1965). **1965** Experiments with holography. *The Railway Station at Perpignan* (p. 356), described by Dalí as his "best work so far," is exhibited at the Knoedler Gallery, New York. **1967** Dalí organizes the exhibition "Homage to Meissonier" at the Hôtel Meurice in Paris, where he shows his recently finished painting *Tuna Fishing* (p. 348). **1970** Critical acclaim for Dalí's exhibition of recent works at Knoedler's, New York, including *The Hallucinogenic Toreador* (p. 352). He announces the creation of a Dalí museum at Figueras. November: first large retrospective in the Netherlands at Museum Boijmans Van Beuningen, Rotterdam. **1971** Another Salvador Dalí Museum, founded by A. Reynolds Morse and Eleanor Morse and comprising their collection, is opened in Cleveland, Ohio. It is transferred to St. Petersburg, Florida, in 1982. Major retrospective at the Staatliche Kunsthalle Baden-Baden.

1972 Exhibition of holograms at Knoedler's, New York. **1973–78** Experiments with stereoscopic works: *Gala's Foot; The Chair; Gala's Christ* (pp. 368–69, 372, 380–81). **1974** The inauguration of the Teatro Museo Dalí in Figueras is the fulfillment of a lifelong wish. **1978** Dalí is elected a member of the French Académie des Beaux-Arts. **1979** Large retrospective starting at the Centre Pompidou, Paris, then Tate Gallery, London. **1982** Gala dies (10 June). Dalí is created Marquess of Púbol. He now lives in the castle at Púbol which he had given to Gala. **1983** Major retrospective in Madrid and Barcelona. Dalí finishes his last painting in May: *The Swallow's Tail—Series on Catastrophes* (p. 411). **1984** Dalí's health, which had begun to fail after Gala's death, further deteriorates after he is seriously burnt in a fire at Púbol. Retrospective in Ferrara. **1984–88** Much of the last part of his life is spent in seclusion, first in Púbol, then in his apartments at Torre Galatea, next to the Teatro Museo. **1989** Salvador Dalí dies on 23 January 1989 in Figueras from heart failure with respiratory complications.

Concise Bibliography

Georges Bataille. "Le jeu lugubre," *Documents* 7 (1929). **Salvador Dalí**. *The Secret Life of Salvador Dalí*. New York 1942. **Salvador Dalí**. *Hidden Faces*. New York 1944. **Salvador Dalí**. *Fifty Secrets of Magic Craftsmanship*. New York 1948. **Ana María Dalí**. *Salvador Dalí, vist per la seva germana*. Barcelona 1949; French ed.: *Salvador Dalí vu par sa sœur*. Paris 1960. **Salvador Dalí**. *Manifeste mystique*. Paris 1951. **André Breton**. *Anthologie de l'humour noir*, Paris 1953. **Michel Tapié**. *Dalí*. Paris 1957. **Robert Descharnes and Salvador Dalí**. *Dalí de Gala*. Lausanne 1962 (2nd ed. 1979). **Salvador Dalí**. *Diary of a Genius*. New York 1965. **Alain Bosquet**. *Conversations with Dalí*. New York 1969. **Carlton Lake**. *In Quest of Dalí*. New York 1969. **William Rubin**. *Dada and Surrealist Art*. London 1969. **A. Reynolds Morse**. *Salvador Dalí. A guide to his works in public museums*. Cleveland, Ohio, The Salvador Dalí Museum, 1974. **Robert Descharnes**. *Salvador Dalí*. New York 1976. *Salvador Dalí*. Exh. cat. Tate Gallery, London 1980. **Dawn Ades**. *Dalí*. London 1982. **Daniel Abadie et al.** *Salvador Dalí: Rétrospective 1920–1980*. Exh. cat. Musée National d'Art Moderne, Centre Georges Pompidou, Paris 1979–80. **Robert Descharnes and Gilles Néret**. *Salvador Dalí 1904–1989. The Paintings*. Cologne, London, Madrid, et al. 2001.

Index of Works

on canvas, 230 x 144 cm, Collection John Theodoracopoulos. **Atavism at Twilight** 134, 1933–34, oil on panel, 14 x 18 cm, Kunstmuseum Bern, Georges F. Keller Bequest 1981. **Atavistic Vestiges after the Rain** 127, 1934, oil on canvas, 65 x 54 cm, Perls Galleries, New York; formerly Collection Carlo Ponti, Rome. **Athens Is Burning!—The School of Athens and the Fire in the Borgo (Stereoscopic work; right component)** 391, 1979–80, oil on panel, stereoscopic work, 32.2 x 43.1 cm, Fundación Gala-Salvador Dalí, Figueras. **Athens Is Burning!—The School of Athens and the Fire in the Borgo (Stereoscopic work; left component)** 390, 1979–80, oil on panel, stereoscopic work, 32.2 x 43.1 cm, Fundación Gala-Salvador Dalí, Figueras. **Atmospheric Skull Sodomizing a Grand Piano** 142, 1934, oil on panel, 14 x 18 cm, The Salvador Dalí Museum, St. Petersburg, Florida, on loan from E. and A. Reynolds Morse. **Illustration for "The Autobiography of Benvenuto Cellini"** 254, 1945, pen and India ink on paper, 28 x 19 cm, gift of Dalí to the Spanish state. **Illustration for "The Autobiography of Benvenuto Cellini"** 255, 1945, pen and India ink on paper, 18 x 10.5 cm, gift of Dalí to the Spanish state. **Automatic Beginning of a Portrait of Gala (unfinished)** 113, 1932, oil on laminated panel, 13 x 16 cm, Fundación Gala-Salvador Dalí, Figueras. **Autumn Cannibalism** 168, 1936, oil on canvas, 65 x 65.2 cm, Tate Gallery, London; formerly Collection Edward James. **Average Pagan Landscape** 192, 1937, oil on panel, 38 x 46 cm, Collection G.E.D. Nahmad, Geneva; formerly Collection Edward James. **Barber Saddened by the Persistence of Good Weather (The Anguished Barber)** 137, 1934, oil on canvas, 24 x 16.5 cm, Collection Klaus G. Perls, New York. **Basket of Bread** 44, 1925, oil on panel, 31.5 x 31.5 cm, The Salvador Dalí Museum, St. Petersburg, Florida; formerly Collection E. and A. Reynolds Morse. **Basket of Bread—Rather Death than Shame** 256, 1945, oil on panel, 33 x 38 cm, Fundación Gala-Salvador Dalí, Figueras. **Bather (Female Nude)** 65, 1928, oil and pebbles on laminated panel, 63.5 x 75 cm, The Salvador Dalí Museum, St. Petersburg, Florida, on loan from E. and A. Reynolds Morse. **Beach with Telephone** 207, 1938, oil on canvas, 73.6 x 92 cm, Tate Gallery, London; formerly Collection Edward James. **Beatrice** 327, 1960, oil on canvas, 40.5 x 30.5 cm, The Salvador Dalí Museum, St. Petersburg, Florida, on loan from E. and A. Reynolds Morse. **Big Thumb, Beach, Moon, and Decaying Bird** 67, 1928, oil and pebbles on laminated panel, 50 x 61 cm, The Salvador Dalí Museum, St. Petersburg, Florida; formerly Collection E. and A. Reynolds Morse. **Bird** 68, 1928, oil, sand, and gravel collage on panel, 49 x 60 cm, private collection, England; formerly Collection Sir Roland Penrose. **The Birth of Liquid Desires** 120, 1932, oil on canvas, 95 x 112 cm, Peggy Guggenheim Collection, Venice. **The Bleeding Roses** 94, 1930, oil on canvas, 75 x 64 cm, private collection, Geneva. **The Burning Giraffe** 189, 1936–37, oil on panel, 35 x 27 cm, Kunstmuseum Basel, Öffentliche Kunstsammlung, Basel; Emanuel Hoffmann Foundation. **Bust of Velázquez Turning into Three Figures Conversing** 374, 1974, painted bronze, 90 x 70 x 38 cm, Fundación Gala-Salvador Dalí, Figueras. **Cardinal, Cardinal!** 143, 1934, oil and gouache on panel, 16 x 22 cm, Munson-Williams-Proctor Arts Institute, Utica, New York. **Ceiling of the hall of Gala's castle at Púbol** 358–9, 1971, oil on primed canvas, irregularly painted, 12.17 x 6.25 m, gift of Dalí to the Spanish state. **The Chair (Stereoscopic work; left component)** 372, 1975, oil on canvas, stereoscopic work, two components, 400 x 210 cm, Fundación Gala-Salvador Dalí, Figueras. **The Chemist of Ampurdán in Search of Absolutely Nothing** 179, 1936, oil on panel, 30 x 52 cm, Museum Folkwang, Essen; formerly Collection Edward James. **Christ in Perspective. Study for "Christ of St. John of the Cross" 284**, 1950, red chalk on paper, 75.7 x 101.7 cm, The Salvador Dalí Museum, St. Petersburg, Florida. **Christ of St. John of the Cross 285**, 1951, oil on canvas, 205 x 116 cm, St. Mungo Museum of Religious Life and Art, Glasgow. **The City of Drawers. Study for the "Anthropomorphic Cabinet" 182**, 1936, pen and India ink on paper, 32 x 41.5 cm, Collection Paul L. Herring, New York; formerly Collection Edward James. **Clothed Automobile (Two Cadillacs) 224**, 1941, oil on cardboard, 39.5 x 27 cm, Fundación Gala-Salvador Dalí, Figueras. **Study for "Colloque sentimental" 252**, 1944, oil on canvas, 26 x 47 cm, The Salvador Dalí Museum, St. Petersburg, Florida, on loan from E. and A. Reynolds Morse. **The Colossus of Rhodes 306**, 1954, oil on canvas, 68.8 x 39 cm, Kunstmuseum Bern. **Study for "Compianto Diabele" by Canova (unfinished) 385**, c.1979, oil and pencil on copper, 37.8 x 25.8 cm, Museo Nacional Centro de Arte Reina Sofía, Madrid, gift of Dalí to the Spanish state. **Composition (Two Harlequins) 225**, 1942, oil on canvas, 23 x 35.6 cm, private collection. **Condottiere (Self-Portrait as Condottiere) 239**, 1943, India ink on white paper, 76.3 x 55.8 cm, private collection. **Continuum of the Four Buttocks (Five Rhinoceros Horns Making a Virgin—Birth of a Deity) 329**, 1960, oil on canvas, 92.5 x 153 cm, Generalitat de Catalunya, Departament de Cultura, Barcelona, gift of the artist, 1980. **Copy of a Rubens Copy of a Leonardo 384**, 1979, oil on panel, 18 x 24 cm, Fundación Gala-Salvador Dalí, Figueras, gift of Dalí to the Spanish state. **Corpus Hypercubus (Crucifixion) 299**, 1954, oil on canvas, 194.5 x 124 cm, The Metropolitan Museum of Art, New York, gift of Chester Dale. **Costume for "Tristan Insane"—The Ship 240**, 1942–43, watercolor, 63 x 46 cm, The Salvador Dalí Museum, St. Petersburg, Florida. **A Couple with Their Heads Full of Clouds 164–5**, 1936, oil on panel; Man: 92.5 x 69.5 cm; Woman: 82.5 x 62.5 cm, Museum Boijmans Van Beuningen, Rotterdam; formerly Collection Edward James. **Cubist Figure (Homage to Erik Satie) 58**, 1926, oil on canvas, 152 x 90 cm, Fundación Gala-Salvador Dalí, Figueras, gift of Dalí to the Spanish state. **Cubist Self-Portrait 30**, 1923, gouache and collage on cardboard, 104.9 x 74.2 cm, Museo Nacional Centro de Arte Reina Sofía, Madrid, gift of Dalí to the Spanish state. **Cybernetic Odalisque—Homage to Bela Julesz 378**, 1978, oil on canvas, 200 x 200 cm, Fundación Gala-Salvador Dalí, Figueras, gift of Dalí to the Spanish state. **Dalí from the Back Painting Gala from the Back Eternalized by Six Virtual Corneas Provisionally Reflected in Six Real Mirrors (unfinished) 366**, c.1972–73, oil on canvas, stereoscopic work, two components, 60 x 60 cm each, Fundación Gala-Salvador Dalí, Figueras. **Dalí Lifting the Skin of the Mediterranean Sea to Show Gala the Birth of Venus (Stereoscopic work; right component) 377**, 1977, oil on canvas, stereoscopic work on two components, 101 x 101 cm, Fundación Gala-Salvador Dalí, Figueras. **Dalí's Hand Drawing Back the Golden Fleece in the Form of a Cloud to Show Gala, Completely Nude, the Dawn, Very, Very Far Away Behind the Sun (Stereoscopic work; left component) 376**, 1977, oil on canvas, 60 x 60 cm, Fundación Gala-Salvador Dalí, Figueras, gift of Dalí to the Spanish state. **Dance—The Seven Arts 318**, 1957, oil on canvas, 84 x 114 cm, private collection; formerly Billy Rose Collection. **Dawn, Noon, Sunset, and Twilight 386–7**, 1979, oil on panel, 122 x 244 cm, Fundación Gala-Salvador Dalí, Figueras. **Day of the Virgin 261**, 1947, ink and watercolor on paper, private collection. **Debris of an Automobile Giving Birth to a Blind**

Horse Biting a Telephone 206, 1938, oil on canvas, 54 x 65 cm, The Museum of Modern Art, New York, gift of James Thrall Soby. **Dematerialization near the Nose of Nero 273**, 1947, oil on canvas, 76.2 x 45.8 cm, Fundación Gala-Salvador Dalí, Figueras, gift of Dalí to the Spanish state. **Desert Trilogy—Apparition of a Couple in the Desert. For "Desert Flower" perfume 265**, 1946, oil on canvas, dimensions unknown, private collection. **Desert Trilogy—Apparition of a Woman and Suspended Architecture in the Desert. For "Desert Flower" perfume 264**, 1946, oil on canvas, dimensions unknown, private collection. **Design for the Interior Decoration of a Stable-Library 235**, 1942, chrome overpainted with gouache and India ink, 51 x 45 cm, Fundación Gala-Salvador Dalí, Figueras. **Design for the set of the ballet "Tristan and Isolde" 249**, 1944, oil on canvas, 26.7 x 48.3 cm, Fundación Gala-Salvador Dalí, Figueras. **Design for "Vulcan and Venus" 268**, 1947, watercolor and India ink, dimensions unknown, Bonhams, London. **Disappearing Bust of Voltaire 221**, 1941, oil on canvas, 46.3 x 55.4 cm, The Salvador Dalí Museum, St. Petersburg, Florida, on loan from E. and A. Reynolds Morse. **The Discovery of America by Christopher Columbus (The Dream of Christopher Columbus) 324**, 1958–59, oil on canvas, 410 x 284 cm, The Salvador Dalí Museum, St. Petersburg, Florida, on loan from the Morse Charitable Trust. **Study for "The Discovery of America by Christopher Columbus" 325**, 1958, ballpoint on paper, 70 x 48 cm, gift of Dalí to the Spanish state. **Disguised Personage Pinning a Butterfly 340**, 1965, oil on laminated panel, 12 x 9 cm, Fundación Gala-Salvador Dalí, Figueras, gift of Dalí to the Spanish state. **The Disintegration of the Persistence of Memory 303**, 1952–54, oil on canvas, 25 x 33 cm, The Salvador Dalí Museum, St. Petersburg, Florida, on loan from E. and A. Reynolds Morse. **Diurnal Fantasies 109**, 1932, oil on canvas, 81 x 100 cm, The Salvador Dalí Museum, St. Petersburg, Florida, on loan from the Morse Charitable Trust. **Don Salvador and Ana María Dalí (Portrait of the Artist's Father and Sister) 40**, 1925, pencil on paper, 49 x 33 cm, Museo de Arte Moderno, Barcelona. **The Dream 101**, 1931, oil on canvas, 100 x 100 cm, private collection, New York; formerly Collection Félix Labisse. **Dream Caused by the Flight of a Bee around a Pomegranate, One Second before Awakening 250**, 1944, oil on canvas, 51 x 40.5 cm, Museo Thyssen-Bornemisza, Madrid. **The Echo of the Void 161**, 1935, oil on canvas, 73 x 92 cm, private collection. **The Ecumenical Council 332**, 1960, oil on canvas, 300 x 254 cm, The Salvador Dalí Museum, St. Petersburg, Florida, on loan from the Morse Charitable Trust. **Enchanted Beach with Three Fluid Graces 208**, 1938, oil on canvas, 65 x 81 cm, The Salvador Dalí Museum, St. Petersburg, Florida, on loan from the Morse Charitable Trust. **The Enigma of Desire—My Mother, My Mother, My Mother 86**, 1929, oil on canvas, 110 x 150.7 cm, Staatsgalerie Moderner Kunst, Munich; formerly Collection Oskar R. Schlag. **The Enigma of Hitler 215**, c.1939, oil on canvas, 51.2 x 79.3 cm, Museo Nacional Centro de Arte Reina Sofía, Madrid, gift of Dalí to the Spanish state. **The Enigma of William Tell 132–3**, 1933, oil on canvas, 201.5 x 346 cm, Moderna Museet, Stockholm. **Enigmatic Elements in the Landscape 144**, 1934, oil on panel, 72.5 x 59.9 cm, private collection; formerly Collection Cyrus L. Sulzberger, Paris. **Equestrian Fantasy (Portrait of Lady Dunn-Beaverbrook) 301**, 1954, oil on canvas, 118 x 135.2 cm, Beaverbrook Art Gallery, Fredericton, New Brunswick. **Equestrian Parade (possibly set design for "Romeo and Juliet") 232**, 1942, oil on canvas, 31 x 51 cm, private collection. **Eucharistic**

Still Life 293, 1952, oil on canvas, 55 x 87 cm, The Salvador Dalí Museum, St. Petersburg, Florida, on loan from E. and A. Reynolds Morse. **The Eye of Time** 287, 1949, enamel, diamonds, and rubies, 4 x 6.4 x 1.5 cm, whereabouts unknown. **The Face of Mae West** 153, mixed media, Fundación Gala-Salvador Dalí, Figueras, gift of Dalí to the Spanish state. **The Face of War** 219, 1940–41, oil on canvas, 64 x 79 cm, Museum Boijmans Van Beuningen, Rotterdam; formerly Collection André Cauvin. **Feather Equilibrium** 270–1, 1947, oil on canvas, 77.5 x 96.5 cm, Fundación Gala-Salvador Dalí, Figueras, gift of Dalí to the Spanish state. **The Feeling of Becoming** 93, 1930, oil on canvas, 32.5 x 26 cm, private collection; formerly Collection Mrs. W. Murray Crane. **Female Nude** 38, 1925, oil on cardboard, 46 x 48.5 cm, private collection. **Female Trio** 353, 1970, gouache and pastel on paper, 153 x 102 cm, Christie's, London. **Festival at San Sebastián** 25, 1921, gouache on cardboard, 52 x 75 cm, Fundación Gala-Salvador Dalí, Figueras. **Figure after William Tell** 114, 1932, red and black ink, 25 x 14 cm, The Salvador Dalí Museum, St. Petersburg, Florida. **Figure at a Window** 45, 1925, oil on canvas, 103 x 75 cm, Museo Nacional Centro de Arte Reina Sofía, Madrid. **Figure Climbing a Stair** 351, 1967, mixed technique on paper, 98 x 58.8 cm, private collection. **Figure Inspired by Michelangelo's Adam on the Ceiling of the Sistine Chapel, Rome** 396, 1982, oil on canvas, 60 x 75 cm, Fundación Gala-Salvador Dalí, Figueras, gift of Dalí to the Spanish state. **Figure on the Rocks (Sleeping Woman)** 53, 1925, oil on plywood, 27 x 41 cm, The Salvador Dalí Museum, St. Petersburg, Florida; formerly Collection E. and A. Reynolds Morse. **Figure with Drawers. For a four-part screen** 129, c.1934, oil on canvas, 52 x 15 cm, Collection Italcambio. **Figure with Flag. Illustration for "Memories of Surrealism"** 365, c.1971, oil, gouache and collage, 61 x 47 cm, private collection. **Figures in a Landscape at Ampurdán** 32, 1923, gouache on cardboard, 105 x 95 cm, Fundación Gala-Salvador Dalí, Figueras, gift of Dalí to the Spanish state. **The First Days of Spring** 88, 1929, oil and collage on panel, 49.5 x 64 cm, The Salvador Dalí Museum, St. Petersburg, Florida, on loan from E. and A. Reynolds Morse. **The Font** 97, 1930, oil on plywood, 66 x 41 cm, The Salvador Dalí Museum, St. Petersburg, Florida; formerly Collection E. and A. Reynolds Morse. **The Forgotten Horizon** 167, 1936, oil on mahogany, 25.5 x 26.7 cm, Tate Gallery, London; formerly Collection Edward James. **The Fossilized Automobile of Cape Creus** 184, 1936, oil on panel, 31 x 37 cm, Collection G.E.D. Nahmad, Geneva; formerly Collection Edward James. **Fountain of Milk Flowing Uselessly on Three Shoes** 257, 1945, oil on canvas, 18 x 22 cm, The Salvador Dalí Museum, St. Petersburg, Florida, on loan from E. and A. Reynolds Morse. **Fried Egg on the Plate without the Plate** 116, 1932, oil on canvas, 55 x 46 cm, Galería Theo, Madrid. **Fried Eggs on the Plate without the Plate** 117, 1932, oil on canvas, 60 x 42 cm, The Salvador Dalí Museum, St. Petersburg, Florida, on loan from the Morse Charitable Trust. **Frontispiece for "Hidden Faces"—I am the Lady** 251, 1944, India ink on paper, 21.5 x 14.5 cm, gift of Dalí to the Spanish state. **Gala and the Angelus of Millet Preceding the Imminent Arrival of the Conical Anamorphoses** 122, 1933, oil on panel, 24 x 18.8 cm, The National Gallery of Canada, Ottawa; formerly Collection Henry P. McIlhenny. **Gala Contemplating the Mediterranean Sea which at Twenty Meters Becomes the Portrait of Abraham Lincoln—Homage to Rothko (first version)** 373, c.1974–75, oil on photographic paper, 445 x 350 cm, Fundación Gala-Salvador Dalí, Figueras. **Gala in a Patio Watching**

the Sky, Where the Equestrian Figure of Prince Baltasar Carlos and Several Constellations (All) Appear, after Velázquez** 394, 1981, oil on canvas, 140.5 x 100 cm, Fundación Gala-Salvador Dalí, Figueras, gift of Dalí to the Spanish state. **Gala Nude Seen from behind Watching an Invisible Mirror** 330, 1960, oil on canvas, 42 x 32 cm, Fundación Gala-Salvador Dalí, Figueras. **Gala Placida** 290, 1952, ink and pastel on paper, 45.7 x 34.6 cm, University of Arizona Museum of Art, Tucson, The Edward Joseph Gallagher III Memorial Collection. **Gala's Christ (Stereoscopic work)** 380–1, 1978, oil on canvas, stereoscopic work, two components, 100 x 100 cm each, private collection. **Gala's Foot (Stereoscopic work)** 368–9, 1973, oil on canvas, stereoscopic work, 60 x 60 cm each, Fundación Gala-Salvador Dalí, Figueras. **Galarina** 245, 1944–45, oil on canvas, 64.1 x 50.2 cm, Fundación Gala-Salvador Dalí, Figueras, gift of Dalí to the Spanish state. **Galatea of the Spheres** 291, 1952, oil on canvas, 65 x 54 cm, Fundación Gala-Salvador Dalí, Figueras. **Geological Destiny** 131, 1933, oil on panel, 21 x 16 cm, private collection; formerly Julien Green Collection. **Geological Echo (Pietà)** 400, 1982, oil on canvas, 100.2 x 100 cm, Fundación Gala-Salvador Dalí, Figueras. **Geological Justice** 166, 1936, oil on panel, 11 x 19 cm, Museum Boijmans Van Beuningen, Rotterdam; formerly Collection Edward James. **Geopolitical Child Watching the Birth of the New Man** 241, 1943, oil on canvas, 45.5 x 50 cm, The Salvador Dalí Museum, St. Petersburg, Florida, on loan from the Morse Charitable Trust. **The Ghost of Vermeer van Delft** 138, c.1934, oil on canvas, 23 x 19 cm, private collection, Switzerland. **The Ghost of Vermeer van Delft** 140, 1934, technique and dimensions unknown, whereabouts unknown. **The Ghost of Vermeer van Delft which Can Be Used as a Table** 141, 1934, oil on panel, 18 x 14 cm, The Salvador Dalí Museum, St. Petersburg, Florida, on loan from E. and A. Reynolds Morse. **Giant Flying Mocca Cup with an Inexplicable Five-Metre Appendage** 263, c.1946, oil on canvas, 50 x 31 cm, private collection, Basel; formerly Collection Marquis Georges de Cuevas. **Girls in a Garden (The Cousins)** 23, 1921, oil on canvas, 53 x 41 cm, André-François Petit, Paris. **Gradiva Rediscovers the Anthropomorphic Ruins—Retrospective Fantasy** 100, 1931, oil on canvas, 65 x 54 cm, Museo Thyssen-Bornemisza, Madrid; formerly Collection Robert de Saint-Jean. **The Grape Pickers: Bacchus' Chariot (The Triumph of Dionysus)** 298, 1953, watercolor, 77 x 101.5 cm, gift of Dalí to the Spanish state. **The Great Masturbator** 87, 1929, oil on canvas, 110 x 150 cm, Museo Nacional Centro de Arte Reina Sofía, Madrid, gift of Dalí to the Spanish state. **The Great Paranoiac** 185, 1936, oil on canvas, 62 x 62 cm, Museum Boijmans Van Beuningen, Rotterdam; formerly Collection Edward James. **Hallucinogenic Toreador** 352, 1968–70, oil on canvas, 398.8 x 299.7 cm, The Salvador Dalí Museum, St. Petersburg, Florida, on loan from the Morse Charitable Trust. **"Hands" Chair** 188, c.1936, mixed media, Formerly Edward James Foundation, Sussex. **Hannibal Crossing the Alps** 354, 1970, gouache and watercolor on brown-gray fibered cardboard, 73 x 99 cm, The Salvador Dalí Museum, St. Petersburg, Florida, on loan from E. and A. Reynolds Morse. **Harlequin** 60, 1927, oil on canvas, 190 x 140 cm, Museo Nacional Centro de Arte Reina Sofía, Madrid. **The Harmony of the Spheres** 379, 1978, oil on canvas, 100 x 100 cm, Fundación Gala-Salvador Dalí, Figueras, gift of Dalí to the Spanish state. **Head of a Woman in the Form of a Battle. Study for "Spain"** 170, 1936, oil on panel, 102 x 12.7 cm, private collection; formerly Collection Edward James. **Hermes** 397, 1981, oil on copper,

22.8 x 17.8 cm, Museo Nacional Centro de Arte Reina Sofía, Madrid, gift of Dalí to the Spanish state. **Homage to John F. Kennedy 339**, 1963, bronze and paper clips, Phillips, The International Fine Art Auctioneers. **Homage to Newton 364**, 1969, patinated bronze, 132 x 70 x 40 cm, Plaza Dalí, Madrid. **Honey Is Sweeter than Blood 226**, 1941, oil on canvas, 49.5 x 60 cm, The Santa Barbara Museum of Art, California, gift of Mr. and Mrs. Warren Tremaine, 1949. **Study for "Honey Is Sweeter than Blood" (Automatic Drawing) 56**, 1926, oil on panel, 36.5 x 45 cm, private collection. **The Horseman of Death 157**, 1935, oil on canvas, 65 x 54 cm, André-François Petit, Paris. **Hyperxiological Sky 328**, 1960, oil on canvas with nails and inlaid gold tooth, 31 x 43 cm, private collection. **Illuminated Pleasures 80**, 1929, oil and collage on hardboard, 24 x 35 cm, The Museum of Modern Art, New York, Collection Sidney and Harriet Janis, 1957. **Imperial Monument to the Child-Woman 82**, 1929, oil on canvas, 140 x 80 cm, Museo Nacional Centro de Arte Reina Sofía, Madrid, gift of Dalí to the Spanish state. **The Impossible Model. Drawing for "50 Secrets of Magic Craftsmanship" 276**, 1947, India ink and watercolor, 32.1 x 21.6 cm, private collection. **Impressions of Africa 210**, 1938, oil on canvas, 91.5 x 117.5 cm, Museum Boijmans Van Beuningen, Rotterdam; formerly Collection Edward James. **Study for the self-portrait in "Impressions of Africa" 211**, 1938, pencil on paper, 52 x 33 cm, Museum Boijmans Van Beuningen, Rotterdam; formerly Collection Edward James. **The Invention of the Monster 202–3**, 1937, oil on panel, 51.2 x 78.5 cm, The Art Institute of Chicago; Joseph Winterbotham Collection. **Invisible Afghan with the Apparition on the Beach of the Face of García Lorca in the Form of a Fruit Dish with Three Figs 209**, 1938, oil on panel, 19.2 x 24.1 cm, private collection. **The Invisible Lovers 262**, 1946, oil on canvas, dimensions unknown, private collection; formerly Christie's, London. **Study for "The Invisible Man" 84**, 1929, pencil on paper, 28 x 20 cm, private collection. **The Invisible Man 85**, 1929, oil on canvas, 140 x 80 cm, Museo Nacional Centro de Arte Reina Sofía, Madrid, gift of Dalí to the Spanish state. **Invisible Sleeping Woman, Horse, Lion 90**, 1930, oil on canvas, 60 x 70 cm, private collection, Paris; formerly Collection Vicomte de Noailles. **Juliet's Tomb 230**, 1942, oil on canvas, 50.7 x 50.7 cm, private collection. **Landscape at Port Lligat 282**, 1950, oil on canvas, 58.5 x 79 cm, The Salvador Dalí Museum, St. Petersburg, Florida, on loan from E. and A. Reynolds Morse. **Landscape of Port Lligat with Homely Angels and Fishermen 283**, 1950, oil on canvas, 61 x 61 cm, private collection. **Landscape with a Girl Skipping 171**, 1936, oil on canvas, 293 x 280 cm (center panel), 261 x 84 cm (wings), Museum Boijmans Van Beuningen, Rotterdam; formerly Collection Edward James. **The Last Supper 312–13**, 1955, oil on canvas, 167 x 268 cm, National Gallery of Art, Washington, D.C., Chester Dale Collection. **"La Turbie"—Sir James Dunn Seated 280**, 1949, oil on canvas, 132 x 89 cm, Beaverbrook Art Gallery, Fredericton, New Brunswick. **Leda and the Swan 335**, 1961, gouache, 6.6 x 6.7 cm (oval), Fundación Gala-Salvador Dalí, Figueras, gift of Dalí to the Spanish state. **Leda Atomica 275**, 1949, oil on canvas, 61.1 x 45.3 cm, Fundación Gala-Salvador Dalí, Figueras. **Study for "Leda Atomica" 274**, 1947, pen and India ink, 60.4 x 45.3 cm, private collection. **Leg Composition. Drawing from a series of advertisements for Bryans Hosiery 242**, c.1944, watercolor and India ink, dimensions unknown, whereabouts unknown. **Leg Composition. Drawing from a series of advertisements for Bryans Hosiery 243**, c.1944, watercolor and India ink, dimensions unknown, Bonhams, London. **Little Cinders (Cenicitas) 64**, 1927–28, oil on panel, 64 x 48 cm, Museo Nacional Centro de Arte Reina Sofía, Madrid. **Lobster Telephone 169**, 1936, telephone with painted plaster lobster in the cradle, 15 x 30 x 17 cm, Museum Boijmans Van Beuningen, Rotterdam; formerly Collection Edward James. **The Lost Face—The Great Masturbator 98**, 1930, pastel on paper, 64.8 x 48.9 cm, The Salvador Dalí Museum, St. Petersburg, Florida. **The Lugubrious Game 89**, 1929, oil and collage on cardboard, 44.4 x 30.3 cm, private collection. **Mad Associations (Board of Fireworks) 102–3**, 1930–31, oil on embossed pewter, 40 x 65 cm, private collection, London. **Mad Mad Mad Minerva. Illustration for "Memories of Surrealism" 345**, c.1968, oil, gouache, and India ink with photocollage on paper, 61 x 48 cm, Galerie Kalb, Vienna. **The Madonna of Port Lligat (first version) 279**, 1949, oil on canvas, 48.9 x 37.5 cm, Marquette University, Haggerty Museum of Art, Milwaukee, gift of Mr. and Mrs. Ira Haupt, 1959. **Study for the head of "The Madonna of Port Lligat" 278**, 1950, red chalk and ink on paper, 49 x 31 cm, The Salvador Dalí Museum, St. Petersburg, Florida, on loan from E. and A. Reynolds Morse. **Mae West Lips Sofa 187**, 1936–37, wooden frame upholstered in pink felt to resemble the lips of movie actress Mae West. Made from Dalí's design by Green & Abbott, London, for Edward James, 92 x 213 x 80 cm, The Royal Pavilion Art Gallery and Museum, Borough of Brighton; formerly Collection Edward James. **Mae West's Face which May Be Used as a Surrealist Apartment 152**, 1934–35, gouache on newspaper, 31 x 17 cm, The Art Institute of Chicago. **Man of Sickly Complexion Listening to the Sound of the Sea** or **The Two Balconies 81**, 1929, oil on panel, 23.5 x 34.5 cm, Museu da Chácara do Céu, Rio de Janeiro, Fundaçao Raymundo Ottoni de Castro Maya. **The Man with the Head of Blue Hortensias 193**, 1936, oil on canvas, 16 x 22 cm, The Salvador Dalí Museum, St. Petersburg, Florida, on loan from E. and A. Reynolds Morse. **Mannequin 59**, 1926–27, oil on canvas, 248 x 198 cm, Fundación Gala-Salvador Dalí, Figueras, gift of Dalí to the Spanish state. **Martyr—Inspired by the Sufferings of Dalí in His Illness 405**, 1982, oil on canvas, 75 x 60 cm, Fundación Gala-Salvador Dalí, Figueras, gift of Dalí to the Spanish state. **Masochistic Instrument 136**, 1933–34, oil on canvas, 62 x 47 cm, private collection; formerly Collection Countess Pecci-Blunt. **Meditation on the Harp 139**, 1932–34, oil on canvas, 67 x 47 cm, The Salvador Dalí Museum, St. Petersburg, Florida, on loan from the Morse Charitable Trust; formerly Collection André Durst. **Meditative Rose 321**, 1958, oil on canvas, 36 x 28 cm, private collection; formerly New York, Arnold Grand Collection. **Mediumnistic-Paranoiac Image 155**, 1935, oil on panel, 19 x 22.8 cm, Collection G.E.D. Nahmad, Geneva; formerly Collection Edward James. **Medusa 337**, 1963, heliogravure and dry-point, Phillips, The International Fine Art Auctioneers. **Melancholy Atomic Uranic Idyll 253**, 1945, oil on canvas, 65 x 85 cm, Museo Nacional Centro de Arte Reina Sofía, Madrid, gift of Dalí to the Spanish state. **Melancholy—Portrait of Singer Claire Dux 236**, 1942, oil on canvas, 80 x 60 cm, private collection. **Memory of the Child-Woman 121**, 1932, oil on canvas, 99 x 119.5 cm, The Salvador Dalí Museum, St. Petersburg, Florida, on loan from the Morse Charitable Trust. **Mercury and Argos (after "Mercury and Argos" by Velázquez, Museo del Prado) 401**, 1981, oil on canvas, 140 x 95 cm, Fundación Gala-Salvador Dalí, Figueras, gift of Dalí to the Spanish state. **The Metamorphosis of Narcissus 202**, 1937, oil on canvas, 50.8 x 78.3 cm, Tate Gallery, London; formerly Collection Edward James. **Moment of Transition 135**, 1934, oil on canvas, 54 x 65 cm, private collection. **Morning Ossification of the Cypress 147**, 1934, oil on canvas, 82 x 66 cm, private collection, Milan; formerly Collection Anne Green. **Morphological Echo 173**, 1936, oil on panel, 30.5 x 33 cm, The Salvador Dalí Museum, St. Petersburg, Florida, on loan from E. and A. Reynolds Morse. **The Mountains of Cape Creus on the March (LSD Trip) 346**, 1967, watercolor and India ink, 57 x 82 cm, Fondation Paul Ricard, Ile de Bendor. **My Wife, Nude, Contemplating Her Own Flesh Becoming Stairs, Three Vertebrae of a Column, Sky, and Architecture 258**, 1945, oil on panel, 61 x 52 cm, Collection José Mugrabi, New York. **Myself at the Age of Ten When I Was the Grasshopper Child—Castration Complex 124**, 1933, oil on panel, 22 x 16 cm, The Salvador Dalí Museum, St. Petersburg, Florida, on loan from E. and A. Reynolds Morse. **Necrophiliac Fountain Flowing from a Grand Piano 125**, 1933, oil on canvas, 22 x 27 cm, private collection. **Necrophiliac Springtime 172**, 1936, oil on canvas, 55 x 65 cm, private collection; formerly Collection Elsa Schiaparelli. **Night and Day Clothes of the Body 174**, 1936, gouache on paper, 30 x 40 cm, private collection. **Nostalgia of the Cannibal 118**, 1932, oil on canvas, 47.2 x 47.2 cm, Sprengel Museum, Hanover. **Nuclear Head of an Angel 292**, 1952, black ink, sepia, and pencil on paper, 56 x 43 cm, private collection. **Nude in the Water 39**, 1925, oil on cardboard, 50.5 x 47 cm, private collection. **Nude on the Plain of Rosas 229**, 1942, oil on canvas, 50 x 50 cm, Yokohama Museum of Art; formerly Collection P. de Gavardie. **Nude Woman Seated in an Armchair 62**, 1927–28, oil on cardboard, 68.5 x 52.5 cm, Fundación Gala-Salvador Dalí, Figueras. **The Old Age of William Tell 108**, 1931, oil on canvas, 98 x 140 cm, private collection; formerly Collection Vicomte de Noailles. **Old Age, Adolescence, Infancy (The Three Ages) 218**, 1940, oil on canvas, 50 x 65 cm, The Salvador Dalí Museum, St. Petersburg, Florida, on loan from E. and A. Reynolds Morse. **Old Man at Twilight 11**, 1918, oil on canvas with gravel collage, 50 x 30 cm, private collection. **Palace of the Winds 362-3**, 1972, ceiling painting, Fundación Gala-Salvador Dalí, Figueras. **Palladio's Corridor of Dramatic Surprise 212**, 1938, oil on canvas, 73 x 104 cm, private collection. **Palladio's Thalia Corridor 194**, 1937, oil on canvas, 116 x 89.5 cm, Collection G.E.D. Nahmad, Geneva; formerly Collection Edward James. **Paranoia 175**, 1936, oil on canvas, 38 x 46 cm, The Salvador Dalí Museum, St. Petersburg, Florida, on loan from E. and A. Reynolds Morse. **Paranoiac Astral Image 151**, 1934, oil on panel, 15.9 x 21.9 cm, The Wadsworth Atheneum, Hartford, Connecticut, Ella Gallup Sumner and Mary Catlin Sumner Collection. **Paranoiac Metamorphosis of Gala's Face 112**, 1932, India ink on Japan paper, 29 x 21 cm, Fundación Gala-Salvador Dalí, Figueras; formerly Collection Boris Kochno. **Paranoiac Woman-Horse 91**, 1930, oil on canvas, 50.2 x 65.2 cm, Musée National d'Art Moderne, Centre Georges Pompidou, Paris. **Paranoiac-Critical Painting of Vermeer's "Lacemaker" 309**, 1955, oil on canvas on panel, 27.1 x 22.1 cm, The Solomon R. Guggenheim Museum, New York, anonymous gift. **Paranoiac-Critical Solitude 154**, 1935, oil on panel, 19 x 23 cm, private collection; formerly Collection Edward James. **Partial Hallucination. Six Apparitions of Lenin on a Grand Piano 106-7**, 1931, oil on canvas, 114 x 146 cm, Musée National d'Art Moderne, Centre Georges Pompidou, Paris. **The Path of Enigmas (second version) 399**, 1981, oil on canvas, 139 x 94 cm, Fundación Gala-Salvador Dalí, Figueras. **The Patio of Port Lligat 355**, 1968, oil on canvas, 60.1 x 77.6 cm, Fundación Gala-Salvador Dalí,

Figueras, gift of Dalí to the Spanish state. **Penya-Segats (Woman on the Rocks) 50**, 1925, oil on olive panel, 26 x 40 cm, private collection. **The Persistence of Memory (Soft Watches) 110**, 1931, oil on canvas, 24 x 33 cm, The Museum of Modern Art, New York (anonymous gift 1934). **Perspectives (Premonition of Paranoiac Perspectives through Soft Structures) 191**, 1936–37, oil on canvas, 65.5 x 65 cm, Kunstmuseum Basel, Öffentliche Kunstsammlung, Basel; Emanuel Hoffmann Foundation. **The Phantom Cart 134**, 1933, oil on panel, 19 x 24.1 cm, private collection; formerly Collection Edward James. **Pi-Mesonic Angel 322**, 1958, watercolor on paper, 40.6 x 30.5 cm, The Salvador Dalí Museum, St. Petersburg, Florida, on loan from E. and A. Reynolds Morse. **Pierrot and Guitar 35**, 1924, oil and collage on cardboard, 55 x 52 cm, Museo Thyssen-Bornemisza, Madrid; formerly Collection Montserrat Dalí de Bas. **Pierrot Playing the Guitar (Harlequin with Small Bottle of Rum) 48**, 1926, oil on canvas, 198 x 149 cm, Museo Nacional Centro de Arte Reina Sofía, Madrid, gift of Dalí to the Spanish state. **Pietà 407**, 1982, oil on canvas, 95 x 65 cm, Fundación Gala-Salvador Dalí, Figueras, gift of Dalí to the Spanish state. **Pietà 409**, 1983, oil on canvas, 60 x 73 cm, Fundación Gala-Salvador Dalí, Figueras, gift of Dalí to the Spanish state. **Poetry of America—The Cosmic Athletes 246**, 1943, oil on canvas, 116.8 x 78.7 cm, Fundación Gala-Salvador Dalí, Figueras. **Port Alguer 13**, 1919–20, oil on canvas, 36 x 38 cm, Fundación Gala-Salvador Dalí, Figueras, gift of Dalí to the Spanish state. **Port Alguer, Cadaqués 33**, 1924, oil on canvas, 100 x 100 cm, Fundación Gala-Salvador Dalí, Figueras. **Portrait of Ambassador Cardenas 237**, 1943, oil on canvas, 61.3 x 50.8 cm, private collection. **Portrait of "Bobo" Rockefeller (unfinished) 331**, 1960, oil on canvas, 59.9 x 56 cm, Fundación Gala-Salvador Dalí, Figueras, gift of Dalí to the Spanish state. **Portrait of Freud 214**, 1938, ink on paper, 29.5 x 26.5 cm, Freud Museum, London. **Portrait of Gala 115**, 1932, oil on panel, 8.5 x 6.5 cm, The Salvador Dalí Museum, St. Petersburg, Florida, on loan from E. and A. Reynolds Morse. **Portrait of Gala 244**, 1941, pencil on paper, 63.9 x 49 cm, Museum Boijmans Van Beuningen, Rotterdam, on loan from the New Trebizond Foundation. **Portrait of Gala (Gala against the Light) 341**, 1965, oil on panel, 37.9 x 34.8 cm, Museo Nacional Centro de Arte Reina Sofía, Madrid, gift of Dalí to the Spanish state. **Portrait of Gala with Rhinocerotic Symptoms 300**, 1954, oil on canvas, 39 x 31.5 cm, private collection. **Portrait of Gala with Two Lamb Chops Balanced on Her Shoulder 130**, 1933, oil on olive panel, 6 x 8 cm, Fundación Gala-Salvador Dalí, Figueras. **Portrait of a Girl in a Landscape (Cadaqués) 54**, 1926, oil on canvas, 92 x 65 cm, Fundación Gala-Salvador Dalí, Figueras, gift of Dalí to the Spanish state. **Portrait of Grandmother Ana Sewing 22**, c.1921, oil on canvas, 40 x 62 cm, Collection Joaquín Vila Moner, Figueras. **Portrait of Hortensia, Peasant Woman from Cadaqués 15**, 1920, oil on canvas, 35 x 26 cm, private collection. **Portrait of Luis Buñuel 37**, 1924, oil on canvas, 70 x 60 cm, Museo Nacional Centro de Arte Reina Sofía, Madrid; formerly Collection Luis Buñuel. **Portrait of María Carbona 43**, 1925, oil on panel, 52.6 x 39.2 cm, Montreal Museum of Fine Arts. **Portrait of Mrs. Isabel Styler-Tas (Melancholia) 260**, 1945, oil on canvas, 65.5 x 86 cm, Staatliche Museen zu Berlin – Preußischer Kulturbesitz, Nationalgalerie, Berlin. **Portrait of Mrs. Jack Warner 281**, 1951, oil on canvas, 111.1 x 94.6 cm, private collection. **Portrait of My Dead Brother 338**, 1963, oil on canvas, 175 x 175 cm, private collection, Switzerland. **Portrait of My Father 19**, 1920–21, oil on canvas, 90.5 x 66 cm,

Fundación Gala-Salvador Dalí, Figueras, gift of Dalí to the Spanish state. **Study for "Portrait of My Father" 18**, 1920, pencil on paper, 32.5 x 26 cm, Fundación Gala-Salvador Dalí, Figueras, Dalí Bequest 1989. **Portrait of My Father 41**, 1925, oil on canvas, 100 x 100 cm, Museo de Arte Moderno, Barcelona. **Portrait of a Passionate Woman (The Hands) 259**, 1945, oil on canvas, 60 x 45 cm, private collection. **Portrait of Paul Eluard 83**, 1929, oil on cardboard, 33 x 25 cm, Formerly Collection Gala and Salvador Dalí. **Portrait of Picasso 272**, 1947, oil on canvas, 64.1 x 54.7 cm, Fundación Gala-Salvador Dalí, Figueras. **Portrait of Ramoneta Montsalvatge 51**, 1926, oil on panel, two components, 60.9 x 38 cm, Fundación Gala-Salvador Dalí, Figueras. **Portrait of the Cellist Ricardo Pichot 17**, 1920, oil on canvas, 61.5 x 49 cm, private collection, Cadaqués. **Premature Ossification of a Railway Station 96**, 1930, oil on canvas, 31.5 x 27 cm, private collection; formerly Collection Countess Pecci-Blunt. **Putrefied Bird 70**, 1928, oil on panel, 37.5 x 57 cm, Fundación Gala-Salvador Dalí, Figueras. **The Putrefied Donkey 72**, 1928, oil, sand, and gravel collage on panel, 61 x 50 cm, André-François Petit, Paris; formerly Collection Paul Eluard. **The Railway Station at Perpignan (Gala Watching Dalí in a State of Weightlessness above His "Pop, Op, Yes-Yes, Kitsch" Work Where Two Awesome Figures from Millet's "Angelus" Appear to Us in an Atavistic State of Hibernation, Seen against a Sky which Can Suddenly Be Transformed into a Gigantic Maltese Cross, and at the Center the Railway Station at Perpignan, Where the Entire Universe Converges) 356**, 1965, oil on canvas, 295 x 406 cm, Museum Ludwig, Cologne. **The Ram 74**, 1928, oil on panel, 50.2 x 61.7 cm, The Salvador Dalí Museum, St. Petersburg, Florida, on loan from E. and A. Reynolds Morse. **Raphaelesque Head, Exploded 288**, 1951, oil on canvas, 43 x 33 cm, Scottish National Gallery of Modern Art, Edinburgh, on permanent loan from Miss Stead-Ellis, Somerset. **Retrospective Bust of a Woman 123**, 1933, China dummy bust, painted, with corn cob, cartoon film strip as collar band, golden-bronzed sponge, and plastic replicas of the figures and wheelbarrow from "The Angelus," with two inkwells and quills, 54 x 45 x 35 cm, private collection, Belgium. **Rhinocerotic Disintegration of Illissus of Phidias 296–7**, 1954, oil on canvas, 100 x 129.5 cm, Fundación Gala-Salvador Dalí, Figueras, gift of Dalí to the Spanish state. **Roger Freeing Angelica (St. George and the Damsel) 371**, 1970–74, oil on canvas, 291 x 144.7 cm, Fundación Gala-Salvador Dalí, Figueras. **Roussillon—French Railways. Poster 357**, 1969, Lords Gallery, London. **Ruin with Head of Medusa and Landscape (Dedicated to Mrs. Chase) 228**, 1941, oil on canvas, 36 x 25.4 cm, Collection Juan Abelló Gallo, Madrid. **The Sacred Heart 92**, 1929, ink on canvas, 68.5 x 50.1 cm, Musée National d'Art Moderne, Centre Georges Pompidou, Paris. **Saint Surrounded by Three Pi-Mesons 310**, 1956, oil on canvas, 42 x 31 cm, Fundación Gala-Salvador Dalí, Figueras. **Santa Creus Festival in Figueras 26**, 1920, gouache on cardboard, 42 x 65 cm, The Salvador Dalí Museum, St. Petersburg, Florida, on loan from E. and A. Reynolds Morse. **Santa Creus Festival in Figueras—The Circus 24**, 1921, gouache on cardboard, 52 x 75 cm, Fundación Gala-Salvador Dalí, Figueras. **Sardana of the Witches 27**, 1921, watercolor on paper, 41.9 x 59.7 cm, The Salvador Dalí Museum, St. Petersburg, Florida. **Scene in a Cabaret 29**, 1922, oil on canvas, 52 x 41 cm, Bénédict Petit, Paris. **Searching for the Fourth Dimension 388**, 1979, oil on canvas, 122.5 x 246 cm, Fundación Gala-Salvador Dalí, Figueras, gift of Dalí to the Spanish state. **Seated Girl from the Back**

42, 1925, oil on canvas, 103 x 73.5 cm, Museo Nacional Centro de Arte Reina Sofía, Madrid. **Self-Portrait 20**, c.1921, oil on canvas, 36.8 x 41.8 cm, The Salvador Dalí Museum, St. Petersburg, Florida. **Self-Portrait with "L'Humanité" 31**, 1923, oil, gouache, and collage on cardboard, 104.9 x 75.4 cm, Fundación Gala-Salvador Dalí, Figueras, gift of Dalí to the Spanish state. **Self-Portrait in the Studio 14**, c.1919, oil on canvas, 27 x 21 cm, The Salvador Dalí Museum, St. Petersburg, Florida; formerly Collection E. and A. Reynolds Morse. **Self-Portrait Splitting into Three 61**, 1927, oil on cardboard, 70 x 50 cm, Fundación Gala-Salvador Dalí, Figueras. **Self-Portrait with the Neck of Raphael 21**, 1920–21, oil on canvas, 41.5 x 53 cm, Fundación Gala-Salvador Dalí, Figueras, gift of Dalí to the Spanish state. **Self-Portrait, Dedicated to Federico García Lorca 73**, 1928, pen and ink on paper, 22 x 16 cm, Collection Juan Abello Prat, Mollet. **The Sense of Speed 146**, 1934, oil on canvas, 33 x 24 cm, private collection; formerly Rothschild Collection. **Sfumato 350**, 1972, paper burned and charred with a candle, 59 x 45 cm, Fundación Gala-Salvador Dalí, Figueras. **Shades of Night Descending 104**, 1931, oil on canvas, 61 x 50 cm, The Salvador Dalí Museum, St. Petersburg, Florida, on loan from E. and A. Reynolds Morse. **The Sheep (after conversion) 234**, 1942, watercolor and chromolithograph, 23 x 34 cm, The Salvador Dalí Museum, St. Petersburg, Florida, on loan from E. and A. Reynolds Morse. **Shirley Temple, the Youngest, Most Sacred Monster of the Cinema in Her Time 216**, 1939, gouache, pastel and collage on cardboard, 75 x 100 cm, Museum Boijmans Van Beuningen, Rotterdam. **Singularities 163**, 1935–36, oil on panel, 40.5 x 51.1 cm, Fundación Gala-Salvador Dalí, Figueras. **Sketch for a ceiling of the Teatro Museo Dalí 360–1**, 1970, pencil, watercolor and gouache on cardboard, 104.4 x 75 cm, Fundación Gala-Salvador Dalí, Figueras. **Skull with its Lyric Appendage Leaning on a Bedside Table which Should Have the Exact Temperature of a Cardinal's Nest 148**, 1934, oil on panel, 24 x 19 cm, The Salvador Dalí Museum, St. Petersburg, Florida, on loan from E. and A. Reynolds Morse. **Slave Market with the Disappearing Bust of Voltaire 220**, 1940, oil on canvas, 46.5 x 65.5 cm, The Salvador Dalí Museum, St. Petersburg, Florida, on loan from the Morse Charitable Trust. **Sleep 196–7**, 1937, oil on canvas, 51 x 78 cm, private collection; formerly Collection Edward James. **Soft Construction with Boiled Beans—Premonition of Civil War 177**, 1936, oil on canvas, 100 x 99 cm, The Philadelphia Museum of Art, The Louise and Walter Arensberg Collection; formerly Collection Peter Watson. **Soft Self-Portrait with Fried Bacon 222**, 1941, oil on canvas, 61.3 x 50.8 cm, Fundación Gala-Salvador Dalí, Figueras. **Soft Watch at the Moment of First Explosion 302**, 1954, oil on canvas, 20.5 x 25.7 cm, private collection. **A Soft Watch Put in the Appropriate Place to Cause a Young Ephebe to Die and Be Resuscitated by Excess of Satisfaction (unfinished) 389**, 1979, oil on panel, 122 x 244 cm, Fundación Gala-Salvador Dalí, Figueras, gift of Dalí to the Spanish state. **Solitude—Anthropomorphic Echo 105**, 1931, oil on canvas, 36 x 26 cm, private collection. **Southern California 277**, 1947, technique and dimensions unknown, Christie's, New York. **Spain 213**, 1938, oil on canvas, 91.8 x 60.2 cm, Museum Boijmans Van Beuningen, Rotterdam; formerly Collection Edward James. **The Spectral Cow 75**, 1928, oil on plywood, 50 x 64.5 cm, Musée National d'Art Moderne, Centre Georges Pompidou, Paris. **The Spectre and the Phantom 145**, 1934, oil on canvas, 100 x 73 cm, Five Stars Investment Ltd., New York. **The Spectre of Sex Appeal 149**, 1934, oil on panel, 18 x 14 cm, Fundación

Gala-Salvador Dalí, Figueras. **Spider of the Evening . . . Hope! 223**, 1940, oil on canvas, 40.5 x 50.8 cm, The Salvador Dalí Museum, St. Petersburg, Florida, on loan from the Morse Charitable Trust. **St. George and the Dragon 336**, 1962, oil on canvas, 22.9 x 30.5 cm, private collection. **St. Helen of Port Lligat 295**, 1956, oil on canvas, 31 x 42 cm, The Salvador Dalí Museum, St. Petersburg, Florida, on loan from E. and A. Reynolds Morse. **St. James of Compostela 320**, 1957, oil on canvas, 400 x 300 cm, Beaverbrook Art Gallery, Fredericton, New Brunswick. **St. John 317**, 1957, watercolor and ink on paper, 15 x 12 cm, private collection. **St. Peter's in Rome (Explosion of Mystical Faith in the Midst of a Cathedral) 333**, 1960–74, oil on canvas, 225 x 163 cm, Fundación Gala-Salvador Dalí, Figueras. **Status, Roman Emperor 344**, 1965, medium and dimensions unknown, Christie's, New York. **Still Life 34**, 1923, oil on cardboard, 50.2 x 65 cm, Museo Nacional Centro de Arte Reina Sofía, Madrid, gift of Dalí to the Spanish state. **Still Life 36**, 1924, oil on canvas, 125 x 99 cm, Fundación Federico García Lorca, Madrid. **Still Life—Fast Moving 315**, 1956, oil on canvas, 125 x 160 cm, The Salvador Dalí Museum, St. Petersburg, Florida, on loan from E. and A. Reynolds Morse. **Still Life and Mauve Moonlight 46–47**, 1926, oil on canvas, 148 x 198 cm, Fundación Gala-Salvador Dalí, Figueras, gift of Dalí to the Spanish state. **Still Life by the Light of the Moon 63**, 1927, oil on canvas, 190 x 140 cm, Museo Nacional Centro de Arte Reina Sofía, Madrid, gift of Dalí to the Spanish state. **Studies for the Air Centers and Soft Morphologies of "Leda Atomica" 274**, 1947, pen, India ink, pencil, and colored pencils on special paper, 54 x 48 cm, Fundación Gala-Salvador Dalí, Figueras. **Study for Rhinocerotic Portrait of "The Lacemaker" of Vermeer 308**, 1955, oil on canvas, 24 x 21 cm, gift of Dalí to the Spanish state. **Study for the backdrop of the ballet "Tristan Insane" (Act II) 248**, 1944, oil on canvas, 61 x 96.5 cm, Fundación Gala-Salvador Dalí, Figueras. **Study for the set of "Labyrinth"—Fighting the Minotaur 227**, 1942, pencil, India ink, watercolor, and gouache, 58.6 x73.8 cm, Fundación Gala-Salvador Dalí, Figueras. **Study for the set of "Romeo and Juliet" 233**, 1942, oil on cardboard, 28.6 x 37.4 cm, private collection. **Study of a Female Nude 334**, c.1962, oil on canvas, 129.5 x 96.7 cm, Fundación Gala-Salvador Dalí, Figueras, gift of Dalí to the Spanish state. **Study of a Foot 28**, 1922, pencil on paper, 47 x 31.5 cm, Fundación Gala-Salvador Dalí, Figueras: Dalí Bequest 1989. **Suburbs of a Paranoiac-Critical Town: Afternoon on the Outskirts of European History 178**, 1936, oil on panel, 46 x 66 cm, Museum Boijmans Van Beuningen, Rotterdam; formerly Collection Edward James. **Study for "Suburbs of a Paranoiac-Critical Town" 158**, 1935, ink and pencil on paper, 32.5 x 20.3 cm, private collection. **Sun Table 180**, 1936, oil on panel, 60 x 46 cm, Museum Boijmans Van Beuningen, Rotterdam; formerly Collection Edward James. **Sun, Four Fisherwomen of Cadaqués 76**, 1928, oil on canvas, 147 x 196 cm, Museo Nacional Centro de Arte Reina Sofía, Madrid, gift of Dalí to the Spanish state. **Surrealist Horse-Woman-Horse 128**, 1933, pencil and pen, 52.6 x 25 cm, The Salvador Dalí Museum, St. Petersburg, Florida; formerly Collection E. and A. Reynolds Morse. **Surrealist Landscape 181**, 1936, oil on canvas, dimensions unknown, Galerie Malingue, Paris. **The Swallow's Tail—Series on Catastrophes 411**, 1983, oil on canvas, 73 x 92.2 cm, Fundación Gala-Salvador Dalí, Figueras, gift of Dalí to the Spanish state. **Swans Reflecting Elephants 198**, 1937, oil on canvas, 51 x 77 cm, Cavalieri Holding Co. Inc., Geneva; formerly Collection Edward James. **Symphony in Red 304**,

1954, oil, pen, and India ink on cardboard, dimensions unknown, private collection. **The Temptation of St. Anthony 266–7**, 1946, oil on canvas, 89.7 x 119.5 cm, Musées Royaux des Beaux-Arts de Belgique, Brussels. **The Three Glorious Enigmas of Gala (second version) 402**, 1982, oil on canvas, 100 x 100 cm, Fundación Gala-Salvador Dalí, Figueras, gift of Dalí to the Spanish state. **The Three Pines 12**, c.1919, oil on canvas, 28 x 38 cm, private collection. **Three Young Surrealist Women Holding in their Arms the Skins of an Orchestra 176**, 1936, oil on canvas, 54 x 65 cm, The Salvador Dalí Museum, St. Petersburg, Florida, on loan from the Morse Charitable Trust. **Topological Contortion of a Female Figure Becoming a Cello 410**, 1983, oil on canvas, 60 x 73 cm, Museo Nacional Centro de Arte Reina Sofía, Madrid, gift of Dalí to the Spanish state. **The Tower of Enigmas. Project for the cover of "Vogue" 398**, 1971–81, oil on copper, 35 x 27 cm, Fundación Gala-Salvador Dalí, Figueras, gift of Dalí to the Spanish state. **The Transparent Simulacrum of the Feigned Image 217**, 1938, oil on canvas, 73.5 x 92 cm, Albright-Knox Art Gallery, Buffalo, New York; A. Conger Goodyear, 1966. **Tristan Insane 200**, c.1938, oil on panel, 46 x 55 cm, The Salvador Dalí Museum, St. Petersburg, Florida, on loan from E. and A. Reynolds Morse. **Illustration for "Trois Papillons" 316**, 1955, watercolor and ink on print, 26 x 18 cm, The Salvador Dalí Museum, St. Petersburg, Florida, on loan from E. and A. Reynolds Morse. **The True Painting of "The Isle of the Dead" by Arnold Böcklin at the Hour of the Angelus 119**, 1932, oil on canvas, 77.5 x 64.5 cm, Von der Heydt-Museum, Wuppertal. **Large Figure for "Tuna Fishing" 347**, c.1966–67, pencil and watercolor on paper, 153 x 103 cm, gift of Dalí to the Spanish state. **Tuna Fishing 348–9**, c.1966–67, oil on canvas, 304 x 404 cm, Fondation Paul Ricard, Ile de Bendor. **Two Adolescents 305**, 1954, oil on canvas, 56 x 65 cm, The Salvador Dalí Museum, St. Petersburg, Florida, on loan from E. and A. Reynolds Morse. **Unsatisfied Desires 77**, 1928, oil, sea-shells and sand on cardboard, 76 x 62 cm, private collection. **Untitled 78**, 1928, oil on panel, 76 x 63 cm, Fundación Gala-Salvador Dalí, Figueras. **Untitled (Female Figure with Head of Flowers) 192**, 1937, technique and dimensions unknown, private collection. **Untitled (Nude Figures after Michelangelo) 406**, 1982, oil on canvas, 95 x 75 cm, Fundación Gala-Salvador Dalí, Figueras, gift of Dalí to the Spanish state. **Untitled—After Canova's "Three Graces" 392**, 1979, oil on copper, 32.1 x 24.3 cm, Fundación Gala-Salvador Dalí, Figueras, gift of Dalí to the Spanish state. **Velázquez Dying behind the Window on the Left Side out of which a Spoon Projects 408**, 1982, oil on canvas with collages, 75 x 59.5 cm, Fundación Gala-Salvador Dalí, Figueras, gift of Dalí to the Spanish state. **Velázquez Painting the Infanta Margarita with the Lights and Shadows of His Own Glory 323**, 1958, oil on canvas, 153 x 92 cm, The Salvador Dalí Museum, St. Petersburg, Florida, on loan from E. and A. Reynolds Morse. **Venus and a Sailor—Homage to Salvat-Papasseit 49**, 1925, oil on canvas, 216 x 147 cm, Ikeda Museum of 20th Century Art, Shizuoka (Japan). **Venus and Sailor 52**, 1924–26, oil on canvas, 198 x 149 cm, André-François Petit, Paris. **Venus de Milo with Drawers 186**, 1936, bronze with plaster-like mount and fur tassels, 98 x 32.5 x 34 cm, Museum Boijmans Van Beuningen, Rotterdam. **Vertigo—Tower of Pleasure 95**, 1930, oil on canvas, 60 x 50 cm, private collection. **View of Cadaqués from Playa Poal 16**, 1920, oil on canvas, 29.2 x 48.3 cm, The Salvador Dalí Museum, St. Petersburg, Florida; formerly Collection E. and A. Reynolds Morse. **Virgin and Child 238**, 1942, watercolor on ivory, dimensions unknown, private collection. **The Walls of Babylon 307**, 1954, oil on canvas, 27 x 77 cm, private collection. **War Fish (Ocell . . . Peix) 69**, 1928, oil and pebbles on laminated panel, 61 x 49 cm, The Salvador Dalí Museum, St. Petersburg, Florida; formerly Collection E. and A. Reynolds Morse. **Warrior 403**, 1982, oil on canvas, 99.8 x 100 cm, Fundación Gala-Salvador Dalí, Figueras, gift of Dalí to the Spanish state. **The Way to Púbol 370**, 1973, oil on canvas, 160 x 189.7 cm, gift of Dalí to the Spanish state. **The Weaning of Furniture—Nutrition 150**, 1934, oil on panel, 18 x 24 cm, The Salvador Dalí Museum, St. Petersburg, Florida, on loan from E. and A. Reynolds Morse; formerly Collection Jocelyn Walker. **The Wheelbarrows (Cupola Consisting of Twisted Carts) 289**, 1951, watercolor and ink on paper, 101.5 x 76.2 cm, The Salvador Dalí Museum, St. Petersburg, Florida; formerly Collection E. and A. Reynolds Morse. **White Calm 190**, 1936, oil on panel, 41 x 33 cm, Collection G.E.D. Nahmad, Geneva; formerly Collection Edward James. **William Tell 99**, 1930, oil and collage on canvas, 113 x 87 cm, private collection; formerly Collection André Breton. **Wine Glass and Boat 314**, 1956, oil on canvas, 20.5 x 25.7 cm, private collection; formerly New York, Carstairs Gallery. **Woman at the Window at Figueras 55**, 1926, oil on canvas, 24 x 25 cm, Collection Juan Casanelles, Barcelona. **Woman in Flames 393**, 1980, bronze, Phillips, The International Fine Art Auctioneers. **Woman with a Head of Roses 162**, 1935, oil on panel, 35 x 27 cm, Kunsthaus Zürich. **The Wounded Bird 66**, 1928, oil and sand on cardboard, 55 x 65.5 cm, Collection Mizne-Blumental, Monte Carlo. **Young Virgin Auto-Sodomized by Her Own Chastity 311**, 1954, oil on canvas, 40.5 x 30.5 cm, Playboy Collection, Los Angeles.

First published in the United States of America in 2003
By UNIVERSE PUBLISHING
A Division of Rizzoli International Publications, Inc.
300 Park Avenue South
New York, NY 10010

Photo credits: Albright-Knox Art Gallery, Buffalo; The Art Institute of Chicago; Beaverbrook Art Gallery, Fredericton; Artothek, Weilheim; The Bridgeman Art Library, London; Museo Nacional Centro de Arte Reina Sofía, Madrid; Christie's New York; Fundación Federico García Lorca, Madrid; Fundación Gala-Salvador Dalí, Figueras; Galería Theo, Madrid; Galerie Beyeler, Basel; Galerie Maliugue, Paris; Galerie Kalb, Vienna; The Glasgow Art Gallery; Ikeda Museum of 20th Century Art, Shizuoka; Kunsthalle, Hamburg; Kunsthaus Zürich; Kunstmuseum Basel; Kunstmuseum Bern; Kunstsammlung Nordrhein-Westfalen, Düsseldorf; Lords Gallery, London; Marquette University, Haggerty Museum of Art, Milwaukee; Moderna Museet, Stockholm; Montreal Museum of Fine Arts; Munson-Williams-Proctor Arts Institute, Utica; Musée National d'Art Moderne, Centre Georges Pompidou, Paris; Museo de Arte Moderno, Barcelona; Museo Nacional, Barcelona; Museo Thyssen-Bornemisza, Madrid; Musées Royaux des Beaux-Arts de Belgique, Brussels; Museu da Chácara do Céu, Rio de Janeiro; Museum Boijmans Van Beuningen, Rotterdam; Museum Folkwang, Essen; Museum Ludwig, Cologne; The Museum of Modern Art, New York; National Gallery of Art, Washington, D.C.; The National Gallery of Canada, Ottawa; Peggy Guggenheim Collection, Venice; Perls Galleries, New York; The Philadelphia Museum of Art; Phillips, The International Fine Art Auctioneers; The Royal Pavilion Art Gallery and Museum, Borough of Brighton; Scottish National Gallery of Modern Art, Edinburgh; The Salvador Dalí Museum, St. Petersburg, Florida; The Santa Barbara Museum of Art; Scala Archives, Florence; The Solomon R. Guggenheim Museum, New York; Sprengel Museum Hannover; Staatliche Museen zu Berlin; Staatsgalerie Moderner Kunst, Munich; Tate Gallery, London; The Wadsworth Atheneum, Hartford; University of Arizona Museum of Art, Tucson; Von der Heydt-Museum, Wuppertal; Yokohama Museum of Art

Designed by Griet Van Haute and Anagram, Ghent

Cover: *The Architectural Angelus of Millet*, 1933 (detail; see p.126).
Museo Nacional Centro de Arte Reina Sofía, Madrid
Frontispiece: *The Ghost of Vermeer van Delft*, 1934. Whereabouts unknown
Page 4: Study for "The Discovery of America by Christopher Columbus," 1958.
Gift of Dalí to the Spanish state

Printed in China

Library of Congress Control Number: 2003104952
ISBN 0-7893-1002-3